THE NATION:

THE

FOUNDATIONS OF CIVIL ORDER AND POLITICAL LIFE IN THE UNITED STATES.

BY

E. MULFORD.

NEW YORK:
PUBLISHED BY HURD AND HOUGHTON.
Cambridge: Riverside Press.
1875.

RIVERSIDE, CAMBRIDGE:
STEREOTYPED AND PRINTED BY
H. O. HOUGHTON AND COMPANY.

To the

MEMORY OF

MY FATHER,

IN THE HOPE THAT HIS FAITH SHALL LIVE IN HIS CHILDREN'S CHILDREN,

I DEDICATE THIS WORK.

PREFACE.

The purpose of this book is to ascertain and define the being of the nation in its unity and continuity. There is moving toward its realization in national laws and institutions, the necessary being of the nation itself. The nation thus becomes an object of political knowledge.

It is no abstraction, but in this alone is the avoidance of abstractions. It avoids, on the one hand, an empty empiricism, that with the recognition of no consistent principle makes the nation only a formal organization, and politics only a succession of random experiments, hits, and ventures; and on the other hand, avoids an abstract idealism, which, regarding the state also as only a formal organization, would shape all things after an imaginary polity and an abstract design. It is this conception of the state as involving unity and continuity which is the condition of political science, that is to be set forth alike against the political empiric and the political dogmatist. It is this alone which can avert the danger which there is in the application of formal and abstract conceptions in politics. It is a logic which is presumed in politics, — if politics be an object of knowledge,

— but a logic formed in the necessary conception and manifest in the realization of the nation, not the barren forms of logic as it is held in the notions of the schools. In this conception that certainly is to be retained which works well, but political science is to apprehend the law and condition of its working.

The apprehension is of the realization of the nation in the United States, its substance, its rights, and its powers, underlying but manifest in its whole form and organization.

This book had its beginning in a purpose to represent the nation in its moral being; to assert this moral being in its true position in politics; but the aim has been throughout as the conception widened, to define in their relative and positive character those principles which are the ground of political science. I do not believe that the teacher of ethics can avoid the subject of politics. I do not believe that there can be a separation of them in the thought of a people, but ethics will become abstract and formal,—the dry product of the schools; and politics be bereft of all its power to become at last even a name of reproach. The book may thus serve to indicate, perhaps, in some measure the sources of the power of American institutions in the formation of character.

I have written in the conception that holds politics itself as a science which is the ground of political education. In its apprehension of the being of the nation, its unity and laws, which form the condition of science, political history, jurisprudence, political economy, and social statics, are separate and subordinate departments; political history is concerned with the rise and growth of institutions, and the comparative value of political constitutions; jurisprudence is the science of the jural law and civil organization; political economy is the science of wealth, of the relations of labor and capital, of the laws of production and exchange; social statics is the science of the laws of health and population; international law may be regarded also as subordinate, since it presumes the existence of separate nations, and is formed mainly in the conception in which the nation is held.

A larger space has been given in some instances to subjects of special interest in the immediate condition of affairs, as the jural and the economic representation of the nation, the relation of natural and political rights, the distinction of civil and political rights, the representative principle, the method and dangers of a representative constitution, and the relation and difference of the civil and the international state, a particular State, and the United States.

I have written with an obligation, which I am glad to acknowledge, to the Rev. Mr. Maurice of London, and to Hegel and Stahl, to Trendelenburg and Bluntschli; while I have sought by reference to them to indicate this, it has been larger than mere notes of reference can trace; and I am never sure but their words may have mingled unawares with my thought; I shall not regret this if it may lead any who may trace them to traverse those rich and ample fields, or if it may be an aid to larger knowledge. This only can be the aim of the worker; and it is much to contribute to the knowledge of the people in any form and in however slight a measure. The saddest of words are, — the people perish for lack of knowledge.

The slight references to the Alabama question I may say were written before the recent discussion of the subject, but I have seen no reason to change them.

The words "nation" and "state" are used as synonymous, and a particular State in the United States is written "State" and is described as a commonwealth, as the commonwealth of Massachusetts or Virginia.

I have sought, however imperfectly, to give expression to the thought of the people in the late war, and that conception of the nation, which they who were so worthy, held worth living and dying for. I know how far it falls short of that conception which went with them to battle and sacrifice; yet I would most care to connect, if I may, my work with theirs, and trust it may be received by Him, who is the head of all, to whom their service was done.

CONTENTS.

CHAPTER XII.

CHAPTER XIII.

CHAPTER XIV.

CHAPTER XV.

The necessary and moral interrelation of the nation and the family.
The obligation of the nation to maintain the moral order of the family.
Note on the representation of the relation of the family and the nation in Shakespeare.

CHAPTER XVI.

The formation of society in, *a.* The family. *b.* The commonwealth. *c.* The nation:
Note on the historical growth of this conception in political science· Aristotle. Hegel.
The commonwealth is
a. The civil organization: it is defined in the jural relations of society.
b. The economic organization: it is defined in the necessary relations of society.
It is constituted in the maintenance of civil rights and civil order. Its procedure is in the *common law.*
a. The unity of the commonwealth.
b. The scope of the commonwealth.
Its historical growth. Its illustration in the constitution of the Commonwealth of Pennsylvania.
The institution of courts. The civil court. The constabulary.
The relation of the nation and the commonwealth.
a. The nation is immanent in the commonwealth.
b. The nation is external to the commonwealth.
The commonwealth is the civil corporation. Its formal rights.
The concurrent powers of the nation and the commonwealth.
The law of their relation.
The commonwealth as defined in theories. *a.* They are vast corporations having their origin in some charter and continuing with certain vested powers. *b.* They are separate political societies, each existent in the original sovereignty of an independent political power. *c.* They form an organic whole, in whose complex political organism the States exist each as an original integer: theory of Mr. Hurd and Mr. Brownson.
On the distinction of a central government and a local administration.

CHAPTER XVII.

The confederate principle.
Its definition by Montesquieu; by Freeman.
Its appearance in the formal constitution in an age of political transition.
The conflict of the confederacy with the nation in its organic and moral unity.
The historical conflict in the United States.

CHAPTER XVIII.

CHAPTER XIX.

CHAPTER XX.

THE NATION.

CHAPTER I.

THE SUBSTANCE OF THE NATION.

The premise of political speculation has been the assumption of the existence of man apart from the state. It has portrayed an age when the conflict of right and wrong was unknown: there was in the lives of men no care, nor toil, nor endeavor; there was neither chief nor law, neither soldier nor battle; there was no judge nor police, no plaintiff or defendant; there was neither marriage nor homes; property was unrecognized, no boundaries of land were traced, and the ample gifts of the earth were held by all in common; the individual existed in the fullness of all his powers, while yet, as in the traditional, and the ancients say derisive, line of Homer,[1] —

"No tribe, nor state, nor home hath he."

[1] This imaginary state is drawn by the old counselor, in the *Tempest*: —

"*Gon.* — I would by contraries
Execute all things; for no kind of traffic
Would I admit; no name of magistrate;
Letters should not be known; riches, poverty,
And use of service, none; contract, succession,
Bourn, bound of land, tilth, vineyard, none;
No use of metal, corn, or wine, or oil;
No occupation; all men idle, all;
And women too, but innocent and pure;
No sovereignty.
All things in common nature should produce
Without sweat or endeavor: treason, felony,
Sword, pike, knife, gun, or need of any engine,
Would I not have; but nature should bring forth,

But this scene, as it is traced in political speculation, soon closed, its course was interrupted and disturbed; the impulses of men arousing, brought them in collision; strong desires came to clash with each other; there was the necessity for toil, and the lives of men were harassed with care; there was division, and distrust was provoked; then some power was required to maintain the imperiled security, to punish fraud and restrain violence; and thus the state came into being; its origin was in necessity, and its form was that of a repressive force in the institution of an external order.

The same premise, in the assumption of the contrasted picture, has represented the primitive condition as characterized by every evil. It was a constant warfare; fear and self-interest directed human action; the grasp of avarice brooked no limit; hatred was the habitude of men; tumult and violence alone prevailed. Then it is conceived that the state came into being, as an evil also, but slighter and sooner to be borne than those which existed apart from it, and as before in the form of a repressive force.

These imaginary pictures divest man of the actual circumstance and the actual relations of life. They are only abstractions. There is no trace of the natural man, and of the primitive age which they portray. They are assumed as the necessary material out of which to construct the

Of its own kind, all foison, all abundance,
To feed my innocent people.
"*Seb.* — No marrying 'mong his subjects?
"*Ant.* — None, man; all idle: whores and knaves."
The Tempest, act ii. sc. 1.

In contrast to this, Shakespeare has represented the actual condition of man apart from society, in the Caliban. This condition is not ascertained from the fragmentary traces of savage life, for in the lowest stage of the actual condition of man, there is the recognition of some relations, some principles of association, and some authority, in the will of a chief or the sanction of custom. The most exact representation of this condition is thus in some assumed character as the Caliban.

artificial systems of political schools. They have no foundation in the nature, or in the history of man.

The position of Aristotle is the necessary postulate of political science, — "Man is by nature a political being." The elements of the nation are in his nature, and its progress is in the development of his nature. The earliest and the widest records of his existence disclose a condition in which there is the recognition of some common relation, and men appear as dependent upon each other, and as seeking association with each other; they make sacrifices for it, and accept obligations in it.

The nation has its foundations laid in the nature of man. It is the normal condition of human existence. There is in it, as the organization of human society, the manifestation of human nature. The nature of man, apart from the nation, is unfulfilled; and in the individual, in his isolation, the destination of humanity is unrealized; the old words are verified, *unus homo, nullus homo.*

The nation, therefore, is not to be regarded as an artifice which man has devised, nor as an expedient suggested by circumstance, to secure certain special and temporary ends. It has other ground and other elements. It is often described as a contrivance of human skill, and government as the cunning or clumsy device for the accomplishment of certain objects in certain transient periods. A recent writer, identifying government with the nation, says it is "a machine for applying certain principles," etc.; but even as an illustration, this conveys a misconception. The machine, when it is made, is apart from the maker, and complete in itself, and separate from the power which impels it; but the nation never exists as a complete construction, and always is in identity with the people. The nation, moreover, cannot be moved as a machine, but has in itself thought and will and power to do or not to do, and capacity to suffer or rejoice. The nation exists, only as men are lifted out of a mechanical existence; in it there is the assertion of their determination, and their free endeavor. And man does not owe the conception of the nation to the genius of an individual, nor is it the invention of a separate age. The highest ingenuity could not have compassed it, and it is not to be counted among the achievements of human wisdom. The machine also wears out, with time and use, when another is made in its stead; but it is not thus with states, and there is no law of physical necessity which thus limits them.

This representation of the nation as a mechanism — the work of human craftsmen — is the root of the confusion which appears in the definition of man's savage or rude condition as the "natural state," and the emergence from it into civilization, as the "artificial state." It is the distinction, on the assumption of which so many social schemes and such vast social theories of natural and artificial society have been built. The law of Aristotle has here its application in political science, — "The nature of that which is, is to be ascertained from its mature condition;" not in its germ, nor yet in its decay, but in its fullness and its perfectness do we discern the true nature of a thing; or, what every being is in its perfect condition, that certainly is the nature of that being.[1]

[1] Aristotle's *Politics*, bk. i. ch. 2.

R. von Mohl, in one of his later works, represents the *state* as only one in the successive spheres of human life which he enumerates as the sphere of the individual, of the family, of the race, of society, of the state, and of the association of states in their international relation. The special characteristic of this description is the distinction of society and the state; the former is described as the common, yet the unorganized and the unformed life of man. But this distinction has no justification, and in it society in itself is undefined, and every trait which is drawn to give to it a positive substance and form is derived from what is represented as another sphere — either that of the individual, or of the state. When it is further said that there is a law and rights belonging to society, as apart from the state, which yet have the character of neither national nor common law, and of neither political nor civil rights, the absence of all ground for the distinction becomes still more apparent, for law and rights presume an organic life and an organized society. R. von Mohl, *Encyklopadie der Staatswissenschaften*, p. 17. See also Bluntschli's *Geschichte*, p. 616.

The nation is a relationship. They who exist in it are not held only by some external force, and are not bound only by some formal law. In the sketches given of existence apart from society, the state was represented as if men entered it from a condition of individual isolation, and as itself the resultant of their individual accession. This isolation is unreal; it is the atomy of the state, which regards it as the collection of so many units. It is a premise which is devised to sustain political systems and political abstractions. The isolation of men presumes a conception which is inhuman, and it is not in its separation but in its relations that humanity is comprehended. If, moreover, this isolation be allowed, it does not furnish the elements out of which the state can be formed, and it can suggest no law in which the transition to the state may be made.

The origin of the state is not in some speculative theory nor in some formal scheme. The entrance to it is not through a reflective process, nor by an act of individual volition. It has the characteristic of all relationships, in that it has not its beginning in a reflective or a voluntary act, while in it the individual is conscious of existence as a person.

It is not, in its normal course, out of a condition which is external that men enter the nation, but they are born in it, and it has the natural condition of relationship.

The recognition of its law, and the obedience to its authority, is not then conditioned upon the arbitrary choice of those who constitute it, but in reference to it the arbitrary action of the individual is precluded.

It is a common relationship, and there are none exempt from its conditions, and none in the nation can make their lives to be as if it had not been. There are none unaffected by it, but each is involved in every moment of its existence.

In the politics of Aristotle, human relationships — the

man and woman, the father and mother and child — are apprehended as the sign and suggestion of society, by which its existence is suspected, and in which its principle is contained. Then the constituents of society are sought in a house, but the family is not therefore the lesser state, nor the state simply a collection of families, since each has its own nature and end, while each as a relationship has therein its elemental principle. It was in the visionary republic of Plato that all relationships were swept away as antagonistic to its ideal unity, but as the nation is apprehended as itself a relationship, these are apprehended as integral in it and correspondent to it.

There is for the family, apart from the nation, a necessary imperfectness, as also they will hold best the relation of citizenship who hold best the relation of brothers and husbands and fathers.

The nation is subject to the conditions of all relationships. If the consciousness of them perish, the art of man can devise no substitute. Their strength can be supplied by no artificial bond, however subtly forged. They are deep as life, and in their mysterious power there is the holiest communion, so that their only illustration in the physical world is in the vine and the branches, and the body and the members.

It is thus that citizenship has its significance as a relationship. It is not carelessly that human lips have called their country the father-land ; nor is it with vague and idle phrases, but in a spirit of holy and son-like sacrifice and in solemn crises, that men have turned to their country as the mother of all.

The nation is a continuity. It no more exists complete in a single period of time than does the race ; it is not a momentary existence, as if defined in some circumstance. It is not composed of its present occupants alone, but it embraces those who are, and have been, and shall be. There is in it the continuity of the generations, it reaches backward to the fathers and onward to the children, and its relation is manifest in its reverence for the one and its hope for the other.

The evidence of this continuity is in the consciousness of a people. It appears in the apprehension of the nation as an inheritance, received from the fathers, to be transmitted unimpaired to the children. This conviction, that has held the nation as an heritage worth living and worth dying for, has inspired the devotion and sacrifice of a people.

The evidence of this continuity is also in the fact that the spirit of a people always contemplates it. The nation has never existed which placed a definite termination to its existence — a period when its order was to expire and the obligation to its law to cease. It cannot anticipate a time when it shall be resolved into its elements, but contends, with the intensity of life, against every force which threatens dissolution. Those who have represented the state as a compact, have yet held it to be a perpetual one, in which the children are bound by the acts of their fathers.

This continuity is the condition of the existence of the nation in history. The nation persists through a form of outward circumstance. Judæa was the same under the judges and under the kings; Rome was the same under the kings and under the consuls. The elements of the being of the nation subsist in this continuity. In it, also, the products of human effort are conserved, and the law of human production conforms to it. The best attainments pass slowly from their germ to their perfectness, as in the growth of the language and the law, the arts and the literature of a people. Chaucer and Spenser, through intervals of slow advance, precede Shakespeare, as Giotto and Perugino lead the way to Michael Angelo and Raphael.

The nation is a continuity, as also in itself the product of succeeding generations. It transcends the achievement of a single individual or a separate age. The life of the individual is not its measure. In its fruition there is the work of the generations, and even in the moments of its existence the expression of their spirit, the blending of the strength of youth, the resolve of manhood, and the experience of age — the hope and the aspiration of the one, the wisdom and repose of the other. There is the spirit which is always young, and yet always full of years, and even in its physical course the correspondence to an always renewed life.[1]

This continuity has found expression in the highest political thought. Shakespeare has it in his historical plays; the continuity of the nation is represented as existing through the years with the vicissitudes of the people, in the changes of scene, with the coming and going of men; and there is as in the nation the unity of the drama in which so many actors move, and whose events revolve from age to age; and thus these plays hold an attraction apart from the separate scenes and figures which present some isolated ideal for the poet to shape. Burke has represented this continuity in the nation as moving through generations in a life which no speculative schemes and no legal formulas may compass: "The nation is indeed a partnership, but a partnership not only between those who are living but between those who are living, those who are dead, and those who are to be born."

The life of the individual is brief, but in the nation it may become a continuous power. The character of Achilles may have a worth for all in its abstract ideal, but in the history of Greece it was always a living energy. They who have been the leaders of a nation in the strength and nobleness of their lives are always in a vital relation to it. The traditions of valor and sacrifice in the memory of a people become the inspiration of its hope.

The work of the individual is brief also, and in its isola-

[1] Nec temporis unius, nec hominis, esse constitutionem Reipublicæ. — Cicero, *De Republica*, bk. iii. ch. 21.

tion would be almost vain, but in the continuity of the nation it is enwrought in the longer social development. Thus, also, a single generation, in its furthest advance, achieves but little in comparison with the long line of the generations in the nation, and if there is laid on any the necessity of battle, still the holiest triumph is that in which the life of the nation in its continuity is maintained.

The nation is an organism. It has an organic unity, it is determined in an organic law, and constitutes an organic whole. There is a political truth whose worth may be measured against the sciolism of many recent theories, in the ancient words, — "As the days of a tree are the days of my people." The nation is shaped by no external force, but by an inner law; its changes are those of a development; its strength appears in its regarding all division as the sundering of life; and the glory of the people has been not in the uprooting, but in the maintaining and advancing of the work of its ancestors. This imparts to the people an energy which does not wholly perish in the waning of its years, it breaks the external bonds which fetter it, and flourishes amid the vastest historical changes.

The nation, as an organism, has the characteristic of every organism — unity and growth and identity of structure. It has not merely an apparent sequence, nor a constructive force, but is a development after an organic law. It is not a confused collection of separate atoms, as grains of sand in a heap, and its increase is not through their accumulation. It has the unity of an organism, not the aggregation of a mass; it is indivisible; its germ lies beyond analysis, and in it is enfolded its whole future. This unity is the postulate of the existence of the people as a nation, and the condition of its independence. An identity of structure also pervades the whole. Thus the defect of a part injures the whole; and if a part be severed it ceases to exist, as the limb which is cut from the body, or the branch from the tree.

The nation, therefore, is not something which can be torn down, and then from the old material built up again in other nations. It is planted, it is not made. It is not constructed out of preëxisting parts, but is an whole, and the law of Aristotle holds, — the whole is before the parts; that is, a whole cannot be made of parts, but the whole is predetermined, to which the parts belong, or it is only in the conception of the whole that the parts appear. A sum or aggregate can be composed of separate units, but it is only their mass, and there can be predicated of it neither unity nor growth, nor identity of structure.

The law of an organism defines the relation of the individual to the nation. They who form the organic whole, in their relation to it, and to each other, are its members. Its bond is not formal; its action is not mechanical. The members are formed in and through it, as they form it, and are not as the wheels in mills, and the shuttles that slide in looms, but the members of a living body. They are affected by it, not as by an external force, acting on component particles, but as by a living spirit working through the whole. The laws of life in the physical body do not act with more unvarying certainty than in the body politic.

The consciousness of this organic relation, is the ground, also, of the normal action of the individual. Hegel says, the mob in a nation is the force which acts without or apart from the organization of the whole. There may thus be an ignorant or a learned mob, a mob of men of fashion or of men of science, but the spirit is the same, and in its severance from the organic people there is the same essential vulgarity. This has an illustration of singular force in one of the political plays of Shakespeare. When Caius Marcius turns to the crowd in Rome and denounces them as the detached and disorganized rabble, in whom there is nothing of the organic unity of the people, the disdain of the Roman is in the words, "Go, get you home, you fragments!" and those who in the conceit of culture or of wealth, or of higher interests, or of spiritual endowments, withdraw from the normal political action of the nation, are obeying the impulse of the mob, and are as the very fragments, for whom the Roman patrician felt such unmeasured scorn.[1]

The antithesis to the nation as an organic unity, is in the conception which frames it upon abstractions. It assumes a certain scheme of rights, or system of laws, and then proceeds to construct the state out of these rights, or sets it forth as the product of this formal law. These assumptions are destitute of an historical foundation, and arise in the empty notion that men by a reflective act can constitute the nation, and that it exists as the sequence of an abstract conception. The most disastrous of political falsehoods is this, which in any form holds the nation in identity with a legal or dialectical system, and then proceeds to its construction, after the design of the abstract reason. It is destructive, and the whole existent order is constantly liable to be razed, in order to substitute an imaginary polity in its stead.

The apprehension of the nation as an organism, is the condition of political science. It involves the distinction of an art and a science; there may be, for instance, an art in building heaps of stones, but there is no science of stone-heaps. The unity and identity of structure in an organism, in which a law of action may be inferred, form the condition of positive science.

This is the source, also, of constructive political power, and of all that is enduring in the work of the statesman. In the recognition of this fact — of the organic being of the state — the most is gained, says Bluntschli, for the practical study of political subjects. And it is significant that political writers of grasp and wide influence, as Spinoza and Hobbes, proceeding from a premise which precludes the organic unity or being of the state, have yet

1 See Maurice, *The Workman and the Franchise*, p. 9.

been led to represent it as a living body, and have described it as some colossal man. This conception, when presented by those whose postulate is the contractual origin and definition of the state, indicates the reality of its existence as an organism.

It is also significant that the assertion of the nation as an organic unity, in modern political thought, should have proceeded from the historical political school. Savigny, who may be named as its representative, describes the nation as "the organic manifestation of the people."[1] Yet, the necessary conception of the nation as an organism transcends the limits of an historical school, and while the roots are traced in the past, there is necessarily a continuous development, and it passes into the future in the unfolding of its own germ. In the forgetfulness of this, the historical school reverts only to the past to dwell among its forms, and, as the sense of a living continuity and energy fades away, it becomes of all schools the most dry and barren.

But although the nation is organic, it is not limited to the definition of a physical organism. Its description in this logical limitation is often repeated;[2] it is said, for instance, that the nation, as the individual, passes through the necessary periods of youth, manhood, and age; that it flourishes, and after maturity ceases to exist — its bloom is followed by inevitable decay. The deeper truth is in

[1] Savigny's *Syst. des Rom. Rechts*, vol. i. p. 22.

"In every separate people the universal spirit of man manifests itself in an individual way, and the growth of rights has a common social ground." — *Syst. des Rom. Rechts*, vol. i. p. 20. See Bluntschli's *Allgemeinen Statsrecht und der Politik*, p. 568.

[2] "As men are born and live for a certain period, and at last die of age or infirmity, so also states are constituted; they flourish for some centuries and then at last cease to exist." — Frederick II., *Antimacchiavelli*, ch. ix.

Mr. Spencer says, — "We find not only that the analogy between society and a living creature is borne out, but the same definition of life applies to both." — *Social Statics*, p. 490. It may be doubted if the elaborate analogy which Mr. Spencer draws, carried as it is through the detail of a minute anatomy, has any justification. The description of an exact correspondence to the physical organism often serves as a display of anatomical science. The literature of poli-

the words of the Roman statesman, — "The state is formed for eternity." [1]

The nation is a conscious organism. It is the conscious life of the people; it knows its own object and the purpose which is given it to fulfill. Its action does not proceed from mere impulse, and it is not directed by a merely aimless energy, but there is in it that conscious spirit which apprehends an object before it, and apprehends it as its own. "The nation," says M. Thiers, "is that being which reflects and determines its own action and purpose."

It has a determinate end, and apprehends in its own conscious purpose its vocation in history. This consciousness of a vocation enters into the spirit of every historical people, and is the basis of its historical life. The nation has in correspondence to its vocation a determinate character: its character is the manifestation of the purpose it has realized in its vocation. Its character becomes thus as clearly outlined as that of its foremost men. Rome has a character as distinct as that of Cæsar, and Greece as that of Pericles.

The conscious life and vocation of the nation appear in the spirit with which it invests its members, and those who are called to the execution of its purpose. There is a quality in its membership which is distinct from that in a life withdrawn from it, and there is a spirit in the fulfillment of its trusts and offices which it alone imparts. When the thought and action of the members and officers of a nation become empty routine, the mere work of functionaries, there is the sign of the loss of a living energy,

tics has many monograms on this correspondence, in which for instance the members of the political society are compared to the cells, and the legislative power to the head, or the economy to the stomach, and so on; but they are mainly subject to the criticism of von Mohl, — "These conceptions of the state and its correspondences based upon physical science appear from time to time, partly through an altogether sickly tendency of thought, and partly through a mystical and fanciful conceit." — *Encyklopadie der Staatswissenschaften*, p. 84.

[1] "Debet enim constituta sic, esse civitas ut æterna sit." — Cicero, *De Republica*, bk. iii. ch. 3.

and the decadence of a people. It has been said that there was in the office of a Roman consul an inherent majesty, which often gave dignity to a person of ordinary character, and ennobled him with its spirit; and there is in the office of a representative of the people a power which may lift the possessor above the divisions of party and the interests of factions, so that he is made to stand in a living relation to the nation, whose work and purpose is to be wrought through him. It is thus, also, that one who is called to a public trust or office in the nation, is not simply a private person, nor to be so regarded.

The conscious life of the people appears in its literature and arts, its manners and laws. These are moulded in the type of the individual life of the nation, so that with the universal element in literature and art and law there is the individual element in which the characteristic of the people is traced. These not only bear the impress of its peculiar type, but there is in its being the field of their growth. The constructive polity, and the art and literature of a nation, thus terminate with its historical course. There may be great works produced after its close, but their root was in the past, and with its decay they soon cease; as there were solitary great Grecians and Romans after the loss of the national life of Greece and Rome, but the line soon expires. Their spirit can survive in no other people, and their work can be resumed by none. The Turks gain possession of Greece, and the French of Egypt, but the monuments and arts do not belong to them, they do not recognize their spirit in them, and cannot continue them. All that England can do with the sculptures called the Elgin marbles, is to place them in a museum.

This consciousness of the vocation of the nation, how ever reluctantly acknowledged or dimly apprehended, has been stronger than the individual intention of its members.

It has determined the course of the greater in the succession of its leaders and its kings, and has turned them from their individual bent, when they could not warp it to their own use. In England and France the greater rulers, as Henry VIII. and Louis IX., have been those who have held the best apprehension of and given the clearest expression to this vocation; and kings and ministers who have sought to thwart it, or even failed to be penetrated by it, have been set aside, or, as illustrative of its weakness in some ages, are left to stand as passive figures in its lines.

In the conscious life and vocation of the nation, there is the ground of its identity of purpose, through the succeeding generations. Its purpose is transmitted from the fathers to the children. The consciousness of its destination becomes clearer in the advance, as it fades in the degeneracy of the people, and is obscured in the precedence of selfish interests, and at last blotted out in stupidity and slavery. Thus, also, the early incident of a people may contain the premonition, and its historical epochs and crises the revelation, of its vocation. There is through all the same great promise, the same memories, and the same hopes. The longer years alone are its measure. The calling of the nation thus may endure through humiliation and defeat, and through evil days, when there is only a remnant left who keep its ancient faith and guard its errand from forgetfulness.

This is held slightly by the teachers of the technic of political art, and by those who would limit politics to political economy, but the consciousness and the fulfillment of the vocation of the people are the condition of its power; this vocation is the postulate of national character and national freedom. The people has in it no external limitation which impairs action, but is strong and free only as it works it out. The people that fails to hold its calling carefully and reverently cannot attain a strong national life, and weakness and inevitable disaster result when its purpose is but feebly grasped, and servility and degradation when it becomes the imitator or the copyist of another.

The nation is a moral organism. In the necessary elements of its existence in history it transcends the merely physical conditions of a physical organism; and in freedom, and law, and order, in the fulfillment of a conscious purpose and vocation, and in the obligation to law, are the very elements of a moral being.

It is a moral organism; that is, its members are persons who subsist in it, in relations in the realization of personality. It is the condition in which a person exists in the fulfillment of the relations of life with those who are persons. There is in it the assertion of a justice, which is the affirmation of a person in the recognition and institution of these relations between the moral whole and the moral parts of the whole. Its law is regulative of the moral whole, and of the parts, in these relations.

It is as a moral organism that the nation is the field of the action of man, in law and in freedom. There is, therefore, in it the education of the individual, the growth and formation of character. There is in its normal development the coming into the world of that which is laid in the nature of humanity, in its true and original constitution.

It is as a moral organism that there are in the nation the conditions of the moral life of the individual. In the assumed isolation of man there is the negation of the moral life which is formed in moral relations. Thus all the relations of life in its moral order are constituted in the nation, and are to be maintained through its institutions and by its enactments.[1]

It is as a moral organism that the nation is the sphere

[1] "Whosoever lays violent hands upon the state, assails the conditions of all moral life, and therefore the crime is regarded as the greatest." — Trendelenburg, *Naturechte aus dem Grunde der Ethik*, p. 286.

of the individual person. The fact of a vocation cannot consist with his isolation. It presumes an existence in a conscious relationship, and its fulfillment is in the relations of a moral order. It is thus that there is formed in the nation the consciousness of the relationship of humanity, and the moral life of the individual is apprehended in it as the life which is truly human.

The process of the nation is only as a moral organism. It is not constituted in the necessary process of the physical world, but it is constituted in the order of a moral world. Its course is defined in law, and in law as prescribing the actions and relations of men as moral agents. Its attainment is in freedom. Its goal is peace, and that not in the barren conception in which there is the negation of purpose and energy, but peace as the conquest of man, in which there is the satisfaction of his spirit and the achievement of his aim.

The conditions of history presume the being of the nation as a moral organism. History is not a succession of separate events and actions, but a development in a moral order, and in the unity and continuity of a life which moves on unceasingly, as some river in its unbroken current. But it is only as the nation is an organism that this unity and continuity is manifest in it, and as a moral organism that this moral order is confirmed in it.

The nation thus cannot be comprehended in the definition in its logical limitations of a physical organism. The distinction of a physical and a moral organism is necessary, and becomes the illustration of the being of the nation, in its necessary conception. It is as follows: —

The physical organism is determined in itself by a law of necessity, as the tree which cannot be other than it is: the ethical organism is determined in a law of freedom, which is the condition of moral action. In the physical organism, each member exists only in its relation to the whole, as, for instance, the hand is nothing without the body, and has no separate significance: in the ethical organism, each member has in itself a necessary significance, and each member, furthermore, has the destination in itself, for which the whole exists, and which the whole has in itself. The whole subsists in the same relation and has the same destination as the individual, and neither the whole nor the individual has a secondary existence, nor can be made only a means to the end of another. In the physical organism, the elements which are atomic, under a law of combination, are taken up and separated again, and as they pass back into unformed nature, it is only to reappear in other and manifold forms: in the ethical organism, the members are individuals existing each in his own identity, and each is so related to the whole that instead of a construction after the exclusive type of the whole, it is indifferent to say that the individual has his type in the whole, or the whole its type in the individual. In the physical organism, the changes are through necessary periods, as youth and age, or spring and autumn, and the elements which are chemical, and so on, are formed after the law of these periods; but in the ethical organism the process is not through the periods of a necessary sequence, and its members exist in each moment of its existence in uninterrupted relations of youth and age. Its life consists in the constantly unfolding life of humanity.[1]

1 The logical fallacy of defining an ethical by a physical organism, and limiting the one to the conception of the other, appears in Draper's *Civil Polity*. The description of the growth and maturity and decay of nations is repeated with a solemn monotony, as if history was an unbroken succession of funereal pageants. But the nations do not exist in history in this limitation in a physical sequence; they appear under the conditions of a moral life, and their growth or decay is traced not in necessary, but in moral causes.

There is in the same school the utter denial of the real freedom of the individual and the nation, when it aims to define freedom only in the limitations of a physical necessity, and the mind of man is regarded only as involved in the physical process of nature. Yet not infrequently exhortations are made in the same school on the beauty, or the duty, or the excellence of political morality, and these may be often the expression of an emotive fervor or of prudent counsel; but they can avail little when they are connected with a merely economic conception of the nation, and are separated from their only consistent postulate in its organic and moral being.

The nation is a moral personality. This is the condition of its vocation, as in the fulfillment of its vocation there is the formation of its character. The moral personality of the nation is determined in its consciousness; in its conscious purpose subsists its independence of other nations, that it is not to be necessarily what they are nor as they are. Its object is before it, which it knows as its own; its freedom is in the working out of its vocation, and in its goal there is the satisfaction of its desire.

The condition of the realization of personality is the same in the nation as in the individual. This condition in each is the clearness and fullness in which it comprehends its purpose and is centred in it. The source of strength is, as with the individual, in working faithfully after the type of its own individuality, and bringing this to its free and clear development. The being of the nation is, therefore, not merely in an apparent sequence, but in conformance with the law which is laid in its being.

The scope of the nation thus is not exhausted by, and its powers are not derivative from a sphere of outward circumstance; it is not comprehended in a summary of enactments nor defined in an abstract system. The only limitation is its self-limitation in its being, as a moral person. In this is the postulate of its law and the line of its progress. There are no bars or barriers before the course of the free spirit of the people, and the nation moves in its advance towards the higher personality which is realized in its vocation, which is of God, in history.[1]

The nation is a moral person, since it is called as a power in the coming of that kingdom in which there is the moral government of the world, and in whose completion there is the goal of history. It is a power in the moral conflict and conquest which is borne through history, to the final triumph of the good. It is a power manifest in

1 "National character ist der gottliche Beruf, einer nation." — Stahl, *Philosophie des Rechts*, vol. i. p. 365.

the judgment of history. But in the formal and artificial conception of the nation this power becomes a fiction, and in the mechanical conception it has no moral ground.

The nation is a moral person, since its development is in an integral moral life. Its character is its own, it is not derivative from any powers on earth; it does not proceed through them, and its responsibility cannot be transferred, nor its obligation rendered to them. It is not the vehicle in which another and a separate power is carried to its end, nor the frame-work in which another life is to be built, nor the shadow which in a disturbed economy falls from some other order or organization that alone is lifted into the clear light, and alone knows the triumph of the good. It is not the instrument for the pursuance of the vocations of separate individuals, which are to be held before it as separate and special ends, nor in the formation of the character of certain individuals, does it alone have its end; but as its vocation is its own, and it is judged in it, it has its own end. Its ground is not in the individual, but in the historical life of humanity. It has for its end not the special but the universal; its assertion is not of the individual will, but of law which is the universal will; its institution is not in the right of one, nor of a few, but in the rights of man.

The nation is a moral person, since it is formed in a moral conflict. It is not merely phenomenal in its moral being. It is not the perfect image, nor yet the passive reflection of righteousness, as of something external to it, but its being and the condition of its being is in righteousness. Yet it is not therefore a self-righteous power, but exists in the institution of righteousness in the moral order of the world. It is formed in a real conflict. The nation, in the attainment of its being, is to strive. There is always in its freedom the possibility of evil, but in evil there is also the negation of its being.

The being of the nation as a moral person has its witness

in the consciousness of men. It has awakened the higher moral emotion, and its response has been from the higher moral spirit. It has called forth the willing sacrifice of those who were worthy. The life of the individual has been given for the life of the nation. The offering has been laid upon that, which in the holiest spirit has been held as an altar, and life has been given in that sacrifice in which life is found. If the nation had only a formal existence, this moral spirit could have no justification, and if its origin was in self-interest, to call for self-sacrifice would be the negation of it; and if its end was only in the protection of the life and property of the individual, this surrender of them would be the immediate defeat of its end.

The nation is a moral person, since it is the organized life of society, and society is formed in the spirit and in the power of a personal life. It is to be governed in the conscious determination of the will, and to act as one who looks before and after. The strength which is to be wrought in it, exists only in rectitude of thought and of will; wisdom and courage, steadfastness and reverence, faith and hope are attributes of it; the highest personal elements become its elements and are moulded in its spirit.

The relation of the individual to the nation presumes, as its necessary condition, the existence of the nation as a moral person. The individual becomes a person in the nation, and this involves the existence of the nation as also a person; for personality, as it is formed in relations, can subsist only in an organic and moral relationship — a life which has a universal end. The nation is thus the sphere of a realized freedom, in which alone the life of man fulfills itself, and it is to give expression to all that is compassed in life. It moves toward the development of a perfect humanity. Its symbol is the city of an hundred gates, through which there passes not only the course of industry and trade, but the forms of poets and prophets and soldiers and sailors and scholars — man and woman and child, in the unbroken procession of the people. Its warrior bears the shield of Achilles, on which there are not only the figures of the mart and sea and field, the loom and ship and plough, but the houses and the temples and the shrines and the altars of men, the types of the thought and endeavor and conflict and hope of humanity.

The condition of the being of the nation, as the power and the minister of God in history, is in its moral personality; in this it is constituted in history as the moral order of the world, and for the fulfillment of that order.

The assertion of the moral being of the nation has been the foundation of that which is enduring in politics, and has been embodied in the political thought and will which alone have been constructive in the state. Aristotle, who gave the furthest attainment of the ancient world, says, "The end of the state is not merely to live, but to live nobly."[1] Hegel, who has given a yet wider expression to modern thought than did Aristotle to the ages before him, — and there is no other name with which the parallel may be drawn, — represents the state as the realization of the moral, and in the moral alone it has its substance and being. He says, "The state is the realization of the moral idea,"[2] and "The state is the realization of freedom, and it is the absolute end of reason that freedom be real,"[3] and "The state is no mechanism, but the rational life of self-conscious freedom, the order of the moral world;"[4] and again he says, "There is one conception in religion and the state, and that is the highest of man."[5]

There is no other conception which has such power in the thoughts of men, and in this age it has the greater significance when it is drawn, not from a school of puritan

[1] Aristotle's *Politics*, bk. i. ch. 2.
[2] Hegel's *Philosophie des Rechts*, p. 312.
[3] *Ibid.* p. 317.
[4] *Ibid.* p. 340.
[5] Hegel's *Philosophie der Religion*, vol. i. p. 170.

politics, but from those most widely separated from historical puritanism, and finds its expression in the literature of a people which is rising to great political might.[1] But those who have been the masters of political science, and it has perhaps fewer great names than any other science, all repeat this conception. Milton says, "A nation ought to be but as one huge Christian personage, one mighty growth or stature of an honest man, as big and compact in virtue as in body, for look, what the ground and causes are of single happiness to one man, the same ye shall find them to a whole state."[2] Burke says, "The state ought not to be considered as a partnership agreement to be taken up for a little temporary interest and dissolved at the fancy of the parties. It is to be looked on with other reverence, because it is not a partnership in things subservient to the gross animal existence of a temporary and perishable nature. It is a partnership in all science; a partnership in all art; a partnership in every virtue and in all perfection."[3] Shakespeare says, —

> "There is a mystery — with whom relation
> Durst never meddle — in the soul of state;
> Which hath an operation more divine
> Than breath or pen can give expressure to."[4]

1 See Rothe's *Theologische Ethik*, vol. iii. sec. ii. p. 900. Stahl's *Philosophie des Rechts*, vol. ii. sec. 2, p. 181. Bluntschli's *Allgem Stats Rechts*, vol. i. p. 140.

2 Milton's *Reformation in England*, Preface to bk. ii.

3 *Reflections on the French Revolution*, p. 368.

4 *Troilus and Cressida*, act iii. sc. 3.

CHAPTER II.

THE SUBSTANCE OF THE NATION AS DEFINED IN THEORIES.

The conduct of affairs in the nation is shaped after the conception which men may have of its origin and end, and yet it does not subsist in the individual and arbitrary conception, and cannot be made the exponent of that. It exists in its necessary conception, and every divergence from that is the building of some abstraction, or, as the French phrase is, "in the air," and through vagueness will result in feeble action, or, through defect, in negative action. The error in thought can involve only disaster in fact.

The representations of the nation, which most frequently recur in politics, and especially in its later phases, are mainly as follows: —

The nation is represented as a necessary evil. It is a sequence of the evil which is in the world, and is incident to that. It is imposed on man to control the desires and lusts, and to curb the tendency with which it is said the inclination of his nature is toward evil. It is made necessary by the disorder and violence, the fraud and enmity of men, and the antagonism of self-interest, and is itself to be endured as only a less evil than these, and to lose its power as they abate, and to cease with their termination. It is simply repressive, and is the restraint which is necessary to check the evil drift of the world. This defines the state as the resultant of the existence of wrong, and necessitated by that; it is to be apprehended only as involved in the sequence of evil, a manifestation of an estate of sin and misery.

This makes a destructive force the constructive cause of society. But evil in its necessary character is not formative. It creates nothing and produces nothing, it only consumes and destroys. It has in itself no elements of order, and can bring forth none. It holds no type after which things are to be fashioned, but only changes and disturbs them. Therefore the nation, its unity and order and progress, cannot be derivative from evil and an evil condition.

Government, which is the central organization of the nation, is not an evil. Its substance is in itself good, and is implicit in the conception of the good. Law, which is the ground and expression of its authority, is in its ultimate apprehension the manifestation of the divine will, as has been said of it in imperishable words, "Its home is the bosom of God, and its voice is the harmony of the world."[1] And freedom, which in the nation is constituted in law, is the sphere of the normal development of man. And the nation is not a mere negation, only a restriction of evil tendencies and an impediment to evil courses, as this theory assumes. It has a positive character and content. It is the manifestation of the life of the organic people, after a moral order, and in the institution of justice and of rights. It is a constructive power in history. It is not a local and temporary expedient, and its elements are not those which the scientific culture of another and a later age may set aside. It is not a fetter and a burden imposed upon the race, in an evil necessity, which it may gradually come in

[1] Mr. Brownson says of government, "It would have been necessary, if man had not sinned, and for the good as well as for the bad. The law was promulged in the Garden, while man retained his innocence. It exists in heaven as well as on earth, and in heaven in its perfectness." —*The American Republic*, p. 18.

"The nation is not only revealed as the power in conflict with evil, but even the beginning (Paradise) looked toward a development into a perfect kingdom." —Stahl, *Philosophie des Rechts*, vol. ii. sec. ii. p. 81.

its progress to discard, and from which it may be ultimately wholly emancipated. It is itself the condition of progress, and in its course there is the striking off of fetters, and the deliverance from burdens, and a constantly increasing freedom.

The representation of the nation as a necessary evil, appears through many periods, and in many forms. It was the prevalent notion of the mediæval age. It arises often from a want of satisfaction in the merely jural and economic representation of the state. The spirit of man demands something more and better than that, his hope and purpose look to something ampler and worthier, and that offers no sphere in which he can fulfill his vocation or unfold his energies, and when thus conceived it comes to be set aside as a necessary evil in the evil of this world, and also as transient in its nature.[1]

[1] Mr. Calhoun makes this conception the base of his political structure. He defines the end of government, "to repress violence and preserve order." He says, "The powers must be administered by men in whom, like others, the individual are stronger than the social feelings," and therefore, "since they may be used as instruments of oppression, that by which this is prevented is called constitution." While this is the postulate of the argument of Mr. Calhoun's essay, it is significant that he should write, in one of its first sentences, "To man the Creator has assigned the social and the political state as best adapted *to develop the great capacities and faculties, intellectual and moral, with which he has endowed him*," but the thought lies upon the page, and has no further consideration, nor does it enter into his construction of the state. Calhoun's *Works*, vol. i. pp. 7, 15, 52. Mr. Spencer is the most recent advocate of this theory, and presents it in its extremest shape. He says, "Nay, indeed, have we not seen that government is essentially immoral? Is it not the offspring of evil, bearing about it all the marks of its parentage? Does it not exist because crime exists? Is it not strong, or, as we say, despotic where crime is great? Is there not more liberty, that is, less government, as crime diminishes? and must not government cease, when crime ceases, for very lack of objects on which to perform its functions? Morality cannot recognize it." — *Social Statics*, p. 230. He says again, "Government is a necessary evil" (*Social Statics*, p. 25), to terminate with the evil which is assumed as the ground of its existence; "it is a mistake to assume that government must last forever. The institution marks a certain stage of civilization, is natural to a particular phase of human development. It is not essential, but incidental. As amongst the Bushmen we find a state antecedent to government, so may there be one in which it shall have become extinct." — *Social Statics*, p. 24. It would scarcely be necessary to notice these statements of this theory, but if they be received in the

The nation is represented as an historical accident. It is the outward circumstance of the life of man upon the earth ; it is a phenomenal phase of society, the form which society in its manifold nature, in some places and some ages may assume.

But the nation has not been in history an indifferent phase of action in certain places, and a transient incident of certain ages, which this implies. As there is in the nature of man the evidence that he is constituted for the nation, so also his normal development has been in it, in the historical life of humanity.

It is not the characteristic of a single epoch, as would follow if it were only an incident in the life of the race, but it is a power in the continuous development of history. It is no ephemeral mode of existence, and instead of being the incident, it is the substance of history.

It is not the circumstance of the existence of man upon the earth, but in it there is the determinate power in which man controls circumstance, and maintains through events the persistent expression of his aim. It is formed in the assertion of a dominion over the external world. Its progress is as it lifts man above the force of circumstance and the subjection to circumstance. Man is weak and dependent as he is isolated or withdrawn from it. It is not the occurrence of some fortuitous scene, to come and go, in the unlimited play of events, some single strand which is caught and woven in the loom of the years, with

thought of a people, they must work inevitable disaster, alike to the individual and the nation, and their repetition of the mediæval conception of the state, which in that age was always given with a certain sadness and regretful sense of loss, involves in this age wider consequences. The characteristics of " the state among the Bushmen antecedent to government," are not further described, and there is no positive presentation of facts on which to rest these " other stages of civilization," which also were rid of government, whose existence the writer assumes, except as the " state among the Bushmen," may be also illustrative of them. When these assumptions are presented, with the pretension of a school that it always keeps a foothold of facts and is characterized by a scientific exactness, they may justify some surprise.

their ceaseless changes, and then not to appear again, but it is the fabric in which events are wrought.

This representation of the nation apprehends it as only an apparent order; not an end in itself, but incidental to the attainment of some other and separate ends; only a scaffolding for some interior structure, which it is to support, or an association for the advancement of the private ends of the individual. But in its vocation and the moral obligation which it cannot transfer nor evade, there is the condition of an immediate moral being. It has not the individual in himself and his advancement as its separate and special end, but in its aim as the universal, it constantly elevates the individual above a separate and special end. It has a life which may call for the sacrifice of the life of the individual in the higher, the universal aim. There is a false egoism, which has its root in selfishness, in this representation of the subordination of the state to private ends, whatever their disguise and whether they be of a so-called spiritual, or of a temporal character, and the necessary sequence of the principle it asserts is the dissolution of society.

In this representation it is common to regard the organization of government as identical with the nation, and to limit it to that conception. Thus the dynasty or the municipality, the tribal, or patrimonial, or imperial power, may be regarded as substantially the nation. But it is not comprehended in the simple fact of government. There is government in the family, and yet the family is not the state. There may be the recognition of and the subordination to authority, in an association which is organized for plunder, as in the brigand's band or on the pirate's ship.[1] When the nation is apprehended as only an external order, the recognition of a certain authority, in a certain locality, and by a certain association of men,

[1] "Quæ est enim civitas? Omnisne etiam ferorum et immanium? Omnisne fugitivorum ac latronum congregata unum in locum multitudo? Certe negabis." — Cicero, *De Republica*, bk. ii. ch. 2.

then it may indeed be assumed as the transient circumstance in a continually changing condition, but there can be for human society no real stability.

The nation is represented as a jural society. Its sole object is the maintenance of private interests and the protection of private rights. Its end is effected in the keeping of the peace among a certain number of men in a certain locality. Its process is a system of police. It is a vast constabulary force, which is to prevent disorder within certain limits of the earth. The nation is only a judge and warden, and that government is best which governs least. Thus one's country is a larger bailiwick, whose boundaries some convenience of administration has determined; the father-land is the circuit of the judge and the sheriff. The exponent of national power is the tipstave. To be a citizen, to be the member of a nation, has no other significance than a certain relation, in which each is held and bound over for the keeping of the peace. The only association recognized in the state is a jural relation, and the nation is only a jural society.

This conception is obviously imperfect, and while, as R. von Mohl says, it is so narrow as scarcely to need criticism, it is yet constantly recurrent. The state certainly has to secure the civil order of society, to repress violence and to punish crime; but this is not its sole nor its whole end. Every state, simply to maintain its existence, embraces a wider sphere and exercises larger powers. The aim of society, in its most meagre form, could not be accomplished in so contracted a principle.

This also regards the maintenance of the necessary relations of the individual, and private rights and interests, as the end of the state. Its law is in necessity, and in the relations which conform to this law, but it subsists no longer in a real freedom. It is no longer the growth of national character and spirit. There is no organic and moral continuity, and its citizenship is no longer a living relation. There is no principle in which it can animate the spirit of man, and it can awaken no reverence for the past nor hope for the future. It cannot inspire the generous sacrifice of the present to the future, by which alone the life of nations is conserved. There is no place for the self-devotion which is the source of public spirit, and in its whole scope there is no ground for public rights and public duties.

This also confounds civil and political rights, or rather the whole province of political rights is denied, and the nation is limited to the definition of the civil organization. It is constituted only of persons in private relations, and only for their protection in these relations. But this is inconsistent with the essential constitution of the political people, and there is no principle in which it can apprehend the people as organic, and therefore as invested with political power, in the will of the political whole.

This conception is also destitute of an historical foundation, and does not serve to describe any historical nation. It is a low and imperfect representation which fails to define the life of the people in its organic unity and organized relations, and makes no history possible in its own limitation. There is no ground for an historical unity and continuity. The historical course of every nation has elements which transcend it. It fails to represent, for instance, the life of Greece or Rome, of England or France, and eliminates from their history all their spirit and all that gives dignity and grandeur to their action.

This proposition has for its postulate necessarily a false conception, both of the origin of society as only an association of men, and of the nature of men as impelled only by selfish interests and toward selfish ends ; and when it reaches its conclusion, as it merges the nation into the civil corporation, it indicates the beginning of a false civilization.

The highest organization of the civil corporation, and

the most perfect jural system, would still not satisfy the spirit of a people. It could not attain toward the destination of those powers which are immanent in humanity. There is in it the apprehension of no moral relationship, and in its last analysis it could apprehend its members only as plaintiff and defendant. The long result of human society it would represent in the institution of a civil court, and the close of history in twelve men sitting in a jury-box. Its final achievement it would reduce to a codification of the laws. The better conception of society and of the individual perishes, and the largeness in the forethought of the statesman, and the heroism in the devotion of the soldier have no place in it, but its representative is only the civil lawyer.

The civil corporation presumes the existence of the political people, that is, the nation in which it subsists; and it has in itself no element of continuity, nor even of continuous action. There is no fact more significant than that the life of the Roman citizen had lost all its strength and nobleness, when it came to be apprehended under relations and distinctions defined only by the civil system. There was no longer in Roman citizenship a vital and a moral spirit, and the individual discipline which had been the secret of her conquest, and her vast organization, perished. It was in the decadence of Rome, and in the later days of the empire, that the thoughts of the greatest of her sons turned only to the civil law, to its system and its codification.

It allows no sphere for the maintenance in it of the relationships of life. They cannot in their normal conception subsist in it, and when the nation is apprehended as only a civil corporation, an administration of the police, then the family, which is organic and is in itself sacred, is elevated above it, only at last, in its necessary relation to it, to be reduced to the same low conception. The nation, merely as a society of jural relations, cannot comprehend the family thus as organic and as sacred, and whenever the one has been represented as a civil corporation, the other has come to be held as only a civil contract.

This proposition has been assumed in the assertion of a necessary separation of the moral and the legal, and the identity of the nation with the latter. It is correct in the assertion of a distinction of the moral and the legal, and the former has never in the latter its perfect expression nor its comprehension; but the proposition assumes their isolation, so that in the state the conception of the one excludes the other. This has its illustration, and has obtained in some respects its more recent influence, through the aphorism of Kant.[1] Kant represented the state as deriving its content and its powers from a formal law, and defined it as, "the association of men under a system of laws." He asserted that the moral cannot be external, since it requires that duty shall spring from the conscience which is within man, and proceed through an inner motive, while the order of the state regards only the conformance of the external act to the law, and to it there is attached also compulsion, the physical force, which belongs to the authority of the state. This was the argument for the definition of the state as formal, not organic and moral, and for its representation as only an external order. It is correct in the assertion that the conscience is within man, and that the inner life is beyond the invasion of physical force, and over it the state has not, nor has any save only God control, but with this it does not follow for one moment that the external act must be separated from the conscience, nor that the external order has no moral substance, nor that the formal law has no moral content and no moral end. The physical force, also, which this asserts as existent in the state, must, as a right, have a higher sanction than this allows, since there is no ground

[1] Kant, *Rechtslehre*, sec. 45.

on which a number of men are justified in the act itself, in compelling one man. The state also acknowledges as legally binding without express enactment, a moral relation and obligation, and the primary obligations, for instance, of patriotism, which in no state have been defined in its system of laws, and cannot be so defined, are necessarily assumed and asserted by every state. In this argument, also, the laws have necessarily no other content than that which is derived from the external relations of life, but if the state is apprehended only in these relations, it becomes merely an external and formal order, and in the institution of these relations as external and formal it would fail of their end, since they presume a moral unity and obligation. And the legal becomes something poor and empty, when it is separated from the moral; and the law, when its invisible sanctions in the conscience are withdrawn, becomes only the contrivance of legislators, and society only the scheme of politicians. The very conception of law as the affirmation of justice, and its universal aim, is lost sight of when it is apprehended as existent only for the individual, and to subserve his private end. It has, indeed, for the individual, no such egoistic place.

This, also, necessarily excludes all consciousness of a divine obligation in the nation to execute justice and to punish crime, to repress violence and to maintain order. The state is merged again into the civil corporation, and in the assumption of the isolation of the legal and the moral, and the subsequent foundation of the nation in the merely legal, society becomes only the form of legists, and its action the precedent of a political pharisaism.

The nation is represented as an economic society. It is a temporary organization for the promotion of the physical well-being of man; it exists only for the satisfaction of certain physical wants; it has its ground in the necessities which arise in the coexistence of men.

This is the merely economic state; its law is in necessity; its relation has a material basis; its existence is contingent upon the securance of certain temporary ends. The bond by which it is attached, is in production and exchange, and its permanence is to provide security for material accumulations. The nation is apprehended only as a joint stock concern, a board of trade, an insurance shop, or a produce exchange. The continuity in which it unites the generations, is the inheritance of their accumulated capital — contracts and wills. The record of its achievement is in tables of commercial profit and loss, and the relation of its members is defined by regulations in bargain and sale. It exists for the protection of persons and property, and is, at the most, only the external and temporary form in which some interior and spiritual structure is built, but it has in itself no corresponding character, and no apprehension of the purpose and spirit of that, and no enduring principle nor universal aim.

It is true that the nation has in its scope the organization of the civil order, in the protection of persons and property, but this is not comprehensive of it. There is to this the same objection which applies to the representation of the state as simply the jural society: it is obviously deficient. It fails to define any historical nation, and there is none in its limitation which could find a place in history. There is no people which has attained an historical existence, but it has necessarily held a moral purpose and aim, beyond any material interest, and in the crisis of its history, it has been called to sacrifice material interests that the nation might live, and has maintained its calling in the rejection of apparent material advantages.

This proposition fails, also, since it necessarily involves the formation of society after a selfish principle, or in self-interest. There is not in this a formative social energy. There can be no unity, since the principle it assumes is the very root of division. It can issue only in disintegration through self-antagonisms, and the result in fact, as it is the necessary sequence of the principle, is the dissolution of society.

There is not in this assumption the condition of permanence; and when the security of material interests has become the supreme end, it indicates the decay of the state. If it has failed to recognize a principle of righteousness, that still has not swerved to allow a way for it, nor fallen to be passed over in its streets.

This conception does not correspond to the apprehension of the nation, in the consciousness of men. It divests its life of all sacredness, and its authority of all obligation. There is no ground left to the people of reverence for its ancestors or of hope for its children. There is for justice no solemnity. It cannot call forth that devotion from its sons, whose measure is the pledge of life and fortune, and their sacrifice would be the subversion of the end ascribed to it. It has no place for the courage of the soldier, nor the wisdom of the statesman, nor even for the love of its children, but exists for the promotion of trade, and is the copartnership of men in a secular concern.

But the defect in the limitation of this conception is apparent. The nation has elements which are not determined in its economy. It is not exhausted in the schedules of its produce and exchange; its unity is not in material interests; its history is written in other books than the tables of its census; its capital is other than the centre of its trade.

This proposition has had a various support, and has determined the position of the most opposite parties, and has united — each holding the state in moral indifference — the secularist and the ecclesiast. The latter has assumed for himself alone the work of righteousness on the earth, to result often in indifference to actual righteousness, and the former has denied the presence and the power of righteousness in history. The inference of each has been the being of the nation, as only an association of individuals in an external order, for certain temporary ends; an existence subsisting only in the secular, and each, therefore, has regarded its course as profane, and the crises of its existence too often have seen their latent or avowed alliance.

The principles of economy have a common ground and application; the laws of commerce and exchange are as wide as the seas on which their ships sail. They are laws which are applied by every nation, but they are not immanent in the organism of the nation, nor determined in its individual existence. Thus the nation may form a treaty of reciprocity in trade, but it can form none of reciprocity in political rights; for the nation, as an organic and moral power, is subsistent in these. There is nothing in the principles of political economy which can become the ground of the separate life of the nation.[1]

This conception, in its premise and conclusion, corresponds to the preceding; and the characteristic of all is the identity of the nation with the civil corporation, and the rejection of its organic and moral being. These theories become the source not of the constructive energy, but involve the elements of the dismemberment of society. They can apprehend the nation only as the field of individual ambition, and selfish interests, and private ends.

[1] "Die burgerliche gesellschaft rein als solche, ist eine Kosmopolitin." — Rothe, *Theologische Ethik*, vol. ii. p. 123.

CHAPTER III.

THE ORIGIN OF THE NATION AS DEFINED IN THEORIES.

THE conception of the origin of the nation is necessarily presumed in the conception of its unity and its substance. They alike shape the action of men in the conduct of affairs, and there has been in modern history no more manifest illustration of the relation between the thought and the work of a people. The response has been given in various theories, to the inquiry, Whence does the nation, that is, the organization of society, derive its being, and its unity, and the authority in its government, and its rights, and its powers.

It is not the beginning of the nation, in its historical circumstance, which is the object of this inquiry; and this has been the same, in no separate nations. Their inception, in their external phases, has been as varied as the infinite life of history. The historical beginning may be, for instance, in the growth of a family, and the accession of other families, or in the planting of a colony, or in the migration of a race, and so on. But there is in this only the incident of their historical inauguration, and we do not attain to the origin of the nation, nor of its unity, nor the authority in its government, nor its rights and powers. The characteristic of these various propositions in review is their lack of consistence with the necessary conception of the nation; they are mere abstractions, and their worth is only in their illustration of the necessary conception.

It is said that the nation has its origin in the development of the family: the family is the unit of human society, and of its organic process in the nation; and in the explication of the family the nation is formed. The right in which the government of the nation subsists, is then also the right of the father, and the people who form the nation are related to the government as its children.

It is true that the family is the unitary form of society, but it is not therefore the only form, nor determinative of the whole. The nation is not the continuation of the family, nor is it the result simply of its extension, nor is it in its form necessarily correspondent to it. The organism in its perfectness cannot transcend its germ or spore, and the family in its widest development is still only the family. The nation is not necessarily implanted in the family, but it is itself an organism; it has its seed in itself, and the condition of its development is in its own organic unity and the conformance to its organic law.

The rights and powers which belong to the nation also transcend those of the family. The authority in each is different from the other, and while the latter in its form is absolute, and obedience is rendered to it as to an imperative, the former is the determination of the organic will as law, and obedience to it is in the conscious obligation to law. The rights of the former, also, are private rights, and its power is private power as an estate, as it is also indeed when power is held as the property and entail, of a patrimonial prince or an hereditary aristocracy; but in the nation there are public rights, and its power is vested as a public trust. The duties of the family are also in implicit obedience to one, who is the father of the house, but in the nation there are public duties.

The right which is the ground of the government of the family, cannot become that of the government of the nation. The government of the family rests in the right of the father to govern his child, but this is necessarily limited to those who are his children, and cannot justify the extension of his authority over those who are not his children. When it is thus extended over the children of another, it conflicts with the unity of the family and its authority in its natural head, and wherever, in the organization of society, it has been transposed beyond its natural limits, it has sought its justification in a civil conception, and in some legal fiction, as that of adoption.

The nation is over the family, and the latter in its relation to it is subordinate. The father is responsible to the nation for the manner in which he may exercise his authority in the family, and the relations of the latter, and the obedience of the child, are to be sustained and enforced by its law. It prescribes the age when the child may be withdrawn from the formal authority of the father, and even in earlier years it may take the child from him when it deems necessary, and institute a guardianship over it.[1] The right of the nation, therefore, instead of residing in the right of the father, holds the latter in subjection.

This proposition is often stated thus, that the nation has its origin in the association of certain separate families. It is derived from the existence of a certain number of families, separated from all others, and connected by marriage among themselves. But this does not necessarily transcend the limits of a tribal relation, and does not attain to the nation. It does not correspond to its historical institution and course. It is, for instance, descriptive of the plebeian or the patrician organization in Rome; but neither of these was Rome.

The evidence of history is, that where society has not passed beyond the development of the family, there has been no national existence. With the long dynasties and vast populations in Asia, where society has adhered to the patriarchal type, there has been no nation, no citizenship,

[1] "Society must suffer if the child is allowed to grow up a worthless vagabond or a criminal, and has a right to intervene both in behalf of itself and of the child, in case his parents neglect to train him up in the nurture and admonition of the Lord, or are training him up to be a thief, a drunkard, a murderer, a pest to community." — Brownson, *The American Republic*, p. 41.

and no political freedom. Their life has been characterized by the absence of political spirit.

There is yet a truth which underlies this conception of the origin of the nation; and while the latter does not exist in identity with the family, and is not formed simply in its continuance, there is still a necessary connection; their origin and end is not diverse. They exist in an organic and moral interrelation, and the nation has its fruition in the life of humanity, in the universal family. It rests in the unity of humanity in the divine fatherhood; and therefore not with vague and unmeaning phrases, but as its end, it looks to the brotherhood of men and the fraternity of the nations, in the order of the world.

It is said that the nation has its origin in mere might: it is founded upon force; it is the right of the stronger, as superior, to control the weaker, as inferior.

But this involves the immediate contradiction to the being of the nation. The nation is constructive of an order in law and freedom. There is the subjection of barren force to right, and authority in it is wrested from the rude hand of power and placed in the hand of justice, and the conquest of civilization is in the manifestation of power no longer, as mere force, but in the recognition of a law of righteousness. The conception is subversive of rights, for these necessarily presume another postulate than mere force.

There is in mere force no element from which progress can be evolved, but in the prospect of its prevalence there is the awakening of dread, and by it man is not ennobled but subdued. There is the rejection of a principle of humanity. The law of justice is unrecognized, and the procedure of justice is leveled beneath its iron tread, and in a condition in which no asylum is sacred from its invasion, the place of equity is usurped by its authority.

It is so immediate a contradiction to the being of the

nation, that the element of law disappears, and there is only the mandate of power, and the relation of a common citizenship is lost, and it is transformed into that of the master and the slave.

The conception, if it were to become actual, would result, not in the institution of the order, but in the constant disturbance of society. The right of the stouter, the claim of the champion, would claim a trial, and as in the lead of a herd of buffaloes, it would involve an incessant struggle. If then the nation, as also an individual or family or race, in any moment be stronger than another, it is at once the justification of the conquest and the subjugation of the weaker. It is the justification of absolutism, but also of anarchy, when that is strong enough to get uppermost.

This proposition has sought an historical justification, but in the empty and superficial notion of history which it assumes, there has not been in mere physical force the institution of the nation. The external circumstance of the nation at its beginning, has not infrequently been in war, and it has had to pass through a struggle for existence ; but it has not therefore been the product of violence, and war has been the incident of its beginning, only as war was in the assertion of the right. The right, then, has not been born of force, but has been asserted and maintained by force. If force has been severed from right it has been not the inception of the order of society, but its devastation, and the progress of civilization has been in the increasing direction of physical force to a moral end. It has not been strong enough to regard the weakest and the lowliest with indifference, and in its course the things which are not have brought to naught the things which are.

Yet there is also a truth in this conception. It is a protest against the notion which apprehends justice as abstract, and denies the power of righteousness. It is the rejection of a spectral idealism, and the recognition of the fact that the right is manifest, and is not the dream of the spirit, but moves to the conquest of the world. The right is no faint apparition, and no flimsy conceit, but a power.

It is said that the nation has its origin in some instinct or emotion in man: there is some element in his nature in the action of which he is impelled toward the nation, and it exists as the product of this impulse. It is the result of a faculty in man, and is constructed as the bee builds his cell and the beaver his dam. This capacity has been variously described as a special faculty, or as sympathy or self-interest or fear, or as their common action. It is the psychological notion of the origin of the nation.

But there is in this no cause from which the being of the nation can be derived. The nation has an integral life, a positive and substantial content, and can have its origin and foundation in no subjective phase. It is as far from the attainment of the instinctive and emotional, as it is from the reflective and volitional act of the individual.

The nation, moreover, cannot have its origin in an impulse or emotion, whose action is necessary, since it has a moral being, and it exists not in necessity but in freedom.

There is, furthermore, in the nation, in its unity, its rights and its powers, that which cannot be derived from the action of an impulse or emotion. There is no power in the nature of man which could result in the right to government which is in a political order and is over men, nor in the organization of law and freedom.

As the self-government of the individual is in the subjection of impulse to the determination of the will, in conformance to a law of right, the principle also obtains in the government of the people. The individual, in so far as he makes a natural impulse his master and obeys that, is not free, and in the yielding to mere impulse there is the degradation of man. It is an animal existence, and the action for man is ignoble and unfree. Civilization which is formed in the development of the state, is the subjection of the impulses and passions of man in a moral order, and is the elevation above the rude condition of untamed and unrestrained impulse and passion which hold the elements of barbarism, and can issue only in violence and anarchy.

Yet there is in this proposition also a truth, and while there is no identity in the spirit in which man is related to the state of which he is a citizen, and the instinct with which the bee or the bird builds his cell or nest, there is yet in the physical order of nature the correspondence to the order of the state. It is also a protest against the merely artificial conception in politics, and illustrates the truth that the foundations of the nation are laid in the nature of man, and it is formed in the realization of his true constitution.

It is said that the nation has its origin in a convention: it is founded in a contractual law, — in the social contract.

The historical genesis of this theory has a separate consequence, and affords the significant illustration of the strength of a legal fiction, of its use, and then also of its risk. It has been the premise for the most opposite schemes and speculations upon society, and has mustered in its support in succeeding periods the most extreme men and parties, serving now as the defense of the established order, and again as the summons to revolution. It has prevailed in countries the most diverse in their political spirit and constitution. It fills the political literature of the last two centuries, and the association of nearly all their great names with it indicates alike the character of the age, the source of the strength and the weakness of its great thinkers and workers. In Germany it claims the names of Grotius, of Puffendorf, of Kant; in England it was with Hobbes the staff of authority, and with Locke the shield of liberty; but its clearest assertion was in France, and its highest influence was obtained through the *Contrat Social* of Rousseau. It became the scholastic tradition of American legal and political theorists. The phase which it took in the French school corresponds more nearly with the thought of Jefferson, while the influence of the form given to the theory by Locke, is apparent in the political writings of Adams.

The inception of the theory has been traced by Mr. Maine, to an imperfect apprehension of the Roman form of contracts, denominated Contracts juris gentium. "It was not until the language of the Roman lawyers became the language of an age which had lost the key to their mode of thought, that a contract of the law of nations came to be distinctly looked upon as a contract known to man in a state of nature."[1] But this is its scholastic and legal derivation, and it could not have obtained its great historical place, had there not been involved with all its error a great truth as to the being of society and the foundations of the state, which was struggling for expression, and which confronting precedents in the confusion of the age, took the form of a legal fiction. The discussion is mainly of interest as an historical study. It has a certain dryness as "a theory which though nursed into importance by political passions, derived all its sap from the speculations of lawyers."[2]

The theory assumes the existence of man in a pre-social condition, which is described as the state of nature. The imagination lays the boundaries of this province, and then peoples it with its unlimited conceits, as the island of the Counselor, in "The Tempest." From its occupancy by a joint contract, men emerge into the social or political state; the latter is thus constituted as the voluntary association of certain individuals who enter it and hold it as the contracting parties. The proposition presumes a universal application; the origin, and in a certain form the continuance

[1] Maine's *Ancient Law*, p. 299. [2] Ibid.

of all states that have been in all ages, are referred to a social contract.

The proposition in its assumption is arbitrary, and proceeding from a condition which is unreal, in its induction it carries the state necessarily into an abstract and formal sphere, — and because it has its inception in an assumption, it results necessarily in a political system, and not in the nation in its organic being. It is this which has limited its recent advocacy to the most barren of political schools, although of itself not the most dangerous, — a technical school of lawyers. It has assumed the existence of the precedent condition, which is called the state of nature. There is of this pre-social state no report, but it appears upon the chart of lawyers, who hold authentic tidings of it, and within it find stable footing. It advances, then, through a continuous series of assumptions, each of which is introduced to prop the preceding. After the assumption of this state of nature, there is assumed to exist in it one who personates the natural man, a fictitious character, costumed with the conceits of the theory. It is assumed that there is, antecedent to the existence of society, the recognition of some law of society, or of some authority in society, and on this exit is made and the passage is bridged over from the state of nature to the social, that is, the civil and the political state. The principle or the authority here consistently assumed is that of a contract or a contractual law. The validity of a constructive consent for the parties who in succession are to be bound by it, and by whom it is to be continued, is then also assumed. The resultant in the social, that is, the civil or political state, is represented as the artificial state whose precedent was the natural state, which man has left. The necessary inference in this antithesis is allowed, and the social state is represented as the unnatural, or more strictly, the abnormal condition of life.

The theory, in its exposition of the nature of man, contradicts at its outset the fact which is the postulate of Aristotle, that "man is by nature a political being." He is constituted for society, and his nature has its development in it. There is in his being, the rudiments of the state. The fact in the existence of man, which it also contradicts, is that he has no existence apart from society. The archaic condition is everywhere one of dependence, and there is, however dimly apprehended, the recognition of some relationships, and obligations are acknowledged and sacrifices are made for society. The postulate of the proposition is a historical fiction.

There is moreover no illustration of the origin of a nation in the voluntary agreement of individuals who enter it from a condition of previous isolation. There is the constant record of contracts or alliances, where two or more communities or nations are the parties, but these exist already as civil or political powers, and enter into obligations for a certain object; but there is no record of a nation itself established by the voluntary pact of separate individuals. The conception of a contract, or of a contractual origin of law, itself appears only at a later stage of civil society, and in its more definite form, is the attainment of a long and elaborate legal culture.

The nation being the natural and normal condition of existence, the individual, instead of entering it with the stipulations of a contract, is born and educated in it. His spirit and purpose are shaped in it, and its influence in his determination may be traced before he is capable of the voluntary choice or agreement which is the condition of a contract.

The theory fails to substantiate its assumptions, which are necessary to it, and leaves them involved in inextricable contradiction. It assumes that the people form a contract, but they are not yet a people, nor even an association of men; it is to ascertain the ground for obedience to law, and yet the contract it assumes is the most definite of laws; its object is to establish the foundations of the state, and yet, in its conclusion, it falls short of the conception of the state. The individuals enter the association, as contracting parties, but the resultant, by the conditions of a contract, is private property. That, for instance, which one obtains by exchange, or holds subject to contract, he owns; it is his property, and as he acquired it, he also may alienate it for a certain equivalent, but the state cannot be found in this conception. The theory fails alike as it carries into the state the notion of a private contract, and as it derives the state from a private contract. The association of individuals, however numerous, is not the state; and the stipulations of the contract, however wide, have not the majesty of law; the concession of private rights, however extended, is not the institution of public rights. The parties to the contract, at the most, are private persons, and it is not possible to arrive therein at the conception of public rights and public duties.

The necessary being and end of the nation, moreover, cannot be brought within the scope of a contract. A contract proceeds from and through a voluntary act, and therefore is in the alternative of the parties, — something which may or may not be. But the process of justice, and the institution of rights, and the conformance to a moral order in which the state is constituted, cannot be thus optional; they must be, and therefore the state is existent as a power, and is invested with authority. The contract furthermore cannot comprehend the spirit, the allegiance, the obedience to law, the apprehension of and the devotion to public ends, which are integral in the state. There is not in it even the moral spirit in which the civil ends can be construed. Beccaria denied the right of capital punishment, on the ground that, as society is formed in a contract between the state and its members, the consent of the party to his possible extinction becomes then one of the terms of the contract, and it is not to be presumed that it would be accorded. The position is good, says Hegel, in the conception of a state founded on a contract, for the conception has no place for punishment in the divine or in the moral sense.

The contract cannot become the ground of the unity or the continuity of the nation; — not of the unity, for it is the agreement of parties in the exchange of equivalents, and each remains a possessor, or as the phrase is, "it takes two to make a bargain," and in the result the parties remain the several proprietors; — not of the continuity, for a contract presumes the positive consent of the parties, but the constructive consent of succeeding generations evades this, while yet the continuance of the formal contract is conditioned upon this contingency.

But finally, the conception does not make valid its own claim, and limited to its own definition, it has no foundation; the contract is good for nothing as a contract. It does not substantiate the agreement of the parties, which is the condition of a contract. The contract which is not clear as to the identity of the parties, and then also as to its extent and character, is a nullity. It could only bring contradiction into the ordinary affairs of life. It could not be recognized or enforced in any court of law.

The principle is not the foundation, but the dissolution of the organization of society. The contract, if it were allowed, would be obligatory only upon those who deliberately and voluntarily entered as parties into it, and unless renewed it would expire with them. It could form only a temporary obligation which could be suspended, and only a joint concern which could be closed up to go into the hands of a receiver. Then any number of individuals could separate or withdraw, and there would be no power inherent in society to justify its prevention. There is then in government no authority, but only an agency limited to the securance of the private interests of the contractors, and in society no permanence beyond their formal bond, and no nation which lives on although the individual dies.

The falsehood in this proposition becomes apparent when it is confronted by the peril of the state. The permanence of the whole, and the supremacy of law, is conditional upon the option of the individual. It is subject to the unlimited play of individual caprice. The state may be rent asunder in the willfulness and whim of one, and beyond this it has no defense in internal disorder or external assault. The proposition is the postulate, not of the unity and order, but of the dissolution of society. It has been truly said, that the social contract should be called rather a theory of anarchy than the doctrine of the state.[1]

The truth which the proposition subverts, as it sweeps to its perilous close is, that the nation proceeds in the divine guidance of the people in history. "And yet there is," says Bluntschli, "in this conception, involved in the most deceptive and perilous error, a certain truth. In opposition to the notion which sees in the state only the necessary product of nature, it asserts the truth that in its normal process the human will can and must act positively and determinately upon the form of the state, and in contrast with an empty empiricism it vindicates the reason of the state and the right in human freedom."[2]

[1] Bluntschli's *Allgemeinen Statsrecht*, vol. i. p. 260.

[2] *Ibid.* 263. See on some of these theories, *Ibid.* vol. i. pp. 250, 270.

Hooker has a statement of the social contract, and the institution of government in it: "Men knew that strifes and troubles would be endless, except they gave their common consent, all to be ordered by some whom they should agree upon," — "for the manifestation of the right to govern, the assent of them who are to be governed seemeth necessary." — Hooker's *Works*, vol. i. p. 187. But this proposition lies upon the page of Hooker in a fragmentary shape, and is the contradiction of the profound conception of law as organic and not formal, which is the fundamental thought of his great work, and places him among the great politicians of his own and of every age. His work is a treatise of laws, as resting in the eternal and divine reason. — Dr. Tulloch has justly said, the expression of laws "valid in authority both in their substance and direct origin, in their conformity to reason and the national will and position. He not only opposed a special church theory which then sought to dominate in Protestantism, but he showed how every such theory must break against the great laws of historical induction and national liberty. It was the rights of reason and of free and orderly national development in the face of all preconception of whatever kind, that he really vindicated." — Tulloch's *Puritanism*, p. 29. There is an impassa-

4

It is said that the nation has its origin in a sovereignty inherent in the people; the people in its own native might is supreme; its power is of itself, and its responsibility is to itself; its right has no limitation, and it recognizes no authority over it and allows none separate from it.

This proposition postulates the very object to be ascertained. It presumes the existence of the people, but obviously it is not of the sovereignty of the people to will its own existence. In its failure to define the political people, whose political action it avers, it is destitute of a foundation, and there is nothing, in the phrase of Locke, "to bottom it on."

The description of the people, which is commonly assumed in this theory, presents the immediate contradiction to the political people. It represents the people as a collection of individuals in a certain locality, but there is nothing in this to distinguish it from the mob. It is destitute of the consciousness of the unity, and of the order in which the political people is formed.

It is also devoid of the elements of political sovereignty, since there is wanting the will of the organic people whose affirmation is law, and whose freedom consists in an organism determined in law. In its conception any collection of men possessing a certain collective force, may assert their intention, and their action is to be regarded as law, and is obligatory upon all, and may rightly be imposed on the whole. Then also any collection of men may sever themselves from the existent political organization, and interrupt its relations, and rend its whole order in the demonstration of their power.

The proposition allows no conception of a country, since in describing power as existent indefinitely in any locality it avoids the necessary relation in its physical condition of the people to the land.

ble way from the position of Hooker to the inferences of Laud, or to the corresponding inferences, in another form, of the ecclesiasts of a recent puritanism.

The state moreover is not derived from the sovereignty of a mere collection of men, since its origin is not in a reflective act. It is not the result simply of choice and design. It would be consistent with this to refer the existence of justice on the earth to the formal deliberation and conclusion of men. And historically, man does not exist apart from the organization of society, that is, the nation, and from that antecedent condition determine its being. The will of man is certainly a necessary element in it, but as it has not its inception in thought, it has not its origin in the individual nor in the collective will.

This proposition merges the nation into the conception of a bare sovereignty. It is the institution of a power which allows no limitation, and acknowledges no responsibility beyond itself. Its sole mandate is law, and in this alone the whole political order subsists. The merest caprice of the multitude is the only authority. In another form it is the foundation of society upon mere might. There is in it no recognition of the state as the institution of justice. It cannot comprehend the rights of the individual. As in the contractual theory, the assumption of the absolute sovereignty of the individual, by whose private act society was determined, could not arrive at the conception of public rights and public duties, so also the absolute sovereignty of the mass cannot consist with private rights, or the freedom of the individual. It is the assertion of unlimited power, the grasp from which it has been the effort of civilization to wrest the supremacy, and to substitute in its stead a moral force. It is not the tyranny of the one, but the tyranny of the multitude; and yet the latter passes indifferently into the former, and in the degradation of the individual through the subversion of individual freedom the way is open to imperialism; the domination over men in one form succeeds to another.

The sequence to the assumption of political power which this proposition involves, has been always the same in every form. The inevitable result of political atheism has been a political absolutism. But the consciousness of the divine principle in political power cannot be wholly effaced, and there follows the apotheosis of the dominant authority. The Roman emperors are worshipped as divine. In the rejection of the moral obligation in political power, with the overthrow of all freedom, and the degradation of the individual, there invariably will come the apotheosis of the emperor or the apotheosis of the people. The sovereignty, as the freedom of man, neither in the individual nor in the people is absolute. It can consist only with the recognition of a divine relation and the consequent obligation to a divine law. The freedom of the people has its postulate only in the organic and moral being of the people, and this is the precedent of sovereignty. As the sequence to political atheism has been political absolutism, so also it is only as it has a divine origin, and is formed in a divine relation, that freedom exists. This has had the clearest expression in the crises of humanity. The voice of freedom, the mighty voice of nations, has not been "The ruler is absolute," "The people is absolute," but it has been "God and the people," and it has confessed its deliverer in Him. It has not been the shout in the host, but in the name of the Lord of hosts.

The truth which this proposition controverts is, that the origin of the nation is not in the will of the individual, nor in the will of the whole, but in the higher will without which the whole can have no being, and its continuity is not in the changing interest of men, but in the vocation which in a widening purpose from the fathers to the children joins the generations of men, and its unity is not in the concurrent choice of a certain number of men, but in the divine purpose in history which brings to one end the unnumbered deeds of unnumbered men.

And yet the truth which underlies this proposition also comes into clearer light in the higher development of the nation. The sovereignty of the nation is from God, and of the people. The representative of its sovereignty is therefore responsible to God and accountable to the people. The power is transmitted through no intermediate hands, the people is invested with it, in all its majesty, in the nation founded in the law of a moral person and derivative from God alone.[1]

[1] The people holding their authority from God, hold it not as an inherent right but as a trust from Him, and are accountable to Him for it. It is not their own. — Brownson, *The American Republic*, p. 127.

CHAPTER IV.

THE ORIGIN OF THE NATION.

THE nation has a divine foundation, and has for its end the fulfillment of the divine end in history. It has its issue in the divine prevision, that is, in the moral nature of man. It is not the continuance of the family, nor the product of force, nor the working of instinct, nor the result of the social compact, nor the creation of the sovereignty of the people; while the truths which underlie these otherwise false assumptions, in the course of providence, illustrate in a greater or less degree the rise and growth and conservation of the nation.[1]

The origin and foundation of the nation has, in certain aspects, its illustration in its analogy with the family. The family is a divine institution, and so also is the nation; the family is the natural condition, and so also is the nation, and as natural it is not of human construction although a human development, its constituent elements are implanted in the nature of man, and as that nature is unfolded in the realization of the divine idea, there is the development of the state. The family also is rude and imperfect in its form in the early period of the race, and it slowly develops into the true and the normal, that is, the monogamic form; thus also the nation slowly develops into the more perfect type.

[1] I assume in this argument, from the outset, the being of God and His connection with the world, and the origin and derivation of the personality of man from Him, that "in Him we live and move and have our being," — subjects which belong immediately to another province of thought; the statement however may be scarcely necessary, since the work would not perhaps have detained so long any reader who may deny these propositions.

The nation exists as an organic and moral being; its existence is a fact, and the apprehension of its existence in its beginning, is in the conscious life of man. There is therefore, outside of this consciousness, evidence which is only indicative of its origin, as of the origin of the individual and of the moral life of the individual.[1]

The evidence of the origin of the nation is in its necessary nature. — The nation is an organic unity; it is not an artificial fabric nor an abstract system, but it has a life which is definite and disparate, and has a development; therefore it has not its origin in the individual nor the collective will of man, but must proceed from a power which can determine the origin of organic being. — The nation is an organic whole; but the whole, in which there is the conception of the parts, cannot be determined by the parts, since there must be the predetermination of the whole to which the parts belong; but the whole cannot determine itself, and must therefore proceed from a power beyond itself.

The evidence of the origin of the nation is also in its being as a moral person. There is and can be for personality, as it transcends physical nature, only a divine origin, and its realization is in a divine relation. The subsistence of the human personality is in the divine personality, and its realization is in its divine relations, and as with the individual personality, so also with the moral personality of the nation, — its origin and its consistence can be only in God.

The origin of the nation has its illustration in the various aspects in which the nation in its necessary conception may

[1] Plutarch says, in a citation by Haller, "In my judgment, a city could be more easily built without ground, than a state could be founded or exist without faith in God."

Cicero says, with a singular and reverent beauty of language, "Nihil est illi principi Deo, qui omnem mundum regit, quod quidem in terris fiat, acceptius quam, concilia coetusque hominum jure sociati quæ civitates appellantur." *Somn. Scipionis*, ch. iii.

be regarded. Thus the personality of the nation is indicative of its divine origin. The necessary elements of personality are freedom and justice, and wisdom and courage, and the like, but these are not physical powers, and as moral, they are in their origin above the sequence of physical nature. Thus the freedom, which is the substance of the nation, is not the mere creation of law, and it is no more in the power of preachers and assemblies than of priestly and imperial hands to bestow it ; it is of no man or collection of men to confer it as a boon, it is a gift which is not in the power of earth. Thus also the justice which is incorporated in the state is higher than the enactment of the law, and more than the impulses of the people ; it is presumed to be the content of the law, and controls the impulses of the people. It is not the device of legislators, and as it exists in the nation, there is manifest its divine origin. The illustration may be traced further in all the necessary moral elements of the nation, as wisdom and courage.

The powers with which the nation is invested, are also indicative of its origin. It is clothed with an authority, and has a majesty which no power of earth may assume. The affirmation of its will is law, but apart from it, the will of no man and no collection of men, is law for another. The right of government is its right, but apart from it no man and no collection of men have the right to govern another, and it belongs to the nation only as it is of divine right. There is no human ground on which it can rest. They who are intrusted with it hold it as the representatives of the nation, and as the ministers of the divine purpose in the nation. The President and the Congress, as the Crown and the Parliament, rule by the grace of God.

The elements which are manifest in the government of the nation, in its moral being, can have only a divine ground. The power, which is in the people forming the nation, is over the people, and while the individual acts in the government of the nation, it is over the individual and he is subject to it, and this is a power which is and can be in the nation only as it is a moral person, and is derivative from God. This alone in government, is the condition also of the reconciliation of law and freedom.[1] The character of the authority of the nation also indicates its origin. It has authority, and is invested with power in the maintenance of a moral order on the earth. But the right thus to maintain authority over men, belongs in itself to no man and no collection of men, and is existent in the nation only as it has a divine genesis.

There is evidence, also, of the divine origin of the nation, in the historical facts which bring out the consciousness of the people. Its expression may be traced in the greater historical nations, and in their greater ages, the crowning centuries of their civilization. It appears in the symbols of all their power, and is reflected in their laws and literature and art. In Judæa it was the central principle of national existence, and was held through all the changes of its institutions as a law of life, which through the vicissitudes of its course exaltation could not bring into forgetfulness, nor humiliation into denial. In Greece it was shaped in the beginning of its history in all its traditions, and is the last word of its philosophy; it was joined with the sacredness of the family; it united in one aim its heroes and its poets; it was wrought in its architecture, and in the faultless lines of the sculpture of its temples; it gave the type of victory to its art. In Rome the very religion was the witness to the sacredness of the family and the state, and the divine obligations in the relations of a father and a citizen. This moulded all her institutions. The recognition in these nations of a divine origin was also

[1] "Government like man himself participates of the divine being, and derived from God through the people, it at the same time participates of human reason and will, thus reconciling authority with freedom, stability with progress." — Brownson. *The American Republic*, p. 126.

clearest in the ages of their strength. It was not in periods characterized by superstition, by prostration and abject fear, when the powers of man were dwarfed by the impending vastness of nature, before he had discovered the harmony in the wide sweep of her courses, and the uniformity in her cycles, and the imagination was bewildered by an apparent discord, but it was in the manhood of the people, when there was the highest self-respect and self-assertion, in periods whose colossal monuments attest the triumph over physical nature, whose noble monuments attest the higher triumph over foes in the spiritual nature. It was not in what are called the pre-historic ages; in these nations there is the constructive course of history. It was held in no individual conception, but the very names Roma and Athene were the names of divinities as well as nations. There was for each in its name a twofold significance, and it denoted not only a political organization, but was the sign of a divinity in whom it was conceived that the people stood.

This spirit in the most varying forms may be traced in every historical nation. In the unity and continuity of the nation, there has been the consciousness of the divine guidance in history. It has united the generations, and the nation in its battles has drawn its inspiration from no lower faith. The great events in its history become the witness to the divine presence, and in the crisis through which it passes there is manifest a divine judgment, consuming the evil which was destroying it, and gaining for it a divine deliverance from the evil. Therefore in Judæa all the great testimonies in its national history, through the procession of its centuries, were repeated, of Him that endureth forever.

The conscience of man also gives the evidence of the origin of the nation. The moral spirit of the people recognizes the life of the nation as sacred. It is apprehended as a life which cannot be trifled with, nor weighed lightly, nor judged indifferently. Its inviolability is affirmed, and the obligation of its members to it. And as there is in the conscience the witness to a divine relationship, if the nation had merely an external or a physical being, there would be no ground in which the conscience could acknowledge a relation and obligation to it; there would be only the individual obligation which one may hold to another. The conscience testifies also to a judgment as coming upon the nation, because formed in a relation involving an immediate and a divine obligation.[1] There is no thought which has had a more intense expression as reflected in literature and art. In Rome and Greece as they recognized in the disaster of the individual a moral judgment, it was still more apparent that the wider disaster that came upon the nation could not be divested of a moral condition.

If the divine origin and foundation of the nation is denied, the authority of its government is resolved into mere force. The power in the nation, as self-subsistent, is necessarily absolute. It may take the form of the absolutism of the individual or of the people, but its principle and result are the same. In a popular absolutism there may be a more utter degradation of humanity and destruction of personality, until all that gives a moral elevation to the life of men and of nations shall expire, and there remains only a level sweep as in bleak and desolated fields. There is, it is said, in the reign of the despot, still one that is free, but here there is freedom neither for the ruler nor for the people. The ruler who recognizes and follows only the popular voice and the popular opinion, becomes himself a slave. And he only is truly a ruler and truly free, who recognizes

[1] Mr. Brownson says of a recent political school, "it has rejected the divine origin and ground of government, and excluded God from the state. They have not only separated the state from the church as an external corporation, but from God as its internal Lawgiver, and by so doing have deprived the state of her sacredness, inviolability, and hold upon the conscience." — *The American Republic*, p. 122.

in the sovereignty of the nation the divine source of its unity and power, and whose action in it is therefore in immediate responsibility to God. If there is for the nation no divine origin and ground, and the ruler is to listen only to the voice of a people in itself supreme, and separate from God, then in that awful absolutism his strength is broken, and his power is resolved in those living atoms. The ruler is silent in the popular clamor, as he is swayed by the agitation of the crowd, and is blind as he is hurried by the popular impulse and passion. But the nation, when it is conceived as separate from God, can have no realization, for in that separation the ground of all unity and continuity is lost, and there is no more a people.[1]

[1] Bluntschli cites the language of President Washington — the first inaugural of the first President — as among the strongest assertions of this principle in modern political literature. — *Allgemeinen Statsrecht*, vol. i. p. 253.

While it is denied by popular schools, and avoided by ecclesiasts and pronounced enigmatic by newspapers, there has been no age in which it has been more clearly recognized in the thought of statesmen. Napoleon III. said at Rouen, June, 1868, "We cannot separate our love of country from our love of God."

"The human authority in the state can never again be confounded with the divine authority (the theocracy), but it must necessarily be founded on the divine authority." — Stahl's *Philosophie des Rechts*, vol. ii. sec. ii. p. 184.

CHAPTER V.

THE PEOPLE AND THE LAND.

THE people and the land form the natural elements of the nation, in its physical unity and circumstance; they exist in a necessary inter-relation.

The people in its organic unity, constitutes the nation. It is not a sum or an aggregate of men, a chance collection accumulated as an heap of fragmentary atoms; (it is not a mob, but a people; not a vulgus but a populus.) It is not a party nor a sect, nor a mere association of parties and sects, nor a combination of separate corporate interests, nor of individuals in the partnership of their private interests, and there is in none of these the consciousness of the unity and of the order which belong to a nation. With the mob, a detached and unformed mass of isolated individuals, it has nothing to do, and they can have nothing to do with it.[1]

The people is not determinate in any enumeration of individuals. It is the people, not the population, which forms the nation. It is not ascertained in any arithmetical notation, and the political order has not this nominal basis. It is a mechanical conception which assumes a certain normal number as its true condition. Rousseau estimated the normal number for the people at ten thousand, and at peri-

[1] French and German publicists,— the former constantly and the latter mainly, — use these terms, the people and the nation, in this significance. The organic people in its physical condition, as the natural element of the state is called the people (Peuple, naturvolk), in its political condition it is called the nation (Nation, statsvolk). But the terms in German political literature are wide away from any other. Bluntschli adopted the above distinction in his earlier writings, while in his later, against the common use, he has followed the strict derivation of the words.

odic intervals it was to be changed to conform to this census, but it has no more an arbitrary ground in the numbers of statistics than in the formulas of lawyers. It may change with successive generations, and in the prosperity and the adversity of its years. It may exist in "numbers as the stars for multitude," or in only a remnant who keep its calling and guard its ancient faith, and endure through captivities, and at last triumph over every conquest. The national type is not obliterated in the vicissitudes of events, nor overborne by the migrations of races, and does not perish, although the individual die.

The people in its wholeness constitutes the nation, and it is to comprehend in its political aim the purpose, and in its end to realize the destination of the people as an whole. It is not of the one, nor of the many, but of the people. There is no individual, as Louis XIV., who can assume to be the state, and no hereditary class, and no party or section can say, it is in us alone. There is no sect and no faction that can claim it as an exclusive possession. The spirit of a party, or a class or a sect in its isolation, subordinates the state to a special or a private end. Thus when he who comprehends only a party or a class or a sect, — a mere fragment, comes to work upon the whole, not comprehending in his purpose the people as an whole, but only the parts and nothing beyond, his work is that of inevitable weakness and corruption.

The people in its normal and moral relations constitutes the nation. There is no arbitrary principle in which the people can define its existence, as if society had an individual or artificial basis. And it is not simply the physical condition which conforms to a tribal law. It cannot make a physical condition the principle of its being.[1] There is

[1] "America, though the best representative of the social and political gains of the eighteenth century, was not the parent of the idea, in modern civilization, that man is a constituent member of the state of his birth irrespective of his ancestry. It was become the public law of Christendom. Had America done less, she would have been not the leader but the laggard of nations." — Ban-

not among its powers any by which it may elect those who shall be in it, but as the normal and moral condition men are born and live and act in it. It is not to restrict itself to those who may be rich or learned. There is no human imperfectness that can be made the ground of exclusion from it, and no human greatness that can justify an exaltation over it. The isolation from it can result only through crime, and this is in the law that crime is in its nature the severance of the relations of a moral order.

The people in its conscious unity, embodies its aim in the nation. Then it apprehends its object in it, and it is set before it in its moral order as the aim of all. It is then reflected in the political spirit of the people, and moulds its character. There is in a mere mass or aggregate, a fragmentary collection of individuals or parties, no ground in which the unity, apparent in political spirit and political character, can subsist.

The people is to work out its own political conception in the nation, after the type of its own individuality. The external circumstance, the limitations and conditions in which it is to act, are as varied as in the development of the individual type in nature, while its life which runs through human cycles, has a wider range than in the sequence of physical nature. The forms through which its spirit is to work, are more manifold than those written in nature's book of infinite secrecy. The life of history is the more opulent in its types; and the forms of the bud and the tree in limitless forests, are not so individual or so diverse as those wrought in the spirit of the people in history. It is to work out its own purpose in a moral world, and in it alone it has the satisfaction of the spirit. It can no more conceive the desire to be another people, than the individual can conceive the desire to be another

croft's *History*, vol. ix. p. 449. "Der zustand der Barberei besteht darin dass eine menge ein Volk ist ohne zugleich ein Staat zu sein." — Hegel, in *Rosekranz Leben*, p. 244.

than himself, — that is, to lose his own identity. The spirit of the people is thus reflected in, as it is formed in and through, the individual and the generation, while its perfect type is in no single individual and no separate generation, but in the work of the people in its continuity.

The people alone in the nation, constitutes in its integral and moral life the political order. It belongs to none separate from it to prescribe its political course. The people can acknowledge no control beyond its own organic law save only that of God, and the law of its being as a moral person presumes that, as its freedom subsists in that. The power belongs of itself to no individual and no family and no class, separate from the nation, as there is also no individual and no family and no class belonging to the nation that is exempt from its authority.[1]

The people, in the nation in its moral being, alone has the right of government. It is in the nation only, of divine right. Its power is from God and of the people. Its authority is therefore in the name of God and the people, and the responsibility of those who bear its authority is to God and the people. The government therefore can claim identity with no special and divine majesty, and can assume no special and divine appointment. It is only as representative of the nation that it is clothed with authority.

The right of government is in the will of the people, while it is only in its being in the nation, as a moral person, that the will of the people subsists. Its authority apart from this, has no foundation, and can refer for its postulate only to a fiction; it can be held then only in an arbitrary assumption, and defined only in an abstract and vacant conception. The being of the nation as a moral

[1] "This authority is not 'the governed,' from whose 'consent' it is so often in a false sense declared 'every government derives its just powers,' but a political people, having the power as sovereign to govern every natural person within a certain territory without reference to his consent." — Mr. Hurd's article on "Reconstruction," *American Law Review*, January, 1867.

person, is alone the positive and substantial ground, apart from which the will of the people is only formal, and its freedom only the empty sphere of outward circumstance. The will of the people in the nation thus is not comprehended simply in its collective act, nor in its momentary act, and these may not always embody the moral aim, nor represent the continuous purpose of the people. It obtains a clearer expression in the exclusion of the caprice, the whim and willfulness of men, and in the latter there is confusion and not order, the creation of chaos and not the state. The assumption of the caprice of men as the condition of power subverts government, and resolves the state into its atomy.

The will of the people in the being of the nation as a moral person, is the organic political power. It is the only unbroken succession. The ruler who is over and separate from the people, is he whose right is disputed, whose authority is transient, whose succession is subject to accident. The will of the people in its succession in the nation, is not limited to the individual or to the generation, but it is transmitted through the individual and the generations of men.

The people forming the nation exists in its physical unity and circumstance, in a necessary relation to the land. The land is the outward sphere of the organization of the political people. The people and the land thus, in common language, become a synonym. Greece is a name which represents a certain definite geographical limit, and again the complex political life of a people.

The possession of the land by the people is the condition of its historical life. The land is the field of its work in history. Nomads may form a horde, but not a state. The historical work of the people has an immediate relation to the land in which its fortunes are unfolded.

The right to the land is in the people, and the land is

given to the people in the fulfillment of a moral order on the earth. It is the possession of the political people. Thus it can regard it only as a robbery, when it is deprived of any part of the domain given to it and associated with it in its history. The crime is the same when it is undertaken by the treachery of a faction from within, or by marauders from without, but in the complicity of evil in the former, the guilt is enhanced and it becomes the greater crime of history.

The people has in its development, the definite determination of the national domain. The description of its boundaries is to indicate its political organization and to conform to its historical destination.

The exact designation of its boundaries is also necessary in its political administration, for the maintenance of its authority and the enforcement of its laws, and the institution of its order, and without it there would be a source of constant confusion.

The boundaries of the nation are laid in nature and in the historical course of the people. This law is universal, and the nations which have violated it, again have been compelled to acknowledge it. Italy has never passed her boundaries so clearly defined in nature and in history, but she has been driven back again with loss; and Germany in its aggressions has overstepped these limits, only after disaster to withdraw again. The law has its illustration with every people. Its boundaries are not as the artificial lines which trace within the nation the occupation and possession of private property.

There is in nature and in history the evidence, that God has appointed the boundaries of nations. They are to be held in the faith that the land is appointed for the people, and the right to it is in its moral order and its historical vocation. In this faith the people will assert them reverently and carefully, will guard them steadily and well. The integral unity of the land will be maintained against all alienation and division. The bounds of the nation which are written in the courses of the mountains and the lines of the oceans, are written also upon the hearts of its children. In their natural distinction these boundaries may be mountains or oceans and seas, and sometimes also rivers and valleys; but rivers and valleys, which are the wide highways of a nation, may become bonds of union rather than of separation, and in the associations of the people, may aid to forge it together. In the words of President Lincoln, it was after the victories of General Grant and Admiral Farragut, that the Mississippi ran "unvexed to the sea." The boundaries in nature become, also, lines of defense, and in the strength with which they are held, form a guaranty for the peace of the people.

It may be only gradually that the people enter and occupy the land which is open before it, and is necessary to its manifest historical vocation. The boundaries thus may be modified in its history, but it can allow no change to weaken it in the centre of its power, or to impair the integral unity of its territory, and no change which will encroach upon the historical domain, or subvert the integral unity of another nation. The change which would have this result would imperil the whole, and would necessarily fail of permanence.

As the land is the possession of the people it cannot be held as the patrimony of a prince, or the monopoly of a class. The land belongs to the people constituted as a nation, and the right to it is in its moral order. The exclusive possession and entail of the whole domain by a few may prevent this object and subvert the moral order, as it destroys, for instance, the life of the family. In England there are those which are called great families, but as its homes are swept away the family life of the people is destroyed. One half of the land is owned by one hundred and fifty proprietors, and the whole number of proprietors is reduced to thirty thousand, while the majority of the people subsist on wages. "The yeomanry," says Mr. Disraeli, "has vanished from the face of the land, while the tendency of business has been to introduce a condition to consist only of wealth and toil."

There is a common conception in which the land is so regarded, as to make simply a geographical position the origin and condition of the existence of the nation. Mr. Maine attempts to establish the state upon the fact of local contiguity.[1] But in an existence in a local contiguity there is not the origin nor the foundation of the political life of men. While the fact of residence and coëxistence is necessary in the historical course of the nation, it does not bear in itself its germ, nor is it the source of its integral unity. It is not the circumstance of neighborhood, but the consciousness of relations to one's neighbor that is indicative of the origin of the nation. The unity of the nation is not in the existence of man in a certain contiguity, but in a conscious purpose and a relation which is necessary to the destination of each and of the whole; its condition is not a merely physical relation, but a moral relation; and it has not merely the existence of the individual for an end, but the whole for an end. There are thus, for instance, vast contiguous populations which have existed for centuries on the plains of Asia and Africa, and in the most diverse geographical positions, and yet they have not formed a state. There are populations by the Rhine strictly more contiguous to the French, in their bulk, than to the Germans, but they would go to battle rather than be wrested from the unity of the German nation. This definition of the origin of the nation in local contiguity, has also no historical justification. There was a people dwelling by the banks of the Tiber before the beginning of that national development which was to determine so widely the world's history, but they were not Rome. There is a population in Judæa, but the stones

[1] Maine's *Ancient Law*, p. 128.

of its temple are broken, and it is not there that we seek the continuity of Israel.

The relation of the people and the land is consistent only with the existence of the nation in its necessary conception. The proposition which represents the people as a mere collection, an aggregate of men, and the proposition which defines the origin of the nation in a contract, cannot embrace this conception of a country, and when the nation is regarded as only the creation of a formal law, it no longer comprehends the necessary relation of the people and the land.

The influence, in this interrelation, which the land has upon the people is apparent, but there is a tendency in a certain school to ascribe to the land a determinative influence, and to refer the constructive and formative power of the people to external circumstance and physical condition — the climate, soil, geology, minerals, fishes, etc. This had a fair consideration in Montesquieu, but there is a school which comprehends nothing beyond. The denial of the reality of human freedom, the assertion of a bare necessitarianism, has its consistent sequence, in the reference to physical influences of a controlling power, in what it yet calls history. With the denial of human freedom it passes immediately to the study and computation of climatic conditions, the soil, the climate, the agricultural products, and the like. The writings of Mr. Buckle illustrate this. But in the existence of the nation, which is the substance of civilization, there is a power higher than the necessary process of the physical world. It exists in the order of the moral world. This cannot be determined by physical elements. The history of the world cannot be deduced from its geography. In the political course of the nation the land is a necessary element, but it is not the creative nor the controlling element. The future of the nation will not be concluded by its relative nearness to the equator. The nation exists historically in the realization of the freedom of man, and his consequent dominion over nature. Mr. Buckle, when he stood in Judæa, avowed that his only interest was in the agriculture of the country; but the soil is the same upon which a people lived who stood in the continuity of a nation, which long captivity in strange lands and under strange skies did not destroy, whose unity was lost in the grandeur of no imperialism, and whose lines of kings and prophets looked to the coming of One in whom was the hope of humanity; but the physical process of nature does not renew that life. The mountains of Attica are the same upon which the Parthenon was built, and their quarries the same which furnished the marble for the sculpture of Athene, and the windy plains are the same upon which an army was mustered at Marathon, and the sea is the same whose waves were parted by their ships at Salamis, but the conflict which in its moral interest made these names immortal, has closed.[1]

Since the land is necessary to the historical development of the people in the continuity of the nation, the nation has supreme authority over it. It is in its integral character the domain of the people. Within its limits, therefore, the people can allow no possession exempt from its control, and no individual beyond its law.

The people and the land exist, in their interrelation, in the historical realization of the nation as a moral order. The land becomes associated with the spirit and the destination of the people. Since it is the external sphere and condition of the life of the people in its moral order, it is holy; and since it belongs to the people in its continuity, it is inalienable. There is thus attached to the land a sacredness which is derivative from the moral being of the nation, and it is held as inviolate.

The land in its integral unity is thus a divine gift, a

[1] Comte has a more exact statement of the influence of the physical world upon man: "The world," he says, "furnishes the materials, and man determines the form." . . . . "Man is not a result of the world, and yet he depends upon it." — *Catechisme Positiviste*, pp. 37, 42.

habitation of the people for all generations. It shares in the sacredness of the life of the nation, historical associations grow up around it, and blended with their traditions it passes sacredly from the fathers to the children, and constitutes in its wide domain the heritage and the homestead of the people.[1]

[1] "The land is the essential condition of the normal and moral development of the state, and therefore it is absolutely holy and inalienable. It is here that the real moral spirit of the love of the father-land rests: originally it is a love of one's native land, and always retains this natural element, but in its completeness it is wholly interpenetrated with this consciousness of a moral relation. Therefore the true love of the father-land exists only when a people has already attained to the life of the nation. The merely economic society has nothing of this." — Rothe's *Theologische Ethik*, vol. ii. p. 123.

CHAPTER VI.

THE NATION THE INSTITUTION OF RIGHTS.

THE nation is a moral person. This prescribes the province of rights and the province of freedom. The ground of these is in no formal system of laws, and no abstract system of thought. On this ground alone, their provinces are removed from the arbitrary limitations of formulas and abstractions.

Personality has its condition and its realization in freedom. Personality is constituted in self-determination; one whose action is self-determined is a person.[1]

The human personality subsists in the divine personality; as it is realized in the moral life, it is derivative from God, and has its fulfillment in God. It comes not in entire forgetfulness; whether it looks within or without, it gazes into no abysmal depths. It is not attained through negations; its necessary being is not ascertained in a law of thought, as in the formula of Spinoza, nor by a rule of subtraction, as in the resultant of Comte. It does not recede into nothingness, it does not pass into vacancy. In its beginning it is formed in relationships, and in its development it is not severed from them, but there is the fuller expression of them. These relations are not the result of the reflection, nor of the volition of man, and man is not their centre. In the realization of these relations man is always brought nearer to Him in whom they have their consistence, and in whom is the perfect unity.

The central attribute of personality is the will. The will in its freedom is defined in no formal or empty notion; it

[1] "A being endowed with self-consciousness, reason, and freedom, is called a person, or has personality." — Ahren's *Naturrecht*, p. 83.

is the self-determination of a person, and that alone is free. The determination, in the realization of personality, acting in freedom, is in the fulfillment of law, but the law thus is necessarily not abstract nor formal; it is not external, it is a law implied in the being and the realization of personality, and the fulfillment of which is the end of its being; it is in its highest conception the will of God.

The mere formal notion of the will and of its freedom, which separates it from its substance in personality and empties it of all content, could not form the principle of rights. It could produce a scheme concerning rights, but not the realization of rights; it could result in a system, but not in the nation.

Rights belong to man, since in his nature he is constituted as a person. Personality, since it has its origin in God, has an infinite sacredness. This is the ground of the sacredness of the rights of man. The individual personality can therefore be apprehended rightly only in this conception, — the life of each must be held sacred, his worth must be allowed, his dignity must be regarded, his freedom must have in the nation its maintenance and its sphere.

It is only in his personality, in his moral being and freedom, that man has rights beyond the other animals. In the necessary sequence of physical nature there is no ground for rights. It is because man exists also in a moral world, which is in freedom, that he has rights.

The realization of personality is manifested in the ampler institution of rights. For rights in the nation are the asserting and the positing of personality, in the external sphere, through its self-determination which is its freedom. They are the process in which personality affirms itself and attains recognition in the nation. Thus also, reversely, the decay and loss or abandonment of rights is connected with a low and a false conception of man, and presumes always the degradation of personality.

Rights belong to man, as man is made in the image of God; they are his by nature; they belong to him in his original constitution. Thus the condition of their existence, as of their sacredness, is in the nature of man, as it is in the divine image.

Rights have their foundation in the nature of man.

Personality manifests itself in the realization of rights; all rights are of a person.

Rights express and define the relation of a person in the nation, to the nation, and to other persons.

The fundamental law of rights is, — Be a person, and respect others as persons.[1]

The nation is the institution of rights. The primary distinction of rights is of Natural and of Positive Rights. Rights are natural, as laid in the nature of man; rights are positive as defined in the nation. Rights are natural as immanent in the nature of man; rights are positive as emanent in the nation.

Rights are natural, as founded in human nature. They are inherent; they are written in the law and the constitution of the being of man. These rights are variously denominated in the various representations of their content and form.

Blackstone calls them absolute rights. But this is inexact and indefinite; the freedom of man is not absolute, and no rights are absolute. The rights which Blackstone enumerates are all subject to modification. There are none which may not be abridged or yielded or interrupted, and none which have a perfect realization.

1 Hegel's *Philosophie des Rechts*, p. 72. Stahl's *Philosophie des Rechts*, vol. ii. sec. i. p. 331. Michelet's *Naturrecht*, vol. i. p. 143.

"The ultimate ground of the rights of a person is therein that man is made in the image of God." — Stahl, vol. ii. sec. i. p. 331.

This law is the ground of social laws, the unwritten laws of manners and the substance of the character of the gentleman. It is the assertion of a personality, and a deference for it in others. This has had, perhaps, its finest illustration in the character of the Quaker. It has no ground in a formal distinction of classes, and the very quality of vulgarity is a respect for the accidents of life and a deference to them.

They have been called inalienable rights, but there is no right which has its institution in the external sphere, that is, the sphere defined by law, that is inalienable. The right of the nation is necessarily precedent to the rights of the individual, and they are all limited by it in its supreme necessity. They must yield also to its force, as, for instance, life is subject to the call of the state in war and its calamities, property is subject to its claim in taxation, liberty may be interrupted in the peril of the whole, and is forfeited by crime or the suspicion of crime, and in its simplest phase is restricted, as when one is compelled by the police, in a stoppage in the street, to retrace his steps, or take another route. The phrase inalienable, as applied to rights, had its source in the theory of the social compact, in which certain rights are regarded as alienated for a certain consideration to society, in order to secure the balance. It had a certain advantage against governments which were denying all natural rights, and encroaching arbitrarily on positive rights, but its consistence is only in the legal fiction which it presumes.

Mr. Hurd describes these rights, while limiting them to the civil sphere, as individual rights, and Dr. Lieber, as primordial rights. But neither phrase is comprehensive of them, and neither has passed into common use. They have no historical justification, and the assertion of these rights in history has not been from academies or courts, but from the common people. The term natural rights is the more simple and the more exact. It is the less likely to allow injury to rights through arbitrary notions. It indicates the origin and the content of rights. It has a better place in the common thought of men, and may be trusted to hold its own, in the long run, against a more scholastic term.[1]

[1] Hurd's *Law of Freedom, etc.*, vol. i. p. 36. Lieber's *Political Ethics*, vol. i. p. 281.

The declaration of principles at the close of the War of the Revolution was,

These rights cannot be referred to the assumed existence of man in an imaginary state of nature, which is represented as the presocial state. Blackstone refers them to an antecedent state of nature, and describes them as rights which every man is entitled to enjoy, whether out of society or in it.[1] But this assumed state is unreal, and if man be represented as out of society, there is no limit to his action which can be defined in rights, and no power by which the title to rights can be conferred. The title to these rights is affirmed and acknowledged only in the organization of society. This definition has its consistency also only in the fiction of the social compact.

These rights cannot be referred to the assumed existence of man in an atomic state. Thus Kent describes them as rights which belong to individuals in a single unconnected state.[2] But this atomic state is also unreal. Man does not exist in this isolation and cannot be rightly conceived apart from relations, and as these relations had not their origin in the volition or reflection of the individual, he cannot make them as though they had not been. The conception rests also upon a fiction.

There is no necessity of assuming an imaginary state of nature in order to ascertain the foundation of natural rights. The consistent result of its assumption has been

in the words of the Continental Congress to the people, — "Let it be remembered, that it has been the pride and the boast of America, that the rights for which she has contended were the rights of human nature." — April, 1783. *Journal of the Continental Congress*, vol. viii. p. 201.

1 "The rights of persons are of two sorts, absolute and relative: absolute which are such as appertain and belong to particular men, merely as individuals, or single persons; relative, which are incident to them as members of society, or standing in various relations to each other.

"By the absolute rights of individuals we mean those which are so in their primary and strictest sense; such as would belong to their persons merely in a state of nature, and which every man is entitled to enjoy whether out of society or in it." — 1 Bl. *Comm.*, 123.

2 "The rights of persons in private life are either absolute, being such as belong to individuals in a single unconnected state; or relative, being those which arise from the civil and domestic relations." — 2 Kent's *Comm.* 1.

always the construction of an abstract system. These rights in their origin and their content can be referred only to the nature of man. Their foundation is in no sphere of external circumstance, and in no estate or condition of life, but in the constitution of man. They are the rights of human nature, and their derivation is signified in the image in which that nature is made. They are the primal prerogatives of humanity. They have not their origin in human enactments, but determine the just content of those enactments. They are imprescriptible; the image in which they are given is effaced by no priestly illusions, and is extinguished in no imperial obscurantism; they are not wholly buried beneath the most artificial of policies, and are worn out by no continuance of customs, although lying "heavy as frost and deep almost as life."

Rights are positive, as enacted in the law and embodied in the institutions of the nation. Positive rights are the determinate expression of natural rights, in the formal Civil and Political process. They are rights as they receive the recognition of the state and are affirmed by it and in it. Positive rights are therefore the institutes in which the progress of the people is actualized, and they define the extent of its advancement.

Rights are positive, since their necessary definition and institution is in law. It is only as they are affirmed in law, that rights obtain their necessary obligation and their common recognition. Their permanence is secured and they become binding upon all. It is because there is in law this authorization of rights, that the law itself in the course of the organic people is never stationary; it does not reach a final enactment; it is not closed in an imperial code. Yet in law there is only the formal recognition, the deposition of rights, it is not creative of them.

Rights are positive, since their attainment is in the historical progress of the people. They are apprehended and then actualized in its development. They are affirmed in the growth of its self-assertion and self-respect. There is in the nation a continuous advance, and in no single moment of its existence can it be conceived as the ultimate and perfect state. The spirit of the people perishes in that oriental immobility. The rights which are asserted in the nation become thus the signs of its progress. They are the landmarks of the march of the people; and since its rights are the realization of an organic and moral being, there is no definite terminus to its advance.

Rights are positive, since every nation has its own vocation in history, and in each, rights are formed in its course, and become the reflex of its aim. They are wrought out in its vocation, and bear the clear imprint of its character. They have in every people the same universal ground and end, as this in each is the fulfillment in a moral order of the life of humanity; but in the purpose and the freedom of the people their manifestation has a definite type, and they are moulded in conformance to it.

Rights are positive, since they are instituted in the nation, in a certain sphere of external circumstance. They are thus affected by the external relations of the people. The laws in which they are established are modified by the age, the race, the association with other peoples, and then also by the physical condition, the soil, the climate, the products; by agriculture, and commerce, and trade; by all those elements which, in the necessary relation of man in physical nature, so clearly affect, while they do not determine, national and individual development. But it is only a recent school which has held this in so narrow and exclusive a notion as to make all human freedom a fiction, and to leave to man only the poor pretense but not the reality of rights.

Positive rights, therefore, are natural rights, as they are ascertained and affirmed in the normal Civil and Political process. It is only in law, in which this process consists, that natural rights obtain their necessary form. They have apart from this neither the requisite precision, nor the obligation which secures their authority and validity. They are the principle to determine the action of the whole people, but in law alone they become the necessary form for the action of the whole people. In certain rights there is always a vagueness, since that which in itself, for instance, is determined in the development of the individual and the nation, is to obtain a formal determination in law. Thus the time when the majority of the individual begins, and the qualifications by which an elector is ascertained, are illustrations of this. But the principle to be regarded in these instances is, that the state shall not determine them arbitrarily but in the reason of the state.

The relation of Natural and Positive rights has been represented in two opposite conceptions, each of which involves an error.[1]

The one proposition isolates the sphere of natural from the sphere of positive rights; they are defined as existent in an external and formal separation. The ultimate ground of natural rights is assumed in the nature of persons, or the nature of things, and from it they proceed; the ultimate ground of positive rights in the determination of the state, and from it they proceed, but there is no necessary relation between them, nor do positive rights, in the normal process of the nation, exist in the recognition and institution of natural rights.

This conception has its source in the antithesis of natural and political society, in which a definite existence is assumed for the former, and the latter is held in its separation as an artificial existence; the foundation of society

[1] Aristotle distinguishes between a natural right which is everywhere alike valid, φυσικόν; and a positive right which is right only as being established, νομικόν; but as Stahl says, so far as Aristotle defines them, they are placed in external and separate spheres. — Aristotle's *Ethics*, bk. v. ch. vii.

is laid in contractual law, and its structure is formed of conventional rights. This distinction was prominent in the thought of the last century. It was the formalism which held the same separation in natural and revealed religion, and then in natural and political rights, in natural and artificial society. It appears in two men who wrought with the deepest influence upon their age, each working steadily and faithfully in it, becoming thereby the teachers of another age, and while wide apart, yet aiding toward the discovery of a deeper unity, — it appears in those in whom was the strength and weakness of the age, — Burke and Rousseau. Burke opposed the notion which founds society upon the dogmas and theories of an abstract speculation, and fabricates it after an arbitrary scheme and an empty metaphysic; instead of this, he maintained its existence as a structure of acquired rights, and held the nation in its life to be identical with these, so that the form itself became sacred, and rights whose origin was in accident or in custom, shared in the permanence and the sacredness of the life of the nation: Rousseau opposed the notion which founds society upon conventional rights, and regards the state as an accumulation of rights, which, originating in an accident, are to be perpetuated inviolate with the inviolateness of the state itself; instead of this, sweeping away the existent organization and the whole existent polity, he maintained the inauguration of a new order, constructed in accordance with the abstract reason. The one merged the nation into the formalism of history, the other into the formalism of thought.

The proposition which thus isolates the province of natural and positive rights, and locates each in a formal and external sphere, has its refutation in that the nation itself is the natural and the normal process of human society. It is the postulate in political science, of Aristotle, whose solid vantage is the defense from so many errors, "man is by nature a political being." The nation is the manifestation of that which is immanent in the nature of man. It is the legal fiction of the social contract which severs the state from the natural life of man.

The proposition, moreover, in the detachment of positive from natural rights, allows to the former no ground but an accidental succession, or a customary law, or a contractual form, or an arbitrary power. It can only be justified in the origin of the nation in force, or in the accident of history, or in the "use which custom bends." But this is the unreason of the state, and it can then no longer be comprehended in the moral order which is history, nor as the constituent of that order. And rights can allow no arbitrary basis, for this presumes a contradiction, and it is not in its own inclination or in its indifferent choice, that the nation may determine their existence and whether they shall or shall not be. If, however, rights do not consist in the being of the nation as a moral person, and if a merely formal limitation be allowed, then in their restriction to a part, they may be always confined to an individual, or a family, or a class, for their only basis is arbitrary.

But this isolation of natural and positive rights is the sequence of a formalism which identifies the nation with its external organization. Positive rights have in natural rights their content, and their immutable ground, and therein alone the nation is constituted in the realization, in a moral order, of that which is immanent in society.[1]

The opposite proposition identifies the sphere of natural and positive rights; it assumes for natural rights, in themselves, a valid existence, and makes them then the necessary and supreme law. In the conception of natural rights it finds the boundary and description of positive rights, and the scope of the latter is held as coterminal

[1] The entire severance of natural and political rights, where Burke in no way appears clear from the confusions of his age, has been maintained in a distinction in which natural rights are regarded as essential, and positive as accidental;

with the apprehension of the former. The distinction of rights in their conception and in their formal institution is obliterated. That which is deemed a natural right is assumed to be already the law, and to possess an immediate validity.

This merges the whole order of the state into the subjective conception of the individual; the organic action of the whole ceases, and its conduct is left to the determination of the private judgment. Its course is no longer defined in the formula of law and in institutions. It is no more the expression of an authority, which is over every individual, and to which each alike is subject; its language is no longer *esto* but only *videtur*. This is the elevation of the private opinion of the individual into the place of the government of the whole. Its only issue is the setting up of a popular absolutist, the dissolution of the state into its atomy, and the inauguration of a conflict of each against all.

As natural rights are held in the subjective conception of the individual, they have not the clearness which is requisite to a law which shall be the form of action for the whole. They are vague, and the condition of rights is that they shall be defined in a form which shall enable them to be held with decision. They are to be sustained against injury, and are to be obligatory upon all, and therefore it is necessary that they should have so clear an expression that they may be enforced over all, but they obtain this only as they are asserted in a positive form in the civil and political organization.

natural rights as universal, and positive rights as limited to a part. But if positive rights are accidental, then the state, as the process of rights, can be regarded only as the accident of history; and personality, moreover, is not determined in accidents, but in its own determination is the realization of order. The definition, also, while limiting positive rights to a part, fails to define this part and the ground in which it is ascertained, and in its separation also of natural from positive rights, it leaves the former a mere abstraction, since rights are valid only in their positive institution.

The proposition is also inconsistent with the existence of the nation in its historical development. There is in its advance a constant outcome of rights. It is not the application of a perfect system of natural rights, for which there is to be assumed the authority of positive law. The whole body of rights can no more come forth complete in a single moment than can the nation itself. And the individual subjective conception can in no moment assume to be the law or the measure of this advance. It is manifested always in the development of the spirit of the organic people, and no single age can apprehend or attain a final and perfect embodiment of rights. While there is in the definition of natural rights in an abstract system, the weak attraction of a certain intellectual proportion, it is yet an empty notion which regards rights thus as complete in a system, which, when received from the schools, is to be analyzed and applied by the people.

There is a tendency, which this proposition illustrates, to forget that rights are and can be real, only as they are established in the civil and political organization. They are slowly, and only with toil and endeavor, enacted in laws, and moulded in institutions. It is only with care and steadiness and tenacity of purpose that those guaranties are forged which are the securance of freedom, and they are to be clinched and riveted to be strong for defense and against assault. The rhetoric which holds the loftier abstract conception, avails nothing, until in the constructive grasp and tentative skill of those who apprehend the conditions of positive rights, it is shaped and formed in the process of the state. The former is often the quality of some individual thinker, whose ideal is cold also in its distant elevation, and who, regarding in events only the conflict of ideas, is indifferent to the real life of men and nations, and this indifference may become, when his own ideal is unrecognized, the ground only of the scorn of an unsympathizing imagination — not the nobleness but the weakness of disdain: the latter is the work of the statesman who alone knows how patient and vigilant is the toil which is the condition of the institution of rights, and how wary and bitter is the antagonism of the forces, from whose selfish grasp the ampler field of rights is wrested, and who forgets in no immediate end the long result to be attained, nor in the exultation of momentary success, or the discouragement of momentary failure, how firmly and how broadly rights, to be secure, must be enacted in the laws, and moulded in the institutions of the state.

There is a tendency, which this proposition also illustrates, to represent natural rights as construed in some system, and to regard the nation as an external structure to be erected in conformance to it. The nation is to be shaped by these political architects after certain speculative abstractions. The whole existent organization is to be destroyed to effect some end of the individual thinker, and again to be built anew in the individual design. Then all institutions that have not the exact proportions of the momentary schedule are to be leveled to the ground, and all that has been achieved in the work and sacrifice of generations must make room for a structure designed in the individual conceit. It is this spirit, which is the evil of fanaticism, that appears as a vain and destructive force. When there follows the wreck of the whole existent organization, it can find in the abstract reason the ground only of a formal order, and its work, out of a prior system of independent rights, can result only in a formal unity. But the nation is not such that it may be constantly taken down and rebuilt again; the city walls, when they are torn away, may be piled up from the quarries of the hills, as gathered stones, but it is not thus in the political life of the people. And when this destructive course is begun there is no limit to it, but, as the nation is reconstructed after some abstract conception, it comes to be regarded as only an external order, and there is the justification for some further change in some new theory. But stability is the condition of growth, and the furthest advance of a single generation is slight in comparison with that which is embodied in the nation, in the long result of time; and the largest design of a single individual is contracted before that which is attained in the vocation of the nation in history. This conception can only appear in an unhistorical age, and in the extremes, — the provincial and cosmopolitan theories which coincide in their denial of the organic and moral being of the nation. Its source is in the false and deceptive exaltation of the individual, and it becomes in its assumption of the individual phase of the conception of natural rights, as the law of the action of the state, the precedent of a mere egoism.

The proposition in defining the relation of Natural and Positive rights, which isolates the province of each, and locates each in a separate and external sphere, and the proposition which identifies them, so that the individual conception or system of natural rights is apprehended as the immediate formula of action in the nation, are alike without justification.

In their necessary relation, natural rights have their determination in positive law, — the formula of positive rights. Natural rights are the content of which positive rights are the form; natural rights are the ground of action, positive rights the law of action. The relation is not one of identity nor of difference, but of development through content into form.[1]

Natural rights in their positive determination, are further defined as they are determined in the Civil or the Po-

[1] Melancthon has a passage, cited by Hegel, — "Verum quia jus positivum determinatio est juris naturalis, facile intelligi potest, jus positum tamen habere aliquam regulam videlicet, ne pugnet cum jure naturali."

"Alle rechtsbildung hat danach ein doppeltes moment, ein Gottlich-nothwendiges (naturrechtliches) und ein menschlich-freie (positives) und beide durchdringen sich ohne abgranzung, bestehen in untrennbarer einheit." — Stahl, *Philosophie des Rechts*, vol. ii. sec. i. p. 220.

litical process in the nation. Civil rights belong to the jural; political rights to the moral organization of the nation: civil rights are those in which the individual obtains protection; political rights are those in which the person obtains a realized freedom: civil rights belong to every one who is subject to the authority of the state; political rights belong to every person who is a member of the state: civil rights define private relations; political rights define public relations: civil rights are asserted in the jurisprudential order; political rights in the constitutional organization of the political people: civil rights attach to the province of private law; political rights to the province of public law: civil rights are resident in the commonwealth; political rights in the nation.

Civil rights are commonly designated as the right of personal security, of personal liberty, and of property; or the right of life, of liberty, of property; to these is to be added the right of access to the course of law, in which the preceding are sustained, or the right to the protection of the law — the equality before the law.

The right of personal security or of life, is simply the right to existence, the same right, as has been said, which one has to be where he is, that Kearsarge or Cape Cod has to be where it is; it embraces the right to the body, to health, to the limbs, to the senses and their use. There is often connected with this the right to reputation, and this as a right is also indicative of the worth and dignity of a person. From real honor, which is in man, it is true that none can detract, and real integrity is beyond earthly moil, but there is the right to the consideration in the external order of the worth of personality, and this right consists in the defense and maintenance in the external sphere of the integrity of the individual.[1]

[1] Mr. Spencer places the right to reputation on the basis of property, — "Reputation, as a thing which men strive to acquire and preserve, may be regarded

The right of personal liberty is the right of external freedom; it embraces the right to locomotion; the right to labor, — to earn one's bread in the sweat of one's brow; the right to unrestricted action in the choice of the vocation and occupation of the individual. There must be freedom to come and go, and freedom of action, and space in the state for the individuality of each to work outward; and none can be hindered or restrained from his vocation, and every occupation is to be opened upon the same conditions to all.

The right of property is a personal right in its strictest form, and is especially illustrative in certain phases, of the relation of the individual and the nation. Its definition in formulas and theories may be traced through the widest range of legal and political thought, and it bears the impress of the spirit of all their schools. It is more complex than the preceding, and appears in more opposite representations; and in historical and in recent theories it has met with strenuous denial.

"Thou shalt not steal," were the words of the ancient Hebrew commandment, but "la propriété c'est le vol," said M. Proudhon, and the inference was reached through the rejection of all ground on which the right to property has been asserted in the schools of economy. The Hebrew commandment presumed the existence of the nation; it presumed a will whose determination was in righteousness, and in which the nation had its foundation; and the existence of property, then, was recognized as an institute of the nation, not its first nor its main institute, but subsequent to many others, as the order of the family, the rest from labor in the succession of the week, and yet it is presumed with them and as sacred as they.

The legal definition which has most widely prevailed, as

as property." — *Social Statics*, p. 162. But the conception is lost when placed on any other ground than the worth of personality. An old writer has said, — "A good name is better than great riches."

to the ground of property and of a right to property, has been stated in the aphorism of Savigny, — that property is founded on adverse possession matured by prescription. This is simply the formula of the course of Roman law. It refers the origin of property and of the right to property to mere force, the grasp of the "strong man armed who keeps his goods in peace;" but force is not the source of a right, nor is the right evoked in holding fast what one has gotten, nor is its claim so matured by the lapse of time, as to win that measure of respect from the adverse that shall overawe their desire, and prevent possession from yielding to the assault of those who at length in turn may prove the stronger; nor can the mere continuance of possession justify the deference of men for the institution of property. The same legal conception is repeated in a more narrow form in the phrase of Blackstone, that in occupancy is the origin of property and of the right to property. But occupancy is only the incident of property, and not the ground of it, nor of its right, and the phrase, instead of characterizing the archaic condition, — the primitive estate of man, from which Blackstone with his speculations journeys forth, — belongs to a later form of society and to a complex system of jurisprudence, and presumes for its recognition an established order.[1]

These formulas indicate the line of legal thought, but there is a wider scope and grasp in the theories which appear in the later periods of political speculation, and there is an advance in the history of political theories beyond the history of legal formularies. The illustration of this is in the theories of Locke, of Considerant, of Hegel.

The proposition of Locke retains only an historical interest. Locke represented the land as originally of no value, and then he made the acquisition of property to consist in the application of labor, by which the land becomes of value to man; the land is valueless, and prop-

[1] See Maine's *Ancient Law*, pp. 244 – 248.

erty originates in work upon the land, and in the growth of population. But this defines only a certain mode of acquisition and not the origin of property, or of the right to property. It evades the origin of property, for the right to work upon a thing presumes the possession of or property in the thing, and then the work put upon it creates a higher value, but not the thing itself. And if the increased value which is the result of labor be allowed to the individual possessor, the increased value in the greater degree may be the result of the growth of population or of the good order and government of the whole; but the individual possessor has no immediate or exclusive right to the latter increase of value. The value may also in many instances have been increased by omitting to put labor upon the land, as in the wooded lands or the mineral deposits of a country which becomes populated. There is certainly in labor an element of property, but not the origin of property nor of the right to property, and in labor as a physical force man effects no result in comparison with nature in her constant change of physical forms, in her ceaseless laboratories.

The proposition of Considerant is connected with this, and starting from another premise holds the same position. It represents the physical world as the common good and the gift of nature, and as belonging to man, but as yet undivided, and open to all to come in and take their estate. Then no individual or generation can claim possession before another, while that which each lays out upon the land by his labor is his own possession, since it is his own creation and thus not of nature. Those, then, who come afterward, not being in actual possession, have also a right to the land, but only to the land, not to the improvement laid out upon it, which has created its higher value. But the defect in this proposition at once becomes apparent when the application is made. If the actual possessors should hold on to their exclusive possession, that would be unjust to the new comers, who are thereby excluded from possession, and have the common gift and good of nature withheld from them; therefore the actual possessors must divide the possession of the land with them, but that would be unjust to the actual possessors, since the result of their labor, and it may be of their fathers' labor, would be taken from them. There is, therefore, a compensation to be provided for them, and this is represented as the security and the equivalent of labor. Then since the land cannot be usefully further divided in this parcelling among all comers, the actual possessors must provide for the later comers employment and means of labor upon the land, and this is rated as the compensation in turn to them for their claim upon the land, as the common good and gift of nature, and is held as the equivalent to them for their deprivation from it. It is represented as more than an equivalent, since it returns more than could be obtained from the original good and gift of nature in fruits, hunting, fishing, etc.

This proposition assumes a law of compensation, and an exchange of equivalents, in order to its justification; but the principle which it assumes is not substantiated. The compensation allowed does not meet the claim of those who are deprived of possession and are kept from their share in the land, and instead of the common gift obtain a forced contract. That which is the postulate of the whole proposition is also immediately evaded, for what is the value of the original land as part of the common gift and good, and what is the value of the improvement laid out upon it by labor, and what is the actual possessor to allow for that which he may have consumed out of the common gift and good, in the depreciation of its original value, as wood or minerals, or the exhaustion of the soil by crops? Then in the providing of an employment, the sphere and means of labor on the land, the claim of those who are kept from possession of the land is not satisfied, for this which gains them subsistence from the land and a return for service, is not the equivalent for their deprivation also from the land itself. The proposition furthermore is inconsistent, since as M. Proudhon in availing himself of its premise has said, if nature be the common gift and good open before all, it does not belong to the actual possessors nor to their fathers to work on it exclusively, nor to hold exclusively its values. It is furthermore defective in its assumption of the common good of nature as alone a gift, and its separation thus from the return of labor, since labor has the gift of nature for its ground or its reward. "The advocates of this theory," says Stahl, "look upon nature as only a treasury of goods, which has not God for its Lord but only men, and so they can divide them up."[1]

The proposition of Hegel has a higher worth than any preceding it in recent politics. According to Hegel,[2] the beginning of property is in the fact of occupancy; but he says occupancy is only the incident, and property exists in the occupancy by a person, and the ground of the existence of property is in the right of a person to a thing. The possession of a thing is in the will, that is, in a person; and the possession of a thing is mine as I assert my will over it, and thus as I withdraw the assertion of my will from over it, I may alienate the thing which was in possession. The first comer is the possessor, not because he is the first, but as he asserts a will over the thing, and he is first only in relation to some second or third person who may come afterwards. The right is in the will, that is, in the person, and the actual possession is in the assertion of the will; and in property there is only the actualization of the right of a person to a thing. This proposition is true in its recognition of the fact that the mate-

1 See Stahl, *Philosophie des Rechts*, vol. ii. sec. 1, p. 370, whose criticism of this proposition I have mainly followed, and whose whole statement of property has the highest value.

2 Hegel's *Philosophie des Rechts*, pp. 78 - 94.

rial world exists for man and man is placed over it; it is true also in its definition of occupancy as only the circum stance, for it cannot be the ground, of the institution of property, nor of the right in property; it is true also in representing possession as in the will, for property belongs to me only as I assert my will over it, and I may alienate or transfer it by an act of will. But this proposition can only be justified, not as the existence of property is left to be determined simply by the circumstance of occupancy, in a precedence in time, but as property is regarded as the gift of God to man in the material world. It is man's only as his personal being; that is, his life in its moral realization is from God, and it is his in and for the fulfillment of his vocation in a moral order in the world, and apart from this there is nothing which is his own. The right to property and the possession is therefore in personality, and the existence of property is of the gift of God. It exists in the sphere of the vocation of man, and it is instituted and maintained in the nation as the nation is formed in the moral order of God in the world.

The common theories of the schools in which it had been the aim to establish the ground of the right to property, were subjected by M. Proudhon, in the approach to his famous inference, to a thorough and vigorous criticism. The right, he said, is not derivative from the fact of occupancy, for the arbitrary seizure of a thing cannot become the ground of a right to it; the momentary possession of a thing still less can become the ground of a continuous right; and occupancy can at the most claim respect only in so far as the individual actually and immediately exercises it; and then, also, possession can be respected only in so long and so far as actual occupancy appears. It is not derivative from labor, for the right and the freedom to labor upon a thing already presumes possession of it, and the labor may create a higher value in it, but not the thing itself; the value may also be diminished by labor upon it, as the detriment that follows the destruction of forests. It is not derivative from positive law, that is, a legal arrangement and cantonment in the beginning of society, for positive law can regulate nothing which does not of itself already exist; the reference of its origin to a formal law would leave still, moreover, only an arbitrary ground. Therefore, said M. Proudhon, since all the theories of your schools fail, since there is no ground in all that you have claimed for the right to property, property is not a right but a wrong; property is robbery.[1]

The argument of M. Proudhon is conclusive against the theories he assailed, theories held often as the idle or the convenient evasion of a deeper truth, and held in the degradation of the nation, as the consequent of the schemes which deny its moral being, and assert its existence, as only the support of private interests in the combination of capital and toil. The error of M. Proudhon is in his premise. The existence of property is presumed to be a wrong, because no title assumed to the acquisition of property is proven to be founded in justice. But as Stahl has said, the title of acquisition is not the basis of property, but the property is the basis for the title, and occupancy and labor and law are indicative of possession, on the ground that apart from them the necessity and justice of property exists. M. Proudhon has proven nothing against the right in the existence of property, nor against the right to property, but he has proven the defect of the weak and false theories in which a foundation for the institution of property has been sought. M. Proudhon has been called an atheist, but those by whom the accusation has been made may have to consider how far their representation of the origin and institution of property, which he assailed so passionately and so conclusively, separates them from atheism. They who hold the tenure of property in these theories may justify themselves, but it may be for

[1] Proudhon, *Système des Contradictions Economiques*, vol. ii. p. 234.

them to ask what they may have in these theories to protect them and their rights; or what the future of society may be which is educated in them; or how they may meet those crises which try the defect in social schemes, and which they may defer in their dogmas but cannot defer in history, the inevitable days in which false theories and false systems are burned up like stubble. It is in the avoidance of the divine origin and subsistence of the nation, and in the indifference to its existence in its moral being, and in the assertion of individual and economic schemes, that these theories have prevailed, and in them they have their consistent assumption. The Hebrew commandment presumed the being of the nation in which it was declared, as a moral order, and as subsisting in the name of a righteous will, from whom the commandment came, and in that conception the tenure of property was defined.

The origin of the existence of property and of the right, is in no formal law or precedence, and law is only regulative and descriptive of it. It is in no external circumstance, and occupancy is only the incident of it, and, in its exclusive apprehension, allows to it no moral significance. There is in neither a formal law nor an external circumstance the source of rights, and it is only as property consists with the nature and vocation of man that occupancy and law follow from it, but its origin is not in them.

The ground of the right in the existence of property, and of the right to property, is in the vocation from God in the world, of the individual and of the nation. Property is the material for the work of man in his vocation on the earth, and in that alone is the ground of its right. If property becomes in itself an end, then personality is subjected to the things which it possesses. If it be held apart from the vocation of man and the moral relations and obligations involved in that, then it becomes mere possession, the instrument of a selfish interest, and the means for the degradation of personality.

To the individual and to the nation God gives his powers and his working field, and these are the talents of each, and in this alone does property consist. It is thus, as it is given in and for the vocation of man on the earth, that its use affords a ground for the manifestation of character, and there may be in it the expression of individuality, and elements of culture and freedom. In this also is the sign of the sacredness of the relation which the individual and the nation bear to the earth. Thus, also, if there be no recognition of a vocation which the individual and the nation are to fulfill, then the origin of property is only in the arbitrary or the accidental; it is in its origin arbitrary — the seizure by force and choice of that which each may lay hold of; or accidental — that which each in his fortune may stumble on or is in luck to obtain, and it is the sign only of the avarice of men who clutch it in their grasp, or the risk of men who find it by the way.[1]

The origin of the existence of property and of the right to property is not in the physical condition of man. There is no more ground in his physical being for property than there is in the other animals for property, as in it man has no more rights than they. Man is dependent upon the physical world, and in his physical being is related to it, through the sweep of all its changes, and it may be in the evolution of all its forms: but in his spiritual nature, he is over it; he exists in a higher sphere; his citizenship is in another world; and in that ampler realm of a realized freedom there is alone the ground of rights. In the physical world man is to find the satisfaction of his physical necessities, and therefore he has power in it and over it. But property is not therefore simply the means for the satisfaction of physical necessities, nor is its ground in the aimless subjection of the material world; in this there can be the source of no right.

1 Dr. Brownson's definition of property is as profound as it is beautiful, — "Property is communion with God, through the material world." — *The American Republic*, p. 15.

In the physical world man has a formative power, and there is in his physical condition the hard necessity for labor, but labor follows from the existence of property and the right in it; not the reverse. It is an element in property, and in the necessary condition of life it appears as the wages for toil and the return for service, but labor itself passes into the higher conception of work in the vocation of man.

The recognition of property on this postulate is alone consistent with the correspondence in the rights and duties of property. When recent economists, as Bastiat, admit that the true condition of property and the relations of capital and labor can be fixed by no adjustment of economic schemes, but by the recognition of a moral obligation in the use of property, it becomes an evidence of this proposition as to the ground of property. It is not simply the purchase by the individual, which is to be held in exclusive use, and suffers an indifference to moral relations; it has a moral aim, and thus the advance in civilization will not be in its negation, and the degradation of all in a mere communism; there will be its better assertion, and in the recognition of the duties of property as correspondent to its rights there may be the coming of the true communism, of which the world once has seen the type.

The relation of property to the family has its basis in the constitution of the family, as a moral order in the world. The fact that in archaic society it is held as a common possession in the family, is consequent on the fact that the family is the archaic form, and the inception of the moral order and relations of the world is in the institution of the family. Thus the relation of property to the family does not cease in the progress of society, but is held with more definite limitations and provisions as society passes into more complex and varied relations.

The process in the realization of a moral order, in the institution of property, appears also in the realization of the nation. The people possesses in the land the external sphere of its vocation in history. The right to the land is not in the fact of occupancy, but in the vocation of the nation as a moral person. The nation has the right to property in its own vocation, and as a moral order it is instituted and maintained, in the nation, in and with the vocation of the individual. Thus property is to be maintained as an institute of the nation, and secured alike to the individual and the family and the nation. The right of property, as it is existent in the nation, has its formal assertion in the right of eminent domain or expropriation. It obtains, not because the right of one man, or of a collection of men, is precedent to the right of another, and there is no ground on which the rights of several should exclude the right of one, but because the right of the nation is necessarily precedent to the rights of the individual. Yet here also the nation in its moral order is to regard and to maintain the existence of property. Therefore in the formal exercise of expropriation, an adjustment is to be made by compensation. The obvious maxims given by Bluntschli in defining this are, first, that the nation maintain the freedom and the security of property; and, second, that it exercise no arbitrary disposition of property. And as an element in property is labor, the nation in the exercise of expropriation is to render compensation to the individual for the return of his labor appropriated by it. It is the fact of the nation as a moral order that makes the maintenance of the rights of property imperative, and while it belongs to it to define values in the issue of money, it is to make this issue the representative of actual values, and while its own right is precedent — and may be exercised in its peril, as in war — in the possession of all property, yet in its normal course, if it fails to sustain the validity of contracts and exchange, in correspondence with their actual values it becomes itself destructive of property, and as the obligation of the nation is higher as its right is higher, every act of national dishonesty is the greater wrong, and is subversive of the moral order of the whole.

The right to the recognition of these civil rights, and to their maintenance in the civil order, is the primary civil right. It is the necessary condition, in which all other civil rights are established, and without it they remain a fiction. To each and all the nation is to leave open the avenue to these rights, and is to allow it to be closed in the private interest of none. This is what Burke has called the right to justice. It is the right, in the organization of justice, of every man to a fair trial for himself and against every other man. The justice of the state is to be for each and all, or it becomes the institution of injustice ; its tribunal is to be open to hear the cause of all, or it becomes the inquisition of wrong. It is the right of all to equality before the law.

This right is implied in the necessary conception of law as universal. It is indicated in the most ancient symbols of justice, and its types are traced in the most archaic of social forms. The earliest traditions are of the institution of tribunals, to which all may appeal, and in whose judgment all may abide. The signature of justice most widely found is the scale held with fair and even balance. It is the figure of one who is blindfold and sees not those who may approach, but whose ear is open to the cry of all. The rich and the poor, the strong and the weak, may all share its protection and must abide its decision. The life of the humblest is as sacred as that of the greatest, and the possession of the poorest in shelter and tools, is as well regarded as the estate of the rich.

It is this principle of equality before the law that appears in the foundation of social order. In the myths of Plato, it is represented in the inception of society. " Man was furnished with all he needed, for his individual life ; but he had not yet the wisdom by which society is formed. This wisdom was kept in the citadel of Zeus, and into that awful sanctuary forethought could not enter. As time went on, the power and weakness of man was seen. He instituted ordinances of worship; he defined language; he invented clothing and procured food for himself. But he lived in isolation and was unfit for social union. Then if men were scattered they were in danger of perishing from wild beasts; if they tried to combine, they were scattered again by mutual violence. Thereupon Zeus, fearing for the safety of our race, sent Hermes with self-respect and justice, that their presence among men might establish order, and knit together the bonds of friendship in society. 'Must I distribute them,' said Hermes, 'as the various arts have been distributed aforetime, only to certain individuals, or must I dispense them to all?' 'To all,' said Zeus, 'and let all partake of them. For states could not be formed, if they, like the arts, were confined to a few. Nay, more, if any is incapable of self-respect and justice let him be put to death, such is my will, as a plague to the state.'"[1]

The wide historical influence of the axiom of the jurisconsults of the Antonine era, "omnes homines, natura æquales sunt," has been illustrated by a recent historian of Roman law. Its auspicious assertion as a principle and aim in the destination of the state, in the beginning of the independence of the republic, will always have an historical significance.

The recognition of an equality before the law is slow to come, and the attainment of an impartial justice is marked by careful and painful steps. It seems so fair an ideal, as to win the thoughts of men. It alone reflects that holy faith in justice, which men feel in their hearts has somewhere its abode, and to which the right does not appeal in vain. It is the only shield of human weakness, against inhuman wrong, and the violence and fraud and oppression

[1] *Theætetus*, sec. 21.

of wicked men, but many have fallen striving for it who have been the prophets of the world whose cry is still "how long?" It is the policy of evil to devise against it, and it is overborne by all the evil elements of our nature, by selfishness and pride and lust.

Political rights are those rights which are instituted in the normal process of the people as an ethical organism. They are those rights which have their ground in the being of the nation in its moral personality, and in them the freedom of the people in its organic unity is realized.

Political rights include the right of every person born in the nation, to be and to remain in its citizenship. The nation cannot arbitrarily determine who shall or shall not exist in it as members of it. "The right of citizenship as distinguished from alienage," says Kent, in defining the law of civilization, "is a national right, character, or condition." This is applied to "all persons born in the jurisdiction and allegiance of the United States."[1] This is irrespective of ancestry, and consists with a national not a racial principle. It is involved in the being of the nation in its moral relations, and therefore, as every other right, is only forfeited by crime, which is in its nature and effect the severance of relationships.

Political rights include the right of every person who is a member of the nation, to participation in its resultant advantage. The strength and power to which it has attained are to be the aid and defense of every member, and the domain of its order is to be open to him. Its historical memories and associations are no more truly the glory and hope of all its members than are its results the possession of all. It has a universal end, and to restrict its advantages to one or to a few, to an individual or to a class, would involve the subordination of the whole to private and special ends.

[1] 2 Kent's *Comm.* 39.

Political rights include the right of every person who is a member of the nation to the actual determination of a person in its destination. The personality of each is to be respected in it, and to act in it, not negatively but positively, not passively to be allowed as if the nation were only some power over it, but it is to act as itself a determinate power in it. Since the normal and moral process of the nation is in the determination of personality, every individual who, being a member of it, has personality, has the right to its determinate assertion in the nation. It is its defect when, by an arbitrary act, certain persons are included and determine its action and certain other persons are excluded.

Political rights include also the recognition and institution of all those rights which are involved in the relations of life as a moral order. These are to be guarded and affirmed by the nation, which is invested with authority to maintain the order of society. Thus the family in its normal and moral conception is to be maintained by it, and the violation of its organic law is to be punished.

Rights have their correspondence in duties; they may be arbitrarily separated, but it cannot be without the defect or the distortion of the one or the other. Since rights have a moral content, to every right a duty corresponds, but it does not follow that a right corresponds also to every duty, since there are immediate duties in the relations of life, as for instance, the duty of a child to its parents.

Rights and duties have the same ground in personality. Rights have not their ground in duties, and do not proceed as if only derivative from them. A right is a condition, in which there may be the fulfillment of a duty; but a right is not simply the means for the fulfillment of a duty, only the instrument by which a duty is performed, and having apart from that no significance. Rights no less than the fulfillment of duties have their immediate content in personality; they are therefore to be held not simply as subsequent to duties, and as if only incident to them. Since rights proceed in their conception from a righteous will, and subsist in that, therefore in the realization of rights there is the fulfillment of duties. The rejection of the immediate foundation of rights and duties in personality can result only in the construction of a formal law of duty and a formal system of rights.

Mr. Caird has said that, "in the philosophy of Kant, the demand for the rights of man first manifested its true nature, because in that philosophy the claim of right was based on the idea of duty."[1] But rights are based in personality, and in that alone can they subsist, and from that alone is their content derived. Kant asserted that the rights of man exist only in conformance to an abstract moral law, and only for an end defined in that law, but this can become the ground only of a formal conception of rights and a formal freedom. It would merge the being of the state into a formal system of laws. The necessary inference of this postulate of Kant, is the derivation of the right of personality from a law of duty, and thus he assumed it to be resultant from the law, — "Let not thyself be used as a means." But this reference of the right of personality to an abstract and formal law, and its definition in the limitations of that law, is not a sufficient ground for the right of personality. This law, for instance, which requires me to guard my own personality, and forbids that I should allow myself to be used as a means to an end, is obviously too narrow; it does not comprehend the right of personality, for this involves the right against other persons, that they also shall respect my personality, and shall not use, nor dare to use me as a means to an end.

[1] *Inaugural Lecture* in the Common Hall of Glasgow College, by Edward Caird, 1866. Kant's *Rechtslehre*, sec. xliii. See Stahl, *Phil. des Rechts*, vol. ii. sec. 1, p. 96.

The rights of the organic people, or national rights, have an integral unity as they are instituted in the realization of the nation as a moral person. They do not compose simply a formal system. They are not a mere accumulation of institutions, to be held by the people, as a miscellaneous budget of receipts, nor do they exist only as proceeding from the duties of the people, and as the resultant of certain obligations. The rights of the people subsist in the consciousness of the people in its unity, and this is the condition of political rights. They bear in their form the imprint of the type of the nation's individuality, and are the expression of its spirit. In their institution they constitute its political order. There is thus in its political course the expression of its aim and the subjection to it of the whole external order. There is indeed apparent in the institution of its rights, the influence of the physical condition of the people, the age, the land, the climate, the races, but these only modify while they cannot determine its process; this is determined only in the freedom of the people, and is the manifestation of its spirit.

The rights of the people have a universal as an individual element, and move toward one end in every nation, and thus there is a correspondence in different nations. But the one element does not preclude the other, they have an integral and individual character. They have no exotic forms, and cannot at once be transplanted from one people to another. They cannot be applied as abstract ideas adopted with some abstract system. Thus, in the development of rights, while they may not always have the harmony of a system, yet formed in the life of the people they have a deeper unity, and, wrought and forged in the great events of its history, they have subtler power and robuster proportions.

There is a certain representation of rights in which

they are defined as original and acquired rights. But strictly there is only one original right, the right of personality, and to this all others may be referred. It is the right which is primitive in the rights of man, the right of a man to be himself. The term acquired rights, when rights are held as the acquisition or private property of certain individuals or families, denotes a condition isolated from the normal and organic being of the nation, and deriving its content from traditional force, or custom or accident; it describes rather the privileges or prerogatives of an individual or a class. These may invade the whole sphere of natural rights, and when encroaching upon them, become in reality the ancient wrongs of a people. Acquired rights are positive, but they have no necessary basis beyond, and exist only as the creation of law.

There is a definition of rights as absolute and relative. The defect in the phrase absolute, as applied to rights, has been noticed; there is, moreover, no necessary antithesis to separate relative rights and the rights of personality, since all rights are the rights of persons in certain relations. The term describes mainly the rights of persons in certain necessary relations, as for instance the rights in the family, of the parent and child, of the husband and wife, and these relations are founded in nature, and maintained by the nation, as belonging to a moral order.

There is sometimes added to the same category the rights of corporations, — "artificial persons created by law, under the denomination of persons."[1] These rights are more exactly defined as franchises and privileges. They are formed by vesting a certain individual, or a number of individuals, in a corporate character with an artificial personality, and attaching thereto certain definite franchises and privileges, which, since the artificial personality is constructed, are described as rights. They are

[1] 1 Kent's *Comm.* 3.

created by the state in its enactment, and have their origin and limitation in positive law. Their accumulation in great monopolies, presumed to be chartered for the public advantage, is to be rigorously defined, and if not guarded may be an injury to the natural rights of the people. They are only the creation of law and exist always in subordination to the law of the public weal, but the strength, which resides in their assumption, by a legal fiction, of personality, is a significant illustration of the real ground of rights.

There is a definition, the most prominent in the history of civil rights, in which they are described as the rights of persons and the rights of things. This had its source in Roman law, which defined rights as *ad personam* and *ad rem*, and it had there a better justification than in later civilization, since in Roman law the definition of humanity, as Hegel says, was impossible.[1] In Roman law, rights *ad personam* are not the rights of a person as such, but the rights of a certain person or of a person in a certain status; personality as distinct from slavery, is represented as only a status or a condition. The phrase in which the distinction appears, remains as a reminiscence of the Roman conception, or is retained as a technical term or as a nice rhetorical antithesis. It denotes, says Christian, "by the former the rights of persons in public stations, and by the latter the rights of persons in private relations."[2] But since all rights are the rights of persons, and things can be only the objects of action, the merely verbal antithesis involves confusion and may become the source of constant error.

The description of rights as existent in some formal

[1] Hegel, *Philosophie des Rechts*, p. 23.

[2] 1 Bl. *Comm.* 123.

"Now rights and obligations are manifestly the attributes of persons, not of

system which the nation is to apply is unhistorical. Rights are represented thus as complete and beyond modification. They are the framework out of which man is to construct society, the house which is so built that one state may move out and another come in. They are the dry anatomy which a political spirit is to clothe with life. This can be justified only as the origin of the nation is defined in a formal law ; it is inconsistent with its organic being.

The nation is the realization of rights. The foundation of rights is in the nature of man, but their positive determination is in the civil and political organization.

The content of rights is in personality; the realization of rights is in the being of the nation as a moral organism.

There is for rights no positive existence apart from the nation. The imaginary state of nature in which rights are represented as existing in their completeness, apart from the civil and political being of society, is unreal, it is only the fiction in which man is stripped of the actual circumstance and relations of life, in order that he may be costumed in the theories and speculations of later schools. There is beyond the civil and political organization no right but might; there is no security, and rights which are primary, as of life and liberty and property, are neither acknowledged or affirmed. The absence of the rights of man is characteristic of his existence, in so far as the germ of the nation is undeveloped and its form undefined.

There is in the nation the institution, not the creation of rights. Since their foundation is in the nature of man, and their affirmation is in the nation, and since no man can take that which is by nature his right, simply as a

things, and to divide rights, as Blackstone, into the rights of persons and the rights of things, if by the latter words are meant rights not over in or to, but belonging to or inherent and vested in things, we have seen evinces either inaccuracy of thought, or is at best misapplication of language." — Reddies' *Inquiries, etc.*, p. 171.

gift, they are formed and maintained in the nation only as the being of the nation has a divine origin and is itself a divine gift. There is, therefore, in the development of the nation the manifestation of the rights given of God to man. Thus, in the representation of the nation as only an external organization, or as an economic association, there can be no just conception of the origin or subsistence of rights. Thus, also, they cannot be regarded as having their origin in law; in law there is their assertion but not their creation, and in law there can never be the perfect measure or expression of them. In the course of the nation their recognition in law, in any moment, is necessarily incomplete, and is never a finality, but is always advancing to correspond to the life and the freedom they represent.

Since the nation has its being in the realization of rights, the highest obligation of the nation is that rights be real. In the institution of rights there is the manifestation of the nature of man as it is made in the divine image. As the origin of the rights of man is in his creation in the divine image, so also is their realization in the nation the fulfillment of the divine will. As the realization of rights is in the vocation and the destination of the people, so also is the righteousness in which they are wrought the condition of the being of the people. The realization of the rights of humanity in the nation is the fulfillment of righteousness. It is in the being of the nation as a moral person that there is the realization of rights, and in this is the affirmation of righteousness on the earth, and therein also the nation, in its personality, can subsist only in the righteous name, and can proceed only in the righteous will of God.

CHAPTER VII.

THE NATION THE REALIZATION OF FREEDOM.

THE necessary being of the nation is in the realization of freedom; that is, its end is to make freedom real, and its development is only as it does make freedom real.

The freedom of the people subsists in the nation as a moral person.

Freedom is the manifestation of personality. Man has in his nature impulses and the power of following them, and desires and the power of gratifying them; but his being is not in these, and deeper than these and beyond these, there is a consciousness of an I — a person. In the assertion and the realization of this, and in the exclusion of all that is alien from this, alone is freedom. It is the realization in man, through his own self-determination, of his true being. The law of freedom is the law which is laid in the being of personality. The act of freedom is a self-determinate act, the determination of personality.[1]

[1] There is a common phrase in ethics, which asserts the existence of law precedent to life — a law precedent to the divine being, or as the phrase is, in one shape, "the throne of justice is above the throne of God; we may appeal from the throne of God to the throne of justice." If there be the assertion of a law as existent "in the beginning," those who postulate a law having a moral content as the *just*, and those who postulate a law which exists only as a formula of thought, — the necessary limitation of conception — may oppose each other, but the bystander can scarcely question the result; the latter has a consistence which the former cannot claim, and the pure dialectic has the start of the ethic.

But the law which has for its substance the good or the right, is in the divine person, the being of God; it is the will of God. The assumption of a precedent law is not necessary to the assertion of the immutability of the good, as it is apparent in moral distinctions, for this immutability is in the immutable being, — the personal being of God; and then it is manifest in the moral order of the world, as the moral order is the realization of the will of God. The good

The assertion of personality is in the will. The will derives from personality its content. The self-determined will alone is free. The will defined in an abstract and formal conception, and divested of personality, and its subsistence in it, allows no freedom, and when thus divested of its content it is without freedom also.

The action which is arbitrary is not free. It is the mere formal act of the will; it proceeds only from the will, not from the conscious determination of personality, — that is, the whole, the real person, — and having no other source, it is only willfulness. This action, separated thus from its subsistence in personality, is mere force, and instead of implying force of character, it is force without character. It is a barren sceptre. It has no more dignity than the operation of a physical power in nature. The will in this conception may be as strong and as unbending as iron, but its quality is no better than iron.

is maintained in the realization of a moral order by the divine will, and this in the relations of a moral order is the just.

"The good is as little a law for the divine will (that is, God wills it because it is already in itself good) as it is a creation of the divine will (that is, that it first becomes the good, because and after that God has willed it), but it is even in itself the original will of God, from eternity to eternity. The good, as the substance of the divine will, is something specific, distinct from the divine reason and the divine omnipotence; not less original than these: it springs originally purely out of the will, but it springs not out of the abstract conception, (abstraktum) of the will (Kant's abstract conception of the principle, be a law unto thyself; or Fichte's abstract conception of pure self-activity); nor from the formal conception (formalismus) of the operations of the will (Hegel's development of the moral out of the (momente) incident of the operations of the will), but it springs out of the eternal positive (inhalte) content of the will.

"The good is, to speak in a general way, nothing else than the substance of a person. Man can therefore endeavor to derive the conceptions which we recognize in the attributes of God, and the virtues of man from the original conception of personality. In the substance of personality there lies the spirituality which contends against losing itself in external objects and in sensual impulses, and of this alone and of nothing else, has the ethic of Kant and Fichte given a scientific representation; in the substance of personality there lies further the unchangeableness of the will, that in relation to the moral order of the world is the just; in the substance of personality is the love that goes forth toward those who are persons; in the substance of personality there is the oneness of all these energies and qualities in the innermost centre — the person; and therewith its impenetrability by all that is external or strange or alien to it — its holiness" — Stahl's *Philosophie des Rechts*, vol. ii. sec. 1, pp. 85, 86.

The action which springs immediately from impulse or appetite is not free. The pursuance of a blind instinct, or the subjection to a strong passion, is the negation of freedom. Thus the animal is unfree. It is determined and limited by its animal nature. The desires and the emotions, the impulse and the passion of men, as separate from personality, are therefore to be apprehended as external to the will, and the immediate subjection to them is ignoble, as the degradation of personality, and unworthy, as the negation of the true and real self in man; there is in it the loss of freedom. Thus Shakespeare says: —

> "I'll never
> Be such a gosling to obey instinct, but stand,
> As if a man were author of himself
> And knew no other kin."

The action which is merely unlimited and unrestrained is not free; the power to do whatever one lists or pleases is not freedom. The most false representation of freedom is this apprehension of it in the absence of restraint. It is then identified with mere caprice. The freedom which in this assumption is called natural freedom is unreal. It is illustrated by the old words denoting the widest and the most unrestrained play of desire, "a boy's will is the wind's will." But in that unceasing motion and that sweep of limitless fields there is no freedom. It is not until the boy has passed on to the life of a personality, realized in its conscious self-determination, that he is truly free. Yet it was only this false conception of freedom which appeared in the later phases of the French Revolution. Freedom was sought in the removal of all that was assumed as a limitation. It was to be attained in the erasure of the whole organization of society, and of all the institutions and associations of the past. The path of the revolution, in its principle, was not far from that of the cloister, and the ideal still was that which had been sought in the *via negativa* of the mystic. It obliterated all that appeared beyond its immediate intent. The existing order was to be determined in the momentary action of the individual. It was not a freedom which presumed the existence of the nation in its organic and moral being, a freedom which had a moral content, but it was assumed to consist in the absence of all limitation and restraint. Then when all the institutions of the past were swept away, and no apparent barrier was before men to check their advance, and there was nothing in the wide blank of the horizon to debar them, there was a painful discovery that they were not yet free. It was the rejection of the moral relations which subsist in the nation, and the striving after freedom in mere vacancy, that opened the way to any influence from without that might take possession of the empty domain. In the denial of all organic and moral relations there arose everywhere the distrust and crimination of men, and there followed what was called the reign of terror, when those who never were bidden, came to the room all swept and garnished, and men became the slaves of fear and of dread, and the way was open to the entrance of an imperial power.

The action which is simply momentary is not free. The will in its freedom has elements of continuity and identity, which subsist in personality and are reflected in character. It is not merely the capacity to vault hither and thither, and to pass and repass from the one side to the other. The power of choice certainly is involved in freedom, and therefore it is to be recognized as existent in it, and it is not to be obstructed nor confined by that which allows no room for individuality to act, and no sphere in which it may have its sweep; but the choice in which freedom is realized is the choice which is in accordance with personality, — it is the realization of personality. The active choice between good and evil in man is brought forward in the contradiction of his nature, and in the issue of the conflict of life, and it appears in his being influenced by a power against himself and by a presence alien to his true and real self; and in this there is manifest, not the freedom of man, but the defect of freedom. The error in the popular apprehension of freedom in the schools of theology, and as it goes out from them in politics, is in representing it as consisting only in a power of choice, only an empty formal possibility in the life of man, but having no determinate moral content. The freedom of man is not simply in this momentary choice, and the realization of freedom is not in the broader road opened before it and the wider scope of possibility in its action. It is not found in the larger alternative between right and wrong, or the longer balance with the more even play between them. It is not found in the perfect suspense between the opposite forces, and it is not won by the people that stand on neutral ground. On the contrary, in the higher freedom of man there is the less choice between the good and the evil, and there is the less possibility of a decision unworthy of one's real and true self, that is an ignoble decision.

When the will is represented as only in identity with the power of choice, which when thus emptied of all moral content is the merely willful, that is, the arbitrary, then the assertion of this power is not freedom, and the maintenance of this power is not among the rights of men. The nation is to realize the freedom of man, and to guard it in the institution of rights, but it is not in any conception to establish the wider province, and to open the more unlimited scope for this power to act, and to guard the exercise of it, and to remove all restrictions from its way, and to keep it from all hindrance and molestation, in the indefinite sweep of its arbitrations. The freedom of the citizen is not defined in the power to turn a traitor, nor is all restraint upon the power of turning to be forbidden. That people would not be the more free, in which the larger choice was left open to its soldiers to desert, and which made such action a principle of rights, as it must become if it be the real freedom of man; but the people is the more free when there is in the spirit of its soldiers no possibility of desertion, and the soldier is the more free to whom even the suggestion of such action does not come, who is beyond its suspicion, and who knows only and determines only to meet and fight the enemy. The soldier who even deliberates, or allows the choice to pass before him, is the less free — the more exposed to subjection to impulse and fear. This assertion of the mere power of choice is not freedom, and its maintenance is not among the rights of men, and its extension does not constitute the progress of the people. In the choice and the assertion of the right, man acts in accordance with his real and innermost being, his own true self, and with the exclusion of all that is alien as external to that being, but in the opposite, man chooses that which subverts personality and subjects him to evil, that which does not belong to his being, which comes out in the contradiction of his nature; but in freedom and the realization of freedom there is no contradiction, — there is in it alone the act and the unfolding of the true being of man.

Freedom is not attained in the negation, in which man without personality, as if all before was a blank, momentarily determines whether to be this or that, whether to do or not to do. In the determination which is in the right, there is alone in the individual and the nation the realization of freedom and the attainment of the being and end of each.

The nation is the realization of the freedom of the people. The freedom of the people subsists in the being of the nation as a moral person.

If the nation be regarded as only a formal organization, an exposition of a barren system of rights and a miscellany of institutions, then only a formal freedom can be

8

predicated of it as also the postulate of a formal freedom has its sequence in an empty and formal conception of the nation. But the real freedom of the nation in which it works out its end as a power in history, the freedom in the attainment of the vocation of the people, in the manifestation of its own character, in the strength and endurance of its own will in the divine will, in whose purpose is the development of history in the moral order of the world, — this freedom can have no ground in a merely formal conception.

The defect in the popular definitions of the schools, of the freedom of the nation or political freedom, is consequent on their proceeding from this formal conception, and while only a formal conception has been assumed, and a formal definition has been allowed, it is not singular that the latter has been, as Mr. Hurd calls it, the problem of publicists. Thus the subject which is central in politics and formative of its whole course, has obtained in this premise no clear definition. Dr. Lieber, in a treatise concerned exclusively with national and political freedom, represents it as "that liberty which results from the application of the general idea of freedom to the civil state of man."[1] In this reference to "the general idea of freedom," the subject is left undefined, and one is sent in quest of the "general idea." And the freedom of the people in its organic and moral being, that is, national freedom, is avoided in these abstractions. It does not exist thus complete in an abstract form, which a people is then to adopt

[1] Lieber's *Civil Liberty*, etc., vol. i. p. 34.

Dr. Lieber, in attaching so great weight to certain institutions of freedom, allows no corresponding weight to the fact that these institutions have their only ground in the organic unity of the people in the nation. This leads to the application of certain institutions of a certain type to all nations, and thus all are to be made to conform to an Anglican type. But while recognizing the worth of these institutions, in themselves, to civilization, the condition of freedom is the national spirit of the people, which will mould institutions in its own strong individuality. While the United States has in its history a lineal relation to some of these institutions, and they are an inheritance of inestimable value, yet work is to be done in new conditions, and in a life which is neither Anglican nor Gallican.

and apply by some induction, and when thus apprehended it can result only in the construction of a formal system or a collocation of institutions. It would be as consistent to represent the freedom of the individual person, as the assumption and application of the "general idea."

The freedom of the people, or political freedom, subsists in the nation in its organic and moral unity. It is the self-determination of the people, in the nation, as a moral person. It is formed in the conscious life, and its process is in the conscious vocation of the organic people.[1]

Freedom has, apart from the nation, no positive existence. Thus among the vast populations of Asia, there is no political freedom, but only the natural freedom of man, and the term freedom can be applied to those peoples only negatively as denoting the absence of a positive system of slavery. Thus, also, in the loss or the destruction of the national unity, that is, the organic and moral being of the

[1] Milton's whole argument rests on the identity of political and moral freedom, and the utter rejection of any conception which does not presume this. He says of the formal representation, — "The way to freedom is without intricacies, without the introducement of new or absolute forms or terms, or exotic models, ideas that would effect nothing." — Milton's *Works*, ii. 127. It is "a real and substantial freedom, which is rather to be sought from within than from without, and whose existence depends not so much on the terror of the sword as on sobriety of conduct and integrity of life." — *Works*, i. 208. "Unless that liberty which is of such a kind as arms can neither procure nor take away, which alone is the fruit of piety, of justice, of temperance, and unadulterated virtue, shall have taken deep root in your minds and hearts, there will not be long wanting one who will snatch from you by treachery what you have acquired by arms; unless by the means of piety, not frothy and loquacious, but operative, unadulterated and sincere, you clear the horizon of the mind from those mists of superstition which arise from the ignorance of true religion, you will always have those, who will bend your necks to the yoke, as if you were brutes, who notwithstanding all your triumphs, will put you up to the highest bidder, as if you were mere booty made in war; and will find an exuberant source of wealth in your ignorance and superstition. You, therefore, who wish to be free, either instantly be wise, or as soon as possible cease to be fools; if you think slavery an intolerable evil, learn obedience to reason, and the government of yourselves; and finally bid adieu to your dissensions, your jealousies, your superstitions, your outrages, your lusts. Unless you will spare no pains to effect this, you must be judged unfit both by God and mankind to be intrusted with the possession of liberty and the administration of government, but will rather, like a nation in a state of pupilage, want some active and courageous guardian to undertake the management of your affairs." — *Works*, ii. 295.

people, its freedom perishes although its external condition and its sphere of external circumstance, for the individual, may not at once be materially changed. The form and external institutions of society may remain as before in so far as individual action and individual pursuits are concerned, but the freedom of the people expires with the national being. It was not in this form nor in these institutions, and it cannot be perpetuated in them alone. The external structure of society in which the individual moved was not immediately subverted nor destroyed in the dissolution of the national life of Greece and Rome, but their freedom, which was of their spirit, immediately perished.

The freedom of the people, or political freedom, is formed in the self-determination of the people. This precludes all external constraint, since an action which is constrained by a power or influence external to the will, is not free. This precludes also the conduct of the people itself, from mere impulse or passion, for since these are external to the will, in so far as it is controlled by them, there is no freedom. The course which is the result of mere whim or willfulness, the caprice of men in its desultory play, is not of the freedom of the people; in it personality is overborne, and the very unity which is the condition of the freedom of the people is lost, and there appears the agitation of the popular tumult, but not the conscious order of the state.[1]

The freedom of the people, or political freedom, involves the assertion of law. It subsists in the nation in its normal being. There is in it, therefore, the assertion and the manifestation of law, but it has not therefore a formal

1 Bluntschli says, "Natural freedom is the power to do whatever one likes. Moral freedom is the manifestation of the will, and the power to do what is becoming to one's own nature and in accordance with the divine economy in the world. Freedom in its political conception presumes the organization of rights, of which it is a part. It is the power and warranty protected and secured by the law to exercise a self-determined end." — *Allgemeinen Statsrechts*, vol. ii. p. 487.

ground which would follow if the law was merely external and definitive only of a formal order. The law which is asserted in it, as the norm of its action, is the law in the foundation of its being and is realized in its being, — in its self-determination, as a moral person. There is thus in law and freedom an inner unity. In the limitations defined in law, there is, therefore, no bondage, but they become the evidence of the emancipation of man. This emancipation is not indeed in the institution of mere external limitations, which are devoid of all content and may be only obstructions, nor in the mere limitations of formal laws, but in a life which is formed in moral relations, and the laws which are asserted are those which define and regulate those relations. Freedom, in the assertion of law, assumes restraint and accepts obligations in the relations of an organic and moral being, and in these there is no limitation in the sense of hindrance, or as the mere impediment to action. There is in them no barrier, but freedom is wrought through them. It is a divinity that doth hedge us in. The law in the being of personality, instead of the terminus of freedom, is its postulate.

The freedom of the people, or political freedom, is the realization of the self-determination of the people in the nation as an ethical organism. There is in it the expression of the self-determination that is the freedom of a person, in an order which is formed in moral relations. There is in it the assertion of the individual person. The order in which he is to act and to which he is to be subject, is to correspond to his own inner being, — to accord with his own real and true self. The sphere in which he is to work must consist with his own aim and endeavor, It is thus that every polity, and all laws which are immoral are destructive of freedom, as they are subversive of the true being of men, and are repressive, and hold the elements of tyranny. But in the increase of the freedom of the nation, its political order becomes always the more perfect expression of the moral being and longing of the individual person, and therefore of his own true and inner self. Then as the self-determination of the people is manifested in the nation, the individual person in his action attains in it his determination, and in his obedience to it he is obeying his own true and inner self. There is in it the correspondence to his own being, and the embodiment of his own aim. That this attainment is at any moment imperfect, is because the individual and the nation have a life which for each is a development; and then also the life of each is subject to the conditions of a moral conflict. But every polity which avoids this end and neglects to regard or to build upon it, or to strive constantly for its attainment, is itself inherently weak, and only increases the action of disturbing forces, and clogs and thwarts the course of the people, and delays, while it cannot prevent, its inevitable coming, in the development of the nation.

The freedom of the people, or political freedom, presumes that the political order shall conform to the will of the political people. It is not to be restricted by forms and institutions which are alien from it, nor compressed into the cast of some exotic mould, and these limitations, while they impede the free course of the people, may induce a spirit not of law, but of legality, which may be the worst tyranny. It is not to be directed by the exclusive aim and interest of an individual or a family or a class, which are over but not of the nation, and in this there is the inception of a despotism, not the freedom of the people.

The freedom of the people, or political freedom, presumes also that the political order shall express the conscious spirit of the people. It is to be open to the knowledge of the people. The policy and laws are not to be kept as the mystery of a craft, or the tradition of a caste, nor as the speciality of a class. The political design is not to be locked up as a state secret, nor to be conducted by hidden bureaus. The laws are not to be withheld, as if written only in volumes where the people cannot have access to them, but the whole course and action of the state is to be open to the knowledge of the people, and its loyalty and its obedience is to be the assertion of a conscious spirit.

The realization of the freedom of the nation, or political freedom, is in rights. Freedom embodies itself in rights, as in rights also there is the manifestation of personality. The institution of positive rights defines in the nation the sphere of a realized freedom. There is in freedom the right which is fundamental in the rights of man; freedom is the eternal right of a man to be himself. It is not the exclusive claim of an individual or a family or a class, but of man, as the nation has no lower nor special end, but a universal end in the rights of man.

The freedom of the people as it becomes determinate establishes itself in rights, and in its advance it raises barriers in the institution of rights against alien forces and evil influences, the principalities and powers that hinder and thwart it. It is only in rights that freedom is actualized in the nation; it is only in positive rights that it gains a sure foothold in its progress; they alone afford the requisite strength and security for it. In rights freedom is guarded against denial, fortified against fraud, shielded against conspiracy and surprise and sudden overthrow. In the same measure in which freedom fails to establish itself in rights, whose institution is in law, it is liable to the whim and the caprice of men, and the highest interest is left to the adjustment of changing circumstance. This secure institution and organization of freedom in positive rights is the work of the statesman. It demands the more comprehensive political sagacity. Freedom does not gain much while it is held in an ideal conception, and is left to the pages of scholars, or the rhymes of poets, or the voices of orators. These are not laws, and the condition of every advance in freedom is its assertion in laws and its organization in rights. It has in their strong guaranties alone protection against selfish interests and private aims.

The identity of freedom and of rights in the nation is implied in their subsistence in personality, and thus we cannot conceive of the actual existence of an individual in a civil or political relation, or of a nation in which there is freedom but no rights.[1] The second clause of the thirteenth article of the Constitution is not superfluous, and the nation necessarily can only enforce the declaration of freedom by the institution and the maintenance, through laws, of rights. To grant freedom but no rights would be fit subject for the fool who is always about the king's court in Shakespeare, and fit work only for some king's jester.

The freedom of the people never attains its perfect expression in the organization of rights. It may strive unceasingly toward this end, and with toil and energy it may shape them in their clearness and strength, and yet in its spirit it is always beyond them. They can thus, in no moment in the history of a people, be regarded as having obtained their ultimate form, nor can the people have in them the perfect satisfaction of its aim. Its endeavor is always to mould the organization of rights toward the expression of its ampler and fairer freedom.

As the freedom of the people is established in rights, these rights, through laws, may be embodied in institutions. There may thus often be traced in the form and growth of these institutions the progress of rights and the line of their advancement. These institutions often have thus of themselves an historical increase, and are wrought into shape and use in the history of the people. They are

1 "Freedom in its civil and political conception, can never be separated from the process of rights which is its ground and its support." — Bluntschli's *Allgem. Statsrechts*, vol. ii. p. 488.

guaranties in which rights are fortified and stand as the barriers against the betrayal of freedom from within, or its invasion from without. They endure against the assumptions of arbitrary power, and in them, as in a retreat, freedom may hold out through evil days of apathy, and is secure against overthrow alike from the agitation of the many and the conspiracy of the few. The illustration of these institutions is, for instance, in the organization and administration of the township; in the trial by jury; in the office of the justice of the peace; in the common law. These institutions have often also their expression, while their exact form is of slight significance, in some sturdy maxim of the people, some "words that have hands and feet," some sentence in whose clear light the way is seen through dangerous channels, and whose signal is the alarm of freedom. An illustration of this is in the phrase which denotes the right to the sanctity of home,—"every man's house is his castle."

There are certain conceptions of political freedom which, in their error and their defect from its necessary conception, can tend only to thwart or delay its progress.

It is represented as in itself a negation, and as appearing in the check or balance of opposing forces, or in the restriction of adverse power. This has its postulate in the assumption that power is in itself essentially dangerous in the state, and that freedom is manifested in the construction of certain other powers to stand against the current and keep it back; and these, then, since danger is inherent in power, require the building of others to offset them, and so the erection is to go on indefinitely, and the degree of freedom is graduated by the successive and alternative restrictions of power. It is indeed true that freedom, in the conditions of history, presumes an unceasing conflict, and must overcome adverse elements, and at every advance intrench itself in positive rights. But freedom is in itself a determinate power, and of itself advancing; rights only denote in their institution its line of march. And checks and guaranties have only the strength which they may obtain from the power which shapes and holds the check, and asserts and maintains the guaranty. Freedom is no negation as is assumed in this conception; it is not found in the construction of the most exact and formal balance of opposing interests or classes or factions. The balance in itself could effect nothing, and instead of the living unity, which is the condition of freedom, it implies the disintegration of society which it regards as only the combination of certain separate interests which are to be pitted against each other. Freedom is not in this negation, but in the positive determination of the people, and conversely the weakness which appears in the decay of national power is in the loss of freedom, when the people can assert no rights, and even in its spirit can apprehend none. Freedom is alone the power of the people in its organic and moral life; it is the might of the living people; it may break in one moment the fetters which centuries of oppression have forged, and throw down prison walls in which evil dominations have labored to immure the spirit of man.

Political freedom is represented also as existent only as some spectral ideal, some remote abstraction. It is described as some imaginary figure, if it have shape or form, which exists, in its perfectness, in isolation from the body politic, and distant from the organization of the nation. But the ideal is not the contradiction of the real; it is in identity with it, and is striving always toward a more perfect embodiment in it; the ideal is not the unreal. There are sometimes those who, in the guise of a specious devotion to freedom, are ready to consent to the dismemberment of the nation, and for some spectral and abstract presentation of freedom would conspire for the destruction of the whole organization in which it has toiled toward its realization, however imperfect its advance. This is that blind fanaticism, that weak egoism, which is the unreason of the state. These visionaries cannot build again in the ruins it was so easy to make; it is only destructive forces that work thus swiftly; freedom will not follow at their behest, nor go and return at their beckoning, nor enter the abodes to which they invite it, and it is only with long and patient toil and sacrifice that the organization is won by the people in which it dwells.

Political freedom is represented as a power formed in external limitations, or as construed in the formal relations of the individual and the nation. Mr. Emerson says it is the largest liberty compatible with the liberty of every other man. But freedom is not described in this external limitation, nor is the freedom of one the restriction of the freedom of another. This confounds freedom with arbitrariness, and it is only willfulness that is incompatible. Freedom is not thus attained through infinite individual antagonisms. The largest freedom in each is consistent with the same in all. This conception empties freedom of all moral content, and it could be constructive only of a formal, not a real freedom. It could not be the postulate of the freedom of the people in its organic and moral being and relations in history. The freedom of one is no limitation to the freedom of another, but an aid toward his emancipation.

Political freedom is represented as something which may be bestowed or withheld by some external power. It is apprehended as the circumstance of a formal law, the consequent in a formal order; it is described as the boon of some priest or emperor, some preacher or convention. It is true that a power on earth may acknowledge or deny it, and may do much to aid its growth or to crush it in the spirits of men, but it belongs to none, neither priest, nor preacher, nor president, nor congress, nor emperor, nor armies, to bestow it. It is not received as a gift; it belongs to the spirit of man, and therefore is only of God; and only as the personality of man has its subsistence in God, is emancipation wrought in it; and only as the nation is a moral person, in the crises of its deliverance, is He recognized as its deliverer.

There is a representation of the origin and nature of political freedom which, as affecting the conception of the moral being of the nation, involves the most false of political sophistries. It is the theory which is built upon the postulate that man possesses a real freedom in a condition precedent to the nation, and that he then surrenders a certain part of it upon his entrance into it. Freedom is represented as existent in this condition which is precedent to society, in its perfectness, and as diminished when man enters society, and to that extent he suffers a deprivation of it in consideration of certain other advantages which are secured to him in its stead. Blackstone says, "Every man, when he enters into society, gives up a part of his natural liberty, as the price of so valuable a purchase."[1] This part is regarded as surrendered in order to secure the residue, or as exchanged for certain other advantages, held at an equal valuation.

This representation of the origin and nature of freedom proceeds on the assumption of the social contract. It is implied, also, in the position of Mr. Emerson, which was also the position of Kant, when the liberty of one person in society is the possible limitation or restriction of the liberty of another person.

But this condition in which man is represented as existing anterior or exterior to society, and in which freedom is conceived as flourishing, has no reality. It is a fiction, and

[1] 1 Bl. *Comm.* 125.

is only a repetition of the picture sketched so many times, and for so many uses, in the imagination of political theorists. In the actual condition of man, in so far as he is withdrawn from the organization of the state, there is no freedom. The records of the actual condition are of a life in which man is most of all a slave, and a slave to the lowest and meanest wants. He seems the subject of nature, and not one who is to assert dominion over it. It is a stage of abject dependence. There is no freedom, and the recognition of no rights, but each is exposed to the open wrongs of every enemy. There is no security for life, or liberty, or property. The freedom, then, which man is supposed to barter away in a certain part, upon entering society, in order to keep the remainder, has no existence. It is an imaginary possession which then afterwards, by an imaginary transfer, is conveyed to the state. The proposition falls with the fiction of the social contract in which it has its premise.

It bears also the conception of private property into the state, and makes freedom itself a concern of formal transfer and exchange. It contradicts the necessary conception of freedom, which is no longer a living and moral power, but apprehended as something which the owner can parcel out and traffic in; and it is by trade in freedom that man is represented as entering the state, and he not only buys but sells out.

To this there are also the same objections as to the social contract; and men do not from a precedent condition enter the state voluntarily, nor with specifications in this style. It contradicts also the necessary conception of freedom as involving law, when it is thus represented, for the nation is the sphere of law. It could then also, if it were an actual occurrence, result only in a formal freedom, since the amount which is retained in the state would have its formal reduction in the amount of the entrance fee, which is the condition of the purchase or exchange.

This proposition is inconsistent also with the common language of men, and there is scarcely any fact of deeper significance, or capable of wider illustration, than that which makes a synonym of citizen and freeman.

This proposition implies also a conception of natural freedom which is not a real freedom, but the arbitrariness of the individual, and the freedom of the whole is then only in the limitation of the arbitrariness of each.

The contrast to this false conception of freedom, was given in words worthy of an inaugural, in the beginning of the history of the nation, by a governor of one of the early commonwealths, — "There is a twofold liberty, natural — I mean as our nature is now corrupt — and civil or federal. The first is common to man with beasts and other creatures. By this man, as he stands in relation to man, simply hath liberty to do what he lists; it is a liberty to evil as well as to good. This liberty is incompatible and inconsistent with authority. The exercise and maintaining of this liberty makes men grow more evil, and in time be worse than brute beasts: 'omnes sumus licentia deteriores.' This is that great enemy of truth and peace, that wild beast, which all the ordinances of God are bent against to restrain and subdue it. The other kind of liberty I call civil or federal; it may also be termed moral, in reference to the covenant between God and man, in the moral law, and the political covenants and constitutions amongst men themselves. This liberty is the proper end and object of authority, and cannot subsist without it; and it is a liberty to that only which is good, just, and honest. This liberty you are to stand for not only with the hazard of your goods, but of your lives if need be. Whatsoever crosseth this is not authority but a distemper thereof. This liberty is maintained and exercised in a way of subjection to authority; it is of the same kind of liberty wherewith Christ hath made us free."[1]

The great epochs in the lives of nations in the modern world, have been the realization of the freedom of man. It has been said that what the German Reformation whispered in the closet, the French Revolution shouted on the house-tops, that man should be free; and the end of the American War was the assertion that the nation in its conscious spirit is the realization of freedom, and that in the freedom of humanity the nation has its conquest and its end. In the nation freedom is real, and as freedom has its subsistence in the nation, so also in slavery is the resistance to the being of the nation. The nation and slavery cannot abide in one house, but at last the one or the other must be driven out. The nation must overcome and destroy slavery, or at last be destroyed by it. There is in history the evidence of this, and as it appears in the ancient and in the modern world, — in the fall of Rome and the uprising of America.

The antagonism with slavery is in the being of the nation. For as the nation is a moral person, and personality is realized in freedom, slavery is its necessary antagonist, and as it is the realization of rights, and in its universal aim of the rights of humanity, slavery with the denial of these rights and with the consequent degradation of humanity, is its immediate antagonist.

There is always a tendency in those withdrawn from the battle, and its "confused noise and garments rolled in blood," to bear its issues into some ideal and abstract sphere. Thus the war is represented as the immediate conflict of the antagonistic ideas, — freedom and slavery. The reality is other than this; the hosts are mustered in no intellectual arena, and the forces called into its field are other than spectral ideas. This tendency to resolve history into the

[1] Winthrop's *Journal*, vol. ii. p. 13.

conflict and progress of abstract ideas, or the development of what is called an intellectual conception, can apprehend nothing of the real passion of history. It knows not what, with so deep significance, is called the burden of history. It enters not into the travail of time, it discerns not the presence of a living Person in the judgments which are the crises of the world. It comprehends only some intellectual conflict in the issue of necessary laws, but not the strife of a living humanity. The process of a legal formula, the evolution of a logical sequence, the supremacy of abstract ideas, this has nothing to compensate for the agony and the suffering and the sacrifice of the actual battle, and it discerns not the real glory of the deliverance of humanity, the real triumph borne through but over death. There was in the war, in the issue which came upon us, "even upon us," and in the sacrifice of those who were called, the battle of the nation for its very being, and it was the nation which slavery met in mortal strife. The inevitable conflict was of slavery with the life of the nation.

There is no vague rhetoric, but a deep truth in the words, — "liberty and union, now and forever, one and inseparable." They are worthy to live upon the lips of the people, for there can be no union without freedom, since slavery has its necessary result in the dissolution of the being of the nation, and there can be no freedom without union, for it is only in the being of the nation that freedom becomes real.

CHAPTER VIII.

THE SOVEREIGNTY OF THE NATION.

THE freedom of the nation has its correlate in the sovereignty of the nation. Political sovereignty is the assertion of the self-determinate will of the organic people, and in this there is the manifestation of its freedom. It is in and through the determination of its sovereignty that the order of the nation is constituted and maintained.[1]

The existence of the sovereignty of the nation, or political sovereignty, is indicated by certain signs or notes which are universal: these are, independence, authority, supremacy, unity, and majesty.

The sovereignty of the nation, or political sovereignty, implies independence; it is subject to no external control, but its action is in correspondence with its own determination. It implies authority; it has the strength inherent in its own determination to assert and maintain it. It implies supremacy; this does not presume the presence of other powers which are inferior, but it is itself ultimate and can be subordinate to none; it is suprema potestas. It implies unity; this belongs to the necessary conception of the will from which sovereignty proceeds, and in the will

[1] The necessary correlation of sovereignty and freedom was expressed in the common illustration of the old Protestant theologians, — "Liberum et voluntarium sunt synonymia, ac voluntatem non liberam dicere, est perinde ac si quis dicere velit, calidum absque calore." Hegel has a very beautiful statement of the proposition (*Philosophie des Rechts*, pp 20–60). "Denn das frei ist der Wille. Wille ohne freiheit ist ein leeres Wort." — *Ibid.* p. 23. Stahl says, "Desswegen fallen auch Freiheit und Wille in ihrem urbegriff vollig zusammen, der Wille ist frei, und es ist nichts Anderes, frei als nur der Wille." — *Philosophie des Rechts*, vol. ii. sec. 1, p. 116.

alone, in which there is the highest and essential unity, is the postulate of sovereignty; the presence, thus, of separate supreme powers, to which equal obedience is to be rendered, involves a moral contradiction. It is characterized by an inherent majesty; it is a majesty which manifests itself in all the symbols of the state; it is not simply the dignity of noble action, but it is the conscious possession of powers and obligations, on which depend the highest issues in the history of humanity. This has had its expression always in the historical nations, appearing in the purpose and action of the people in its higher national development.[1]

These are the indices by which the presence of political sovereignty is indicated, and in them there is its external manifestation. There are in its content also certain capacities.

It is inalienable; the state cannot transfer it to another nor divest itself of it, except that in the act itself its own existence and its own freedom terminates.

It is indivisible; a divisive sovereignty is a contradiction of that supremacy which is implied in its necessary conception, and inconsistent with its subsistence in the organic will.

It is indefeasable;[2] it cannot, through legal forms and legists' devices, be annulled and avoided, nor can it be voluntarily abdicated to be voluntarily resumed, but involves a continuity of power and action.

It is irresponsible to any external authority; there is

1 The peoples which were made subject to Rome, were thereby divested of a separate sovereignty, and to all terms made with them, the Romans added, — "Imperium majestatemque populi Romani, conservato sine dono malo. — Livy, bk. 38, sec. 2.

"Majestas est amplitudo ac dignitas civitatis. Is eam minuit, qui exercitum hostibus populi Romani tradidit, — minuit is, qui per vim multitudinis, rem ad seditionem vocavit. — Cicero, *De Oratore*, bk. ii. sec. 38.

2 It is incapable by any juggle based upon legal analogies, of being defeated or abrogated. In the expression of James Wilson, "sovereignty is and remains in the people." — Jamison's *Constitutional Convention*, p. 20.

none on earth over it to whom it has to justify its course, or in whose conclusion it has to abide.

It is comprehensive of the whole political order; it acts in its determination as organic through the whole political body, and its authority is conterminus with the whole; it works through all the members, and in all the offices and all the organs of the state.

The sovereignty of the nation, or political sovereignty, primarily presumes the power in the political people to determine the form of its own political life. This cannot be imposed upon it from without. It cannot be referred to the dictation of any power over and separate from the nation, as some imperator. It cannot be restricted to certain special formulas, and the nation is not to be compelled to shape its order and organization after some theory and preconception of state forms which may be alien from it, and thwart the purpose or defeat the hope of the people. The oppression of a mere form or system in politics, may become the extremest tyranny, and far more crushing than an imperial power; for the will of the solitary tyrant cannot have so universal a sway, and there is always hope of change, but the tyranny of a form or a system of itself precludes change, and prevents progress, while it outlives men and generations. In its own sovereignty and in its own free spirit, the political people is to mould its own political life, and to embody in it its own ideal, and to apprehend in it its own aim.

There have been certain theories, which have only a formal and historical interest, as to the residence of the sovereignty of the nation in its normal process. These assume the identity of its sovereignty with a certain form, for which then a universality is claimed, and in their conclusion, they have become the assertion of a sovereignty external to and against the nation, which in any form, whether of an individual or a system, is the very definition of despotism. Their interest is merely illustrative.

It is said that the sovereignty is inherent in a family or a certain number of families constituting the special aristocratical or regal organization, or caste, whom the possession of certain qualities or some circumstance may at the outset have designated, and thereafter it is to remain continuous in them by the necessary and organic law of the state.

This is the contradiction of the real sovereignty of the nation and its freedom, and is the assertion not of a sovereignty in and of the nation, but a sovereignty external to it. It is this which has dragged the people to war after war to decide a disputed succession, where the whole was embroiled with individual claims and family divisions. There is no family or number of families which have an original and indefeasable right to govern. It is not subsistent in the ancestry of a family, or a tribe, or a race, but continues only in the nation. It belongs to no individual or family save only as they are invested with its exercise of and by the nation. The right of government, which is alone of divine right, the right in the nation as a moral person, is of no uncertain succession and of no transient tenure. It is not the exclusive heritage of a family, and is not transmitted in the entail of its estates. "The patrimonial doctrine of the state," says Bluntschli, "which regards it as the property of the prince, and therefore ascribes sovereignty only to him, and the absolutist doctrine of the state which identifies it with the individual ruler, both forget that all the might of the prince is only the combined might of the people, and that the people and the nation as the organization of rights remain, although princes and dynasties change and perish."[1] The recent justification of this proposition has been in some representative principle, as for instance the sovereignty is regarded as representative of the unity of the nation, — Coleridge; or of the permanence of the family in the nation, — Maurice; or of the personality of the nation, — Hegel.

[1] *Allgem Statsrechts*, vol. ii. p. 11.

It is said that the sovereignty of the nation is resident in certain abstract ideas or principles, as justice or reason. This has been assumed by publicists who have sought thus to modify the conception of popular sovereignty. Royer Collard gave a definite statement to the theory: "There is an individual and a moral element in society. To make the majority of individuals sovereign, is popular sovereignty. When, with or without their consent, this blind strong sovereignty passes under the control of an individual or a class, without changing its character, it becomes a wiser and more temperate authority, but it is yet rude force, and remains always such, and becomes the root of absolute power and privileges. If, on the contrary, society be founded on the moral element, that is, on justice, then is justice sovereign, for justice is the law of rights."

This assertion of sovereignty as existent in an abstract principle or law, whatever its quality, as justice, or reason, or love, is illustrative of the tendency to convey the whole subject of politics into a realm of mere abstractions, and to merge the state into a formal idealism. The nation has certainly in justice, the law which is implied in its being as a moral person, and the condition of its being, and must conform to the reason of things, but the nation is itself an organic being, and invested with actual powers. Sovereignty is existent in the nation only as it is an organic and moral person, and in it and through it, justice is asserted and realized in a moral order.

This proposition is the assertion of a specious and abstract ideal, and becomes the substitution of a law or a system for the determination of the organic will. It is inconsequent, since an abstract conception, however high, which is thus asserted, can have no real strength. It is moreover perilous, since it avoids the foundation in an organic being, of the organic and moral relations of the nation. It creates a tendency to regard with indifference the real life and conflict of the nation, in comparison with the barren conceptions of the idealist, and to consent, on the pretense of an abstract reason or justice, to its destruction and to conspire with its dismemberment.

This proposition is also sometimes connected with the assumption of popular sovereignty in its lowest and crudest form; — in disregard of the being and government of the whole, — the assertion of what is represented as the reserved sovereignty of the people, is assumed by some individual, on the ground of his subjective conception of justice, which is exalted in this unlimited egoism. This was the attitude of those who regarded the battle for the nation and its unity and authority, at least with indifference, and as devoid of moral content, until it should become an immediate war against slavery.

It is said that the sovereignty inheres in the people simply as the collective people, in a certain locality. This is the premise in certain phases of the preceding proposition, and, as in each of them, in its ascribing sovereignty to the collective mass in a certain locality, it is the assertion of a sovereignty apart from the organic people.

This proposition, as before stated, postulates the power of the will of the people in its organic unity, and ascribes it to the inorganic mass. This formless crowd is destitute of the consciousness of unity which is implied in the will and is the condition of sovereignty. The state is resolved into its atomy. There is no ground for the continuity which is presumed in government and in law, and as sovereignty is apprehended as existent in the momentary action of the multitude, then in some momentary change the authority in government and law expires. As sovereignty is represented as resident in a mass of individuals who may coexist in any locality, and as determined by their momentary action, the conception of the whole is precluded, and any section, or faction, or sect, may withdraw if it have the momentary strength.

The proposition fails, also, because it cannot make clear

what the will of the many is, nor by what law its sovereignty or its reserved sovereignty is to be ascertained, nor how it is to be exercised. The existence of a law, giving authority to a political majority, cannot be assumed in the multitude, since the proposition places before us only a collection of individuals, an inorganic mass, in whom there is no consciousness of a common political principle, nor of the authority of a common political law. It is, as before, the assumption of the mob and not of the people.

These theories are the assertion of a sovereignty, external to the nation, not in it nor of it, and identical only with a formal organization.

The sovereignty is of the organic people, constituted as a nation. It has its condition in the consciousness of the people, and it is the manifestation of the nation in its moral personality, and therefore, as subsistent in personality, it is from God; — it is from God and of the people.

The form and the circumstance of sovereignty in the beginning of the historical life of the people, are as manifold as the incidents of the individual existence. But in whatever form, and however slow the development of its power, the sovereignty subsists in the organic people, who in the consciousness of their unity and order form the nation.

The sovereignty has not its ground in the empty conception of the people with no conscious unity nor vocation in history. There is no conception of sovereignty, and none of the state, attaching to this mass. The numerical accumulation of men by no multiplication could attain to the sovereignty of the organic people. The sovereignty whose normal expression is law, and whose realization is freedom and order, is not in the multitude, nor in the momentary action of the multitude,[1] but in the will of the

[1] When Rousseau asserts an absolute sovereignty as resident in the momentary volition of the individual, and regards it as always justified by the act it-

organic people ; it is the majesty of a people, the sovereignty of a nation.

The sovereignty of the nation is the original power through whose self-determinate action the political order is established, and in it all the other powers subsist and from it they proceed. It is not merely the supreme power, in respect to which others are subordinate, but it is the original power which determines all others. Its affirmation is the supreme law.

The sovereignty of the nation has an external and an internal manifestation. The external sovereignty is manifest in its independence of, and in its relation with, other nations. It is its own right to be and to be itself; it exists as a power on the earth, with other powers, equal and self-subsistent. In its external sovereignty the nation is manifest as a power in the historical order of the world. It is its highest being; it is conscious of the authority with which it is invested, and the obligations in which it is involved, but it recognizes no human control, and acknowledges none nearer than very God, none over it but only God.

The internal sovereignty is manifest in its assertion in its self-determinate action, of its political order and organization. It ordains its constitution and laws, and prescribes its political course. As all the powers of the nation, as an organic whole, proceed from and in conformance to its sovereignty, so its constitution and its laws define the order and administration of the whole.

self, in setting aside the whole existing organization, and renouncing obedience to the whole existing authority, and repudiating all obligation which has its source in a past action, it contravenes the necessary conception, both of freedom and sovereignty. The will is emptied of all moral content, and apprehended as identical only with a transitional action — the immediate power of choice.

The will in this conception is not sovereign and is not free, when its whole determination is construed in a momentary action, and its freedom is exhausted in the play of caprice. Thus, also, the repudiation of past national obligations has its precedent in the denial of the being of the nation in its continuity.

The sovereignty of the nation in its determinate form is law. Law, in its political sense, is the formal assertion of the will of the political people. The common definition is thus, a rule of action made obligatory by the state upon all who are subject to its authority. It is the formal affirmation of the will of the people as regulative of the action of the whole in its civil and its political process.[1]

The ground of law is not formal nor abstract. It is the affirmation of the will of the people, and therefore consequent from no empty conception of the will. It is the will of the people in the nation, as organic and moral. It is the formal expression of the purpose of the nation, but it is none the less the continuous purpose which is implied in its being. The conception of justice, the reason and law of right is implicit in the nation as a moral person. It is in the will in its sovereignty and the realization of its freedom, and therefore all willful and arbitrary action is in its nature lawless. The law is laid in the foundation of the being of the nation. It is then the assertion of justice, which is the fountain of all law, not as the illusion of visionaries, nor as the scheme of theorists, nor as the device of legislators, nor as the compromise of interests, nor as the trade of parties, but as implied in the being of the nation in its necessary constitution, and the realization of its being.

Law, in its political determination, has certain characteristics which are necessarily presumed. There are, in

[1] Rome, through all the successive periods in her history, represented as the source of law, the "majestas populi Romani," and asserted as the law, the "voluntas populi Romani."

"The will of the state, indicated in some form of expression, is the law, and no natural rule which may exist forms a part of the law, unless identified with the will of the state so indicated. What the state wills is the coterminous measure of law; no preëxisting rule is the measure of that will." — Hurd's *Law of Freedom, etc.* vol. i. p. 4.

"Law is the direct or indirect, explicit or implied, real or supposed, positive or acquiesced in, expression of the will of human society represented in the state; or it is the public will of a part of human society constituted into a state." — Lieber's *Political Ethics*, vol. i. p. 98.

the distinction of laws with reference to their object, general and special laws, but there are certain elements implied in all law in the civil and political order.[1]

The law presumes the being of the moral person from whom it proceeds: it presumes a consonance with reason and justice. It cannot contravene the nature of things, this would involve the unreason of the state; an incongruous law is inoperative.[2]

1 The definition, which is most prominent in the history of law, is that which, after the Roman law, defines the provinces of public law and private law. The distinction of these departments, as given in the Digest, would serve as the definition of the nation and the commonwealth, — the political and the civil order. "Hujus studii (juris) duæ sunt positiones; publicum et privatum. Publicum jus est quod ad statum rei Romanæ spectat; privatum quod ad singulorum utilitatem." — *Dig.* lib. 1, tit. 1, sec. 2. But with the apprehension of society only in its civil relations, that is, as the commonwealth, these boundaries, in fact and then in law, became obliterated, and the conception which underlies their distinction was lost: the division has been held by later writers vaguely and again not inconsistently rejected by some, and its reason denied.

The Roman juridical writers thus regarded public law, in the imperfect development of this distinction, as inclusive of criminal law. Savigny, *Heut Rom. Recht.* bk. i. ch. 2. Austin rejects the distinction, but his definition of public law is worth noting: "Public law, in its strict and definite significance, is confined to that portion of law which is concerned with political conditions; that is to say, with the powers, rights, duties, capacities, and incapacities, which are peculiar to political superiors, supreme and subordinate." — *Lectures on Jurisprudence*, vol. ii. p. 435. Mackeldey describes the province of each, "The public law comprehends those rules of law which relate to the constitution and government of the state; consequently it concerns only the relations of the people to the government. The private law comprehends those rules which pertain to the juridical relations of citizens among themselves." — *Civ. Law Comm. Introd.* p. 8. Falck, as cited in Pomeroy's *Constitutional Law*, p. 3, has defined them with more precision. "Public law embraces those precepts which impose duties or confer rights upon the political superiors in the state, those who organically represent the state. Private law includes the civil law proper, police law, the law as to crimes and punishments, the law as to civil and criminal procedure. It embraces the rules which define the rights, powers, capacities, and incapacities of various classes of persons, private, domestic, or professional; the rights of property; the rights which flow from contracts and obligations between private persons; the description of the delicts and offenses called crimes; the means by which civil rights are secured and enforced; the means proper to maintain good morals, order, health, etc., in general all those means which augment the convenience and promote the tranquillity of social life." — *Courc d' Introduction Générale a l'Etude du Droit*, ch. i. These citations indicate the historical scope of the distinction, and in its application to the relations of the political and the civil order — the nation and the commonwealth — it has the utmost value for American publicists.

2 "Lex spectat naturæ ordinem." The law respecteth the order of nature.

The law is personal; its presentation is to persons, and its obligation is imposed upon persons. Its direct assertion in its simplest expression is, — thou shalt, and thou shalt not. It takes every man apart by himself, and appeals to him, and evokes his responsibility.[1]

The law has in its conception a universal aim. It presumes a principle of action which is applied in it; it is then set forth as regulative of all action and appertaining to all cases which fall within this conception.

The law is the definition of relations to be maintained as constituent of a moral order and is regulative of them. The law assumes the existence of man in moral relations, as of the family.

The law has no retrospective action, it is the on-going determination of the organic will. There is an injustice in an ex post facto law; when one in conformance to existing laws has done his whole duty, and certain consequences have ensued, it would be manifestly wrong to adjudge him and reverse the procedure, because the lawgiver had changed his mind.

The law is subject to amendment, to change or repeal. It is not immutable; it is not stationary, but always presumes a progress toward the more perfect attainment of its end.

The law is inclusive of the nation in its physical unity and being, as a whole. The nation is the domain of law; the law is of the nation, for the nation. It is thus, in its inclusive character, an authority over the individual lawgiver through whom it is set forth. It is even its own

"Lex non cogit ad impossibilia." The law compels not to the impossible. The argument "ab impossibile," is valid in law. "Impossibile est quod naturæ repugnat." — *Dig.* lib. i. tit. 17.

1 "Law is always in its nature personal, or a law for certain persons." — Hurd's *Law of Freedom, etc.*, vol. i. p. 22.

"The law relates to persons as its basis and aim, that is, it has an essentially personal character. All law is throughout a law of persons. The law necessarily has also reference to things, since these compose the physical conditions of human development. But the law in reference to things, constitutes only a subordinate division of the law relating to persons." — Ahren's *Naturrecht*, p. 83.

necessary interpreter, and while the private judgment of the law-giver may be allowed as an aid to ascertain, it cannot absolutely determine its import; the reference to it, is only private judgment.

The law is an affirmation; it is positive. The subjective apprehension of right and wrong cannot assume the place of an objective rule. Private opinion is not to be elevated into the position, nor invested with the authority of the nation.[1] The law itself is the standard by which the will of the nation is to be ascertained. This is requisite to the necessary obligation and validity of law. While the antithesis is superfluous, the aphorism of Hobbes is valid, "authoritas non veritas, facit legem." There is in law alone the formal assertion of the will of the nation, and through it alone its will is ascertained, and the private judgment of no man can be the authority for another, nor control his action.

The sovereignty of the nation, in its affirmation in law, and acting through its normal powers, constitutes the government. The government is the institution in which the sovereignty of the nation is realized. It is the order in which the will of the political people is inaugurated and established.

[1] This applies also to the practice in equity, and the procedure in it is based upon the assumption that it is the will of the nation. Of the application of natural law in jurisprudence, Mr. Hurd says: —

"Whatever rules or principles, tribunals may apply as law, they apply them as being the will of the supreme authority, and as being themselves only the instruments of that will.

"The will of the state is to be ascertained by the tribunal in one of the following methods: —

"First, direct and positive legislation is the first and ruling indication of the will of the state, whether it acknowledges or refers to any rule of natural origin or not.

Second, since the will of the state is to be presumed to accord with natural law, when the positive legislation of the state does not decide, the tribunal must ascertain the natural law which is to be enforced as the will of the state. But this law can only be determined by such criteria as are supposed to be recognized by the supreme power of the state, if such criteria exist; and this law when so determined becomes identified in its authority with positive law." — Hurd's *Law of Freedom, etc.*, vol. i. p. 24.

The government is of the people and it is over the people. There is in this no contradiction, but it is predicated in the being of the nation as a moral person. The government is therefore, in its highest conception, the self-government of the people, — of but over the people in every moment of its action. It is the will of the people in its self-determination, that is its sovereignty and its freedom.

The government is the representation of the political people as a whole. It asserts the authority of the whole over the individual; then only the will of the whole is law.

The government is often described as a government de facto and de jure. The former is strictly the force which at a certain moment may get and hold possession in the state, without reference to its origin or character, and it may maintain itself by foreign influence or by fraud; the latter is the power in the state which exists in conformance to its organic law, although the term is sometimes more narrowly applied to define a government which has an antecedent claim in mere legality. This is strictly described as a legitimate sovereignty or government.

This, as the claim of a pretender, may contravene the sovereignty of the people, that is the nation, and that government in the higher sense is only legitimate, which is the exponent of the will of the people, and in conformance to its organic law.[1] The term has been mainly connected with the patrimonial conception of the state.

If the government is deficient in its power, and its authority is no longer in the security of rights, and of free-

[1] Bismarck says of these minor pretensions of sovereignty in the German nation, in reference to their claims of legitimacy, — and it applies as well to the theory of legists of separate sovereignties here: "There are many pedantic people who want Prussia to protect the principle of legitimacy. But this principle of dynastic and conservative legitimacy is a fiction, and that a most pernicious one. Unless the conservative party renounce this principle we shall have to go the length of applauding the hallucinations of the petty potentates, who supposing they are powers, avail themselves of the pedestal of our own might to play at kings. And yet all this swindle is unauthorized by the history of the past, is quite new, unhistorical, and equally opposed to the teachings of God, as to the rights of mankind." — September 10, 1861.

dom, it is consequent on the decay of its internal sovereignty, and while then through certain changes its external form may remain, the ultimate result is the overthrow also of its external sovereignty. If the domain of law is not maintained, and crime is left unpunished, and justice is not executed, and everything falls into disorder in the lapse of internal sovereignty, there is no basis for an external sovereignty. It can no longer claim recognition as a nation by other nations; the self-determination, the moral spirit in the people is gone, and the government perishes in sedition and crime.

The government cannot be imposed upon the nation by any power which is external to it, nor can it be inaugurated by a clique, nor instituted by a bureau, nor by the decree of an individual, and in none of these is there the assertion of the organic law. If in some transition, when the order is interrupted by the violence of revolutions, the authority is assumed by these powers, as in events recently in Spain, it yet can be only temporarily, and the ultimate reference must be to the people.

The government is the manifestation of the sovereignty of the people. It rests on no contract. The nation and the government are not two separate parties who enter into a joint agreement. The people ordains and establishes the government, but does not contract with it. The description of it as only a party to a joint agreement repeats the fiction of the social contract, in which some ground was sought to establish the obligation of the feudal prince to his subjects. When it is applied to the government of the people, instead of a constructive principle, it becomes a source of division and is inconsistent with the unity of the people.

The government as the representative of the will of the people as a moral person, has its strength in the will. The strongest government is that in which there is the higher assertion of personality, — that is, the realization of the freedom of the people. In the common phrase a strong government is too often identified with an arbitrary rule, which is inherently weak. The government which is without strength, lacks the constituent principle of government. It is in its true conception stronger in the development of the people, in the maintenance of law, the institution of rights, the realization of freedom. For this it is clothed with power and with majesty on the earth.

CHAPTER IX.

THE NATION AND ITS CONSTITUTION.

THE constitution of the political people has a twofold character: there is a real and a formal constitution. The one is the development of the nation in history, — the historical constitution; the other is the formula which the nation prescribes for its order, — the enacted constitution; the one is the organism; the other is the form for the organization of the nation; the one is in identity with the nation in its organic being, it is written only in the law in which the members are fashioned; the other is the method which the nation establishes for its procedure, and the order to which the whole is to conform.[1]

[1] When it is not otherwise mentioned, the term is used strictly of the constitution in its formal character, the constitution as a legal instrument, and the institute of the government.

"The written constitution is simply a law ordained by the nation or the people instituting and organizing the government. The unwritten constitution is the real or actual constitution of the people as a state or as a sovereign community and constituting them such or such a state. It is providential, not made by the nation but born with it. The written constitution is made and ordained by the sovereign power and presupposes that power as already existing and constituted." — Brownson's *American Republic*, p. 218. See Hurd's *Law of Freedom, etc.*, vol. i. p. 296. Jamison's *Constitutional Convention*, p. 67.

"The more we examine the influence of human agency in the formation of constitutions, the greater will be our conviction that it enters only in a manner infinitely subordinate, or as a simple instrument, and I do not believe there remains the least doubt of the truth of the following propositions: —

"1. That the fundamental principles of political constitutions exist before all written law.

"2. That constitutional law is, and can only be, the development or sanction of an unwritten preëxisting right.

"3. That which is most essential, most intrinsically constitutional and fundamental, is never written and could not be without endangering the state.

"4. That the weakness and fragility of a constitution are in direct proportion to the multiplicity of written constitutional articles." — De Maistre, *On the Generative Principle of Political Constitutions*, Boston, 1847.

The comparative value of a written constitution has been the subject of wide

The sovereignty of the nation has its first formal expression in the convention. The convention represents the constructive power and intendment of the people in the formation of its constitution. It is the assertion of the will of the people in the ordination and institution of its government. The power existent in it is not then withdrawn, but as has been truly said, the convention persists in the constitution and never expires. It is the people forming the nation that ordains and establishes the constitution, and acts in and through it.

The nation is before the constitution. It precedes and enacts the constitution as the determinate form of its political life; it establishes the constitution as the order in which it will realize its determination.

The constitution, which defines the formal organization of the nation, is the law which is regulative of its normal action, and then also of the institutions which are its normal powers. The law is the formula of its process, the institutions are the structure of its process. The law and institutions, in their positive character, become the firm support of order, and the muniments of freedom. They are established, and in them the people recognizes its own stability. The constitution stands as the continuous expression of the sovereignty, the freedom, and the rights of the people. It has the authority of law, and there is the defense of the whole from arbitrary action; it has the stability of institutions, and there is the defense of the whole from individual action. It is constructive of the course of the people in its entirety, and in the constitution in its true significance, "we stand altogether, and we march altogether." It is the impregnable barrier against the assault of a mere individualism, and

discussion, but, if the proper limitation of a constitution be regarded, as simply the definition of the order of the nation, and if it does not assume the functions of the legislative power, the argument for it may be justified, and at least has the higher historical support.

the stable basis of the whole against the strife of factional, and the pretension of provincial supremacy. It remains while parties rise and disappear, and while systems change, as the constitution of the whole, stable in the power and supreme in the majesty of the people.

The constitution, as established by the will of the people, is of the nature and authority of law, and in its necessary process is the supreme law of the land. As law it is the assertion of the will of the people, and yet it is over the people, and obedience is to be ren dered to it. It is instituted in the self government of the people. It has therefore, as the law which is the expression of the moral being in the nation, the sacredness of law. But this sacredness is derivative from its content. There can be no sacredness attaching to the abstract form, and neither devotion nor sacrifice for the constitution when it is regarded only as an abstract formula; it is sacred only in so far as it is affirmative of the law which is implicit in the nation, or as the life of the nation may be affected in its maintenance.

The constitution is to have the style and language of an instrument of law; it has the intendment of positive law. It is ordained of the people as the law of the land, the will of the whole people, and the authority over the whole land. It is not in its scope, since it is an instrument of law, to present any theory or speculative notion of the origin and substance of the nation. The presentation of any theory is superfluous, in the presence of the being and sovereignty of the nation itself.

The constitution defines the formal organization of the normal powers of the government. But while these powers are established in conformance to the constitution, it is not to be so construed as to become the substitute for their normal operations. The distinction between the convention and the congress, the constitution and the laws, is fundamental; the one is the definition and construction of these powers, the other is their action in the condition and circumstance of the people.

The nation forms the constitution, in its own conscious determination. It is not a necessary physical sequence, as if the product of physical causes; it is not the result of aimless forces; it does not come into existence apart from the conscious thought and action of the people, as if it were to be had without effort, and sustained without vigilance, or as if it were to be held in a superstitious reverence. It is not attained without thought; it does not increase as the trees in the wood. It is not formed, and it cannot be sustained in the lethargy and passivity of the people. It is the assertion of the will of the people, and it subsists in the conscious and continuous determination of its will. It consists in an ethical and not a physical organism, and proceeds from, as it is maintained by, the sovereignty which exists in a conscious freedom.

The nation is to realize in the constitution the determination of the sovereignty of the people. It is not to be formed in the working of some sect or party. It is not to express the intent only of certain individuals; and while in isolated individuals there may be the longing for a better constitution, it must pervade the whole and become a common conviction before it can be realized. The constitution thus also in its completeness, cannot be the work of a single generation or separate age; it can be promulgated on the adjournment of no convention, as ample to embrace all events and all times. This is the oriental conception, and could result only in Chinese stability, not national permanence. It cannot consist with the existence of the people as a living power, and civilization as a living principle. It belongs to oriental immobility, not occidental spirit.

The nation is to apprehend in the constitution its object and aim. The formal constitution must correspond to the real. It is the order in which the people are to act, and the people must find therefore in the constitution the expression of its spirit, and its purpose must not be fettered nor perverted by it; but it must be able to act in and through it with entire freedom, in the furtherance of its aim. There must be reflected in it its own spirit, and in so far as it fails of this it has elements of weakness or of peril. The life of the people cannot be sacrificed for a political form, or a political dogma. The nation is not to perish that a political theory or a political abstraction may strive vainly for realization. There is thus danger if some conception which belongs only to the past is adhered to, and none the less, if some which is too far in advance, is insisted upon. The value of the constitution is relative as well as positive. Napoleon I. gave to Spain a constitution which was abstractly better than she had before; but it worked badly, for it was not adapted to the people, and they held it as something strange and alien. In modern English politics there are the most frequent illustrations of the neglect of this principle. They have furnished constitutions ready made for all communities. They are the same empty and stereotyped form, and struck in the same mould, and with the same trade stamp. The spirit of all peoples is to find embodiment in Anglican forms and institutions, and to realize an Anglican freedom. England, which never has apprehended the spirit of another people, and holds forms as immutable when of her own cast, has always had those which she regarded as the only hope of other countries. In the organization of society in India, the native farmers of the revenue, as the best material to be had, were taken by force to be made into squires. It was necessary to society that there should be squires, and that they should be of the Anglican type. In the last century an English minister proposed a plan for the introduction of the whole feudal system into St. Johns; in this century the Dominion of Canada has been designed in the same device. The constitution is to be the exponent of the will and spirit of the people, and that which is over it, but is not of it, or no longer of it, has elements of weakness or of tyranny. It is the weakness of an empty form, or the hard tyranny of an abstraction or system, and repressing but not expressing the spirit of the people, it crushes its energies and consumes its freedom.

The neglect of the distinction between the real and the formal constitution and the consequent identification of the nation with its formal organization, becomes the most dangerous of political falsehoods. The nation not only is before the formal constitution, but the events in its history, which it holds in highest honor, may be precedent to it; as the war of the Revolution was fought and brought to its close before the adoption of the existent formal constitution.

The nation continues in its identity, while constitutions are changed or abolished. Rome was the same under her kings and under her consuls. France is the same through all her revolutions, and under her feudal and republican and imperial organizations. The nation, in her formal constitution, has not always even the indication of her real condition, but under the same constitution may advance or decline. The constitution has, in itself, no inherent power and no abstract virtue to deliver the people. It is not for the individual nor for the nation to be saved by any system, however complex, nor any dogma, however subtle. The constitution may become itself only the mask which hides from an age its degeneracy, or the mausoleum which conceals its decay. The pedantry of systems may be made the substitute for living forces. The nation is not comprehended in its formal organization. There is a political truth in the rude verse of a poet of the Republican Age in England: —

> "Let not your king and parliament in one,
> Much less apart, mistake themselves for that
> Which is most worthy to be thought upon;

> Nor think *they are essentially the state.*
> Let them not fancy that the authority
> And privileges on them bestowed,
> Conferred are, to set up a majesty,
> Or a power or a glory of their own;
> But let them know *it was for a deeper life,*
> *Which they but represent;*
> *That there's on earth a yet auguster thing,*
> *Veiled though it be, than parliament or king.*"

The nation may amend or alter the constitution which it has formed. The course of history in which the nation stands is a development; and there is to be in it always the better institution of rights, and the broader domain of freedom, and these are to have their assertion in the constitution. The constitution must be open to recognize the advance in each age, since in each the work of the people is to be carried on under the changed conditions of an historical life. Neither the individual nor the nation can in any moment regard its course and order as perfect; and, with entire subjection to the constitution, there must be in it always the expression of an higher historical development. It is here that the relation of the permanent and the progressive element in the organization of society becomes apparent; the one involves the other, and is even its condition. The new is to be built in the old. It is not to be the isolation from the old; but it is wrought out of the old into the new. The change which comes is to be ingrooved in that which flies. The retention of all that is good in the past is to be held as no hindrance to advance, but its precedent. There is to be no divergence from the old, as if it were necessary to take from the outset a new start. The wise change is not in the weak conceit of the ability to construct out of one's own political materials the best constitution, but with carefulness, lest, from the acquisition of the past, anything of worth shall be allowed to perish. While Rome has bequeathed to the world the universal terms of law,—and her civil law has become an institute in history of the world's civilization, — she yet held, in undying deference, the tables on which her first law was written. There must be thus always in the constitution itself forms to enable its amendment, and, while it is open to no sudden change in the momentary action of the people, it is not to prevent the freedom of the people. It is to assert the continuous will of the nation in its organic continuity, and it must, therefore, possess permanence. It is to be open to the expression of progress, also, for it is to be the institute of freedom and of rights.[1]

If there be in the constitution no provision whereby the political people in its normal action can effect an amendment, or if the mode provided be such as to obstruct its action, there yet subsists in the people the right of reform; and if, while yet there is no way open to it or only some inaccessible way is indicated, the hope of reform shall fail, and the constitution and the government which is instituted in it be wrested from their foundation in the consent of the organic will, there is then, at last, the right of revolution. This, in the supreme peril, is the supreme necessity of the people. If the people no longer finds the correspondence to its aim in the constitution which it has once established, if its advance is thwarted and it is being deflected from its course, and its life is being deformed, although under the form it once enacted and alone has the right to enact; if the government becomes thus subversive of its ends, and the future holds no hope of a reform which may effect those ends, then revolution is a right. This maintenance

[1] President Washington, in his farewell to the people, which, in its political wisdom has, in modern political literature, no parallel, asserts, as a fundamental right, "the right of the people to make and to alter their constitutions of government;" but, since the constitution has the form of law, the mode of amendment which it provides may be so intricate or so difficult, as to so restrict the action of the people, that this fundamental right shall be more effectually wrested from them, than by the most consummate tyranny.

"A constitution which has no place for amendment is absolutely immoral, for it sets itself forth as absolutely perfect; it is far more immoral than the unlimited power of the monarch." — Schleiermacher, *Christliche Sitte*, p. 270.

of the continuous life and continuous development of the nation, against that which is hindering its growth, or sapping its energy, is not strictly a revolution. It is rather the reverse, since there is in it the maintenance of the organic being of the nation and it is in conformance to the organic law. It is not anarchic, for it is the only possible pursuance of the order of the nation, and its vindication from the false order which is interrupting it. It is the spirit of the people in its real strength which breaks through the system by which it is gyved. But it is only to be justified in the supreme necessity of the nation, and as itself the act of the nation as an whole, the work of the political people. It is not to be the act of a part only, as a section or faction. The development is only of the nation as an organic whole, and conditional in its organic unity, and it is this alone that is thwarted or imperilled, and in this alone the right subsists. Thus a revolution is not an insurrection, since the one presumes the action of the people as an organic whole, and is justified in proceeding from the people, whose determination is law; the other is the act of individuals, a section or a faction, in revolt from the will of the whole.[1]

The revolution which is thus a necessity is not the discord, but it is more strictly the concord of the nation, and when thus a necessity, the order which is set aside will be

1 "The moral condition of a revolution is that it express the conviction of the common people and the common will." — Fichte, *Naturrechte*, p. 238.

"The right of revolution must be grounded in the living conviction of the whole." —Schleiermacher, *Christliche Sitte*, p. 265.

"Regarded abstractly, revolutions are always moral anomalies; but actually they are to be regarded as unavoidable and therefore only apparently moral anomalies. For in human history, through the power of sin, the development cannot continue to proceed in a continuous sequence, but only through many throes and crises. The revolution which is really the work of the nation itself, can only be regarded as such a crisis, which, through external impediments, becomes the condition of the maintenance of the moral life of the nation; and such a revolution therefore can only be justified when it rests on the living conviction of the people in its totality." — Rothe, *Theologische Ethik*, vol. iii. sec. 2, p. 984.

succeeded immediately by the real order of the nation, in its new form, with the return of the energy of the people, and its ampler freedom. It is not therefore of any to glorify revolution, which can appear only in a disturbed order; but when in the mystery of evil, the energy of the people is impaired and its life withering, although its path can be only through violent struggle, it is yet to rejoice in the power which may resist and overcome the evil. It is thus that epochs of national revolution have been those not of despair, but of hope and exultation, and there has been in them, as there is not in the triumph of parties or factions, the renewal of the strength and spirit of the people.

The nation thus may be the stronger in the crisis in which its constitution is swept away, and there may be in it the evidence of a power which opposing evils could not wholly destroy. It is the life which could not be utterly crushed, and the strength which could not be entirely consumed by fetters forged through lapse of time, in which privileges assumed to be alone the precedents of action, and were girt by legal forms and devices, until they barred out the rights of men. The transition from the feudal constitutions of Germany, has been in every crisis the development in its higher unity of a national life. The age of the commonwealth, when the same result in part was effected in England, was the last great age in her history. The French Revolution bore throughout the deepest devotion to the nation, and in its tumultuous changes no voice was lifted against the unity and glory of France. The American Revolution was the act of the political people of the whole land, in the endeavor toward the realization of the nation. These crises were in the development of national life, and the constitution displaced was foreign to the political people.

The constitution is primarily to define the structure and the mode of action of the normal powers in the nation.

It is the enumeration and the limitation of these powers, and is then simply the norm of their action. It is to regulate the form, but it is not to specify the content in their action. It is to prescribe the organization of the nation, and not that which shall be in the action of the organs. It is as the chart of a ship, and the order of its company; but it knows not the voyage it shall make, nor the storm nor mutiny it may encounter, nor those whom it shall carry, nor the seas it shall sail.

The prescription of the action of the people in all events and circumstances, is not in the scope of the constitution, and it would not be possible. It is not requisite to its stability, nor to the firm order of the government; but in the effort of the past to control the future it would induce elements of conflict which would impair the whole. The constitution which sought to predetermine the future, and to forestall the conduct of affairs in the infinite change of time and circumstance, would presume that a people was already beyond the conditions of history. If the people possessed a living energy, and was not itself as dead as the past, the object, if attempted, would be as vain as the insistance that men in a real battle should listen, for the word of command, only to the echoes of the voices of commanders on some battle-field of the past, whose banners are folded, and from which the ranks have long since marched away. It would be, against the inevitable current of events, which still would sweep on resistless as time, the building of "parchment barriers," and in the real crises they would be thrown aside, as the impediment in the path of a free people in its necessary course.

To attempt to make the constitution the formula which not only shall define the order of the people but mould the events in its history, to make it determinative of the course of the people in these events as they arise, to make it the substitute for the process of laws and statutes which become in their immediate enactment the embodiment of a living will, is itself possible, only as the nation is no longer a living power, and has no longer a living will. The constitution which the convention has formed, and which has been adopted, is in its nature the supreme law, but in its own provision, to make its amendment difficult or well-nigh impossible, and then to assume that it shall be exclusively and exhaustively definitive of the action of the people in all events, involves the denial of the organic and moral being of the people. It is directly immoral, since in its necessary inference the people no longer exists as a power in the moral order which is the life of history. It does not honor the past, nor is it joined with it in living relations. Thus in the strict historical school there is always a regretfulness, as that the convention of 1787 should have adjourned, and that there is now no Hamilton and no Madison; but this deference does not honor them. We may only know of them that they had the strength to do, knowing that things were to be done, and that their strength was as their days. Of this spirit, which may become a weak superstition, the age has to learn, in the words of another, that the bones of the giants of old have been found and they measure no more than ours. This conception enslaves the present to the past instead of emancipating it with the past. It is the worst tyranny of time, or rather the very tyranny of time. It makes an earthly providence of a convention which has adjourned without day. It places the sceptre over a free people in the hands of dead men, and the only office left to the people is to build thrones out of the stones of their sepulchres. The spirit is immured in the walls it has built. It is in politics the thought which in history had its expression in Egypt. It is said by Hegel, that as it is reflected in her monuments, the Egyptian was in love with death, and thus there was always a skeleton at the banquet, but this places the same image not only in the assembly of the people, but in the power of the majority in it. It elevates the past to a throne over the present, of irreversible decrees.[1]

The constitution determines the order, but it cannot predicate the course and destination of the people. It is not providence, nor destiny. The years and what they bring, are withdrawn from the gaze of conventions as well as of men. They have no more a horoscope to forecast the future in the lives of nations than of individuals, nor can they outmaster time, nor wrest the secret from the years. The constitution is to provide that the people shall stand together, and march together, but their line of march is hidden from it. The nation is formed in the changing conditions of history. It must pass through conflicts which the prescience of no assembly can anticipate, and they will not regulate their coming by the action of any convention, nor conform to its project, nor abide in its provision. The aim of the constitution is to leave each generation free to do its own work to which it is called, but in the continuity of the nation, and in its normal process, and therein, it becomes the assertion of the unity of law, with the realization of the freedom of the nation in its being in history.

The constitution, when it transcends its province, and, from the enumeration of powers and the exposition of rights proceeds to the specification of their content in the immediate direction and adjustment of events, becomes imbedded in political theories, which are introduced to supplement its literal articles, or encumbered with minute detail. Since it is in its form a positive law, it becomes, then, through judicial interpretation, complicated with precedents and opinions, and is tortured by judicial decisions, until, instead of representing the will or the freedom of

[1] "Whosoever will have a government that cannot follow its living conviction, sets the dead over the living, and denies the moral development of the state." — Schleiermacher, *Christliche Sitte*, p. 273.

the people, it is only the field ground for lawyers; the people no longer recognize their aim nor their stability in it, and its intricate and complex character tends to produce ignorance of, and then indifference to it.

The constitution has a positive and a relative value. It has the elements of a universal as well as an individual character, since the nation has a universal aim as it has an individual life. In the critical study of a constitution its comparative advantages are therefore to be regarded, and there is to be applied to it a common as well as special estimate. There is thus a high value in the comparative study of the constitutions of nations.

The constitution is to become in the progress of the people the institution of an ampler freedom, and a more perfect organization of rights. As the sovereignty of the people attains a more determinate expression in it, that which is vague and incomplete, or inconsistent and incongruous, is set aside. The arbitrary can find in its vagueness only the cloak for tyranny, and the treacherous the mask for secession and anarchy. Its language is, therefore, to be plain, to express the purpose of the people. It is in its high conception, the evidence of the stability and the instrument of the freedom and the assertion of the sovereignty of the people, in whose will it is ordained and established.

The more perfect constitution is always to be the aim of the whole as it is the indication of its advance. But the formal constitution is not to be an end in itself, and its worth is derivative only from the life it conserves. To reverence it for its own sake, may create a spirit not of law but of mere legality. The superstitions of lawyers are more perilous than the superstitions of priests. It is the adherence to a political formula, to which it attaches a separate sanctity, and refuses all change, while its spirit is wasting and decaying. It holds the form above the life and being of the nation which it was instituted to maintain. There is here the contrast of a righteous and an evil conservatism; the true conservatism aims at the maintenance of the being and the unity of the nation, although the form be changed or destroyed; but there is a false conservatism, — there are those who, in their regard for the constitution of the nation, deny the nation itself.[1] They would sacrifice the nation to maintain the constitution. They hold the constitution as something above and separate from the people, to be looked upon with another reverence. They place the symbol above the reality, and adhere with a blind attachment to the letter, when it is dead to the spirit. It is at last the conservatism of a political hypocrisy. It is the conservatism of the scribes and pharisees and lawyers; but they neither knew nor cared for the calling of the ancient nation. It is busy reading the inscriptions and repeating the legends upon the stones, while the fires upon the altar are dying, and it will build and adorn the sepulchres of the prophets, while the great Prophet of humanity stands unheeded in the streets of its Capital.

1 "Conservatism consists not in that the old form be retained, but that the substance be maintained." — Stahl, *Philosophie des Rechts*, vol. ii. sec. 2, p. 200.

"Conservatism, when it rightly understands itself, will in no way hold on to the exact form of the state as hitherto existent; but will hold fast the preservation of the state itself, under the development of its form." — Rothe, *Theologische Ethik*, vol. iii. sec. 2, p. 995.

"We have heard of the impious doctrine in the old world, that the people were made for kings, not kings for the people. Is the same doctrine to be received in another shape in the new, that the solid happiness of the people is to be sacrificed to the views of political institutions of another form? It is too early for politicians to presume on our forgetting that the public good, the real welfare of the great body of the people, is the supreme object to be pursued; and that no form of government whatever has any other value than as it may be fitted for the attainment of this object." — President Madison, *The Federalist*, No. xiv.

CHAPTER X.

THE NATION AND ITS SOVEREIGN RIGHTS.

THE nation, in its sovereignty, is possessed of certain necessary rights. These are rights which are involved in the attainment of its necessary end in history. They subsist in the unity of the nation, and in their historical manifestation, they become the indices of its sovereignty. They have thus an integral character; they are not an indiscriminate and incongruous collection of powers, but are formed in a necessary correlation, as the sequence of the unity in which they subsist. They exist in the correspondence of rights and duties, and there is resident in them the necessary responsibilities of the nation.

Firstly; the sovereignty of the nation involves the right to its own existence. The right which is precedent to all others is the right of the nation to be; the law which, in the conflict of laws, abrogates all others, is the law of its supreme necessity. It may, therefore, in its necessity, interrupt and suspend the ordinary course of rights in their reference to the individual or the community.

The supreme object of the government is to care for the preservation of the nation. In this end, it is justified, in its necessity, in the suspension of the ordinary procedure of its law and order, which then becomes the assertion of its higher law, and the maintenance of its enduring order. The principle of action is then, *salus populi, suprema lex.* When the necessity of the nation thus demands it, it is not the negation of rights and of laws, but in the deeper sense and sequence their maintenance. But in this action, the necessity of the government is the exponent of the necessity of the nation, and of and for itself, the government has no right to interrupt the process of laws.

It is justified only as the peril of the nation is actual or imminent. There is no consideration of a resultant advantage that can become its ground, since then it would presume to be itself the normal law and condition of the land. It is a power so high, and yet so imperative, that there should be in the constitution itself the careful provision for its exercise, and the protection from its abuse.

The right has been recognized as necessary by every historical people. In Rome, it was asserted in the words, "videant Consules ne quid detrimenti capiat respublica"; in England, it is construed in the right to suspend the habeas corpus; in France, Italy, and Germany, in the right to declare martial law; in Rome, it could be formally exercised only by an act of the senate, and in England, by an act of parliament.

The nation may call for the willing sacrifice of the life and property of its members, and this has its precedent, in the being of the nation as a moral person, to whom is given a vocation in the moral order of the world. The sacrifice of the individual is for the longer life, and the surrender of material wealth, is for that in which the moral acquisitions of humanity are conserved. But this is consistent alone with the being of the nation as a moral person, and when the nation is assumed to exist only as a necessary evil, or only for the protection of property and persons, this right becomes a contradiction, since in the one instance it would be the deference to a mere fate, and in the other its exercise would presume an immediate negation of its end.

Secondly; the sovereignty of the nation embraces the right to declare war and to conclude peace.[1] The nation

[1] Rothe says, "Every war which is morally justifiable, is a national war." — *Theologische Ethik*, vol. iii. sec. 2, p. 958.

is the investiture on the earth of right with might; it is constituted as a power in the moral order of the world and for the maintenance of that order. The right to declare and make war belongs only to the nation, and to that only as the minister of righteousness, the power which in its normal being is to assert justice against violence, and law against anarchy, and freedom against oppression. The nation in its sovereignty alone can declare war, and alone can conclude peace, to which all surrender is made. The nation has therefore the supreme command of the physical force of the people, — its military. In the armed might of the nation there is the manifestation of its power, but the might is to be one with the people in its unity and its totality, and then there can be no danger to the freedom of the individual or of the whole, but there is the immediate security of that freedom. Therefore every member of the nation that can bear arms, and not a separate order and organization, must be trained to arms.[1] This belongs to the education of the whole people, and should be the instruction of its schools and universities; there is in this the moral significance of the world discipline, which the study of the technic of science and of abstract propositions inclines to forget, and which always has so singular beauty in its significance in the pages of Roman literature. This discipline is presumed in the nation in its being as a moral person, and is inconsequent in education only as instruction is limited to a formal or an individual conception of the nation. It is as one army that the people becomes conscious of its power as a nation. There is then the apprehension of righteousness as no abstract principle or spectral ideal, but as invested with might on the earth. Then there appears that spirit of sacrifice in which the unity of the nation is laid, and in which its

[1] "The army must not only be national, but be the nation, — the nation in so far as it is capable of bearing arms, in its totality, must form the army." — Rothe, *Theologische Ethik*, vol. ii. sec. 2, p. 964.

life is gained. Then the prophecy of the future of the nation is not in those that are, but in those that have given themselves for it, and its continuity is in those that died that the nation might live.[1]

The declaration of war, therefore, can be justified only as it is national, or the act of the nation. Its end is to be that which is involved in the being of the nation, and in its vocation in a moral order. This indicates the spirit in which war is to be conducted. It is to be waged with no individual hostility, nor against private persons, nor with a subordination to private ends. It is not the destruction of the lives or of the property of men that is its object; it is not the destruction, but the defeat of the enemy that is sought; and all destruction is justified only as necessary to its prosecution, or to the public defense, or as effecting a more speedy termination, and a more sure peace.[2]

The formal declaration of war and conclusion of peace must be the act of the nation in its sovereignty; a company or a division of an army may, with no immediate authorization, in certain circumstances, commence hostilities, but it cannot declare war; and the enemy may lay down its arms, before a company or a division of an army, but it cannot conclude peace.

Since there belongs to the nation the supreme command of the physical force of the people, the nation can allow, within its limits, the accumulation of no force which is not subject to its ultimate authority. The commonwealth

[1] "The meaning and the end of the military power of the nation, is found not merely in the conquering of enemies, and the suppressing of rebels, and the preservation of an undisturbed order, but in that the nation itself in its might shall stand forth as a righteous warrior." — Stahl, *Philosophie des Rechts*, vol. ii. sec. 2, p. 180.

"This might is not merely the outward means, for the maintenance of public order, but it is also in itself the moral energy of the nation." — Stahl, vol. ii. sec. 2, p. 140.

[2] A very striking definition of war is cited by Rothe from Wirth, — "the power of one people against another people in its whole might, its totality."

Pomponius, — "hostes sunt quibus bellum publice populus Romanus decrevit; cœteri latrunculi vel prædones appellantur."

necessarily cannot declare war, nor conclude peace, and it has in its direction the physical force, only as a constabulary for the maintenance of internal order, and for operations only within its confines. The nation, in its sovereignty alone, can appeal to the issues of war. in which the existence of the whole is involved.

The nation, in its physical as in its moral unity and being, is a power over the individual, and must effect its purpose, notwithstanding individual caprice or intent. But in the basis of the state, in a mere individualism, there is the foundation for none of its rights of sovereignty, nor can it justify their necessary action. It is not the security of property and persons which is primarily involved in war; but it is the direct reverse; and the call of the nation, in its right in war, belongs to no individual and no collection of individuals, but it is an authority in and over the whole.

The end of war is peace, "a peace that will come, and come to stay." A universal peace is the goal of the nations in history. But it is assured only in the realization of the unity and of the being of nations, and in their higher development and power there is the advance toward peace and its surer prophecy.[1]

[1] Napoleon III. has often expressed this, but it is not in the empire.

Rothe says: "That end which is a universal peace is approached in the same degree in which the idea of the nation — the political idea, fills and penetrates the consciousness of the people." — *Theologische Ethik*, vol. iii. sec. 2, p. 954.

The recognition of the Rebels as belligerents, by England, and their consequent investiture with the rights of war, indicated the spirit of an hereditary aristocracy, a governing caste toward the nation, and its want of all consciousness of national rights and duties, and the subordination of national to private interests. It was not the act of the people of England, if there be a people. The neutrality, which England professed between the nation and the ebels who were seeking to destroy it, in the nature of things and in the moral order which is the precedent of the laws of nations, was no neutrality; but her recognition of them as belligerents, and their investiture with the rights of war, threw around them the protection of rules and regulations which were formed in international law only for nations, and placed a rebel force, in the view of Roman law — *latrunculi vel prædones* — on the same footing with a nation, and the advantage was secured to them of the rights of nations, while the hazard of their political recognition as a nation was avoided.

Thirdly; the sovereignty of the nation embraces the right to form and sustain international relations. This is in history the immediate sign or note of political sovereignty. It is the formal manifestation of the external sovereignty of the nation. It belongs to the nation alone to enter into those relations with other nations which are in the province of international law; it alone can make treaties with them, and send ministers and embassies to them, and receive them in turn.

Thus, also, the members of a nation can have no public or official communication with another nation, excepting through the representatives of the nation to which they belong, and can receive from another no mark of honor or consideration without its consent. Thus, also, no representative of another nation can be accredited to, nor recognized by, nor in his official character hold communication with any individual or section of a nation, excepting through the constituted authority of the nation.

Fourthly; the sovereignty of the nation embraces the right to adopt in its citizenship, and to invest with political rights and powers, those whom it may for this object elect, of those who may emigrate to it. Thus, also, each citizen has the protection of the nation, in the rights it has conferred, not only through its whole domain, but among other nations in so far as these rights are defined by treaty; and, wherever he may go, he may claim, in his integrity, its defense. It throws around each its entire majesty, and an injury to the least who is its citizen is an injury to the whole.

There is for every person who is in the nation, or may travel or reside in it, security in civil rights,—the protection of life, liberty, and property, in conformance to its civil administration and subjection to its civil authority,—since these rights subsist in the necessary relations of life; but it belongs only to the nation, in its sovereignty and its freedom, to invest those who may come to it with political rights,—its citizenship and its freedom.

But the citizens of another nation, who may travel or reside in it, or acquire and hold property in it, are subject to the conditions of its civil order. They hold property on the same conditions with its own citizens, and subject with theirs to loss incurred by accident, by the possible interruption of order in social crises and by the vicissitudes of war. No nation can invade the domain of another on the pretense of the maintenance of the civil rights of its citizens, nor obtain any reparation for loss or injury to persons or property which may arise in these circumstances, except that which is allowed by the nation itself to its own citizens. The opposite principle would involve not only an unequal preference of aliens, but would concede to them an increased security,—that of the land to which they belong, in addition to that of the land in which they choose simply to reside and hold possessions.

Fifthly; the sovereignty of the nation embraces the right to coin and issue money—the representative of all values within it. The signature of the nation which is stamped upon the money it issues, is the sign of its power in its original right of possession, and of the maintenance of property, as an institute of the nation, whose value it is to sustain. The description of money is not limited to a single style, as gold or silver or copper, which form in common the accepted standard of values, and which in the transaction of exchange are less rude than an exchange in cattle, but are not of themselves stable.

But the nation, in the exercise of this power, does not and cannot by any formal act create values, and as it is to maintain the institution of property by its laws, so in the issuing of money there is to be the representation of actual values. The issue which does not represent actual values, but is made a legal tender in the formal exchange of values, as in the liquidation of contracts, may be and is justified in the temporary destruction of war, while yet it is destructive of actual values and can have no justification in peace. It becomes then, not an appropriation of a part by the nation, in its supreme necessity, when the nation in its original right owns the whole, but a fraud, and involves the robbery not only of the poor but of all men.

The crime of issuing counterfeit money is also twofold, and is not only a fraud and a robbery, but in a higher degree is a crime against the state.

Sixthly. The sovereignty of the nation involves the right which is described in its formal phrase, as the imperium or eminent domain. The organic people holds the possession and inheritance of the land, as one and indivisible. The supreme authority over the whole land belongs to the people in its organic and moral being, and it has a right correspondent to its authority not only over persons but over the land and all things in it.

It is to maintain the authority and the supremacy of its laws through the whole domain. In this rests the right of the nation to interdict the assumption of authority or the exercise of power by another nation within its territory. Therefore no foreign government can perform within it an office, even of civil police, without its consent, and can hold no possession or private estate within it, but as subject to its authority. This is the occasion for treaties of extradition.

The right appears also in the levying of taxes, which are a prior lien upon all property within it. A tax is not, as in false representations of the state, primarily a certain amount paid to the nation in consideration of the advantages obtained from it, nor as an equivalent for its protection, nor is it a certain sum donated to it in order to secure the remainder, but it is the taking by the nation, for its own necessary use, of that which it alone holds in full in its original right.

This right forbids the alienation of any part of that which by nature and in history constitutes the domain of the people in its integral unity.[1] In the barbaric constitutions and in the feudal system, the ruler could divide or transfer the domain, as in the administration of a private estate; but, in the public character of the domain of the nation, it is held, as constituted in nature and in history, as one, and as inalienable and indivisible.

This right includes the immediate, that is, the proprietary right, to certain places and parts which are the immediate possession of, and are to be held by, the nation in its sovereignty. This includes, — Firstly, All that which by its nature is withdrawn from private possession, or is of immediate necessity for the public use. The rivers, lakes, bays, and harbors or ship-homesteads, and the great highways, the military and post-roads and telegraph-routes, are of this description. The line, for instance, of the Ohio or the Mississippi, the bay of New York or San Francisco, or the passes of the Atlantic and the Pacific Railways, are the possession of the whole people, and belong to the nation. They do not belong to those who are resident by them, but are the domain of the people. Secondly, This includes all places and parts which by nature are formed for the defense of the whole. The cliffs or outlooks which are suited for forts or signal-stations, or the lines adapted to military fortifications, or places for naval yards are of this description. Thirdly, This includes all waste and unoccupied lands and places throughout the whole; thus, the territories are in the immediate ownership of the nation. Fourthly, To this may be added the immediate possession, by the nation, of its capital. This is not a city simply of certain municipal privileges, but belongs to the nation, and, in its central position, should be free from immediate social and commercial influences and their agitation. It is

[1] "The mere rectification of a boundary is not to be regarded as the alienation of the domain of the state. A part of the domain of the state is not alienated thereby, but the whole is more exactly defined." — Bluntschli, *Allgemeines Statsrechts*, vol. i. p. 217.

the place of the government and of the ordained and representative majesty of the nation; it is the witness of its unity; it is connected with the long line of its presidents and representatives, and judges; and around it gather the armies of the nation; and over it, always, the nation's flag is floating; to it the ministers of all other nations must proceed; from it there goes forth that law which is an authority over the whole people and through the whole land. It is around its capital that the deepest associations gather; its peril stands for the peril of the people, and its deliverance is the sign of the deliverance of the people.

In the necessary correlation of rights and duties, there is also attached to this right the duty of the nation, in its physical progress, to undertake and execute those works which are necessary to the well-being of the people, and which by their nature are beyond private enterprise, and are removed from the immediate scope of individual interest and individual power, such, for instance, as the construction of military and post roads, the improvement of rivers and harbors, the survey of coasts, the building of lighthouses, the planting of forests, etc.

The fact that whenever the nation may assume possession of any place and part, compensation is rendered, involves no contradiction of the right of eminent domain. The national right is asserted in the right to effect a cession of the property, and the private right the nation itself sustains, in the allowance of an adequate compensation to those in immediate possession.

This right comprehends, also, the right in the nation to the extension of its domain by purchase, by occupancy, or by conquest. The extension of its domain is the act of the nation in its sovereignty. When another nation is affected, it may be by treaty, and this is a free and peaceful cession. To this Grotius first added as a condition, the consent of the present occupants of the parts annexed; but the interests of the nation are in no comparison with those of an isolated and detached territory in which there is no political organization and no political life, and the former cannot be conditioned upon the latter. The requisition of an inquiry, as to the consent of the existing occupants, has only a formal justification, and is a pedantic compliance with a formal political theory.[1]

The inquiry as to the residence of the right of eminent domain in the United States has an interest for lawyers, as the phrase is strictly technical; but it has only a formal interest, and the fact is determined in the political being of the political people. The evidence of the subsistence of the right in the people of the United States rests in the fact, firstly, that the organic and historical people is, and can only be, the dominus or lord: secondly, that the defense of the whole domain is in and of the United States alone: thirdly, that all acquisition of territory, by purchase or conquest, is by the United States alone, and the immediate transferal is to the United States, as in Louisiana and Alaska: fourthly, that all rectifications and determinations of boundaries are made in and through the United States alone: fifthly, that treaties of extradition are made by the United States alone, and from it alone can the extradition of any person be obtained: sixthly, that all vacant and unoccupied territories are held by the United States alone: seventhly, that taxation by the United States is a prior lien upon all property throughout the whole: and finally, on the other hand, the fact that no commonwealth can enter upon or effect an acquisition of territory, nor alienate territory to a foreign power, and that no common-

[1] The principle which is to govern territorial extension has been stated as follows: " The government has long since laid down its principles in respect of territorial extension. It comprehends, it has comprehended, those annexations which are commanded by an absolute necessity, uniting to the country populations having the same manners and the same national spirit as ours. France can only desire such territorial aggrandizements as do not impair her territorial cohesion, but she should always labor for her moral and political aggrandizement by using her influence to advance the great interests of civilization." — Napoleon III. *Circular*. 1868.

wealth can of itself determine its own boundaries or effect their rectification; these considerations, from a simply legal position, are decisive. But if there is a legal doubt, let it be supposed that, in fact, some commonwealth begins a course of territorial aggrandizement, or attempts the alienation of any portion of territory to a foreign power, and the error in the claim becomes apparent.

The legal confusion has arisen from the fact that while the right of eminent domain is in the United States, the formal administration of the power implied in the right, as a civil procedure, is referred to the commonwealth in conformance to its normal constitution. The evidence assigned for the residence of the right, primarily and exclusively, in the commonwealth, has been in the fact that all private escheats fall to it, but this conforms to the province of the commonwealth, since private interests are constituted in it; but no general or public escheats fall to the commonwealth, and it has within its confines the right to vacated lands, but it has no right to vacant lands. There is the fact of the possession of unoccupied lands by Texas, but this is anomalous and ought not to be allowed to remain.[1]

[1] "The dominus is the United States, and the domain of the whole territory, whether meted into particular States or not, is in the United States. The United States do not part with the domain of that portion of the national domain included within a particular State."—Brownson, *American Republic*, p. 300.

CHAPTER XI.

THE NATION AND ITS NORMAL POWERS.

THE sovereignty of the nation has its institution in the powers in which the government is constituted. The will of the organic people, in its normal action, works through different members, to which are attached different functions. The nature of these powers and these functions is implicit in the nation in its organism, — their manifestation is in the process of freedom and of rights.

The formal organization of these powers has obtained its higher construction in the modern age. The distinction of their different organs and their functions, is illustrative of its higher development. In the political body, as in the physical, each organ has its separate use for which it is formed, and each has no separate existence, but they subsist as the organs of one body.

The distinction of these powers, although in imperfect outline, is traced by Aristotle. He describes, firstly, the assembly for public affairs; secondly, the chief magistracy, — the executive power; thirdly, the judicial power. The decision in regard to all crimes of a public character is referred to the first or the legislative power and the chief magistracy or the executive power is made subordinate to it. "It is the proper work of the popular assembly to determine concerning war and peace; to make or terminate alliances; to enact laws; to sentence to death, banishment, or confiscation of goods; and to call the magistrates to account for their behavior when in office."[1]

In modern politics the distinction has been held in a

[1] *Politics*, bk. iv. ch. 14.

clearer and firmer conception, and obtained a wider actualization through Locke and Montesquieu, but it has been defined by none with greater fullness than by the earlier American publicists, and especially in the writings of President Madison. Its genesis forms one of the most significant pages in the history of modern politics. The assertion of legislative and judicial powers, as original in the civil and political organization, against the sole and exclusive prerogative of a king, to the exercise of all powers, has been indicative of the advance of freedom; and the assertion of the distinction of all these powers, and their ampler development, has been indicative that the more perfect organization of the nation is in the realization of freedom. The distinction of the normal powers of the nation in its civil and political organization has been principally as the Legislative, the Executive, and the Judicial.[1]

[1] There have been various analyses of these powers, but their value is chiefly illustrative, and they have no correspondent historical justification. The description of Locke, and of Montesquieu, and also of Hegel is, I. Legislative. — *Pouvoir législatif.* II. Executive, — *Pouvoir exécutif.* III. Judicial, — *Pouvoir judiciare.* B. Constants added to these, IV. An intermediate power, — *Pouvoir modérateur.* This was an attempt to define more clearly their unity. The executive power has also been further divided into (a.) An administrative power, — *Pouvoir administratif;* and (b.) A supervisory power, — *Pouvoir inspectivé.*

Trendelenburg designates four powers, — *vier functionen,* — I. The Government, — *Die Regierung.* II. The Military power. III. The Legislative power. IV. The Judicial power. But it is obvious that the Military is not a power corresponding to the other powers, since it is simply the organization of the physical force of the whole; it is in subjection to the political power, and its necessary principle of action is that of entire subordination in the political whole. — Trendelenburg. *Naturrechte,* p. 160.

Bluntschli's description indicates the tendency of recent German publicists. The common distinction is criticized as too formal and abstract, as something dry and pedantic, and this also is the criticism of Stahl. In Bluntschli's statement the legislative power is necessarily precedent, and is over against all others and is regulative of them, but in the organization of this power, the Crown and the Parliament, or the President and the Congress form each an integral and inseparable element. The powers are thus defined, as, I. The Government, — *Die Regierungsgewalt, das Regiment.* II. The Court, — *Die Richterlichegewalt, das Gericht.* III. The Public Instruction, — *Die Statscultur.* IV. The Public Economy, — *Die Wirthschaft.* The presentation of these powers is given with great fullness of historical illustration. — *Allgemeines Statsrecht,* vol. i. pp. 446, 503.

These powers in their origin and content are not determined in some historical accident; nor are they merely the expedient of human ingenuity, for which some substitute may be found in some other and better expedient, whereby, for instance, legislative or judicial functions shall be superseded; nor are they the sequence of some formal law. They are the manifestation of that which is immanent in the organism of the nation.[1]

These powers represent the will of the organic people in its civil and political organization. Their origin is in the necessary being of the nation, and their action is its normal process.

The necessary characteristics of these powers may be traced in their structure.

These powers are organic. They are not the mere incident of the action of the state, their distinction is not accidental nor arbitrary. They are not merely an artificial contrivance; their connection and their action is not as in some ingeniously devised mechanism, but as subsistent in the civil and political organism their action is unitary and organic, and in the civil and political development is their ampler organization.

There is an abstract conception which represents the state as simple not complex, as arbitrary not natural in its structure, but the law of organic life appears in it also —

> "More complex, is more perfect, owning more
> Discourse, more widely wise."

[1] Kant finds the source and the necessity for these powers in the formula of logic, and they are presented as corresponding to its sequence. But they can have their ground in no formal or empty conception, either in logic or law; their ground is in the organism of the state, that is, the political organism, and their correspondence is to its real constitution. The presentation of Kant is consistent, however, with his formal conception of freedom and of rights. — *Rechtslehre*, sec. xiv.

"The exercise of power, whether by an individual or a nation, is naturally divided into thinking, judging, and doing. Action implies all three: thought to originate, will and force to execute a conceived purpose, judgment to compare it with rules of conduct." — Fisher. *The Trial of the Constitution*, p. 41.

The tendency which this conception constantly induces, in its correspondence with an empty and barren conception of freedom, is to eradicate those institutions which have been established in the ampler organization of the state.[1] The substitute, when all are swept away, is the reconstruction of the whole after some abstract scheme or some formal design. But freedom is not found in the vacant spaces which this devastating force has opened, nor in the sweep of their bleak and windy plains; the assumption again combines the conceit of individual egoism with the limitless caprice in which freedom is feigned to exist.

There is also a representation of these powers, as simply a well adjusted balance, when each is of itself negative or merely restrictive of the other. A trivial and superficial description of their origin and relation is formed after this pattern. The nation is represented as identical with the formal construction of its government, and described as simply an association of men under laws; then a power to make its laws must exist; and as some power is required to execute them, an executive is established; and then as an arbiter is required between them to regulate and settle their differences, a judiciary is established. This representation is defective, since it fails to define the content of these powers and their relation to each other and to the nation, and their subsistence in the unity of the nation. It is also destitute of an historical justification; there has been no people the process of whose government it could presume to describe. Its postulate is a formal and mechanical conception of the state.

[1] "Nothing is more deceptive or more dangerous than the pretense of a desire to simplify government. If we will abolish the distinction of branches and have but one branch, if we will abolish jury trials and leave all to the judge; if we will then ordain that the legislator shall himself be that judge; and if we place the executive power in the same hands, we may readily simplify government. We may easily bring it to the simplest of all forms, — a pure despotism." — Webster's *Works*, vol. iv. p. 122.

These powers are coördinate; that is, neither is so related to another, that it could be defined as in itself a negation, and as existent only as the instrument of another. Such a definition would make the action of a power mechanical, and would leave but one or two actual powers in the state. It would be incorrect to represent the judiciary as existing to receive the opinions and to justify the actions of the legislature, or to represent the executive as only the passive agent and pliant tool in the hands of the legislature, and neither of them as having a determinate character of its own.

Since these powers subsist in the organism of the whole, one cannot proceed from another, nor derive its content from another; each subsists in the being and immediately in the sovereignty of the nation. They are, each in its own sphere, invested with the power and formal sovereignty of the nation. Each is not determined from or through another, but, within the limitation of its necessary sphere, exists in the determination of the whole. Neither can assume to represent, in its isolation from the others, the sovereignty of the whole.[1]

These powers are coextensive; they do not exclude each other, but each implies the other and the action of the other; and each acts in and through the whole. Thus, no individual and no section can be entirely isolated from them.

These powers are correlative; not only neither has its ground in the other, but neither has its ground in itself; its ground is only in the whole. Since they subsist in the nation they cannot be regarded as isolated and self-subsistent, but as existent in a necessary correlation. They are not separate sovereignties, but each is subsistent in

[1] "It should be remembered as an eternal truth, that whatever power is wholly independent, is absolute also; in theory only at first, while the spirit of the people is up, but in practice as fast as that relaxes." — President Jefferson, *Letters*, Sept. 6, 1819.

the sovereignty of the nation in its unity. They are constituted not in a formal but an organic unity, and therefore each is in necessary relation to the other, and is necessary to the completeness of the other.

The common phrase, "a division of powers," may become the source of error and disaster. An actual division would imply the division of the nation itself, and the severance of its sovereignty. The very assumption of a sole and entire sovereignty, by each or either power, would tend toward the dismemberment of the nation, through the ultimate strife of the one necessarily to subject the others to itself. The isolation of powers, neither of which subsisted in the sovereignty of the nation, but each of which, as complete and self-subsistent, held a barren sovereignty in itself, would make the realization of a national unity impossible, since the unity involved in sovereignty, would still strive to attain its necessary realization; but this would become the occasion of conflict, and the actual and entire sovereignty of the one power would be attained only in the subversion of the others. In the constant recognition of this fact there is the strength of each, and each is sustained in its normal action.[1]

[1] The argument in *The Federalist* has for its object the refutation of the assumption of the entire isolation and severance of these powers, — it is the assertion of their necessary correlation. President Madison stated as its aim the proposition, — "that unless these departments be so far connected and blended as to give to each a constitutional control over the others, the degree of separation which the maxim requires as essential to a free government can never be duly maintained." — *The Federalist*, No. xlviii.

Of the consequence of their entire division Calhoun says, "Instead of a government it would be little better than the régime of three separate and conflicting departments, ultimately to be controlled by the executive in consequence of its having the command of the patronage, etc." — Calhoun's *Works*, vol. i. p. 374.

There is no exception to this statement in the writings of any eminent modern publicist. Bluntschli says, "The entire division of powers would involve the dissolution of the unity of the state, and the dismemberment of the political body." — *Allgemeines Statsrechts*, vol. i. p. 450.

"The error involved in the maxim 'a division of powers' is almost universally recognized in the science of politics, but it has not been until it has wrought the

There is thus in the government, no aggregate of powers, but the manifestation of an inner and an ideal unity as it exists in the sovereignty of the organic people.

These powers are the distinct powers of the civil and political organism. There is for each a distinct function. As the error which would isolate them is destructive of unity, so also the error which would identify them is destructive of freedom.

They are distinguished in their nature, in their content, in their form and object of action, and in their institution. They are also vested in different persons. To identify one with another, so that its own normal action should be suspended and its content determined by another, would subvert the development of the whole.

The distinction of these powers, in the organization of the nation, tends toward the realization of freedom. It is in the formation of these relations that the freedom of the people is established. When the organization is imperfect, when, for instance, the sole power is vested in a popular assembly which enacts the law, and then enforces and administers order under it, and judges all cases that arise from it, the result, in the construction of a power of unrelated and unlimited action, is an absolutism. And

greatest confusion in theory and disaster in practice. It is refuted alike by the facts which have been adduced to sustain it, by logic and by the prudence of the state. Instead of the common endeavor toward the common good, it would result in conflict, and the antagonism of divided powers, and instead of stable freedom it would lead to anarchy." — R. von Mohl, *Encyklopädie der Staatswissenchaften*, p. 112. See also R. von Mohl's *Literateur und Geschichte der Staatswissenschaften*, vol. i. p. 397. Stahl, *Philosophie des Rechts*, vol. ii. sec. 2, p. 198. Hegel, *Philosophie des Rechts*, p. 272.

The interrelation of these powers in the constitution of England, in some respects, is one of its best results. The obligations of Montesquieu and of Hegel to its study are well known. It is to be noticed that their closer interrelation increases the actual power and capacity of the Parliament, through its ampler organization. Thus the Parliament and the Crown together constitute the government; and the ministers of the Crown are the members of the Parliament, and the judges sit also as members of the Parliament, but with no vote, and the action of each may modify but does not control the action of the other, and the realized sovereignty of the state is only in their unity.

when one power destroys the others, or assumes their offices and capacities, or usurps their functions, and there remains only the unrelated and unlimited action of a single and separate power, the consequence is again the same,—the destruction of freedom.[1] In the French Revolution, the legislative destroyed the executive power, and then the executive in turn destroyed the legislative, and this subversion of the organization of the whole left the way open to an imperialism.

The distinction in these powers is illustrated in the fact, that while in each there is a field for the highest attainment, the special qualifications for each are different. He who excels in deliberation, is often lacking in executive force, and a speculative breadth of thought often brings a larger hopefulness than is justified by events; and he who is clearest and firmest in action may often be without largeness of discourse; and each may be wanting in that fair judicial spirit which is open to all sides.

These powers therefore are not to be vested in the same persons, since they are so distinct that each demands for itself an exclusive vocation, and their offices in the modern state are obviously beyond the capacity of the same persons. Their reference in their offices to different persons, who are resident in different chambers, is itself, in the careful maintenance of their distinction, a guaranty of freedom.

These powers in their organization cannot be too strong nor too great, since they have their origin in the civil and

1 "Through Locke and Montesquieu, the great truth has been won, and it constitutes their undying renown, that the participation of the different elements, in the exercise of the power of the state, and that too in its threefold functions, is the foundation of civil and political freedom; and on the other hand, when one and the same power, whether a prince or a popular assembly, alone exercises all functions, despotism is the inevitable result." — Stahl, *Philosophie des Rechts*, vol. ii. sec. 2, p. 203.

"The accumulation of all powers, legislative, executive, and judicial, in the same hands, whether of one, a few, or many, and whether hereditary, self-appointed, or elective, may justly be pronounced the very definition of tyranny." — President Madison, *The Federalist*, No. xlvii.

political organism; but it is a merely formal conception, which is the premise of the phrase "an equality of powers." It assumes their division and then aims to establish their equilibrium, regarding them as external forces to be pitted against each other. This predication of a formal equality, as if between mechanical forces, fails of the necessary conception of the nation as organic. The phrase has no real significance nor consistent application, and it has to learn again the wisdom well nigh as old as the state itself, of the political fable of the belly and the members. In the political as in the physical organism, each member has its own functions, and the full and normal action of each is necessary to the normal action of the other and the normal being of the whole.

The representation of the equality of these powers has moreover no historical justification, and when they have been thus held and balanced against each other, the balance has always been a varying and disturbed one, until in their entire separation, which the proposition assumes, an inevitable conflict has demonstrated the greater strength of some one power. Thus in periods when the people is summoned to meet insurrection or invasion, the strength of the executive is more manifest, while in the subsequent construction of order the strength of the legislature appears. In these succeeding periods, the assumption of a formal equality of powers would tend to produce weakness or conflict, or to impair and retard the action of the whole. In the prudence of the state it is not the feigned or the constructive equality of the powers which should be sustained, but their necessary correlation, so that the action of each may promote and modify and not subvert the normal action of the other.

The representation of these powers each as the necessary restriction to the other is imperfect. It has its premise in the distrust of power as in itself evil, and implies not a spirit of unity but of latent hostility and dread of each other. This proposition, as Hegel says, makes ill-will and aversion the foundation of the powers of the state.

The result is also negative; there is only the formation of a system of checks, which also require other checks without end. The object set before each power is to reduce the other to a negation; their construction is the adoption of the economy of a political house that Jack built. Since each, to use the common illustration, is the offset to the other, each is to be placed as a makeweight in the opposite scale, but the balance, if evenly held, is a dead weight. It is constructive of nothing. Power implies energy, and each must act in its own normal conception, and is not to be apprehended primarily as restrictive of the action of the other.

The character of these powers, and of their necessary relation to each other, appears in their relation to the physical force of the nation, — its military. This embraces some of the most important principles in politics, and in the administration of the state.

It is evident at the outset, that the organized physical force of the nation does not constitute, in correspondence with these powers, a distinct power in the government, since instead of being constituted in the moral organism of the nation, it is the physical force wielded by the nation, and it is not existent in a sphere in which it is self determined as are the necessary and normal powers, and the law of its action is that of subordination.

It is the organized might of the whole, — the nation in its unity and entirety; in it men move in the highest personal spirit and freedom, and this is the root of valor, but the many as one, and therefore they march as an host, and with the accordance of music, and the ensigns and symbols of the unity of the nation.

But its determination is in the nation in its political organism. Its members are citizens before they are soldiers; if they were not citizens they would not be soldiers. Its action is in conformance to a strict discipline. The authority which immediately directs it is by command.

Of the normal powers of the nation, it is evident that the judiciary has no immediate relation to the military, and the military has none to it. The action of the judiciary, is only through a constabulary.

The executive is the head of the physical force of the nation, — the commander-in-chief of the army and navy. This belongs to his office as the representative of the unity of the nation, and of its external sovereignty. The army and navy in actual service must also have a single commander-in-chief, since it cannot be directed in the field by a council or an assembly. But the executive, as commander-in-chief, is a part of the army, and in that capacity, as entirely in identity with it as any officer or private, and thus all that refers to the army and navy refers to him as officially included in it.

If now this power of the executive as commander-in-chief were sole and supreme, the whole force of the nation would be constituted no longer necessarily in conformance to law which is the normal expression of the will of the nation, but in subjection to a single individual will, and the result would be the institution in and over the nation of an imperial power. There would be in the formal constitution only a formal but not an actual limitation to this power, since on this assumption it could suspend the actual operation of the other normal powers. The power instituted would be imperial, whether hereditary or elective in its origin. Its possessors might succeed each other as rapidly and irregularly as the elective emperors in the catalogues of the annalists of Rome, or each continue for a certain term of years or for life, but this would not change the character of their power.

The subjection of the physical force of the nation, whose

principle rightly is that of subordination, to a single individual will upon whose action there is in the organization of the whole no limitation, would tend to the subversion of the nation. It would no longer exist as an organism whose subsistence was in freedom, but there would be the sway of an individual will, to whose intent there was no limitation.

The nation is constituted not in subjection to a single individual will, but in the organization of and the obedience to law. Its freedom and rights have their institution in positive law. Its force is to stand in and maintain the authority of law. To open before it another course would be the construction of a power which, in the exercise of its private opinion and fiat, would be above and separate from the law. The only and the ultimate authority which the nation recognizes is the law, and no citizen, nor soldier, nor lawgiver, nor ruler can be above and separate from the law.

The clear discrimination of the military from the civil and political powers, appears first in the later periods of Roman history. In so far as it places the soldier before the citizen, or makes the duty of the soldier precedent to the duty of the citizen, it indicates the utter destruction of national life and the construction of a physical force which had no ground in a moral order. But in the higher organization of the nation, the relation of the military — the organized physical force — to the law must be clearly defined. The imperialism which would leave it to the ultimate and unlimited control of a single individual will, also separates the soldier from the citizen, and is necessarily the subversion of the nation and its freedom.

The military is therefore constituted and organized by law. Its immediate direction, which is by word of command, is necessarily with its commander or commanders, but the ultimate direction of the whole, as the organized force of the nation, must be through law, and by no command can it be carried outside of the law. The ultimate direction then must be with that power, which, in the normal process, alone can affirm its will as law. The legislature certainly cannot assume executive functions, and the immediate direction is necessarily with the executive, but the executive in the capacity of a military commander is in identity with the army and navy and simply a soldier of of the nation, although in rank the first soldier. The legislature is not to command the army, since its action is in the form of law and not of command, but since the assertion of the will of the nation is in the form of law and not of command, the ultimate direction must still be with the legislative power, and the military can never be carried beyond nor removed from its ultimate control.

This object has been guarded and secured in many ways, and its constitutional guaranties and securities form the amplest illustration of the relation of the legislative power to the military. The legislative power alone can declare war[1] and as implicit in this, alone can conclude peace. The military in all its ranks, and in the person of a private or captain or commander-in-chief, is immobile, until, as regards the operations of war, it is called to act by the declaration of the Congress. The legislature alone can "provide for the common defense,"[2] and "raise and support armies."[3] The army and navy has no existence until the Congress shall form it. The legislature alone can provide for the "organizing, arming, and disciplining"[4] of the army, and alone can "make rules for the government and regulation of the land and naval forces."[5] To its government and regulations the whole force is necessarily subject. There is no officer, who by command can authorize their violation, and no member, either officer or private, is exempt from their operation, and as a soldier the executive is subject to the government and regulations which the Congress may adopt. The President certainly is the exec-

1 Art. I. sec. 8, cl. 2. 2 *Ibid.* cl. 1. 3 *Ibid.* cl. 12.
4 *Ibid.* cl. 16. 5 *Ibid.* cl. 14.

utive before he is the commander-in-chief, and has power which is external to the latter office; and no action by Congress in reference to the latter can encroach upon the sphere, or interfere with the immediate action of the presidential office. The legislature also alone can provide for the calling out of the military to "execute the laws, suppress insurrections, and repel invasions."[1] It alone has control "by exclusive legislation, in all cases, over forts, magazines, arsenals, and dockyards."[2] There is certainly in the executive the power necessarily in every nation, to call out its force to execute laws, to suppress insurrection, or to repel invasion, and this becomes his immediate duty in the supreme necessity, but the constitutional limitations to this authority become the evidence of the residence of the ultimate direction of the military in the legislature. The Congress alone can maintain the army, and furnish the means and munitions of war; it alone can "support armies,"[3] and make all appropriations for their sustenance, and thus the very condition of their existence is in the act of the Congress, and in the house which is in the more immediate control of the people. It is thus only by an act of the legislature that any soldier of the nation, from the commander-in-chief to the private, may obtain a single requisition of the war-office, or own a sword or carry a gun. Then also the appropriation which the Congress may grant is restricted to the term, when it again is subject to the election of the people; "no appropriation for that use shall be for a longer time than two years."[4]

The legislative power alone has the ultimate determination, as to the declaration of martial law, or what in substance corresponds to it, the suspension of the *habeas corpus*. Martial law, in the celebrated charge of Cockburn,

[1] Art. I. sec. 8, cl. 16. [2] *Ibid.* cl. 17. [3] *Ibid.* cl. 12.

[4] *Ibid.* In the constitution of England, to which this clause corresponds, the army and navy in this respect is subject to the Parliament, and the Mutiny Bill, by which the army is organized, is limited in its operation to one year, and is annually enacted at the session of Parliament.

C. J., is defined as "either the law of necessity, which will always warrant the use of violence by a state in self-defense, although the imperative nature of the case must be shown as a justification of the act, or on the other hand, military law to which soldiers alone are liable, and which is a system of fixed rules laid down by the articles of war; beyond this," he adds, "there is no such law in existence as martial law, and no power in the Crown to proclaim it."[1]

The power to establish martial law, in the latter sense, belongs expressly and exclusively to the Congress, since it alone can "make rules for the government and regulation of the land and naval forces." The power in the former sense must belong also in its ultimate determination to the Congress. The declaration of martial law in this sense, is in substance the same as the suspension of the *habeas corpus*, since each is the formal assertion of the right of the nation in its supreme necessity, the one being the form in which it is established in Germany, France and Italy, while the other is its form in England and the United States.

The declaration of martial law, or the suspension of the *habeas corpus*, is the intermission of the ordinary course of law, and of the tribunals to which all appeal may be made. It places the locality included in its operation no longer under the government of law. It interrupts the process of rights and the procedure of courts, and restricts the independence of civil administration. There is substituted for these the intent of the individual. To this there is in the civil order no formal limitation. In its immediate action, it allows beyond itself no obligation and acknowledges no responsibility. Its command or its decree is the only law; its movement may be secret, and its

[1] The Queen *vs.* Nelson and Brand. London: 1867. Martial law is defined as "the will of the general who commands the army."—*Digest*, p. 130. War Department, 1866.

decisions are open to the inquiry of no judge and the investigation of no tribunal. There is no positive power which may act or be called upon to act, to stay its caprice or to check its arbitrary career, since judgment and execution are in its own command, and the normal action and administration is suspended, and the organized force of the whole is subordinate to it.

The power which appears in the suspension of the *habeas corpus* is a necessary right. It is the assertion of the right in the supreme necessity of the state and in the imminent or immediate peril of the people to suspend the ordinary process of rights. It is the right of the nation which is precedent to the rights of the individual or the community. The inquiry has been, as to its residence, in the legislative or the executive power. The evidence of its ultimate residence in the former, appears in its nature, in its historical institution, and in the conditions in which it may be formed.

It is a right of the nation in its sovereignty. But there is always implied in sovereignty the conception of law, and the legislative power is the only one which in its action can affirm its determination as law. Thus Blackstone says: "sovereignty and legislation are convertible terms, and one cannot subsist without the other." This power, moreover, is the only one, the nature and method of whose action tends in itself to exclude the arbitrary. Thus, as the act of the sovereignty of the nation in its highest expression, it is to be presumed that this is not wholly withdrawn from the legislative power. Its reference to the legislature would also correspond with the residence of the sovereign rights of the nation, in immediate analogy with it, as for instance, the declaration of war.

The government is, morever, in its normal structure, a government of laws. If then the legislature by its own enactment suspends the ordinary action of the government, there is still, in its ultimate conception, the continuance of law, and as the power from which the law proceeds declares, by its enactment, the suspension and then the restoration of the *habeas corpus*, there appears still, in the permanent and substantial order, the maintenance of law. The act is divested of its apparent antagonism, and wears no longer the appearance of a civil cataclysm. But to refer the suspension of the *habeas corpus* to the executive, seems an immediate contradiction to the normal process of the nation and the subversion of its order.

To refer this office to the executive might, in fact, occasion the negation of the other normal powers, as in their process they became subject to the single power in whose exclusive control this act was placed, and by whom it might alone be exercised. The form might remain, and the judicial power could still open its courts, but the act of the executive would decide if any might seek their protection, and the legislative power could continue its sessions, but all laws might be rendered inoperative by the sole actual power, the executive, — "the will of the commander-in-chief as general, commanding the army." It is not implied that, if the action were vested in the executive power, it would remove the other powers, since this would be the subversion of the organization of the nation, and the destruction of its constitutional order; but this would not be requisite to its design, since the act of the executive, in so far as it might elect, would be, in fact, an absolute veto upon the action of the other powers, and would enable the executive to avoid all laws enacted by the legislature and all decisions of the judges.

If, moreover, the executive alone held this office, it would allow an individual to originate a condition of affairs, in which not only an individual will could act without control, but the will would be the same which originated the condition. The act and the whole subsequent power resultant from it, would be referred to the same department of government, and that resident in an individual. It would not be possible for a people to construct a broader highway for a tyrant to come in. It would concede the assumption of all power beyond all actual limitation, to an individual. The political body can scarcely contemplate the possibility thus, of the accumulation in the hands of one person of all its powers, beyond its normal control and in the cessation of its normal process.

The whole body of rights, moreover, in which freedom subsists, both civil and political, is in the process of positive law, and to allow its suspension to an individual who then could alone determine the continuance of the period of that suspension, is not only what the nation could not concede, but it is a power which no member of the nation should possess, since the inevitable disaster which follows all arbitrary action is too great and the contingency of such action in the weakness and the aberration of the individual is too near.

The highest guaranty of the freedom of the nation, and the prudent limitation to this act is in its being so construed that the suspension of the *habeas corpus* by one power shall require the immediate transfer of all authority under it to another and separate power. The legislature in suspending the *habeas corpus* does not assume the resultant authority, but refers it to the executive, from whom in its discretion, it may withdraw it.

There is the necessity for the most careful and yet the most ample provision, for this act and the exercise of this right, in the constitution. It is a right of the nation in its sovereignty, and it has been held and exercised by every historical nation. There has been none but has been called to pass through crises, when the evil forces assailing its life and unity were so many, or their attack so sudden, that the omission to exercise it would be the abandonment of the plainest political obligation, and the impotence and crime of government itself, and might involve the ultimate and lasting subversion of all rights. And yet, since the legislature cannot always act with the immediate energy which may be demanded, and does not act continuously, in its supreme necessity, in the actual or in the imminent peril of the nation, it becomes not only the office but the imperative duty of the executive to assert it. But the action of the executive in its assertion is here subject to certain definite limitations; firstly, it should assume under no pretense whatever control over the legislative and judicial powers, to obstruct their organization, or to approach the persons of those in whom these powers are vested by the people; and secondly, the legislature should be summoned, if not in session, it may be by the act itself, and the imperative necessity of it should be made to appear, and its justification presented; and when the latter has been rendered, an act of indemnity may be granted by the legislative power, the process of whose action has been suspended, and the further conclusion as to the continuance of the suspension of the *habeas corpus* revert to the legislative power.[1]

But the investiture of the legislative power with this right illustrates, also finally, the residence in it, of the ultimate direction of the military, since, excepting as the duty, with definite limitations, is for the moment imposed upon the executive, the legislature alone can call the military into action. There can be between these normal powers indeed no actual conflict, except in the most awful crime,

[1] In the constitution of England, the Parliament alone has the power to suspend the *habeas corpus*, but, in the interval of its session, or if necessity demanded sudden and secret action, during its session, the ministers of the Crown have exercised the power; but it has been always followed by the solicitation of a bill of indemnity, and the consent of the Parliament has been held requisite to justify it, and since the statute 31 Charles II., this has been always asked and allowed.

Sir Edward Coke said in the first Parliament of Charles I., of the king's claim of a right to imprison, and of the decision of the judges, "What is it but to declare upon record that any subject committed by such absolute command may be detained in prison forever? What doth this tend to but the utter subversion of the choice, liberty, and right belonging to every freeborn subject in this kingdom? A Parliament brings judges, officers, and all men into good order."

and then, in the destruction of the organization of the nation by the very powers called to act in its constitutional order, the individual is thrown back upon himself, and each has only to remember that he is a citizen before he is a soldier, and only a soldier because he is a citizen.

The more perfect organization of the legislative, executive and judicial powers in the government is attained in the long historical development of the people, but their institution is the first object of the constitution.

The immediate aim is that they shall not be severed, so that there shall be an isolation that induces alienation between them, and that they shall not be merged, so that their separate functions shall be impaired, but their construction is to conform to their nature and correlation. Since they are the manifestation of that which is immanent in the civil and political organism, the constitution may define, but, as it did not create, it cannot change their nature nor their attributes. They are not the product of a political empiric, and the ingenuity of no individual and no convention can make them other than they are. The change of these powers in the being of the nation would presume the change of the nature of the reason and judgment and will in man. They are as in a musical notation, where the separate notes are necessary to a full harmony, and yet these notes are not the creation of art, nor could art change them, and it is thus that the powers of the state are described by Shakespeare, "as converging to one natural close, like music."

The constitution is to describe these powers and their limitation, but their strength, in which each is involved with the other, is in their construction, according to their unity and necessary correlation, and their formal description apart from this will not avail much. Their action can be determined in the words of President Madison, by "no mere demarcation upon parchment." Mr. Hamilton says, also, "as all external provisions are found to be inadequate, the defect must be supplied by so contriving the interior structure of the government as that its several constituent parts may, by their mutual relations, be the means of keeping each other in their places." [1]

The sphere of each in its limitations is to be so construed, that the legislature shall not execute its own laws, nor decide in a conflict of rights under the laws; and the executive shall not decree its own will as law, nor decide in a conflict of rights; and the judiciary shall not establish its opinions as laws constructive of the political order. The legislature alone can enact laws, and its act, by the veto allowed the executive, is detained and restricted, but it is not imperatively determined, and its enactment is to be thereafter enforced by the executive, and to be applied by the judiciary in judgment on cases where controversy arises under the laws, but the legislature cannot assume the execution of laws, nor intervene to conduct their immediate administration; it can not render judgment between parties, nor forbid a judicial procedure so as to impair the vindication of rights, and the only case which can be brought before it, is that in which the senate is constituted as a court, if the people shall appear with charges against the executive or the judges. The executive is to execute and administer the laws, and it has in its veto the qualified restriction of legislative action, and is to communicate to the legislature whatever may concern the state of the nation, but it cannot be summoned before the legislature, except on the presentation of charges for its impeachment. The judiciary has its province most clearly defined, since its action is in judgment, and judgment is only of force as the expression of conviction, and as subject to no external control; its decision in all cases is final of those cases, and in its final judication is open to no revision.

These powers in their organization are to be shaped

[1] *The Federalist*, No. ii.

through history, in the patient toil which will care most that nothing of value received from the past be allowed to perish, but will hold their construction in any moment as very far from perfect.

The interrelation of the powers is to be so defined, that neither shall be isolated from another to become its opponent, nor subjected to another to become its instrument. The action of either, when, in its alienation, it becomes the impediment to another, will result in the weakness of the government, and tend to the corruption of the whole. If their interrelation is not clearly defined and established, there will be, through vagueness, a greater risk of divergence, or their action will proceed without dignity or decent respect, or through irregular channels, or with undue influences.

There will be the resort also to special and temporary devices and contrivances by the one power to hinder or control the other. While the mode of communication between them is not clearly established, slight and irregular means will be introduced. Then the condition of affairs is ascertained through private channels, or the casual testimony of investigating committees. The executive becomes only the man at the other end of the avenue; but the legislature is then only a crowd of men at this end of the avenue. The confusion is increased, and the relative strength of the powers is disturbed by the neglect of the legislature to organize a civil service, so that the executive has a vast preponderance given to it in certain intervals. But the most obvious danger is in the too wide separation of the legislative power from the executive and the judiciary. The isolation of the latter from the legislative power, becomes the source of indifference in the legislative power to them, and then of their weakness, and in the consequent disorganization, there is the defect of the whole. Thus Stahl says, "the complete isolation of the executive strips it of everything and makes it the tool of the legislative power."

The high offices of a minister of a department of administration, are imperfectly organized. Their growth and number are beyond the provision of the constitution, and are to be determined in the historical necessity of the state. While their immediate relation and administrative responsibility is to the executive, they are more than merely its registrars. It has been suggested that the ministers of the executive, in conformance to some modern political constitutions, should sit in the chambers of the legislature, but without a vote, and a member or attorney of the judiciary should also sit with them, but without a vote. This might improve legislation, since it would give to the legislature a higher strength in its ampler and more complex organization, and aid toward the removal of the breach between the powers, and open clear and definite means of communication between them, instead of the vague and indefinite, and therefore perilous ways which now alone exist.

The legislative, executive and judicial powers, in their formal organization, constitute the government.

The legislature is the precedent power in the government. Since the government is of law, and the assertion of the sovereignty of the nation is in positive law, the power which can alone constitute its determination as law, in its relation to the other powers, is necessarily precedent. It is not, that these powers do not each subsist immediately in the sovereignty of the nation, and it is not, that the other powers are subordinate, since the action of each, in its own sphere, can neither be directed nor determined in its content by another; but in the normal process the inception of civil and political action is in the legislature. It is not the power which executes the law, nor the power which interprets the law in adjudging cases under the law, but the power which in its nature can enact its will as law, that in the formative process is precedent.

The legislative power has the definition of its sphere of

action and the enumeration of its special powers in the formal constitution, but the objects of its action exist only in the change and circumstance of history. It alone is constructive, and alone can act with a reconstructive power in the historical crises which come to every nation, for which it is not in the capacity of a formal constitution to provide, and for which it could no more prescribe than it could predict the circumstance of history, — epochs which no individual prescience could anticipate and no expiring convention could forestall. The political course is not to be shaped by an executive decree, for this, apart from law, is authority for no man, nor by a judicial decision, for this has only a revisionary power, but in the process of law, and therefore by the power which alone can enact its will as law. The recognition of authority, in the formative course of the nation, in any other form than as law is anarchic, and is the inauguration of an imperial power. It is to law alone that every individual, both the power that makes and the power that executes the law, is subject.

The distinction between the constitution and the laws is indeed fundamental; but it is to be considered that the formation of the constitution is in its nature a legislative act, as the constitution, when formed, is the supreme law, and every amendment is also in its inception a legislative act.

The legislative power is regulative of the order and organization of the other powers, in so far as this is not defined by the constitution, but is left to be determined in the continuous process of the state. The other powers, indeed, subsist with it in the organic constitution. It did not create them, and it can neither nullify them, nor assume their functions. Because they are subject to its action as law, it does not follow that they are subordinate to it, since it also is subject to law; this does not reduce the executive simply to an instrument of its intent, and the judiciary to a registrar of its opinions.[1]

[1] "To prevent collision in the action of the government, without impairing

There is also, in the representative structure of the legislative power, a vested authority, in relation to the other powers, which they have not to each other nor to it. Thus, on an alleged violation of his trust, it may summon an executive or a judicial officer before it, and if a high crime or misdemeanor is proven, he may be convicted by it; but no other power has a corresponding office, and it alone can judge its own members, and determine their qualifications. It also holds those who are to fill the judiciary subject to its confirmation, and a vacancy in the executive, in certain circumstances, may be filled by it, but if any occur in itself, it must be referred immediately to the people. It also is to receive from the people the announcement of an election of the President, and to induct him into office.

The more perfect structure of the legislature has been the index of the progress of the political spirit of the people. In the higher political development its organization has become ampler and it has embodied more varied elements of strength. This has been the principal aim of modern political constitutions. The effort has been also to make it more free, and less subject to repressive legislative codes and rules, without impairing its power of coming to a conclusion. But the construction of the legislative power, its history, its order, its system of rules, the number of which it should consist, the form of election, the duration of office, the dual system of houses, and the like, is a special study.[1]

the independence of the departments, all discretionary power was vested in the legislature. Without this, each would have had equal right to determine what powers were necessary and proper to carry into execution the powers vested in it, which could not fail to bring them into dangerous conflicts."—Calhoun's *Works*, vol. i. p. 346.

Bracton said, " The king ought not to be subject to man, but to God and the law." Christian cites *Year Books*, 19 Henry VI. 31: " The law is the highest inheritance which the king has: for by the law he himself and all his subjects are governed, and if there was no law there would be no king and no inheritance."

[1] Bluntschli says, but it is to be noticed that the executive is regarded as in-

The executive is the power to which belongs the execution of the laws and the administration of affairs. It is in immediate direction of all the departments of administration. It is the head of the army and navy, and in command of them for internal order and external defense. But the name — the executive — imperfectly indicates the character and dignity of the office and even its relation to the other powers. While it is entirely in subjection to law, and cannot pass beyond the law, it far transcends the office of a merely executory instrument of the legislature. Nor can it be described even as the exclusive executive, since in the ordinary course of affairs the law is not executed, but is pronounced and applied by all concerned, or more strictly, the law may be said to execute itself, since the proclamation is presumed to be identical with the execution.[1] The name still less indicates its relation to the judicial power, since the execution of the judgment of the court is in the immediate authority of the court, which acts through its own constabulary, and it is only in its discretion that it may call for the aid of the executive. While imperfectly denoting the relation to these powers, the name is itself dry and formal, and suggestive rather of a pedantic and scholastic distinction; there is in the office a far larger conception that embraces higher duties and trusts.

It is representative of the unity of the nation, and its unity in personality. It is therefore vested in one person. It is representative of the majesty of the nation, and it is to preserve and protect and defend the constitution in the unbroken supremacy of law. It is representative of the

tegral with the legislative power, " Die gesetzgebende Gewalt bestimmt die Stats-und-Rechts-ordnung selbst, und ist ihr höchster, das ganze Volk umfassender Ausdruck. Alle andern Gewalten üben ihre Functionen innerhalb der bestehenden Stats-und-Rechts-ordnung in einzelnen concreten und wechselenden Fallen aus."— *Allgemeines Statrecht*, vol. i. p. 452.

[1] The signature of the executive is always presumed to be upon a law, and indicates something of its necessary relation to the legislature, and while it is only a form, it yet has a significance, and would be insisted on by one who guards the executive office.

organized might of the nation, the power of the nation in its totality. It is therefore the head of the army and navy. It is representative of the nation in its external sovereignty, and the nation acts immediately through it, in its relation to other nations. It is through it alone that all communication with other nations proceeds, and it alone is to receive ministers and embassies from them, and is to send its own to them. It is representative of the nation in its unity, beyond all interests and sections and factions and parties, and is in identity with none of these, but in immediate relation to the people in its entirety. It is representative of the relation of the nation to every person who is a member of the nation. This has had no higher exemplar in the life of nations, than President Washington and President Lincoln. They kept a conscious relation to all, and they heard the petitions of all the people.

In the conscious life of a free people, it is a power which is not left to be determined — if that word may be applied in this connection — by any accident, and it is not restricted to a single line of family descent, but he who is called to it is to be called of the whole people. There is no form in the barbaric constitutions, and no type drawn from the confusion of the changing conditions of the feudal age so noble as this, in which the nation is manifested in its moral being, and no imperialism has such elements of strength as this, in which there is the representation of the nation in its conscious purpose, and in the recognition of the majesty of law. The inauguration of its power, is the expression of the conscious determination of the people, and in the fulfillment of law.

It is to guard the unity of the nation, and to protect the people and the land in all perils. Since the judicial power is withdrawn by its process from immediate action, and the legislative power is without the continuous action and the capacity for immediate action, which some sudden or imminent peril to the nation might demand, it becomes its duty and power, in the emergency, in the defined limits of the constitution, to suspend the *habeas corpus*, and to call out the armed force of the nation; but the provision for this act is to be so clear that it may not become in itself a source of peril.

It represents the might of the whole in its relation to the individual, and in it the nation stands forth in its unity on the approach of insurrection from within or invasion from without. It holds for the individual the power of pardon, and this is always its prerogative.

There has been through all the conflicts of history the exhibition of no quality in the sovereignty of nations, which does not belong to it, and there has been no tyranny but is alien to it. Its authority is in the supremacy of law and its power is in the majesty of the nation. The phrase is, the king can do no wrong, and it has a deep significance in the assertion of the sovereignty of the nation as subsisting in its being as a moral person; and every act which does not proceed from this, or is in variance with this, is unkingly.[1]

The construction of the executive power was widely considered in the formation of the constitution. The conditions of its organization were, that he who was called to it should be called from the whole people, and that it should be left to no accident. There was the suggestion of various forms, as its entrustment to an elect council, or to a person elected from the legislature and responsible to that, and its duration for life or for different terms. The proposition adopted was its investure in one person, elected by a college, which was elected by the people; and the term of office, open to a reëlection, was four years. The project of an electoral college failed, continuing only as a form, and it remains as an illustration of the want of inherent strength in a constitutional form which

1 "He that does injustice dishonours the king." — Samuel Mulford, 1714. *Doc. Hist. of N. Y.* vol. iii. p. 371.

does not correspond to the purpose of the people, since in every election some name has been immediately before the people. This course alone has an historical justification. It has been truly said, that the people can best appreciate great services to the nation, and great qualities in action, and they are without the envy and the prejudice of the narrow circles of cliques and parties, and no separate interest as of a certain family or a class prevails with them, and they are indifferent to the private ambitions of great men.

The executive power in its organization is vested in one person, and no other form is consistent with it. The plan of an executive council was sustained by Milton in his description of a free state. It was the constitution of the executive in the triumvirate of Rome; but its internal dissension illustrated the defect of a plural system. It was established in France, in the directory of five; but the want of unity and decision, and the variance in this collegial rule, opened the way to the power of the First Consul. There is an inevitable weakness in the assumption of executive power by a college, as a senate or parliament.

The higher organization of the executive power comes in the historical development of the people, giving to it greater strength, and a more perfect correlation to the other necessary powers in the nation, and its better conception is gathered from the work of those who fill it best.

The judicial power has its sphere in the interpretation and application of laws in a conflict of rights. It renders judgment in a controversy in law between man and man, and man and the state. Its conclusion is an opinion in pursuance of which decision is made, which is final in respect to the status of the parties concerned. In order to its action, a case must be laid before it, and judgment is given between parties in dispute. Its procedure is in a court.

It is withdrawn from the military, and can execute its decisions only by a constabulary. "The judiciary," says Mr. Hamilton, "has no influence over either the purse or the sword; no direction either of the strength or of the wealth of the society; and can take no active resolution whatever. It may truly be said to have neither force nor will, but only judgment."

Its decision is not a law, but a precedent from which its subsequent action in all corresponding cases is presumed, but by which it is not imperatively determined. Its decision is a finality, in the case considered, and is beyond even its own revision. It would be a digression to inquire into the nature and philosophy of a precedent in law; but as the conception of rights is widened in the increasing freedom of the people, and courts change, and the wisdom of the application of the law is not perfect and does not reach a finality, it may follow that precedents are annulled or avoided with the process of time, as with the action of courts; and yet, in a conflict of rights, a precedent is rightly presumed steadfast, and to settle affairs for all time.

The inquiry of special importance as to the judicial power is in reference to its relation to the other powers, and the political sphere which has been assumed for it.

The organization of this power, in conformance to its nature and end, is judicial. Its structure is that of a bench of judges, and not of a representative order. It is established as a court, and not as an assembly of the people. If it were invested with positive political power, it would necessarily be formed as representative in the political constitution; if it were invested with ultimate political power, it would be formed from and of the whole political people. In the election of those who were to exercise its office, the people would not be restricted to a single profession or class, as that which is variously described as solicitors, proctors, attorneys, counsellors, lawyers, but it would be composed from the whole people, and from them there would be drawn scholars and artisans, and farmers, and tradesmen, and economists, who, no less than lawyers, have their sphere in the process of the political people, and are to act in its decision.

The concession to the judiciary of an ultimate decision in the political sphere, would be the reference of the destination of the state to a regime of lawyers, and, as it is now organized, to a power which is not responsible to the people, and holds its position for life, and whose action is a precedent which is presumed to be final and beyond reversal, and whose opinion is a decision from which there is no appeal. Then the historical progress of the people would be traced no longer in the better institution of rights, and the broader freedom, and the more varied organization of its powers, but in judicial decisions rendered, it may be, upon feigned issues and pronounced over contending litigants. Then the crises in the political life of the people would await for their event, the process by which a case could be made up and brought into court, and the development of the state would be shaped by an exclusive profession or class, and that one which is of all the most superstitious, and superstitious of the letter. It is the poet, and not the historian of laws, who says that freedom broadens from precedent to precedent.

The nation also exists in the conditions of an historical development, and therein is the on-going of its power, but the action of the judiciary is retrospective. It is invested with a revisionary but not a constructive power. It can only consider a case which is brought before it, and pass judgment upon that. It is, in the rendering of judgment on a case, to say what the law is, but not to say what the law shall be. The formative political power belongs only to the power which is representative of the political will.

The form and procedure of the judiciary also precludes

its exercising an ultimate political determination of the destination of the political people. It is incapable of the functions which the proposition demands. "It is," says Kent, "to determine the supreme law whenever a case is judicially before it." The fact that its action is limited to the case before it, is the evidence that this power is beyond its capacity. The vastest changes and crises might follow in swift succession, and yet give rise to no case, nor involve in a special controversy, contending litigants. The actual course of events would not await the constant construction and conclusion of feigned issues, and yet, the judiciary is silent, until the consideration of a case opens its lips. These feigned issues would also render the house of judges only the moot court for the examination and trial of political theories.

The construction of feigned issues by the legislature, which it is to refer to the judiciary, is indicative of the bias of jurists, and not the constructive grasp of statesmen. It would be as consistent, in the difference of opinions by the judges, to refer the conclusion to the legislature. It would involve peril, also, in the subversion of the integral character of the legislature, since, while it might avail as a temporary device, there must be but one power to enact laws, and this power can suffer no evasion of its responsibility.

The reference of this office to the judiciary is inconsistent with the normal institution of law in the political organism. In the political order law subsists in the consciousness of the political people. The determination of the individual must be the assertion of a conscious power, and obedience to the law must be a conscious act. Therefore the deliberation of a political assembly is public, and the law is published and presumed to be in the knowledge of all. But the formation of judicial opinions is private, and the study of these opinions and precedents, and the examination of the decisions of courts, demands the prolonged and laborious research of an exclusive profession. To allow to these opinions and precedents the ultimate determination of the political order, is to dissever it from its basis in the conscious spirit of the political people. It is as if the laws were to be hidden in costly and obscurely written tomes, and required the interpretation of a special craft. They would be as completely withdrawn from the conscious life of the people, as the laws of the tyrant which were recorded, but so high that none of the people could read them.

The special scope of the judiciary is indicated also by the qualities demanded for it in contrast with the work of the statesman. These qualities can only be described as judicial. The breadth of thought and the prescience of the statesman have not in the judiciary their immediate field.

But the opinions of the judiciary cannot be regarded as the power determinative, in its ultimate action, of the destination of the state, nor accepted as the finality in its course, since this would be inconsistent with its existence in the realization of the freedom of the people. To make the opinions of the judiciary a finality in the political order, would fetter the free spirit of the people, confining it, not in the assertion and recognition of law, as the determination of the organic will, but in the conformance to a mere legality. The past by its precedents would impose its authority upon the present. The energy of the people perishes when precedents become the substitute for the action of a living will and the strength of a living spirit. The Israel which once had kings and prophets, has then only Rabbis of the law.[1]

[1] "The law spoke to each man individually, bound him to his fathers, bound him to those who should come after him; it united him to every member of his nation. Suppose that law reduced to a mere collection of letters, written on stone or in a book, yet invested with all its traditional sacredness; suppose it changed from the witness of a nation's vitality, into the witness of a glory that has departed; suppose a set of men possessing hereditary claims to reverence, untiring diligence, much acuteness, devoting themselves to the task of expounding this law, — suppose this and you have probably the best conception you can get of the Rabbinical casuistry, and its immediate influence upon the mind of a people, crushed and fallen, but full of grand memories, seldom quite deserted by an inspiring hope."—*Inaugural Lecture*, by the Rev. F. D. Maurice Cambridge, 1866.

There is a proposition connected with this which refers to the judiciary, the preservation of the constitution, as an exclusive province, regarding its final interpretation as obligatory upon the other powers, and placing it as an arbiter over them, to confine them in their constitutional limitations. This also is inconsistent with its character, and is an office which belongs to no separate power, and involves a misconception of the relation of each and of the whole. It is in its province to interpret the law in every controversy in rights which is brought before it, and it may hold a law invalid in a certain case, because in conflict with the constitution which is also a law, and to which every enactment of the legislature must yield. Its decision is final only of the case in controversy, although held to apply to all corresponding cases. Its decision is to be received by the executive and by the legislature with the highest deference, but it is to be accepted by them, in their action, only in so far as their judgment may approve and confirm it.

The judiciary would also fail as a final arbiter, since no power is constituted to act as arbiter over the others, but each is to conform to its own normal sphere, and the avoidance of conflict is to be found only in their interior structure and their interrelation in the whole. This would also impose upon it a duty which it could not fulfill; it would refer the final arbitrament to the inherently weaker power. It is withdrawn from the military, and has the least ability to enforce its decisions. Its endeavor would be futile, since the mandamus of the court, if issued to the President or the Congress, would of necessity be disregarded.

To ascribe this province to the judiciary and to impose its decision upon the legislative power as a finality would make the latter subordinate. The judiciary would control the legislature, and its opinions might become the substitute for laws in the political order, and its decisions supersede legislation. It would be as consistent to give the legislature the revision in certain cases of the opinions of the judiciary, and to make that revision obligatory.

The reference of this province to the judiciary is a political solecism, and has no historical justification. Its only parallel would be the power of rabbinical opinions, in the decay of the national life of Judæa, and the influence of the jurisconsults in the decadence of Rome. Blackstone, in defining this assumption, says, "To give to the courts the power to annul the laws of parliament were to set the judicial power above that of the legislature, which would be subversive of all government."[1]

It would be also an imperfect arrangement, since the judiciary, when involved in a conflict, is left with no arbiter over it, and there is no provision against its encroachment upon the other powers, and its assumption for instance, of legislative functions. It places an arbiter between two parties; but it is a third party and is also concerned. Story says, "a declaratory or prohibitory law would be the remedy;" but the judiciary alone would be the interpreter of this law, and might set it aside, and in a decision beyond appeal.

To allow to the judiciary a decision upon the validity of a law itself, and that before it had involved a wrong to any, would give to the judiciary an absolute veto upon the legislature. It would have no parallel except perhaps in the tribunitial veto in Rome,[2] the *ultima jus tribunorum*

[1] 1 Bl. *Comm.* 91.

[2] Argument of the Attorney General, 1867.

The exclusion of the judiciary from the constructive political power of the nation, has been recognized in an opinion of the Supreme Court. It states that when the national government acts, for instance, in reference to the concerns of a commonwealth, "the constitution, so far as it provides for an emergency of this kind, has treated the subject as political in its nature and placed the power in the hands of that department," *i. e.* the legislature. It continues, "its decision (*i. e.* the legislature's) is binding on every other department of government, and cannot be questioned in a judicial tribunal."— Luther *v.* Borden, 7 Howard's R., 1.

"Invested with political power to keep the other departments in their prescribed limits, such a doctrine must destroy the judiciary. The people will not bear a political power which is independent of their control. If the judici-

of the republic, and the illustration still would be imperfect, for the tribunitial power was of the people and was held only for short periods.

The decision of the judiciary is authority in all courts, and this is necessary to the unity of a judicial system and the uniform interpretation and application of the laws;[1] but the decision is in no respect binding as a rule of legislation upon the legislature.

The judiciary demands for its strength exclusion from all legislative and executive functions. It has the indication of its independence in the tenure of its office. It is not a representative body, and therefore is not to be constructed as representative. The call to it is to be from the government of the nation, in its authority. It demands also exclusive qualifications, and the study requi-

ary exercises such power it must become representative, which is the nature of all political power under free institutions. A branch of government which can dictate to the legislature is legislative." Fisher, *Trial of the Constitution*, p. 82.

"By the Constitution of the United States the President is invested with certain important political powers, in the exercise of which he is to use his own discretion, and is accountable only to his country in his political character and to his own conscience. To aid him in the performance of these duties he is authorized to appoint certain officers, who act by his authority and in conformity with his orders. In such cases their acts are his acts, and whatever opinion may be entertained of the manner in which executive discretion may be used, still there exists and can exist no power to control that discretion. The subjects are political. They respect the nation, not individual rights, and being intrusted to the executive the decision of the executive is conclusive." Marbury *v.* Madison, 1 Cranch's R., 137.

"The Supreme Court of the United States, like all other courts, is simply a court of judicature, to decide controverted cases, in law, equity and admiralty, that are brought before it by actual litigants. It is not charged with any special function conservative of the constitution, like the so-entitled Senate of the French Constitution of December, 1799. In cases before it the Supreme Court has no other jurisdiction over constitutional questions than is possessed by the humblest judicial tribunal, state or national, in the land."

"The court does not formally set aside or declare void, any statute or ordinance inconsistent with the constitution. It simply decides the case before it *according to law*, and if laws are in conflict, according to that law which has the *highest authority*, that is, the constitution." — Wheaton's *International Law*, Dana's note, p. 79.

1 "And the judges in every state shall be bound thereby, anything, etc. Art. 6, sec. 2.

site to its higher attainment often withdraws men from direct intercourse with the people.

The judiciary must always resist in so far as it can, arbitrary action or usurpation in every form and by every power; but it is not invested with superior or special functions for this end, and its resistance is simply that which belongs to every degree of power.

The judiciary has, in fine, no power of origination, but only of judgment and comparison. But it subsists in the nation in its sovereignty, and therefore, while it is not constitutive of the political order, it has not merely a formal relation to it. Though it cannot make its opinion a law constructive of the political order, because then it would be a legislative power, it is yet in its sphere to interpret and apply the law. It cannot determine what shall be the law, but only ascertain and define what is the law. The fact that it is to interpret and apply the constitution as law, and then also the laws of the legislature, has been the occasion of the advancement of the judiciary, and of the reference to it of public or national law. If it be allowed that nations stand related and their rights and powers and obligations are comprehended in public or national law, as individuals stand in their private relations in common law, it is then in the apprehension and explication of the former that the province of the national judiciary appears. And the strength and consistency of the judiciary in its historical course has been in the fact that it recognized the necessary being of the nation, as subsistent in the sphere of public or national law; and its greater decisions were formed in the conception of the nation in its necessary being, — the organic power which in its sovereignty asserts itself in the constitution, and enacts its will as law.[1] The

[1] The illustration of this is, for instance, in the decisions of Gibbons *v.* Ogden, Martin *v.* Hunter's Lessee, Luther *v.* Borden, McCulloch *v.* Maryland, Ogden *v.* Saunders.

The constitution is interpreted in no exclusive or restrictive sense. "It did not suit the purposes of the people, in framing this great charter of our liberties, to

office of the national judiciary is necessarily the explication of those principles, in which the necessary being of the nation consists, and in which alone national rights and powers can be construed. The terms of the constitution which presume the being of the people, and the law as the expression of its organic will, can only be rightly construed in conformance to the necessary conception of the nation. It is certainly to allow the proper authority to the historical interpretation of law; but this can be only as it apprehends the actual history of the nation, and in so far as it substitutes for the actual facts in this history, its own abstractions, its opinions will become as worthless and vain as all abstractions are, which cannot be allowed to thwart or to stay the organic course of the people, and the realization of its historical life. The earlier decisions of the Supreme Court were characterized by their profound and lofty conception of the nation. There was, in that period, in the varying conflict of rights, a conception of the nation, its being, its rights, its powers, its capacities, which places the names of the earlier justices by those of the earlier presidents. Chief Justice Marshall is second only to President Washington, and the services of Mr. Justice Wilson were no less than those of Mr. Secretary Hamil-

provide for minute specifications of its powers, or to declare the means by which these powers should be carried into execution. Hence, its powers are expressed in general terms, leaving to the legislature from time to time to adopt its own means to effectuate legitimate objects, and to mould and model the exercise of its powers as its own wisdom and the public interests should require." — Martin *v.* Hunter, 1 Wheaton *R.* 304.

"This instrument contains an enumeration of powers, expressly granted by the people to their government. It is said that these powers ought to be construed strictly. But why ought they to be so construed? Is there one sentence in the constitution which gives countenance to this rule? In the last of the enumerated powers, that which grants expressly the means for carrying all others into execution, Congress is authorized to make all laws which shall be necessary and proper for the purpose. But this limitation to the means which may be used is not extended to the powers which are conferred, nor is there one sentence in the constitution which has been pointed out by the bar, or which we have been able to discern, that prescribes this rule." — Gibbons *v.* Ogden, 9 Wheaton R. 1.

ton. In their decisions, there is the foundation of a national jurisprudence, which Kent has justly described as "a solid and magnificent structure." It is in later decisions that a provincial theory or a partisan scheme or a narrow legal dogma succeeds to that high conception of national powers and rights; it is in recent decisions that there is displayed the conceit of a power, which in its historical interpretation may ignore all the facts in the history of the nation, and proceed to determine the issue of the gravest historical crises, by the application of certain pedantic formulas, which the spirit of the people does not know nor recognize.

The legislative and executive and judicial powers, in the exact significance of these terms, are but imperfectly defined. The distinction has a scholastic style, and is suggestive rather of the terminology of science than of the powers in the civil and political organism. These phrases become the occasion of error, when they are assumed to define powers which have not their source in the organic unity, and their development in the organic relations of the nation. When they are described as proceeding from a formal law, it has been truly said that they make of the nation only a great law machine, and the government a necessary contrivance for making laws, where one power institutes the law and a second executes and a third applies it. But these powers, in their immanence in the civil and political organism, and in their institution in the realization of rights and of freedom, transcend this empty conception. There is beyond these terms a significance in the words which always will denote these powers with the people, — the Congress, the President, the Judges.

CHAPTER XII.

THE NATION AND ITS REPRESENTATIVE CONSTITUTION.

THE sovereignty of the nation has its normal assertion in representative government. The representative principle is illustrative of the higher political organization.

The representative constitution is the realization of the sovereignty of the nation in its necessary conception as a moral organism.

Government is necessarily of and through a person. There is in its action the assertion of personality, and sovereignty is existent as the determination of personality.

In the normal process of the nation in its representative organization, in whom does its sovereignty rightly exist? The common answer is in two forms: —

Firstly; it is said that it is existent in the whole people. This embraces each and every individual in the nation, with no further discrimination. This is merely indefinite, and can admit of no actualization. It does not presume even the consciousness of a political unity and order, which is the precedent and condition of the action of the political will. It does not ascertain a real sovereignty. It is physically impossible, since the whole population comprises a certain proportion who are not capable of performing what the proposition presumes. It is unhistorical, since there has existed no political organization where the power was held in common by the whole population; some law regulative of political action in the consciousness of the people must be assumed. The proposition is inconsistent with the organic and moral being of the nation, and has its premise in the conception which identifies the contiguous population in a certain locality with the nation.

Secondly; it is said that it is existent in the qualified electors. But who, in the normal representative constitution, are qualified? What qualification may be rightly assumed by the nation as defining an elector? It is said that the nation of itself has a right to define the qualifications of its electors. This is evident; for as the act of the elector presumes the being of the nation, and the consciousness of unity and order, that is a political spirit, so the nation alone may define the qualifications of its electors; and the act then of the elector is that of one in whom there is the political spirit which subsists in the nation. The act of each — the nation and the elector — is primarily involved in the other, there is a logical, but not a formal, precedence. But since, then, the nation alone has the right to define the qualifications of its electors, in what principle may it rightly proceed to define them? In what principle may it ascertain the real sovereignty of the nation, so that in the designation of its qualifications its sovereignty may have full and free exposition? The nation cannot be left to define these arbitrarily, since that would contradict the reason of the state, and would imply injustice in the nation itself; its process would become the expression of the willfulness of men, not of the will of the people. It cannot be presumed that they are to be left for their definition to the adjustment of accident, since the conception of sovereignty precludes this; and the nation can allow no accident to shape its course or determine its end.

In what principle, then, is the nation to proceed in its representative constitution, — in the realization of its sovereignty? This inquiry may be carried further. What is the quality of the act of an elector for which qualifications are requisite in order to define it? In other words, what is a vote? A vote is the formal assertion, in conformance to certain political prescriptions, of a free will in the determination of the government of the civil and political organization. It is the act of a person in the political process of the people of which he is a member. A person is one who has a free will, — one whose action is free and self-determined. This is the substance of personality, and in this personality is in identity with sovereignty. The existence of personality is therefore necessarily presumed in the qualifications of an elector.

The inquiry, then, as to the principle of representation is resolved into the further inquiry, what is the organization of the nation, — the normal political organization, in which a person acts as an elector, in the determination of its sovereignty? The answer to this inquiry has always been in correspondence to some antecedent assumption, as to the being and end of the nation.

It is said that the nation is formed in the representation of interests, which in their combination are assumed to constitute the political organization. This is the postulate of Mr. Calhoun. He says: "There are two ways in which the sense of the community may be taken. One regards numbers only and considers the whole community as having but one common interest throughout, and collects the sense of the greater number of the whole as that of the community. The other, on the contrary, regards interests as well as numbers, considering the community as made up of different and conflicting interests, as far as the government is concerned, and takes the sense of each through its appropriate organ, and the united sense of all as the sense of the entire community."[1] This is defined as a universal principle and applied to all forms of government. "In a republic, in consequence of the absence of artificial distinctions, the various natural interests rise into prominence and struggle for the ascendency;" and he says of the restriction of each by the other, "it is this negative power which in fact forms the constitution."

[1] Calhoun's *Works*, vol. i. p. 221.

This identifies the nation with the commonwealth or the civil corporation, while in that it is imperfect, since it allows no real ground for its continuance. It apprehends the organization of society only as the combination of conflicting interests, each struggling for the ascendency, and the constitution is the negative result which is obtained in the balance of these repellant forces. This theory of selfishness, or of enlightened self-interest — *l'interet bien entendre*, which is assumed as the basis of society, cannot become the foundation, nor, in the balance of its endless antagonisms, constitute the authority of the nation. There is no combination of private interests or private rights which can attain to the conception of public rights or duties, or create a public spirit; no accumulation of special interests can form the whole, and the nation does not exist for the furtherance of private or special ends.

Interests, even in the low and evil conception of life in which this theory proceeds, do not form the stronger motives to human action, but are overborne even by the habits and impulses and passions of men. These interests moreover, centering in self, cannot become constructive of unity, for unity can subsist only in the consciousness of moral relations. There is also in the foundation of the nation the manifestation of a spirit and law of duty and sacrifice, and there has been none but has been called to crises in which no interests could be weighed against the sacredness of its life, or the obligation of maintaining it.

While each interest is thus constituted as a negative against every other interest, these negations can form nothing positive; they are constructive of nothing.

The proposition assumes also a representation "through their appropriate organs," of various interests, whose value is to be regarded, and which are weighed and counted against each other, and estimated by some special consideration. As this becomes the ground of representation, it would consistently require a representation of interests proportionate to their value and extent, and form a constantly changing schedule.

It is deficient even as a description of the commonwealth or the civil corporation, and in it the organization of society is severed from its moral ground; its bond is only the maxim of expediency, and its permanence the dictate of some separate and private interest seeking its own end. There is no longer a higher authority for government, nor the recognition of a divine obligation to maintain order and to punish crime. It is the disintegration of society; and the subversion of the whole, by the secession of any interest which deems the action justified by the grievance it may suffer, or by the profit it may anticipate, is its logical and historical sequence.

It is said that the nation is constituted in the representation of families. The family is the integral and formative unit of the nation; each family is to be represented in it, and only one who is the head of a family is to be an elector.

But the nation as an organism is distinct from the family. Instead of being limited and defined in its end by the end of the family, and in its order subordinate to it, it is constituted over it.

The proposition would conform to an oriental type of society, and instead of consisting with the organic and moral being of the nation, it would be constructive of a state in which there was no political spirit, and no citizenship or law or freedom. It would also, unless supplemented by a fiction, obviously exclude some who have wrought with the highest power in history.

It is inconsistent with the nation in its necessary conception, as itself a moral organism, to which the individual has an immediate relation, and not merely a relation formulated through the family. But the error in the premise of the proposition, is the implication of the identity of the family with the nation.

It is said that the nation is constituted in the representation of numbers. The whole number of inhabitants as enumerated by a census, is to be represented.

There is no more reason why men should be estimated by their numbers than by any other physical quality, as for instance their bulk. There would be the same consistency in basing representation upon the stature or color or gesture of men, and these might with the same justice enter into the representative government. There is no clearer discrimination of sovereignty in numbers than in any physical proportions. This also assumes the identity of the nation or the political people simply with the population.

It is said that the representation should be of certain capacities or properties or accidents attaching to men. This regards certain powers of mind, or incidents of life, as for instance, occupation, as the ground of representation. The practical application of this proposition has been attempted in the scheme for a plurality of votes. Mr. Mill denies the proposition, "that all persons ought to be equal in every description of right recognized by society," and therefore demands a distinction in the number of votes which each should give; "if every ordinary unskilled laborer ought to have one vote, a skilled laborer ought to have two, a farmer, manufacturer, or trader should have three or four, a lawyer, a physician, or surgeon, a clergyman of any denomination, a literary man, an artist, a public functionary, ought to have five or six." These proportions are laid down, "putting aside for the present the consideration of moral worth, of which, though more important even than intellectual, it is not so easy to find an available test." If then this consideration of relative moral worth were added in this arithmetical estimate, the difference between the single vote of the workman, who knows enough to cast one vote but not more than one, or is good enough to cast one but no more, and the higher grades of social and intellectual acquisition would be very great. But the proposition, in its application, would be unjust upon its own premise, while this condition is omitted, and of this the external condition gives no test. If the power of each as an elector was made thus proportionate, in a numerical scale, to certain external signs of relative moral worth, the standard would inevitably be so imperfect, as to make the actual process corresponding to it the most complex system of injustice. It not only would revive the maxims of the Pharisees, but it would attach to their schedule of virtues a power beyond any compensation that has been assumed in their estimates. If it were joined to a merely economical conception of the state, there could be for a people whose moral strength had any living energy or spirit, no agent of debasement so potent.

But the principle which the scheme assumes is false, for it is not the occupations nor the acquisitions of men, nor literary attainment, nor official place, nor artistic nor professional skill that is the ground of rights, but it is personality itself, and in the infinite worth of personality — the worth of manhood — is alone the foundation of rights. The state can compute this by no arithmetical notation, nor by any addition or subtraction can it find its numerical equation. It cannot set against some intellectual or professional acquisition in one person the whole determinate action of another person. The proposition proceeds from a merely artificial notion of personality, a mechanical standard of duties and rights, a formal scheme of morals, the empiric of virtue; it is the "excellent foppery of the world."

It may be further said of this scheme, that none of the properties and powers enumerated in it correspond to the nation as founded in the nature of man, and as the normal and moral order of human existence. If it were a great utilitarian organization or machine, a cutlers' association, or a railway or gas company, or a produce exchange, or an economic society, and it were required to choose those who should be its foremen or directors, then it might better give to skilled labor or to professional attainments, and to these in their strictest estimate, the sole or the substantial choice ; and if it were only an academic society, a school or sect, then literary culture or scholastic habit might chose its dean or doctors.

But it is none of these; the principle, moreover, in so far as these estimates have been applied, has been disproved. The literary and scientific class, to whom in this estimate, and perhaps, on its premise, no better could be made, a power sixfold beyond that of the unlearned is allowed, have only too often been betrayed by whim and caprice, and subservience to political abstractions. They are men withdrawn, perhaps, in the narrow circle of some ethnic or linguistic theory, and blind to all facts beyond its narrow horizon, or scholars who draw their political precedents from the ideal world of Homer's heroes, and not the grander world of to-day. The Universities, when a special representation is open to them, are more often represented by lower men; as Oxford in England, whose later representatives could scarcely justify the working of the representative system in comparison with the greatest of its medieval politicians, William of Occam, or might suggest, in the comparison, some question as to the principle itself. A fact often noticed, is the tendency, also, to defect of political spirit and loyalty, in men of an exclusively scientific or mathematical culture; it may be in the latter, because their study is merely formal; there is the depreciation of the moral or political world, the life of man in history and the order of society, in comparison with the physical world.

But this empiric standard would require also for its consistency the adoption of a negative scale, by which the number of votes should be diminished, as, for instance, one who lives in idleness, whether in poverty or with inherited wealth, whatever be his profession or his attainment in it, should have his number of votes correspondingly reduced; this rule of subtraction would require constant changes with the changes of condition or character, as on some weather-gauge with its shifts; and in the representation of professions, the difference between the better and poorer members is more than the difference between separate professions, and this also would require representation.

While the aim in this proposition may be well enough, the principle assumed has no foundation, and therefore fails of any clearly defined practical application. It is at the outset in conflict with the foundation of rights, or it may be said, that it allows its inconsistency with an equality of rights. The proposition has its premise in the mechanical notion of psychology, which classifies and divides the will and the affections and the powers of the mind, so that, as in Hegel's illustration, a man is represented as carrying one faculty in one pocket and one in another. It is after the distinctions of the school-men, who pronounced their judgment upon the masters in the medieval schools by a fixed scale, representing for instance genius as four, learning as five, imagination as six, judgment as seven, and striking the balance in order to arrive at their comparative merit. When Mr. Mill, to maintain his proposition in opposition to "equal suffrage," defines the latter as an "equal claim to control over the government of other people,"[1] it resolves the state into its atomy, and is the merest individualism; for no man has a claim to control over the government of another, but the nation has the claim to government over the whole.

The nation, then, is not constructed in the representation of interests, for it is in itself before each and every separate and special interest, and can be formed by no accumulation of them; it is not of numbers, for these may

[1] J. S. Mill, *Dissertations, etc.*, vol. iv. p. 160.

exist separately from it, and no aggregate of numbers, however vast, is in identity with it; it is not of families, for it is other than the family, and no collection of families can attain to it; it is not of special acquirements or capacities, as an association of trades, or arts, or schools, for the state is in none of these; it is not to interests or families or numbers, or special and exclusive professions and attainments, that the right of government in the nation belongs.

The nation is constituted in its normal political order, in the representation of persons; and the right to representation is the right of a member of the nation who is a person.

Government is and can be only of and through a person. The vote is the right in the nation of a person, as the act can be only the act of a person. This is no abstraction to be newly applied in the sphere of politics, and no scheme for which from the outset an actualization is sought, but it is the principle which has the broadest ground in history, and the only ground in reason, and the necessary ground in justice.

Firstly; this principle has the broadest ground in history. It alone can claim an historical justification in the representative constitution. It has not infrequently passed into the order of the state without a direct or avowed recognition, as if of itself coming forth. There has been a constant endeavor, in some shape, toward its assertion. The most common tests which have been established have had no other consistent basis, and without the recognition of this law fall to pieces as a miscellaneous bundle of terms and conditions. Thus, in the most common conditions for instance, a universal principle being assumed, the child, or the dependent, or the demented are not allowed to vote, since they have not the will, the conscious self-determination and freedom of a person; and in the conception of the law they are constructively, but not actually persons; and they, also, who have been proven to have taken a bribe, or made a wager on the issue of an election, are not allowed to vote, since their act, as controlled by an external consideration, is regarded as no longer free, that is the act of a person; and they who have committed a high crime are not allowed to vote, not because this privation is an immediate punishment of crime, but because through crime they are regarded as having lost their freedom, as in wickedness men are no more free, and there is in it the destruction of personality. There are no other tests which have been established so widely as these, and in this principle alone they have their consistent ground. The qualification of property might claim as wide an application, but that refers to this also for its ultimate justification. Blackstone, in a passage of great breadth and significance, concedes this. He says, "The true reason of requiring any qualification, with regard to property in voters, is to exclude such persons as are in so mean a situation, that *they are esteemed to have no will of their own. If it were probable that every man would give his vote freely, then every member of the community should have a vote.* But since that can hardly be expected in any of indigent fortunes, or such as are under the immediate dominion of others, all popular states have been obliged to establish certain qualifications, whereby some *who are suspected to have no will of their own are excluded from voting.*" Again he says, "*only such are entirely excluded as can have no will of their own.*" While this presentation of human nature, which makes property the sign of personality, is neither just nor edifying, the principle of representation is conceded in it. There is, therefore, in all these tests, which have had the widest institution, the recognition of this principle and the endeavor to establish it. It alone has the broadest historical ground, and only in their reference to it are the common conditions justified.

Secondly; this principle has the only ground in reason. It has its precedent in the being of the nation as the natural and normal order of human society. In personality, man has the condition of all rights, and a realized personality is to have its normal expression in the nation, as the nation is the natural and normal condition of human society. The right to vote is therefore a natural right, — the right of a member of the nation. It is still the induction, in fact, of the postulate of Aristotle, "man is by nature a political being." If the nation was only a formal or an artificial association, then it could allow any formal qualification and any artificial test, and the political artificers constructing the fabric could elaborate them after their own device; but if it be the natural order and condition of human existence, as there is in personality the realization of the true nature of man, so in the nation, as the manifestation of the true nature of man, there is to be the expression of it. There is no other conception of government which is not inextricably involved in the arbitrary or the accidental.

Mr. Brownson says, "The elective franchise is not a natural right, because it is political power, and political power is always a trust, never a natural right, and the state judges for itself to whom it will or will not confide the right." It is evident that the nation is to judge for itself to whom it is to confide the right, but the whole inquiry is, as to what principle it may rightly act upon, in the assertion of this right, and what is to be the premise of its judgment. It is a right as well as a trust, but the position of Mr. Brownson assumes as the condition of the process of the nation, the isolation of positive from natural rights, and the severance of the sphere of each. It is a trust and a right, and there is an inherent weakness in its separation as a trust from its conception as a right. In it, as it is nowhere else apparent, there is the correspondence of a right and a duty, as they subsist in personality; it is a trust vested only in an actual or realized personality, and in this only is it a right.[1]

In this the nation is constituted in conformance to its necessary conception, as a moral organism. There is evolved in a moral organism the affirmation of personality, and the nation is formed in the realization of personality. The person who is a member of a nation is not to be regarded as a negation in his relation to it. For personality no negative condition is to be postulated, in which its being is ignored, and its aim is disallowed; but it is to be regarded, as the nation strives toward the realization of a moral order.

It is not alone the passive right to the advantages resultant from the nation, for in this there could be neither the satisfaction of the moral longing nor the fulfillment of the moral aim of man, and this would indicate only the defect in the moral condition of the nation and its degradation, but it is the right to recognition as a person and the correspondent affirmation of personality in the process of the nation.[2]

In this the nation is constituted in conformance to its necessary conception, as the realization of freedom. Freedom is no negation; it is not found simply in the security which is obtained by restrictions imposed upon an external power, nor in the uses resultant from the checks and guaranties constructed against an external power. It is not attained in a condition of indifference to the nation. It is not in the acquiescent reception of its common advantages, nor in the permissive participation in the things in which it has profited. Personality is not regarded in the nation when it is restricted to some special end, nor has it

1 Brownson, *The American Republic*, p. 379.

"No man has a natural right to be a voter without qualifications or conditions, but every man in a republican state has a natural right to become a voter." — *Mr. Taylor Lewis.*

2 "Die volksvertretung ist im Staat absolute sittliche Forderung, nämlich genau in demselben Maase, in welchem der Staat, bereits wirklicher Staat ist." Rothe, *Theologische Ethik*, vol. ii. p. 125.

compensation in the partnership of its accumulated gains. The personality of man is not in the multitude of things which he possesses. Freedom is only in the realization of personality; it is only as there is in the nation, in its process and order, the expression of personality that there is in it the realization of freedom.[1]

Thirdly; this principle has a necessary ground in justice. In this, government in the nation is constituted in conformance to its normal law. It rests in the conscious consent of the people. It is the assertion of the political will of the political people. The more perfect expression of the will of the people is in the government, and it embodies in it its purpose, and has in it the satisfaction of its aim. The government in the determination of its sovereignty is not a mere order apart from the people; it is not an abstraction having no ground in the organic and moral being of the people, but it is the determinate life of the people in the realization of a moral order.

The government in its necessary conception is over the people, but it is none the less the determinate action of the people, and of the whole people in its realized sovereignty. The individual person is not simply to exist as a subject to the government of the nation, while yet he is in perfect subjection to it, but he is to act determinately in it. The self government of the people is then no speculative pretense, and no legal abstraction; it is no formal order and no aggregate of institutions, but there is in it the realization of the self-determination of the people, the asser-

[1] Franklin asserted these two theses: "That every person of the community, except infants, insane persons, and criminals, is of common right and by the laws of God a free man, and entitled to the full enjoyment of liberty." "That liberty or freedom consists in having an actual share in the appointment of those who frame the laws, and who are to be the guardians of every man, of life, property and peace; for the all of one man is as dear to him as the all of another; and the poor man has an equal right, but more need to have representatives in the legislature than the rich one." — Franklin, *Works*, vol. ii. p. 372.

"Auch in der rechtlichen Freiheit, ist demnach, die Wahl, ein unentbehrliches moment, — ja, sie ist die Blüthe der Freiheit, denn die Wahl ist eben die Ausserung der Individualitat." — *Stahl*, vol. ii. sec. i. p. 327.

tion of and the obedience to law. The right of government in the nation is not then merely prescriptive; nor is it derivative from any convention; nor is it to be construed as a private right, to become the privilege of a caste; nor is it to be restricted to a succession in a certain family or a certain number of families to be accounted only as some domiciliary right, vested in its present occupants, and to descend as their estate, but it is the right of the people in the realization of its moral being.

If any other principle be assumed, it must justify itself in another and a lower conception. If for instance, the nation is based upon property or has for its end the security of property, then property may control it, and money, not men, may rule it, and those who have their highest accomplishment in the making and keeping of money may represent it;—if it consist as a private possession in the privileges of the few, a family, or class, or race, whom force or accident has placed in power, and if it be only the increment of their privileges to be held against all comers, until some may come with stronger and more subtle force to oust them, and hold these privileges against the former proprietors, then, those holding them alone may determine the course and destination of the whole. If any form be assumed by which the expression of personality is denied, then in so far, the government is defective, as the form is arbitrary, since it exists not in the affirmation of that which yet, in a realized personality, has in itself the spirit and the determination in which government subsists. It becomes the suppression and not the manifestation of the power immanent in the nation in its moral being. And as the form in which the affirmation of personality in its normal process is denied is arbitrary, it may assume the form of the determination of an individual, or family, or class, and becomes the support of the power and privileges of one or of a few, who hold only a formal and legal precedence. It establishes the government in an exclusive, and not in a universal principle, and it is formed in a narrow separatism, as if the individual personality were to act in the nation for some special end which is placed before each, but not in its being, in the realization of the universal end.

The representative government is therefore constituted in the representation of the people, in the realization of its moral being. It is the representation of persons. This principle has had its assertion in the progress of the nation, and with the higher result of history. It is in the being and order and sovereignty of the nation, in the institution of rights, in the realization of freedom, that common men as a fact have proven themselves to be men. The succession in the authority of the nation, since its inauguration, has been maintained unbroken, and has triumphed over anarchy, when allied with the hate and the secret assault and support of aristocratic and imperial powers. It has been the ordination of a mightier sovereignty, and the institution of an ampler freedom, and the realization of the noblest political order which the world has seen. The line of the Presidents, the elect of the people, from President Washington to President Lincoln, has been greater than any line of kings. In the succession of events, the self-determinate purpose, the moral strength of the people, has been tried in its integrity and firmness of resolve, through the crises of the most mighty insurrection, and it has sought the maintenance of the authority of law, and the consistence and continuance of order, and with the love of peace in its steadfastness it has followed them with an unselfish end.

The right to vote is the right of every person who is a member of the nation. It is the birthright of freedom. It is the right only of a person, that is one in whom there is the realization of personality, one whose action is self-determined, — one who has the consciousness of law and of freedom in the self-determination of his own spirit, and in that alone is the power which can shape the course and destination of the state. It is the right of every person who is a member of the nation, that is, who is born and educated in it, as the nation itself is not simply a physical but a moral organism. It is in the assertion of this right alone, that there is the expression of the political will of the political people. In this alone the government of the nation has also the manifestation of its divine origin and institution; as personality has its realization only in the realization of divine relations and the fulfillment of the divine will. In the institution of righteousness and of freedom is the being of the nation, and in this in its highest conception, government in the nation is manifested as a trust and a right.

The aim of the political constitution should be, to give to every member of the nation who is a person, representation in it, that is, every actual person should vote, and none beside. This and this alone ascertains the actual sovereignty of the political people. The qualifications which proceed on this ground, which is also the nature of the act itself, — and no power can make it other than this, — alone give expression to the political thought and political will. These qualifications may become more exactly defined in the historical development of the political people; but their aim will be always the same. These qualifications as defined in law have necessarily the form of a general law. Their intent is the exclusion of those only who have no will of their own, that is, no personality. Thus children and minors, and those who have taken bribes or made wagers, and the imbecile and insane, and all convicts or criminals are not allowed to vote. The government of the nation is founded then in the determination of its manhood and in the spirit of the people, and not in the accidents of life, as property or occupation, or rank, or color, or race.

The vote then, as the representation of a person, precludes all special distinction. There is an infinite worth in personality, and therefore every person in its representation counts one. It is representative of the whole personality. There is no graduated scale in which to estimate the relative worth of real manhood, or the valuation of the whole moral determination. If the personality of man could be made secondary, then by a graduated standard the most extensive system of a plurality of votes could be adjusted to the proportionate worth of the moral determination of men, and many votes could be given to one, and few to another; but the personality of none can be held thus as itself inferior and its all, the entire moral determination in its integrity, as of a diminished quality.

To confer the power of an elector upon one who in the course of nature is not a member of the nation, belongs only to the nation in its sovereignty. There is for every individual as such, whether citizen or stranger, all rights subsisting in the necessary relations of life, that is all civil rights; but all rights subsisting in the nation in its freedom, that is all political rights, are only of the political body, and if an alien be received and made a member of it, it must be by the act of the nation in its sovereignty. The homely phrase of the law is — to get naturalized; but this is not a slight nor easy thing; and nature works, even as in the life of states, slowly and patiently, and is not subject to the act of legislatures, or the administration of courts. The Republic is indeed to welcome the stricken and the oppressed for conscience sake out of every land, and is to be as the city whose gates are open by night and by day, and not the least among its titles is that of the name of the home of the pilgrim; and if it be forgetful of this, it loses some of its noblest historical traditions. But to admit to immediate representation whoever may come to its shores, who have no consciousness of the aim and destination of the nation, and no participation in its political spirit, becomes a defect of government and is a detriment to the Republic. To bestow upon these the same political power with those born and educated in the nation and animated by its design, is no more just, than to refer the decision as to the direction of a house or the disposal of an inheritance to some transient guest who may come to lodge over night or take shelter in a storm. They have no apprehension of the unity and continuity of the nation, and do not partake of its conscious spirit; it is elsewhere that their thoughts turn to cherish the memory of their ancestors, and elsewhere that their hopes look for the home of their children. Thus, there are Keltic and Asiatic populations who have been educated under an imperialism, and bring with them imperial tendencies which involve the degradation of the individual personality. They have thus no clear conception of freedom and of rights which subsist in personality, nor of what constitutes a nation; there is thus often among the Keltic populations a merely tribal feeling, and the nation is conceived as itself vested in a race, and in the want of personality they fall under the control of some priest or demagogue. The immediate characteristic of the Asiatic populations is this want of personality. Through customs which have a weight which the occidental mind can scarcely apprehend, they retain their attachment to the land of their nativity. They have here no enduring home, and regard another land as alone sacred. Thither they turn with reverence to the graves of their ancestors, and look forward themselves to finding a grave in it, avoiding to fall in battle elsewhere, and refusing elsewhere to be buried. There is an evil in the accumulation of masses of populations whose thought and spirit separate them from the nation, and who are subject to a foreign ecclesiastical or political influence; but the evil is not obviated by conceding to them a political power which has no root in devotion or sacrifice, and is inspired by no love. There may and should, in the prudence of the state, be some form or law of naturalization; but to refer to these populations political power, with no discrimination, involves danger to the political whole.

It is thus, also, that Indians are excluded from voting; not because they are not taxed, but because, as they are subject to the will of a chief and absolutely controlled by it, they are without freedom; they also exist in a tribal relation, the organization of a race, which isolates them from the organic and moral being of the nation; but in withdrawing from this tribal relation, they come upon a national position and should be regarded as members of the nation.

There have been some qualifications defining the right to vote which claim a separate notice. The qualification in property, maintained by Blackstone as the sign of a conscious freedom and independence of character, has an historical presumption. But property is no more the evidence than it is the basis of manhood. It has always in itself too great power, and there is always danger that it may seek to subvert character, and to subordinate the whole to selfish ends. This pecuniary condition of suffrage tends, also, to an estimate of the nation itself by a pecuniary consideration. It induces the disposition to regard the government as the agent of special interests, and in the crises of its existence there has been the inclination, in great divided interests and monopolies, to pursue exclusively their own separate ends.[1] When it is said that the owner of property should vote, because possession gives a stake in the nation, it makes self-interest the condition of the nation, which it cannot be; and as in these

[1] Mr. Brownson says, "The mere men of wealth, the bankers and brokers, are those who exert the worst influence upon the state; their maxim is, let the state take care of the rich, and the rich of the poor, and not let the state take care of the weak, for the strong need it not." — *The American Republic*, p. 383.

crises the nation may call for the sacrifice of property and of the life of the individual, there is the negation of the so-called stake in it.

But a property qualification has its premise in the assumption that the nation exists primarily to protect property. It regards security as the only end, and prefers Babylon to Judæa if only the ducats are stowed away more safely in it, though they never are. But the residence of government in property is consistent only with the organization of the nation in certain private rights, the barbaric or the patrimonial constitutions, where power is a private estate. Thus when property has been made the exclusive qualification, there has been the disposition to regard a vote as something which one possesses, as itself property, something which may be held at a pecuniary valuation, and bartered or transferred.

A qualification in education, or more strictly, a literary qualification, as the ability to read some state document or to write, has obtained a recent advocacy. In so far as intelligence is implied in the conscious freedom and self-determination of the will, that is, in so far as its action has a rational content, this test has a higher worth than the preceding, and the real education of the people, in which there is a moral more than an intellectual element, is, in another phrase, the realization of personality. But the inquiry is, how far a strictly literary qualification is indicative of this. If it was the only qualification, then lads at school, on passing their examinations, could vote. The qualification is then assumed as but one, with certain others, and the ability to read or write, and a certain technical or scientific acquisition, is held as indicative of fitness for the offices of a citizen, so that all lacking this are precluded from its highest exercise.

But the test is a superficial one, and perhaps of all is the most artificial. A technical or scientific acquisition is not the evidence of the real education of the people.

Mr. Hare says justly, that "no science can reach the depths of the knowledge painfully won in the daily life, and the experience of man and woman." The life of the workman, the fulfillment of human relationships in the family and the community, the endeavor of men in the realities of life, is a deeper education; and in work rather than in a certain literary or scientific acquisition, is the evidence of the capacity for political power.

There is nothing in the political action of a distinctly literary or scientific class to justify the application of this test.[1] They have seemed more often to be controlled by notions or theories, or by some vulgar conceit withdrawn from politics and the organic life of the people, to become only a learned mob. The elements of character, clearness, foresight, and the self-determination of the will, are not always among the acquisitions of literature or science. Even Comte says, "clear-sightedness, wisdom and even consistency of thought, are qualities which are very independent of learning."

A qualification of a literary or scientific form for political action has also no historical justification. Some of the most intellectual periods in the course of a people have been the most corrupt; they have been characterized by the destruction of personality and the coincident decay of national life. Greece in her dissolution was crowded with the most fluent rhetoricians and the most subtle sophists, and her citizens became at once the slaves and the tutors of other peoples; and the Greek still with his intellectual acuteness is destitute of the most primary civic virtues. The age in Rome which was marked by the

[1] See Milton's reply to the grammarian, "Whosoever therefore he be, though from among the dregs of the common people, that you are so keen upon, whosoever I say has but sucked in this principle, that he was not born for his prince, but for God and his country; he deserves the reputation of a learned and an honest and a wise man more, and is of greater use in the world than yourself. For such a one is learned without letters; you have letters but no learning, that understand so many languages, turn over so many volumes, and yet are but asleep when all is done."—Milton's *Works*, vol. i. p. 30.

transition from a nation to an empire, although its creative power in literature in certain forms may be traced to a preceding national development, was yet characterized by a wide intellectual culture, and a rare although superficial refinement in letters. The movement for Secession was marked by a skill in its leaders that could ransack history for their legal and diplomatic precedents; and the growth of imperialism in England has drawn to itself the almost entire support of the literary class of the English race; but literary and scientific culture is not always indicative of the moral strength and determination of a people, and the intellect divested of moral spirit is not a power working in the institution of righteousness, which is the condition of national being.

But a literary or scientific test fails, because the act to which it is to apply is not of a literary or scientific character, and the qualification must be conditioned upon the nature of the act. These qualifications, to the effect that a certain amount of property or a certain degree of literary acquisition shall determine the fitness for the duties of a citizen, proceed from the notion that the character of man consists not in what he is, but in what he possesses; that in the conditions of his action what a man has is to be preferred to what he is.

The real education of the people is to be provided for in the organization of political power. They for whom, in the want of a realized personality, the exercise of electoral power is not possible, yet have a right to the aid of all in the nation that may tend to its development. They are not to be left in political indifference because destitute of the capacity for political power. They have the right to be educated by the state for the state. Their education is to be regarded as the necessity of the state, and in the endeavor toward the development of their personal power, the nation advances toward its destination. It is the formation of an independent manhood, so that he who has reached his majority in years, is always in his political majority.

The correspondent evidence of the law of representation is in the fact that every divergence from it, as the sequence of a false premise, issues in disaster. The sovereignty and representation of numbers, and the entrustment of political power to those, who have in themselves no ground for it, has only this result. There is no basis for electoral rights, when there is no capacity for electoral action. The force which is impersonal in the state, cannot be called upon to shape the destination of the state. The crowd, that is, the disorganized elements, the anarchic fragments, are not to be called to the government of the state. The power referred, on the premise of some abstract notion of rights in representation, to this impersonal mass, is a contradiction. This force does not and cannot offer a vote, when the occasion is open to it by electoral laws. Its action is expressive of no free and conscious purpose; and called to act in the institution of freedom, and to incorporate it in the state, it moves only as some fate. In the construction of a moral order, it sweeps on as a physical force, not as if directed by an inner will, but by a mere momentum. It is the casting into the scales, when the highest issues are to be decided, of a dead weight. It drifts, and like all forces not guided in human life by a personal power, it drifts downwards. Its course, apart from the real will and freedom of the people, is so inevitably toward the wrong, that the language of a clear and self-determinate spirit is, "I have not gone with the multitude to do evil." It is the building not of an order, but of a pandemonium; it makes the nation the confusion of strange tongues, and the Babel of incoherent and unmeaning voices. It creates a power which is not the will of the people, but is without the consciousness of the unity and order of the people.

The object of every political constitution is to exclude this element, that is, the impersonal mass, from authority in the state. The reference of power to it subjects the organization of society to brutal force, while the whole effort of civilization has been to wrest it from that blind and unthinking sway. It is this which has been the constant aim and the condition of freedom.

This reference of power to mere numbers, that is, the impersonal mass, is justified by no right. It is a barren sceptre, and in the defect of sovereignty in itself it cannot act for its institution in the state. It is not the assertion of the sovereignty of the people, but the negation of sovereignty and of the people. Its exclusion is no violation of the law of democracy, but is necessary to the assertion of democracy. Its exclusion is not despotism, but its inclusion is the worst despotism, — the absolutism of a multitude, not the government of a free people. It is a rabble of men which is called to the expression of the thought and purpose of the political people. It is a formless waste, out of which the determination of the form of the state is sought. It is the necessary degradation of the whole, and the state supplies in itself the instrument of corruption. It does not act with freedom, and it will not act for freedom. It falls under the influence of parties and sects, to be used for their special ends. It becomes subservient to men who will employ it for the accomplishment of selfish schemes, or the furtherance of their own ulterior interests. Its subjection is to the domination of those who can rule masses, but cannot rule freemen, and it becomes the instrument of the designs of the demagogue or the priest or millionaire.

The multitude is everywhere dangerous to the state; but the bestowal of power upon it is to place the arms of her arsenals in the hands of the blind. It is the unreason of the state when it calls upon ignorance and vice and crime to determine its career.

This investiture of the impersonal mass with political power, — the mere representation of numbers, — justifies all the scorn which has been spoken of it by the best of men. There is a comprehensive truth in the words, so exact, as the political expression in Shakespeare always is, — where

> "Wisdom
> Cannot conclude but by the yea and no
> Of general ignorance, — it must omit
> Real necessities, and give way the while
> To unstable slightness. *Purpose so barr'd, it follows,*
> *Nothing is done to purpose.*"

The result is, that it —

> "Bereaves the state
> Of that integrity which should become it,
> Not having the power to do the good it would,
> For the ill which doth control it." [1]

The result of the bestowal of political power upon the mass appears in the government of the municipality of New York. With the qualifications prescribed by electoral laws, the danger disappears in a great commonwealth, while it is apparent in a city where large numbers are congregated, whose education under an imperial or ecclesiastical domination has left them without freedom. The people are used to increase the wealth of a few individuals.

There has been a special justification sought for this bestowal of electoral power in its educational influence upon the individual, as invoking a sense of responsibility. It is true that the nation, without reference to the exercise of electoral power with this object, is the mightier power in the education of the race; but the bestowal of electoral power, with the special design of the education of certain individuals, avoids the content of the act and considers it primarily in the interest of the individual apart from the state. Its value as an educational influence upon the mass is not apparent, since in the want of independent action it

[1] *Coriolanus*, act 3, sc. 1.

becomes the instrument of any who may get dominion over it; it induces also a low conception of a vote and of the government itself. The gain which may appear in some instances is at the most slight, in comparison with the detriment to the whole. The education of the few by this method becomes also as costly as it is perilous, as for instance in the municipality of New York.

This bestowal of electoral power has been justified also as a means of protection, and has been called by a senator "the protection of ignorance and weakness." To call upon ignorance in this way to protect itself, is to impose upon it an office of intelligence and decision of character. It is only in justice and foresight that the protection of ignorance and weakness is found. When the control of the state is given to ignorance the safeguard of rights is destroyed. The vote of the city of New York is cast blindly against the public interest, and subserves the private schemes of men. If protection alone, and not a realized freedom, were the end of the state, power assigned to ignorance and weakness would not ensure it.

The necessary nature of electoral power discloses the evil of a condition of affairs which, in the abandonment of character and freedom and the degradation of personality, is fraught with the deepest corruption. In the absence of the organization of the civil service and administration, it is the condition in which public offices and trusts become the instruments of power, so that their places and pay are held to further private and partisan designs, and as agents or tools to control men to certain special uses and ends. The profits of office are used to buy voters, and the promise of office is held before them as an equivalent for their vote, or the threat of removal is used to intimidate them in their vote. Their vote is unfree and of itself is made the instrument of their corruption. It works with injury alike to the individual and to the whole. It is the more immoral, for it is the use of the powers of the nation to subvert its moral order. Thus there are those who refrain from the thorough organization of a civil service upon the simplest maxims of economy and prudence, because they can use its offices to further private and partisan ends and to build up their own power, and an imperfect civil organization becomes the pretext for their course. It is the undermining of the freedom and the defeat of the sovereignty of the people.

The public offices and trusts of the nation are held as patronage. The word is consistent with the barbaric constitutions in which power was held as a private estate; the ruler was a patron and the place belonged to his patrimony. Yet however democratic the pretense of the form of the state may be, to hold these positions as a means for private or partisan ends is beneath the barbaric constitutions, for if they allowed this patronage to the prince, it was because he alone was presumed to be in identity with the state. In the existing condition, the offices and trusts are held, not as in the service of a free state, but as an imperial boon. It is, in the interest of a class of so-called politicians, the building of a power independent of the people, and to become a means of their degradation. To allow these men to offer offices as a recompense for action in their behalf, or to remove or threaten any with removal from offices they have faithfully administered, on account of their independence of political action, is bribery. And when workmen in national armories and navy yards, who are dependent for their daily support upon their daily labor, have their places used as an instrument to control their vote for private or partisan ends, the political crime can scarcely be surpassed. The national offices and trusts are employed to control men as evil dominations control them, in the subversion of their freedom. They are driven to vote as a gang. It is the same in result, when the bribe is tendered by an individual or a party, and in money in hand, or a place of corresponding pecuniary value, and there is no distinction if the workman be discharged from a plantation or a navy yard, or driven from a farm or an armory on account of his vote.

The public service is conducted not only without regard to prudence and economy, and honest and efficient administration, but national offices are used by those in power to retain power and promote their private ends; or in the triumph of a party, they are held as booty won on the field, to be divided among its retainers. The consequence is also the filling of public offices with bad and irresponsible men. The vote of those who are thus controlled is no longer a free, that is, a responsible act, but is the service of a dependent and the assent of a valet. It has no more worth than the act of a slave, the man who does not know his own mind and cannot call his will his own. The corruption works in those who give and those who take the bribe, and one who uses these means to control men becomes destitute of self-respect as he destroys the self-respect of others. It frustrates the free and independent purpose of the people, and there is in it the degradation of character.

The nature of electoral power is inconsistent, also, with the singular proposition, that in certain sections or districts, representation should be made necessary, and a vote should be compulsory. It has been said, that men might be required to send representatives to the government, but this would be a form with no representative character. It would be only the authority compelling the act which was represented, and this could act immediately with better consistency. The action when thus required would not be the representation of free men, and would not have the worth of the power which in some *plebiscite* obeys an imperial will.

The necessary principle of representation illustrates the strength and also the weakness, in that conception which describes the government as the representation of public opinion, or public opinion as the basis of the representative constitution. It is true that public opinion appears only in the organization of society, and there is in it the indication of an aim beyond the private and separate end of the individual. But government is not constituted in the representation of public opinion, and there is not in this the sovereignty or the freedom of the people.

There is in public opinion the unformed thought of men, or thought as it is being formed. It thus takes its color from the changing impulse and emotion and passion of the moment, and reflects its hopes and fears. It denotes, indeed, in some phases, the purpose that will endure and assert itself with irresistible might; and in this is the expression of the conviction of the people, that will hold on against the treachery of those who have been called to power. It is thus that it indicates often the course and tendencies of historic movements. But it denotes often the confused agitation rather than the stable purpose, the impulse instead of the deliberation of the people. It is the rude and crude thought, often obscured by prejudice, and it acts often in an imperfect knowledge of events. Its organs thus are informal forces, and not recognized in the constitution of the state; as, for instance, the popular rumor, that is, the mere "report of a report," the public lecture, the newspaper, the course of the exchange, the talk of the street. It is always undefined, and there is no power whose authentic expression it is so difficult to ascertain, or which is so open to imposition, since some alien purpose may often raise the noise and counterfeit the voice and assume all the guises of public opinion; there is no vehicle of public opinion, as the newspaper or public lecture, but may be set in motion by an alien power. It is indeed the secret or anonymous form of these agents, as the common rumor or newspaper article, that thus enables them to serve a foreign opinion.

The statesman must learn to estimate the strength and the weakness of public opinion, and when and how to regard and to disregard it. It is always to be considered and weighed as a positive force in the conduct of affairs, and those who acted in indifference to it, would expose their measures to the unnecessary risk of disaster. It is to be regarded in any course of action, with respect to what it may indicate in the mind of the people. But so far from an immediate representation of it, it is always to be held as a force which has not even a law of discrimination, whereby its own thought and purpose may become clear. The disposition to overestimate it is a characteristic of weakness. It is more often not itself clear, and instead of being the guide of the state, needs a firmer intelligence to guide it. He who would have even its support in the long run, must be strong alike to lead and to resist; he must learn to apprehend the enduring purpose of the people, and to hold it against betrayal. The danger is that men who are untrue to themselves, and thus without self-respect or rectitude, will listen for it blindly, and follow its uncertain voices, until in their weakness they lose their foothold, and are swept away by its current.

To regard the representation, therefore, as that of public opinion, is obviously defective. It cannot and is not to govern. To regard the government as only its representative, would argue a defect of will. There would be in it the subversion of personality. The power which became its exponent to indicate its courses and the shift in its changes, would be no longer a real government. It would open the way to "unstable slightness." It would yield in the panic of unformed thought. It would be the regiment of those who start at the shaking of the leaves. In the agitation and surging of its crowd, they that would aim only to follow it must leave the place of leaders, and become lost in its multitude as their call is drowned in its tumult. If they rise for a moment upon it, it is only to be swept away by its tide.

The peril is thus in regarding public opinion, not to consider what it may indicate, nor what may be its force, but blindly to obey it. Then in this servility there is the prostration of manhood. Then it is made the substitute for the conviction of duty, and a foundation is sought in it instead of the steadfastness which is "buttressed in conscience and invincible will." To turn from a central rectitude, and the inner light, and the eternal word, to this uncertain voice, which has in itself no law by which it may become clear, is to follow the shout of the multitude. It is the abdication of government when statesmen look only to the popular voice in its momentary changes, and seek the oracles that peep and mutter, and join in the common superstition that calls for its favorite magicians and soothsayers. At last the inevitable weakness of these men incites only the contempt of the people whom they could not govern, and whom they could not guide when called to go before it.

There is another phrase which has become the formula of a certain scheme in representation — the representation of minorities. This presumes an arbitrary division of the majority and the minority, and then asserts an injustice in the reference of the conclusion in political action to the former. The principle which it aims to establish is the actual representation of persons; but it has been made complex not only by not apprehending the necessary principle, which alone gives it consistency, but by the introduction of extraneous notions, as for instance, the proposition for a plurality of votes.

While the aim is always to be an ampler and more perfect organization in the representation of persons, this principle demands the exclusion of whim and willfulness, the mere caprice of men. It also demands the clearer determination which is implied in the representation of persons; and as the principle is embodied in the nation, the government becomes more resolute and more positive. The government is necessarily to have strength and energy of purpose, and authority is to have a clear and unequivocal assertion; and so vast an impersonal mass is already allowed to act, that the form of the political decision of the majority alone may give a positive and conclusive expression to the political will. In another form there might result the most grave disaster in a paralysis of power and will.

The charge which is associated with this phrase of a tyranny of the majority, has no justification on the postulate assumed, nor in the course of government. There has been in history no power so devoid of tyranny as the political majority; and the more frequent invasion of tyranny in modern nations has been in the effort through violence to override the will of the majority of the political people, when asserted in the order of law. If the majority is actually tyrannical in its spirit and intent, no scheme for the protection of minorities, which alone can be sustained by the majority, would avail, and tyranny in some form would be inevitable. It might be inferred from the assault upon the political majority, that the oppression of the world had been consequent upon the political action of the majority of the political people; but the fact is that the tyranny has always been the power of the minority acting with no conformance to a constitutional order, as the despot or dynasty, the hereditary or monetary class, some family or collection of families, bound by a tie among themselves; and these have held the whole as their possession, and subordinated it to their own special ends. The majority also is constantly changing and being resolved in the people, but these powers perpetuate themselves. The assault upon the political majority has often seemed to start from the premise that its act is held as the standard of truth, and not as the form for ascertaining in the political order the determination of the political people, and for the enactment of laws which are over all. The political majority has always been the method of ascertaining the conclusion of a representative body, as for instance in England, where not only the sovereignty of the parliament is assumed, but where there exist no limitations upon its power corresponding in force to those in the United States, and its members are elected by a majority, and while its law is enacted by a majority, submission is commonly rendered to it, while of course no just effort is prevented, to effect its change or repeal.[1]

In the past the will of the majority has been the most beneficent form in which the government of the political people has been instituted. There has been in it a more constant recognition of a principle of right which is over all, and an endeavor to substitute it for the arbitrary action of an individual or a class; and it has sought, though far from its better realization, more steadily the well-being of the whole against the design of a few as an individual or a class, and far more unfrequently than they has it been diverted from its end.

There is an illustration often drawn from the action of the mass, or the fragments of a disorganized society, against the action of the organic people. The cry of a Judæan mob or a Roman rabble is made an argument of accusation against the nation and the expression of the organic will. But in these instances, the illustration is of

[1] The form of representation was a subject of discussion, in the Colonial period. "The Governor, Commissioners, and Council took upon them the legislative power, and the People were governed by their Ordinances until an assembly was called which privilege was then declared to be the People's Right." — "A great part of the injustice done in the Colony may be ascribed to an unequal proportion in representation." — Samuel Mulford, 1714. *Doc. Hist. of N. Y.*, vol. iii. p. 367.

the influence of imperialism. It was when the national spirit and life of Judæa was lost, and her unity was broken in the increase and pretension of parties and sects, that a mob was gathered, and the crowd, that shouted for the release of Barabbas the robber, and for the condemnation of one who came to manifest the power of a king in the service of humanity, appeared when the multitude had already learned to cry, "Cæsar is king; we have no king but Cæsar." This is no illustration of the action of a people, but of the mob which is not a people; it is no argument for accusation against the people, but is the evidence of the degradation of men under an imperialism.

In this principle the political spirit and political will has its true expression. It is to be held as a constant aim, and there can be no estimate of the higher power which it will bring. But the change in the application always in larger and nobler forms, can be the result of no laws, and it is to come in the wisdom of the state. It is to come in the development of the state, and not before its time, when it could involve only peril and disaster to the whole.

In this period, as in every period of transition, when the order of things is disturbed by a vast migration of races, there is so large and indefinite an impersonal mass casting its heavy weight in elections, that its uncertain increase is to be guarded against, and the change which has elements of progress must be in reality as in form, and in the development of the nation in its moral being. The conditions and qualifications of electoral power have a universal premise and law, but the aphorism *de minimis non curat lex* is necessary, and while this in individual instances and to certain persons may involve an apparent wrong, yet the extension of political power to the inclusion in electoral action of a vast number who have no freedom of will, and no capacity for political action, involves a far greater wrong to the higher personality of the nation, and the detriment of the whole.

The electoral right is a political right, and affects primarily the political people, and it should have in the constitution of the whole its enduring guaranties, and its sanctions should be established in the supreme law. The constitution defines the conditions of electoral power, and the writings of President Madison indicate that it designed this, but it defines them as inclusive of the conditions established in the administrative order of each commonwealth for the election of its lower house, and the more definite description is referred to the commonwealth. It is true that there is a certain advantage in this, since an extension of suffrage might be made in the commonwealth, which in its limited sphere, would not involve the peril that might result in an extension through the whole, and the method of amendment in the constitution of the commonwealth is more free; but there is often wanting in the separate commonwealths the spirit which pervades the political whole, and there is a want of the comprehension of the well-being of the whole, and the conditions in each commonwealth may differ so widely as to impair the unity of action in the whole.

By an ingenious exegesis and collocation of clauses in the constitution, the specific designation of the qualifications of an elector may now be claimed as within the power of the Congress, but the assertion of political rights must require no ingenious argumentation. There is not in that the stable ground necessary for the institution of rights, and the argument on which they are assumed to rest may be met by some other argument, and argument is not conclusion. The indifference of this school to the securance of clear and express guaranties for rights in the positive law, is the source of the distrust of its statesmanship with the people. The disposition to be satisfied with some argument, however subtle, indicates the defect in the thought of those who dwell in the abstract conceptions of rights, rather than toil for their substantial realization in institutions.

The Republic is constituted in the representation of persons. There is in this the institution of the actual sovereignty and freedom of the people. It is the organization of the republic in the democratic principle. There is strictly no democratic form of the state. There may have been at a certain interval, in some of the municipalities of Greece, in the organization of the whole people in a public assembly, some correspondence to it, but it was necessarily limited, and there is no historical nation but transcends the possibility of a democratic form. But while there is no democratic form of the state, there is a democratic principle. It is the principle, in which every person who is a member of the nation is to be called to act in the normal determination of its government, and the government is to be in the name of the whole. The form of the state in which the democratic principle is realized is the republic.

The electoral law is the law of the Republic. This law has in the most varying forms the wider historical justification. The only comparison would be with the law of hereditary succession, and the latter claim can scarcely be sustained, even with the long monotony incident to its periods. The latter has assumed an apparent security, since it has an immediate provision for the future; but to leave the government to the accident of birth, and to restrict it to the line of a certain family descent, with the contingency of the intervals which are described as a regency, is not the most provident constitution. It has been from century to century interrupted by a disputed succession; and where the hereditary principle has been maintained, as in England, in historical crises it has been disavowed, as in the revolution of 1688; and these crises have been more often the precedents of national power. The sovereignty in certain families, as in England, has also become only a formal sovereignty,[1] that is, only the institution of sovereignty. There was courage and chivalry in the house of Plantagenet, and there was strength to rule in the house of Tudor, and there was always a courtly dignity and recognition of public duties and public offices in the house of Stuart, but it is difficult to associate a conception of sovereignty with the existing house, and in this aspect the later line of its kings seems a sad and fantastic procession. The families which have held the government as an inheritance, have not differed from other families; they have not been exempt from the law in which the sins of the father are visited upon the children, nor could they claim more than the blessing which showeth mercy unto thousands. A recent writer has said that the constitution of England, its king and peerage, rest upon a power of great influence, although held slightly by the philosophers, the power of visibility. It is rather the opposite, the power of illusion. The haze of old political traditions veils them from the sight, and in their elevation above the people they are not visible as they actually are. The hereditary principle is thus maintained in a sovereignty with indifference to the actual character of the monarch, or it is an institution without reference to a person; negative qualities conform to it, and there is in it no representation of the nation as a person, and only by some figment it is described as a national device, — "only the dot over the i."

[1] In the constitution of England, the crown has not the strength which the executive has in the United States. Mr. Disraeli is one of the few statesmen who have noticed the increasing incapacity or lapse of executive power. The crown is a power without reference to the character of its occupant. It is said the Parliament has become the sovereign, but the Parliament, in certain respects, is not sovereign; it is destitute of the power which should be vested in the legislature, as, for instance, the power to declare war and conclude peace.

The electoral law was the form of the Roman empire and of the German empire of the middle age. It was the law of the church; and the popes, as also the bishops and abbots of the middle age, were elective. In Venice the doges were elective. In Rome the hereditary law was modified by a form of adoption.[1]

It is as the representation of persons, that the republic is formed in the moral determination of the people. Its necessary foundation is in the virtue of the people. Montesquieu defined this as the principle of the republic. It is the foundation of society in every form; but it is the very condition of the order of the republic.

It is said that the republic is a monotony, and its level a low and dead level. The contrast is then the formal gradation of society, the construction of lower and middle and higher classes. The greatness which appears here is comparative. Its aim is the formation of a conventional type. But in the republic the political people hold their own conscious aim, and reflect and determine their own end. It is then a necessity that the republic should have more of life. Its life is always necessarily one of endeavor and conflict, or the government must lapse into some other form. Its greatness is only that of a realized personality. The long monotony of a despotism is in contrast to the ceaseless movement and agitation of the republic, and the latter in its stability demands a higher energy, a more constant vigilance of the people. But the moral life must necessarily follow this law, and in its advance is always

[1] Macchiavelli says that "most of the lineal successors of the Roman emperors turned out badly, while those who were adopted did comparatively well."

Aristotle maintains a partly elective law, rather than a strictly hereditary monarchy. — *Politics*, bk. ii. ch. 8.

Cicero says in a passage of singular force, "Novus ille populus, — Romanus, — vidit id, quod fugit Lacedemonium Lycurgum, qui regem non diligendem duxit sed habendum, qualiscunque is fuit, qui modo esset Herculis stirpe generatus. Nostri illi etiam tum Agrestes viderunt, virtutem et sapientiam, regalem non progeniem quæri oportere." — *De Republica*, bk. ii. ch. 12.

the more quick, and the more unresting and unsatisfied, and borne into higher and intenser conflict. This has its illustration in the energy and devotion and sacrifice which give nobility to the pages of the history of nations. This, says Rothe,[1] is the nature of an holy life, and that it is the more unresting, and that as a consequence there may be the loss of some apparent material advantage to the state, is not to become an argument of opposition to it.

The offices and powers of the republic constitute a public trust. They are not held as a private estate. In England the higher positions are held as a private investment, and in the army and navy commissions are open to purchase and sale.

The representation of the Republic is of a person by a person. It is not of one person in substitution for another, but in community with another. To regard one person as in the place of another, would be the negation of personality, the representation of a person by a form or symbol. The representative violates his own personality, if instead of standing in his own free and conscious self-determination, he aims to follow a constituency and to stand in identity with that. Then he is no longer free in his own will and knowing his own mind, and the result can be only the weakness and instability of government.

The representative is a person, and is the representative of the moral personality of the nation, and therefore in the realization of that acts immediately only in relation to the nation and to God. It is the law and the majesty of the nation, in its unity and its freedom, and as a government over the whole, that is to be realized in his determination. He is not the blind and mechanical instrument or exponent of an external will, as a constituency or a party, but stands in the will and determination of the

[1] Rothe, *Theologische Ethik*, vol. ii. p. 126.

state, which is not external to him, but is to be realized in him; but every formal notion of the nation forbids this, since then the representative has only a formal relation to the nation, and is representative only of separate parties or certain persons in it.

CHAPTER XIII.

THE NATION IN ITS SOVEREIGNTY, IN RELATION TO OTHER NATIONS.

THE sovereignty of the nation, is the manifestation of its power, in the historical life of the world. Its external sovereignty is apparent through its relations to other nations, and in its sphere in history. While its internal sovereignty appears in its government and order, and the assertion of its will, as the supreme law ; in its external sovereignty it exists in its unity and independence in relation to other nations.

The recognition of a nation becomes thus one of the most impressive events in history. It rests on the consciousness, in each of those who act in it, of its sovereignty, as a power in history. It reflects the majesty of a power existent in its unity, in the moral order of the world. This recognition of one nation by another as thus existent with all the sovereign rights of a nation, can never be divested of historical solemnity. From the unformed life of men existing with no consciousness of political unity and order, and sustaining only some tribal relation, there emerges a new nation, to be recognized in its sovereignty by other nations and to enter its course in history. The appearing of a new planet in the wide fields of space, to be followed in all its circles in the physical order, is not so impressive as the appearance of a nation which is to exist as a power in history, and to act upon the destiny of man in that grander order, the order of a moral world. From the vacant centuries that have furnished no element of unity or freedom or fraternity, there rises a power which is to hold a conscious moral aim, and to act as a conscious moral energy.

The sovereignty of the nation has thus its immediate external manifestation, in the recognition of nations. It is the moment in which there is a conscious realization of the historical power of a people, and each stands toward the other in a recognized sovereignty in the world. This recognition presumes in the power which is recognized the capacities which belong in its necessary being to a nation, and in which it is constituted as a nation. The nation recognizes in another, that which it is conscious of possessing in itself, in its own necessary being. It recognizes not a mere association of men in a certain locality, under a certain form of government, but a people as a nation. There can be no recognition which does not imply this.

This recognition presumes then respect toward the nation recognized as a nation. It must concede to it the rights, which in its own necessary existence it asserts for itself. There is the application here of the fundamental law of rights, — be a person, and respect others as persons. This law is implied in the being of the nation as a moral person; it is the necessary postulate of rights and of duties. From this then proceeds the recognized right of a nation to determine its own political end; the right to establish its own political form; the right to exclusive legislation in its domain; the right to self-preservation, to independence, to property; the right to exist in a common relation to other nations. In the existence of the nation as a moral person, is the postulate of the sacredness of the principle of non-intervention. The recognition of it, in its sovereignty, necessarily presumes a deference for its self-determination and its freedom. It is to control its own order, and is to be respected in this, and no other nation is to intervene in its internal administration.

This recognition presumes that the nation which is thus recognized, shall itself respect the rights and powers of other nations. There is the assumption of the formal obligations of a nation. It is to yield respect to others, as it asserts its own self-respect. The principle which is here also the ground of action, is the identity involved in the necessary being of nations.

The recognition of a nation is thus a continuous act, and so long as there is moral integrity of action, it is limited only by the formal existence of the nation itself. It is not therefore to be momentarily offered, nor to be arbitrarily withdrawn. It is the expression of the continuous relation of nations in their existence in history, and proceeds from the postulate of continuity in the nation.

While the recognition of one nation by another nation is one of the highest acts of external sovereignty, the right to recognition is a formal right and the demand for recognition can be only formal. A people may exist with a manifest unity and sovereignty, and with entire independence and freedom, and be in reality a nation, although it receive no recognition from other nations. Whether it be in reality a nation, is to be determined only by its content, that is, the internal sovereignty which is manifest in law and freedom, and the external sovereignty which is manifest in independence and self-subsistence, but its recognition depends only upon the determination, in the judgment of another, whether it be a nation.

This recognition of a nation is not simply the recognition of a certain succession in government, although it is necessarily through a government. It is the recognition of the nation, which in its sovereignty may determine its own government. The act is through the government which the nation ordains for itself, and the government thus constituted, whatever its form, is alone legitimate. It does not follow, therefore, in any event, after the recognition of a nation, that communication is to be opened with some transient power which, perhaps through the aid of a foreign imperialism, may be imposed upon a people from without.

The sovereignty of the nation in its external relations is indicative of the place and vocation of the nation in history. It is manifest through it as an integral power in the moral order, which is history. This is the premise of normal international relations, and the system of international laws. Since the nation has its vocation in a moral order, and its end in the realization of the destination of humanity in history, the nations exist in an international relation, which has for its condition a moral relation, and the system of international laws is definitive of the moral order in which these relations come forth. The nations, in the attainment of their necessary end, are constituted in a moral order. They cannot therefore, in the development of national life, remain in isolation and indifference. While a collection of men has no consciousness of national life, it does not and cannot concern itself with other peoples which exist as nations, except as some fragmentary mass is concerned in the pursuance of some private interest; but if there be the development of national life it is brought into a relation to other nations. The formal definition of these relations is the office of international law. As these relations consist in the moral order of history, their ampler expression will come in the higher realization of the being of the nation in the moral order of history. But the merely formal character which the science of international law has in the work of its yet greatest master, bears the impress of his whole political conception, and of the formal political tendencies of his age.[1]

The science of international law has its foundation in the being of the nation as a moral person; this is the condi-

[1] "Grotius was not a generative thinker. If the difficult problems of the duties which one nation owes to another had been discussed in a Baconian spirit for the purpose of ascertaining what those laws are which bind voluntary agents — if it had been shown historically how these laws, though they may be broken by men with arms in their hands, nevertheless avenge themselves, something would have been gained. But mere maxims which define accurately and peremptorily what should and what should not be done, must be rather hindrances than helps

tion of the rights and obligations which it is to embrace and define. And as the nation advances in the realization of its being, the science which has for its province the definition of the law of international relations will become constantly the expression of a development in wider and more varied relations. It is regulative of relations deeper than those formed simply in the adjustment of controversies arising among nations out of a state of war, or those which are the dictate of a mere international courtesy, although the principle of rights presumes this courtesy. It is this conception of the nation as a moral being, which has given to the work of Wheaton an almost historical position; and however briefly defined, its clear apprehension of it has been the source of an influence which can attach to no mere manual of rules or collection of precedents, in a science which has no acknowledged tribunal. Wheaton says, "every state has certain sovereign rights to which it is entitled as a moral being; in other words, because it is a state;" and again, "every state as a distinct moral being, independent of every other, may freely exercise all its sovereign rights in any manner not inconsistent with the equal rights of other states;" and again, "all sovereign states are equal in the eye of international law, whatever may be their relative power." These propositions are constructive in the work of Wheaton.[1]

The progress in international law can come only in the clearer apprehension of the being of the nation, and the

to an actual moral science. Yet the value of the work," the writer adds, "is in its evidence that these relations have some moral ground; that they cannot be left to be determined by accident, nor commercial cupidity, nor a Macchiavellian policy." — Maurice, *History of Philosophy*, vol. iv. p. 324.

1 Wheaton, *International Law*. Dana's ed. pp. 52, 89, 100.

R. von Mohl has criticized the work of Wheaton as unscientific, a confusion or miscellany of law, contemporary politics, and history; but whatever may be its defect of method, — and that certainly is obvious enough, — its moral spirit and conception has given it an historical influence and position beyond almost any modern work on the subject. — *Literateur und Geschichte der Staatswissenschaften*, vol. i. p. 399.

consequent assertion of the rights and correspondent duties involved in that. It will await the institution of no tribunal, whose formal judgment will be a finality. In the nature of the nation in history, there can be no tribunal and no congress which shall be in itself supreme, and possess over the course of nations an ultimate and imperative control. As the nation is constituted as a moral person, it cannot abdicate its responsibility which is given in its being, and can, in its ultimate determination, be responsible to none on earth, but only and immediately to God.

The nation will hold in its own determination, so long as it exists in the conditions of history, the issues of war, on which it enters in its entire being. It may act in certain circumstances through another, and it may refer the exposition of certain principles, or the estimate in the adjustment of certain concerns, to the judgment of another; but in this it may not act so as to impair its sovereignty, or to surrender its moral responsibility.

In the realization of the being of the nation in history, there will be manifest among nations a deeper relationship. In their greater strength, and as their end is apprehended in the realization of the destination of humanity, there will come a more enduring peace. The advance of humanity is indeed slow; but in the solidarity of nations they will discern the sources and conditions of their aid to each other, and that all must suffer in the detriment of each. Then will come the sympathy and the helpfulness, which there is among men, who march toward the same goal, and at last must march all together if at all. It is therefore no dream, but the coming of a new life, which holds the prophecy and the realization of the fraternity of nations. In the development of history this relation is becoming more perfectly apprehended, and as mankind recognizes more deeply the universal fatherhood, there is manifested in the Christendom of nations the family of nations.[1]

[1] Napoleon III. pronounced the award in the Universal Exposition, "in the name of the family of nations." Thiers and Guizot have shown the course which would have represented the selfishness of France; but the idea of the fraternity of nations has always awakened in the spirit of modern France an emotion, and has stirred it with hopes beyond any appeal to selfish interests.

The tendency of modern diplomacy is, to become more open, and the old devices and disguisements of merely sinister schemes and tortuous courses constantly avail less. But there is no estimate of the danger and disaster involved in the weakness and cowardice of nations, in not meeting as men.

The premise of international rights is given in the postulate of Heffter, as cited by Wheaton: "Law in general, is the external freedom of the moral person. This law may be sanctioned or guaranteed, or may derive its force from self-preservation." — "The *jus gentium* is formed on reciprocity of will."

The refusal of England to submit her action in recognizing the Confederates in rebellion as belligerents, to arbitration, proceeds upon the ground that it was an act of England in her sovereignty, and may in itself be referred to no arbitration; but it was a deliberate act, within her control, and the injuries to this nation which were resultant from it are therefore within her responsibility, and may be submitted to an arbitration.

Their recognition as a belligerent power, by a nation, before the circumstance of war involved any necessity for it, tended necessarily to elevate them to an equality with the nation, and gave them all the advantages which arise from regulations shaped to apply to nations, in defining national rights in time of war. This was the constant security of the *Alabama* in British ports. The neutrality of England in the circumstance of war became nominal.

Mr. Gladstone attributes many of the recent difficulties of England to her recognition of any power as a nation, when a transient interest may dictate. There was more than this in the eager manifestation of satisfaction at the peril approaching the American people. It would seem to have been a sudden disclosure of the spirit of the English toward the United States. If the disclosure was terrible, it would be weakness to forget it and peril to overlook it.

Mr. Gladstone, who seems never to have heard the Hebrew national psalms said or sung, said, as a minister of state, that "Jefferson Davis had made the South a nation," and the remark is mainly significant as indicating among the statesmen of England the conception of what constitutes a nation. The sympathies of nations are more subtle and profound than are those of individuals, and the causes of the sympathy of Prussia and Russia and Italy for America, and the active sympathy of England for the rebellion, lie deep in the springs of history.

The strength of the political course which Mr. Burlingame has inaugurated in the East, is that it does not regard these peoples merely as those with whom we are to open economic relations, — a policy in the interests of the sovereignty and of the freedom of trade, nor to begin a scheme of conquest in which all the elements of national life in the people, however imperfect, are to be crushed; but it is the institution of a policy in which these elements, in the unity and spirit of the people, are developed, and is the investiture of them with powers and rights which have a moral content, and consist with international law.

CHAPTER XIV.

THE NATION AND THE INDIVIDUAL.

THE tendency of the political speculation of the old world, in Greek and Roman thought, was to regard the state as above and before the individual, so that the existence of the latter was subordinate and secondary; — the individual existed only for the state, and the state alone existed as an end in itself. There was the assumption of a necessary contradiction, and the solution was in the negation of the individual. In Greece, the state acknowledged no moral, and allowed no formal limitation to its power. It took upon itself the immediate and exclusive conduct of life. It was to dispose of all, and not only to prescribe the avocations and regulate the affairs, but to direct even the thoughts and affections of men. It compelled the individual to engage in public pursuits and fill public offices and execute public trusts in the same manner as if subject to a military discipline.

In contrast with this, the tendency of modern political speculation, in its abstract systems, has been to regard the individual as above and before the state, so that the existence of the latter is subordinate and secondary; — the state exists for the individual, and the individual alone exists as an end in himself. In these conventional schemes, the state is apprehended as only the form which the individual adopts in the pursuance of his private ends; it is an artificial and temporary association, formed by a collection of certain individuals; it is established and maintained by a certain number of men, as private persons, and is subservient to their interests as individual or collective.

It is secondary to the individual in the assumption that it is only an artificial and temporary organization, and in the rejection of the unity and continuity involved in its necessary conception, and manifested in its organic life.

In the course of history, there has been through the Christian centuries, in the realization of the being of the nation and the individual, the evolution of no antagonism, but there has been the manifestation of their necessary foundation and unity.

Firstly, The nation and the individual are existent in the conditions of history, each as a necessary and integral element, in the normal development of the other. The nation is no abstraction. It is not a formal and external order apart from the people. It is organic, and in its necessary process as a moral organism it presumes in the individual the realization of freedom. In this, it is constituted in its freedom. There is in this, instead of a source of variance, the postulate of its moral strength and its spirit.

The individual, conversely, has his normal development in the nation; it is formed in the institution of a moral order. This has been the course of history. The transition from the unformed life of man, the barbarous condition, has been in the realization of the truly human, that is, the normal and the moral condition, and this has been formed in the relations of the nation. The isolation of man is the representation, not only of an unreal, but an undeveloped existence, and the institution of the normal relations of men, that is, the organization of society, is in the nation. There has been thus for the individual apart from the nation, no realized freedom. The nation has been the precedent of the realization of freedom.

Secondly, The nation and the individual in their relation, exist each in a real and integral moral life and each as an end. The necessary conception of personality forbids that it should exist only as a means to an end, and its realization in the nation and in the individual forbids that either should be apprehended as merely secondary and subordinate. The nation, as a moral personality, has its law of being in itself, and its own vocation and its own end in history; the individual in his own personality has therein also his own law of being, and his own vocation and end.[1]

The personality of the individual has not its origin nor its foundation in the nation; the personality of the nation has not its origin nor its foundation in the individual, but each has its origin and foundation immediately in God, and its vocation is only from Him. There is therefore no necessary antagonism, but in the law of their being an inner unity. There can be, therefore, in their normal development no real conflict, and there can be no apparent or external conflict which does not involve in the one or the other the precedent contradiction of its own nature, and of the law of its own action, as determined in personality. The actual conflict of either with the other, is in its precedent a conflict with itself. That there should be the possibility of an apparent or an external conflict, lies in the fact that through the power of sin, and through the ignorance and the weakness of men, the course of each is agitated and disturbed, and the realization of its being must be through many crises; and in the fact also that the existence of each in itself is a development in the moral conditions of history and of life; but in the realization of the being of each, the possibility of this antagonism is diminished, elements of external opposition are eliminated, and all that separates or occasions variance is being constantly excluded in the course of the development itself.

1 There is the representation of the individual personality in the consciousness, in the dramatist: —

"I am a nobler substance than the stars:
Or are they better because they are bigger?
I have a will and faculties of choice, and power
To do or not to do; and reason why
I do or not do this; the stars have none.
They know not why they shine more than this taper,
Nor how they work, nor what?"

The organism of society is thus construed as an ethical organism, that is, an organic whole in which that which exists in it is both a part and a whole, — a part in relation to an existing whole, and yet each a whole in itself.[1] In the Greek representation, Aristotle justly places the nation in relation to the individual as the whole to the parts, and this relation exists for each individual comprehended in it; but the defect in the Greek thought is in not regarding the individual as a whole and an end in himself, and also in apprehending him as immediately related only to the state, and therefore as secondary and subordinate. This was the fault of the Greek thought; it had not the revelation of the divine origin of man in the image of God, which has been from the beginning of history the ground of the positive Christian development.

Thirdly, The nation is withdrawn from the individual by a vocation, and the individual is withdrawn from the nation by a vocation; but this instead of being the premise of an inconsistence, because the fulfillment of the relation of each is in the realization of personality, and in the will of God from whom it proceeds, is the condition of an inner and a necessary unity, as this unity has its subsistence in God. There is in this apprehension of the moral order existent in the vocation of the nation and the individual, the presentation of no abstract ideal, but it is the very ground of the unity and progress and solidarity of society.

The nation has its own vocation which it is to apprehend and to realize in history; it has not its origin in the volition of the individual, nor its end in the object of the

1 "The nation must apprehend its moral aim not exclusively as the universal but as this in inseparable unity with the individual. Every individual must be an absolute end also to the state. The individuality of none can be engrossed by society as an whole to perish in it, as if crushed through the grinding of the wheels of the state machine, for the sake of the common good." — Rothe, *Theologische Ethik*, vol. iii. sec. 2, p. 903.

"It has often been said that the well-being of its citizens is the end of the state; this is certainly true: if it is not well with them, if their subjective aim is not satisfied, if the state as such is not the means for this satisfaction, then the state stands on lame legs." — Hegel, *Philosophie des Rechts*, p. 321.

individual, since as a moral person, it has its origin in the divine will, and its end in the moral order which is set before it. There is thus manifest in its progress, a purpose in which it is borne toward the divine end in history. There is an aim which in its completeness in history, transcends necessarily the existence of the individual. There is a continuous spirit which is apparent in the succeeding moments of its existence, and these are not merely the changes in a physical sequence, but in the development of a moral being.

The individual is to work in his own vocation, and this consists with a moral order. This vocation, in its external phases, is incident to the realization of personality. The nation cannot determine the vocation of the individual, though in its moral order it is to maintain its sphere. It can assume nothing which devolves upon the determination of the individual, but while existent with it in the relations of personality, it is external to it. The individual cannot transfer to the nation that which is involved in his vocation. Since it is in the realization of personality, there can be no transferal of it, but the individual is to work in it, and to work it out. The individual has necessarily to work in his own purpose, and after the idea given in the type of his own individuality. He can only apprehend that which is his own, and an end which was alien to his being would be for him an abstraction, or would have necessarily to be rejected as an evil. It is thus alone, in conformance to his vocation, that he can work with a conscious spirit and freedom.

Personality is inalienable. The rights of the spirit alone are inalienable rights. They are the rights of the spirit in itself, and are not as those which can be instituted through positive law in the external sphere. They are rights which are not won by force of arms. They are not to be numbered in the conquests of earth. The inner spirit is beyond the assault of force; its life is not touched, and its strength does not yield to mortal wounds. A man may alienate an outward thing, but personality he cannot alienate. Its alienation would presume its negation, the very abdication of the will. The surrender thus of the individual will and the conscience to that which is external, as to a priest, and the faith which calls one on earth a master, is the degradation of personality, and its consequence is superstition and slavery.[1] Since personality has its origin in God, its spiritual and inner life is immediately with God. Its course is in the light in which no shadow falls, as it is unmeasured by time; it is the path which the vulture's eye has not traced, and is as "the flight of one alone to the Only One." "Over the soul," says Luther, "God can and will allow no one to rule but himself." The authority of the state cannot control the inner life, it can judge none for opinion's sake, it can by no enactment direct the course of the spirit; it is not to invade the conscience and thought, it is not to regulate the dispositions of men; it cannot determine their love or hate or thoughts. These are withdrawn from the state, and over them the state neither has the power, nor is it called upon to rule. As the freedom of the inner spirit is beyond external power, the rights of the spirit cannot therefore embody themselves in the formal sphere of positive rights, but the nation is to guard them from all attempt at invasion from the external sphere, and to forbid every attempt to bring force to bear upon them, and is to secure and maintain the freedom of conscience and of thought, the freedom of worship and of science.

Fourthly, The nation and the individual exist in an organic and moral relation, in which the normal development of each has as its condition the development of the other, and their unity is formed after the law of a moral unity. The development of the individual has instead of

[1] Hegel speaks of personality as "die hochste zugescharfste spitze." —*Logik*, bk. iii. p. 349. Rothe says, "Personlichkeit ist die rechste, concreteste, und intensiviste Bestimmtheit." —*Theologische Ethik*, vol. i. p. 66.

its restriction, its necessary condition in the nation. It has its postulate in no merely external order, and no formal complex of laws and systems, but there is in these its limitation. As it is formed in relations, it subsists in a relation to the nation, as a moral person. The life that proceeds in conformance only to an external and formal postulate — the life that in morals is under rules, and in art under manners, and in religion under dogmas, and in politics under systems — is devoid of energy and of the strength and satisfaction of a living spirit. It is because the nation is not merely an external and formal sequence or system, but an organic and a moral person, that it consists with the development of the individual person.

The nation indeed exists in its freedom in the realization of a moral order, but that order is correspondent with the real, the innermost being of the individual personality, and therefore the individual may strive to embody his moral determination in it, and may have in it the satisfaction of his aim. But it is in consistence with this that the nation may always require from the individual, in the external sphere, an external moral life, and the individual may demand from the state that no law determining the external sphere shall be in itself immoral, or destructive of the rectitude, or conviction of right of the individual, or impose obligations which are an offense to conscience.[1]

[1] The conscience is not simply a certain faculty, as the memory and the judgment, to be occupied with the perception and contemplation of good and evil, as the memory, for instance, is occupied with the recollection of the past, or the judgment with the comparison of objects. It is not simply the capacity for the wider knowledge of good and evil, and the higher, — the better conscience is not the wider acquisition of knowledge of the fruit of the tree of good and evil, and the discernment of the quality of its fruitage. This can account for none of the facts of conscience, as they are attested in the consciousness of the individual; or in the writings for instance of Shakespeare and the older dramatists, in whom there is the most profound analysis of these facts; or in the history of the race; or in the witness of its great moral teachers. There is in the realization of personality the conquest of evil and the separation from it. The conscience presumes the communion of a person with a person ; it is represented thus as the inner voice, the eternal word which speaks to the spirit of man.

It is a duty to obey, but if the law to which obedience is enjoined is in violation of the law of conscience, its rejection is a moral necessity. The individual may not in his action controvert his own conscience, as if for instance the state demanded his participation in some superstitious rite. But the state in every law and regulation of this sort, not only passes beyond its province, but the requisition of such acts is in violation of the law of its own being, as there can be no actual conflict of the individual and the nation but it is preceded by, and in itself involves, the variance of the one or the other with the law of its being. The rejection of an immoral requisition may be therefore the conformance to the higher law, the law of the being of the nation, but the rejection can only be justified in the individual, when it is followed by an effort and endeavor to repeal the law or regulation itself.

The development of either the individual or the nation is in so far the condition of the higher development of the other, that the ages of their higher historical development have been coincident. They become associated in the spirit of the people. In the life of the nation, the very names of its members, in whom there has been the higher personality, become the synonym of its strength. Thus Dante becomes identified with Italy, and his name becomes a sign of its national hope; and Shakespeare with England, and Luther with Germany; and in the struggles of the peoples for national life, their names become the symbols of national unity and national spirit.

It is thus, also, that in the decay of the nation there is the correspondent degradation of the individual. This has its historical evidence in many forms. As the strength of the organic life of the nation is impaired, and its spirit is

There is in the conception of personality, the significance in ethics of the golden rule, as a comprehensive law, — "do unto others as ye would that they should do unto you." This alone removes it from a mere negation; the law of action is in no abstract idea of justice, nor in love of itself considered, but the content of the law is in personality.

broken, there is an increase in the assumption and domination of sects and parties, and the individual personality is weakened as the people become entangled and trammeled and ridden by them. The tyranny of opinion is stronger in the decadence of law and freedom. The moral energy and vigor of the people is sapped. The armies are no longer armies of men, but masses moving mechanically, as if impelled by some power external to themselves. They become converted into the passive instruments of an imperial force.

It is in the law of a moral unity — the unity in which the realization of personality subsists — that the foundation of the unity and continuity of the nation is laid. It is the law which has its highest manifestation in sacrifice. It consists with the consciousness of the vocation of the nation, as the fulfillment of humanity in God. A historian of the state, as he presents, in the exclusion of all theories, the facts of history, says,[1] "The glory and honor of the nation have always elevated the hearts of its children, and inspired them with sacrifice. For the being, the freedom, and the rights of the nation, the noblest and the worthiest have always offered their lives and their all. The whole great thought of the Fatherland, and the love of its children to it, would be inconceivable, if this moral personality did not belong to the nation."

But as there is in the moral unity which is manifest in sacrifice, the recognition of the moral being of the nation, there is in it also, the preclusion of the postulate and induction of individualism. It can find no reconciliation with the assumption that the nation exists only for the institution and protection of private interests, and the furtherance of private ends. The unity which subsists with the sacrifice of the individual for the nation, as it is formed in the manifestation of the law of the highest moral unity in the life of humanity, can proceed only in the conception of

1 Bluntschli's *Allgemeines Statsrechts*, vol. i. p. 40.

the being of the nation as a moral person. It cannot consist with a mere individualism in its principle or result; and it is abhorrent that the sacrifice of those who had the higher moral spirit — the worthier going forth in their prime with joy and trust — should be counted only to serve the private and special ends of the individual, and to secure or promote their pleasure or possession; and when the names and sacrifice of these are kept in the memory of the people, it is abhorrent that any should regard the nation as existent only to subserve their private and special interests and ends. But this is the necessary assumption of individualism.

It is because there is an inner moral unity in the nation that the higher realization of personality consists with it. The ideal state of Plato regarded the freedom and personality of the individual with dread, and found no place for it; but in the realization of the nation it becomes the element of its strength. It is as the temple whose building is of living stones. The very substance of the nation is in identity with the realization of personality; but this can be conceived only as the nation is a moral person. It is thus in its history, that those in whom there is the higher realization of personality testify in themselves to the higher realization of the nation. The will that strives for the prevalence of righteousness on the earth, in obedience to the divine Will; the spirit that communes with the inner voice to follow the divine Word; — as there is in these the source of the personality and freedom of man, so there has been in these, also, the building of the nation. The historical forces, with which no others may be compared, in their influence upon the people, have been the Puritan and the Quaker. The strength of the one was in the confession of an invisible presence, a righteous and eternal Will which would establish righteousness on the earth, and thence arose the conviction of a direct personal responsibility which could be tempted by no external splendor, and could be shaken by no external agitation, and could not be evaded or transferred; the strength of the other was the witness in the human spirit to an eternal Word, — an inner voice which spoke to each alone, while yet it spoke to every man; a light which each was to follow, which yet was the light of the world; and all other voices were silent before this, and the solitary path whither it led was more sacred than the worn ways of cathedral aisles. There was in this the foundation of the personality of each, and the secret of the power in which they have wrought upon the nation.

Fifthly, The conception which defines either the nation or the individual as subordinate and secondary, is in its error the postulate of an inevitable antagonism. If either be held not as an end in itself, but only as a means having the other for an end, there can be no principle of unity and no form of reconciliation; there can only result the negation of the one by the other. Society, then, in its irregular course, moving from one contradiction to another, sweeps through the extremes of socialism and individualism. It alternates between a communism, in which there is the destruction of the individual, and an imperialism, in which as in anarchy there is the exaltation of the individual. There is in each of these phases of discordant action, the contradiction to the nation as an ethical organism, — the subversion of the organic and moral being of the people. The result in each is the decay of public spirit, which is the reflection of the moral aim of the people, and the loss of even the conception of public duties. Thus in an individualism, — where society is apprehended as having its origin in the volition of the individual, and its continuance subject to his option, and government is only the temporary agency of certain individuals, its right only the combination of private rights, its will only the momentary choice of private persons, its end only the furtherance of private ends; and in socialism, — where the individual is apprehended as subordinate, and is related to the government only as its subject, and in himself and his services is held as if owned by the state, — there is in the principle and result the comprehension only of private capacities and private obligations, and in each there is no foundation for public duties and public rights. Their conception is apparently preserved in the latter assumption, but in it, the necessary rights of the state itself can only be apprehended as private rights, and in relation to the individual the state is only a private person.

There is wanting also in the artificial conception of the state, that is, its conception as only a formal sequence or order, the necessary condition of the individual development. It is necessarily restrictive of the individual. This has been conceded in the induction from the theory itself. Those who have assumed the origin of the state in a compact, have regarded its existence as the necessary and formal limitation of the individual, and therefore it has been assumed that the individual surrendered a part of his actual freedom and actual rights on his entrance into it, and in so far suffered the deprivation of them.

The organization of a merely formal association, as the organization of a sect or a party, is necessarily restrictive of the individual; but it is not thus in an organization formed in an organic life, and as freedom has no formal ground, it cannot subsist in a merely formal association, and it is only as the nation is an organic and moral person that freedom is realized in it, and that the freedom of the individual may be wrought in and with it, in its normal development.[1]

Sixthly, The nation is to institute and maintain for the individual the sphere of an individual development in its external conditions. It is to enable each to bring all that is in the type of his individuality to its fresh and free expression. There is to be room for each that he may do

[1] See Bluntschli's *Geschichte des Staatsrechts, etc.*, p. 622.

all that is in him to do, so that if there be failure in any attainment it is in the homely phrase, because it was not in him. The state by no enactment is to thwart or restrict the working out of the individuality of each in its own type. It is not to hamper or debar any in the creative use of the talents given to him, but in its external conditions is to guard them against let or hindrance. The individuality of each is to be so left, that each may work after his own idea, as all that is alien to this must necessarily be rejected as abstract or evil.

This is the condition of the moral life, and its real achievement. In this alone, as the individual works freely and steadily in it, is the only sureness of strength and repose of character. It is in this that the manifold riches of life, more varied and opulent than in the process of the physical world, are wrought. There is thus to be open to each, the expression of his own conceit, his own disposition of things, his own fancy alike in the work and play of life. There is to be also the freedom of work, and freedom of thought in every form, in theology, in politics, in science, and freedom of study and research, and freedom of communication and association, and freedom of coöperation in industry and economy. There is to be freedom of action, the choice of a home, the choice of a vocation, the choice of a wife. This freedom in every field is the condition of moral strength. In it the bondage of the animal is overcome, and "the ape and tiger die."

The higher individuality is always advancing toward the universal, as universality is a necessary element in personality. Thus the mere eccentricity of style, the singularity of manner or oddity of action which do not belong to individuality, tend to disappear, as all mere mannerism ceases in the work of the greater artist.

In the necessary conception of a moral organism, the nation is to regard the individual as in himself a whole, and its aim is to be, that his powers shall have a development in a consistent whole. Since the nation comprehends in its aim the universal, not as an abstraction, but in the realization of personality, it diverges from its own aim, and impairs its power in every course which is restrictive of the individual personality. Its attempt immediately to control and direct it, is an incursion always marked by the devastation of human energy. In its encroachment it can only mar the work and baffle the purpose of men. It can only make men by it the agents of imperial dominion and the subjects of priestly superstition, the tools of sects and the trade and stock of parties, not the members of a free nation. It is the course of principalities and powers, not of the government of free men.

Seventhly, The nation is constituted as a power in the education of the individual. The individual first becomes a person in the nation. It acts as a power in the realization of personality. It works as an organic energy. The elements of a moral order in it are formative of character. In the nation the individual apprehends the authority of law in an order which is over self will, and he has before him an aim which transcends a selfish end, and is lifted into the consciousness of a life which has a universal end. In the nation there is wrought into the life of the individual the apprehension of a purpose formed not in momentary and transient desire, but a purpose transmitted through the succeeding generations with its sacred memories and mysterious sympathies and quickening hopes. The nation thus becomes for the individual an heritage, and not his alone, but to be held for those who shall follow him. The wealth of its historical associations, and the grandeur of its historical epochs, are its gifts. The majesty of its law, and the authority of its government, and its conquering power are around him; its acquisition is his vantage-ground; its domain is his home; its order is his working field; its rights are the armor it has forged for him ; its achievements are the nobler heights he treads; its freedom is the ampler air he breathes.

The evil of things is in the degradation of personality, and in that men sink into the undistinguished mass. But the nation in its being as a moral person penetrates the whole, and transfuses it with its spirit. In its relationships it becomes the realization in humanity of the brotherhood of men; and in its continuity, it takes hold upon that which is eternal, and man is lifted into the clearer consciousness of the being and the eternal "I am," the foundation of all. But no theory of interests, and no scheme of economy, and no sect in its exclusion, and no imperialism in its dominion, have power for this, and it belongs not to the nation as these, but to the nation because it is other than these.

There is in Stahl a suggestive and beautiful illustration of the representation of the state in the fundamental thought of Plato and Rousseau. The true postulate and the real object, it is admitted, is the perfect unity and relationship of men in a moral kingdom, and with this the perfect freedom and conscious self-determination of each; it is this that has inspired the loftiest conceptions of the state. The fundamental thought of Plato is the perfect unity of the state, but as involving the surrender of the individual will; and yet it is this which casts a marvelous light upon the pages of the Republic, — the feeling that the true condition of humanity is only realized when the individual wholly and without reserve loses himself in the unity and the harmony of a higher moral whole: the fundamental thought of Rousseau is the perfect freedom of the individual, and he asserts as the problem a condition in which every man remains perfectly free, so that when he obeys the state he obeys only himself; and this statement of the problem is the deep and eternal truth, but it is only to be solved in the conclusion, that the will of the state and the will of the individual hold substantially the same determination, and that each hold a moral determination.

There is a faith in the destination of the state which makes the highest moral endeavor no vague and empty dream. There is a faith which while it may call for the willing sacrifice of the individual, yet makes it not all in vain; and they that in the strength of that faith pass though the suffering and sacrifice of prisons and of battle-fields, find in the realization of the life of the nation that the words are justified, "He that loseth his life shall find it."

NOTE. Mr. Mill says: "The tendency of all the changes taking place in the world, is to strengthen society, and to diminish the power of the individual; formerly men lived in what might be called different worlds, different ranks, trades, etc. at present in the same. They now read the same things, see the same things, have the same rights and liberties, and the same means of asserting them. The assimilation is still proceeding; all the political changes of the age promote it since they all tend to raise the low and lower the high." — *On Liberty*, pp. 8, 43. This proposition that the political changes taking place in the world, — the political changes tending to increase the power of society, operate to diminish the power of the individual, is the necessary induction of Mr. Mill's conception of liberty; but it is presented with no historical evidence. These changes, it is admitted, are towards the realization of a stronger life in the nation, that is, the organization of society; but the ages of national development have always been characterized by a higher individual development. These changes have been the greater in the United States, in Germany, in Russia, in Italy, in Spain; and the most superficial survey of these countries makes it apparent that the greater unity and power in the realization of the being of the nation has been coincident with a higher freedom — a higher realization of the individual personality. A wider illustration might be drawn from the history of preceding centuries, as for instance, the age of the higher national development of England was the age also of Shakespeare, of Raleigh, of Bacon, of Milton.

To read the same books, to hear the same truths, to see the same ideals in art, to become conversant with the same facts in history, does not diminish individuality; the same books does not mean books of sameness. That all men, for instance, read the Bible, or Homer, or Dante, or Shakespeare, or in the facility of travel, have opened before them the whole world of art, does not diminish individuality. If these truths, or books, or works of art, were limited by an exclusive patent, it would not aid in the development of individuality. In so far as any production in literature or art has a universal element, the personality of each is elevated, instead of being depressed and diminished by it. It would be inferred that individuality is apprehended in the preceding citation as only a formal variety or contrast. The artificial distinction is the description of a personage, and not of personality.

When Mr. Mill assumes a diminution of individuality as the result of the institution of the same rights, the fallacy is more apparent, but is most dangerous, for these rights have their consistent foundation in no artificial representation of the state, but only as they are recognized as the rights of personality — the rights of man. And individuality is not founded in, nor developed by, artificial distinctions and grades in rank, or caste, or by various trades, or by the isolation of provinces; these impair it as it is compressed in their external moulds. The force of custom and circumstance weighs upon the spirit, as it is cramped and bent to run in these grooves. The country may be called the more free which has roads open through it; but it is not the more free when one is always required to take a road through the valley and one always to ride on the hills. The stronger individuality comes to hold these distinctions which are cited, only as an accident. And the formal distinctions of rights and liberties, as it severs them from their only true foundation, instead of elevating crushes the individuality of men and fetters their free action; for the further statement, it is a law of unvarying force, that when in the nation the low becomes high, it is not by the degradation of the high, but in the elevation of the whole.

Mr. Spencer has a representation of the state, in which education and the institution of public schools by the state is regarded as an infringement upon the sphere and rights of the individual; and recognizes among the rights of the individual "the right to ignore the state." — *Social Statics*, p. 229. The meaning of this term is made further apparent. Mr. Spencer says: "Government being simply an agent, employed in common by a number of individuals to secure to them certain advantages, the very nature of the connection implies that it is for each to say whether he will employ such an agent or not. If any one determines to ignore this mutual-safety confederation, nothing can be said except that he loses all claim to its good offices and exposes himself to the danger of maltreatment." — *Ibid*, p. 229. It may be well to have the induction of an out and out individualism, which holds the state only as a "mutual-safety confederation," — a joint-stock insurance office, and regards government as a private "agency," and recognizes for the individual, "the right to ignore the state." Then when not only one but two or a crowd assert their rights and ignore the state, and in this condition rob or murder, or in any sort maltreat each other, the state may not act in reference to it, since it is only the agency in the employ of other individuals. If then, — if the illustration may be allowed, — Mr. Spencer assert and exercise his rights, and while maintaining his right to ignore the state is robbed by some vagrant, of course he cannot recover through the aid of the government the property which he has lost; or the vagrant, not having determined himself to ignore the state, may bring the power of the government, being the agency in his employ, to secure him in his actual possession, — it of course refusing to admit the claim of one who had ignored the state. Mr. Spencer further describes this right as the attitude of "a citizen in a condition of voluntary outlawry." — *Ibid*, p. 229. It is difficult to imagine "a citizen in a condition of voluntary outlawry;" and one fails to recall the political position of any whom it depicts, unless it be not the least significant among the political characters in Shakespeare, — Sir John Falstaff. The satisfaction with which Sir John would receive this presentation of the state, as defining his position, can readily be imagined, and it is not surprising, in the unshrinking conclusions of the writer, to find on the following page a repetition of Sir John's inveterate opinion, — "The state employs evil weapons, soldiers, policemen, jailers, to subjugate evil, and is alike contaminated by the objects with which it deals and the means by which it works." — *Ibid*, p. 230. The difference between evil doers and deeds, and this use of so-called evil weapons, is not defined; and a people who have reason will not regard the soldiers of the nation as justly described as "evil weapons," nor believe that it was contaminated by them. These statements need no discussion, and if there be an illustration of a barren logic applied to the state, or in Milton's phrase, "ideas that effect nothing," it is in these positions. Their significance is mainly in their evidence that at the outset a mere individualism loses the conception of a country, and the relation of the people to the land. They are the induction of empty formulas; and they do not touch the solid ground, nor comprehend any fact in the life of an historical nation. And it is the peril of a people if these theories mould its thought; the right to ignore the state becomes the justification of secession and rebellion and of every political crime, and these principles in the thoughts of men are the dissolution of society and destruction of the nation.

CHAPTER XV.

THE NATION AND THE FAMILY.

THE nation and the family exist in a necessary and moral correlation. They do not exist in identity; the family has its own unity and order, and the nation has other powers and obligations, so that when society is constituted after a patriarchal type, and does not pass beyond that, there is no political life, nor the institution of an historical power.

The family is the natural and the normal condition of human existence. It is not the unit of society, that is, the ultimate and integral element, but it is the unitary form of society. In its beginning it is rude and imperfect in its structure, but with the progress of society it passes on to a higher development and a more perfect conformance to its type in the true and monogamic organization.

The family is of divine institution, and is constituted in and with the nation in the moral order of the world. It is a relationship, and there is thus in its growth the education of the individual and the formation of character.

It is as a moral order, and as constituted in moral relations, that the family has its origin and foundation, not in impulse and desire and transient choice; but it presumes in its beginning and its course the assertion and continuity of a moral determination, and therefore impulse and transient choice must be brought into subjection to it. It is as a moral order that it has its own law, and is to be formed after its own necessary conception. It is as a moral order that it is related to the whole order and organization of society, and therefore its violation affects not only the individual but the nation.

The family, in its divine origin and in its formation in the relations of a moral order, and in its consistence with the determination of personality, is a holy estate. It has its beginning in the "I will" of those who enter it; and it cannot therefore consist with the transient desire, nor the momentary act of the will, and these are excluded by its law, and the continuous character of the moral determination of the will is apprehended in it. It is in conformance to the relations of a moral order; and as these relations, while they consist with the moral determination, had not their origin in the transient volition of man, they cannot be made subject to it. Since man did not create this order, in the possibility of sin, he may interrupt or violate it, but he cannot change it. It is not therefore existent only in the momentary choice of separate parties, to be continued or dissolved, as the inclination of either or both may dictate. This would consist only with an arbitrary and unfree, and therefore an immoral, constitution of society.

The family is organic; it has not its origin in an enactment or a contract; it is not a construction in conformance to a speculative theory or scheme; it is not a formal relation, but an organic and moral relation; it is not a formal order, but the natural and normal order. This precludes its assumption by a certain section or a certain class as an exclusive or a proprietary right. This precludes also the representation of the origin of the family in a contract. The contract also could not become the ground of the unity involved in the family, since those who form a contract remain separate parties to it.

The necessary analogy of the family and the nation illustrates their necessary structure, and there is in it the avoidance of the error of many political abstractions and the infidelity of many political dogmas. The representation of the nation as only a formal organization, or as an external order, or as the exclusive possession of a few, or as formed in a contract, or as the scheme and expedient of legislators, is inconsistent with the necessary analogy of the family and the nation.

In the organization of society the family is precedent to the nation, while in its continuance it is subordinate to it. It is through its precedence and through its necessary constitution in organic and moral relations, that it appears in an historical relation with the beginning of the nation, and subsists in a continuous relation with it. The nation has not its origin in the family, but it exists in a necessary correlation with it, and in the development of each this relation must always have a deeper recognition. The first indications thus of the organization of society, are in the family, the life of the patriarchs and the patricians; and the notions of a formal and conventional origin of society disappear in the study of the historical beginning of things.

There has been in no age the record of the foundation of the nation, but there has been coincident with it the witness to the sacredness of the family. In the ancient world, or rather in the beginnings of the historic world, this conception is central and prevails in its art and literature and laws. The book of the Genesis is mainly filled with the record of the foundation of the family, and the incident of its history; and with its close the transition is made to the nation. The Iliad, in which there is the deepest reflection of the spirit of archaic life, is the story of a war for the vindication of the purity of the marriage bond, and its heroes are those who go to battle to vindicate the sacredness of the family; the Æneid is the story of filial duty and reverence, and in each the spirit of the family blends with the nation, and in each there is the unfolding of a national life. In Judæa the family, in its primitive law, is declared to be holy, it is to be maintained as an institute of the nation in its order, and its violation is to be punished as a crime. In Greece, its earliest institutions, the phratriæ and gentes, are the evidence of the power and the dignity of the family. In Rome the reverence for the family is reflected in all the observances of its religion, moulding all its institutions and its laws. The law has a universal attestation, that when the life of the nation has been the deeper, and its moral aim more clearly apprehended in the consciousness of men, there has been a clearer recognition of the sacredness of the family, and conversely when the family has been regarded as formed in a contractual law, or a momentary obligation, it has impaired the power and spirit of the nation. In its higher development, the people have apprehended in the nation the glory in the work of its ancestors, and in its future the enduring heritage of its children. It is thus that the symbols of the family have been inwrought with those of the nation, and its services have been recounted in the inscription of ancestral honors. Its glory has been in its devotion to the nation, and it has kept the names of those whom it has given for it in its holiest traditions. It is thus that reverence for the fathers and their work is involved with the continuity of the nation, and therefore the law which is so deep a revelation of the conditions of national life, "Thou shalt honour thy father and thy mother," is made the premise of the permanent possession of the land by the people.

It is thus that in the decadence of national life there is a loss of the consciousness of the sacredness of the family, and a consequent increase in the violation of its law. It is the degradation of the family, and the lower apprehension of its obligations, that is represented alike by all her annalists and her satirists, as the cause and circumstance of the ruin of Rome. When the sacredness of the family is not regarded, when it is no longer apprehended as a moral order, but as devised by men and shaped only by a law of expediency, and subject to caprice, the life of society is corrupted in its sources.

Thus also the system of slavery, in its antagonism to the nation, was in conflict with the law of the family; and among the slaves in certain commonwealths, family life was unknown, and many on emerging from slavery had no family name, but only the designation given to identify the individual.[1]

In the family a child is educated for the nation. It is a relation which has a moral content, and character is moulded in it; and the individual grows into the consciousness of a whole, in which he is borne beyond his own separate and selfish end. In the advance of childhood there is also the consciousness of a continuous relation, and in its obedience there is the education for government and for freedom. It has been truly said, that government so depends on the life of home, that for a homeless community, anarchy or despotism would be the alternative.[2]

The conception which prevails of the nation shapes the family also. When it has been regarded only as a formal relation, and its origin referred to a contract, the same law has been assumed as defining the family; when it has been apprehended in a mere individualism, the conception of the family as organic and as a divine institution, has also perished, and in this formalism and individualism, there is not only the rejection of the organic and moral being of the family, but its necessary relation to the nation.

The necessary relation of the nation to the family is the condition of the rights and obligations existent in that relation. The nation is to guard and maintain the family, in

[1] Slavery, in its necessary antagonism to the organic being of society, destroyed the family before it sought to destroy the nation; and there is nothing in the reconstruction of society more important than the assertion of the sacredness of the family and the unity of the household. There might be the highest value in a homestead act of some sort, but no legislation can maintain an accumulation of property without a deep assertion of the family, and with it, in the ordinary administration of civil rights, nothing can prevent that accumulation.

[2] Rousseau says, "The family is the primitive type of political society." "Prima societas in ipso conjugio est, proxima in liberis, deinde una domus communia omnia. Id autem est principium urbis, et quasi Seminarium Reipublicæ." — Cicero, *De Officiis*, i. 17.

conformance to its normal and moral conception, and to punish its violation, which is in a higher measure a crime against the whole. The nation fails in its office, in which it is clothed with power and authority for the realization of a moral order, if it regards with indifference, in any form, the infraction of that order. It is thus that it is in conflict with a system of polygamy, which has in itself the elements only of an imperfect development of society, or elements at variance with the moral unity of the family, so that it becomes an impulse toward barbarism. It is thus, also, that it is to prescribe and regulate the forms and conditions of marriage, and to require that it be undertaken not slightly nor hastily, but with a definite form and the attestation of the obligations of the state, in and for its maintenance. It is thus to punish the violation of the law of the family, and is not to leave it to the wild justice which acts in private revenge, which is the defect of government; and it is not to omit adultery from the calendar of its crimes, nor to intermit the judgment of it as crime; it is an abandonment of its trust if it fails in this.

In its civil rights the family is to be sustained by the nation acting in and through the order of the commonwealth, and its inheritance in property, and the guardianship of its members left dependent, is to be observed by the nation, and if parents themselves are derelict in duty to their children and to society, even the right of parental control must be superseded by the *parens patriæ*.[1] But the maintenance of the family in its moral order is the immediate obligation of the nation, and although it acts in and through the process of the commonwealth, yet its obligation is not limited to the latter sphere, and while in certain periods or phases it may act more effectually through it, yet in others the same method might imperil the order and being of the whole; thus, if divorce is allowed it may devolve immediately on the nation to prescribe its

[1] 4 Whart. R. 11.

conditions. And as the family is in itself a moral order, and has not merely a formal origin, the government of the state cannot simply by a formal act annul it, and the divorce it grants is not the ground of the dissolution of marriage, but the authoritative recognition of the fact that the bond of the family has been already dissolved by crime.

The hope and the blessing of the family and the nation is one. Their foundations are not laid with human hands. The years do not erase them from the record of human lives.[1]

[1] In *Troilus and Cressida*, Shakespeare has indicated the deep moral relation of the family and the nation, and its significance, in the story of Troy. The war had its origin in the violation of the purity of marriage life, and it was this which involved the city in destruction. The doom then which overtakes Troilus and Cressida is the reflex borne on through the years, and on to the close of the city, of the moral judgment upon Paris and Helen. There is an expression not only in the catastrophe, but through the whole drama, of the organic and moral relation of the family and the state, and it shapes the discourse and even lends its coloring to the imagery of the play. It is thus that its thought dwells upon the

"Unity and married calm of states,"

and thus the deepest lessons of political wisdom are no digression, but are naturally connected with the conception and import of the play, and the tragedy in its close consists with the unity of the whole. This political significance alone justifies the drama from the criticism of Mr. Verplanck, which has the assent also of Mr. White, that "the effect of the play is impotent and incongruous." Mr. Verplanck yet says the drama "displays all the riches and energy of the poet's mind when at its zenith;" and Mr. White places it "among the most thoughtful of all his plays." White's *Ed.*; vol. ix. p. 10. One may then be reluctant to admit the conception which regards the conclusion as impotent and incongruous, and the political lessons as only detached discussions on politics, and the awful fate at the close as arbitrary and misplaced. But if, in the close of the history of Troy, there is to fall upon the life of its own members — on Troilus and Cressida, — with scarcely an immediate premonition, the shadow of the guilt which was the beginning of the war and the destruction of the city, then in the relation in which the family is involved with the nation in its whole course, and from which no individual member of it can be wholly exempt, there is the unity of the drama, and then the same doom is repeated in the close of Troy which impended over it in the beginning of the war, as if in that alone the burden of the city was ended.

CHAPTER XVI.

THE NATION AND THE COMMONWEALTH.

THE nation in its internal order and administration, is constituted in the commonwealth. The family is the primary form of human society, but in the natural growth of society the family does not remain single; it branches outward, forming other families, or in the course of time other families become connected with it. These have as separate families certain relations; they are subject to certain common necessities, they hold certain common lands in occupancy, and with labor and its result in the satisfaction of necessities, there may come into use some mode of exchange in that which they have separately obtained. The return of labor is scant and irregular, and often is subject to the disposition of the stronger, but in this archaic life some uses, in forms however rude, prevail, in which interests are recognized, and although they may be shaped at the outset by the will of some patriarch, these uses obtain a certain force. It is the community which has been formed in the transition of the family, through common necessities, and the adoption of common uses and the accumulation of common interests. There is in this the beginning of the system of civil rights, and the building of the commonwealth.[1]

The commonwealth may be regarded thus in its formal organization as precedent to the nation.

[1] In defining the character and relation of the United States and a particular State, the international and the civil state, — the nation and the commonwealth, this term is used in a strict and limited significance. Yet it is not arbitrary, and may claim both a literal and historical justification; it is the style of many of the earlier and larger communities, as the commonwealth of Massachusetts, the commonwealth of Virginia, the commonwealth of Pennsylvania.

In the process of society, the family exists in an organic, and the commonwealth in a formal relation to the nation.

The distinction in the organization of society, of the commonwealth and the nation, has been recognized by the great masters in political science. Aristotle describes (1.) the family — οἶκος, the house; (2.) the commonwealth — κώμη, the community; and (3.) the state — πολις, the political body; the city state. The commonwealth, he says, is formed for mutual advantage, but the state is formed for a moral end.[1] The conception is represented by Hegel, with great clearness and completeness, and forms one of the most masterly subjects in his politics. Hegel maintains the distinction through the whole structure of his work. He defines (1.) the family, — *Die Familie;* (2.) the commonwealth, *Die Bürgerliche Gesellschaft*, the civil state; and (3.) the nation, *Der Staat*, the international state.[2]

The commonwealth is the civil order of society. It is a formal organization, and is based upon external and necessary relations, and its action is through a civil system for the security of the private rights of persons.

1 *Politics*, bk. i. ch. 2.

2 *Philosophie des Rechts*, p. 66. Hegel defines the commonwealth as "an association of men as private individuals, and thus as existent in a formal relation, — a relation formed through their wants, and in the civil constitution as a means for the security of persons and property, and in an external order for their special and common interests;" he says, "the commonwealth as an external order, in its realization recedes into and subsists in the state." — *Ibid.* p. 215. The commonwealth, he says, has three phases, the satisfaction of the individual through labor and exchange, or "the system of wants;" the security of liberty and property, or "the jural process;" and the care of special interests as a common interest, or "the police and corporation." *Ibid.* p. 248. He says the commonwealth "is constantly apprehended and represented as the state, but the state is other than this, and its law is higher than this, it is the righteousness," etc. — *Ibid.* p. 69. The representation of the commonwealth, *Die Bürgerliche Gesellschaft*, in Hegel, may well be described by Rothe as *meisterhaft.* It is in no respect open to the criticism of R. von Mohl, that it is introduced simply in conformance to a threefold logical sequence. — *Geschichte u Literateur des Staatswissenschaften*, vol. i. p. 82. The distinction is maintained with certain modifications by Rothe. — *Theologische Ethik*, vol. ii. pp. 101–120. Bluntschli rejects the formal distinction of the civil corporation and the state, but the

It is the society of men existing in jural relations, and in associations which are defined in jural forms. Its members exist in no organic unity and continuity, but in a formal relation, through the existence of private interests in their individual or collective character. It embraces the administration of civil justice in its formal order.

The commonwealth, since it is formed, in the necessary relations of life, has the law of its action in necessity. It is thus that its characteristic is order, and its object is security through the integrity of the collective whole.

The commonwealth has for its end protection, — the protection of private interests, as individual or collective. Its organization is for the protection of interests involved in the necessary relations of men. It exists for the securance of life and liberty and property, through the institution of the system of civil rights. It embraces those wants which are necessary in life and their satisfaction. It is the same which those who have held only a negative and formal notion of the nation have apprehended and sought to embody in that.

The commonwealth has for its province the economic organization of society. The system which is ordinarily described as public economy belongs to it, and writings on economy are mainly occupied with subjects which are its concern. It comprehends the relations of the vast and complex industrial processes of society. There is in its immediate scope the separate and the coöperative interests of agriculture, of trade, of mining, and of the mechanic arts. It is to direct the movements of production and of

position he afterwards assumes may be allowed to justify it, since he is there under the necessity of establishing in the organization of the state a separate power or department, which is immediately concerned with private or civil rights and the economy of the state. — *Allgemeines Statsrechts*, vol. i. p. 458.

The present historical tendency indicates that in the unity of the German nation the separate states, as Prussia, Saxony, Hanover, Bavaria, will exist as distinct commonwealths or civil societies, forming in this respect a very close parallel to the United States.

exchange. The adjustment of the relations of labor and of capital which represents the accumulated result of labor, is to be referred to it. It is to regulate the division of labor, and that which is of higher value, the union and coöperation of labor, and that which is of still higher value, it is to maintain the freedom of labor.

The commonwealth has, in connection with the economic interests and laws of society, the department of social statics. The enactment of sanitary laws and regulations, and the foundation of sanitary institutions, belongs to it. It is to take necessary measures for the protection of health, and to secure society against whatever may be a public nuisance or a public peril.[1]

The commonwealth is formed in the institution and maintenance of civil rights. The individuals composing it are private persons, and as such they are comprehended by it; they have each their end in the necessary relations of life to secure, and the security of their private interests is the necessary end for which the commonwealth exists. The individual, therefore, may require the security of his necessary rights from the commonwealth, and the commonwealth may require from each that he also hold these rights for others secure. There is, therefore, to be established through it the protection of each in his necessary rights and his necessary avocation, with no undue hindrance or unequal restriction.

The commonwealth is instituted in the maintenance of justice in the necessary relations of life, or civil justice. This is the law which is formative of its whole organization, and is defined in a jural system. Justice is to be recognized as necessarily involved in the organization of society, and is to be affirmed as law, and to be adminis-

[1] The establishment of a quarantine and quarantine regulations, thus falls naturally within its object, but this ought not to be regarded solely as the concern of a separate commonwealth, and is not subject to internal administration. Its institution in the harbor of New York, is of no more consequence to the people of the commonwealth than to the adjacent territory.

tered between man and man. Its violation is to be set forth as crime, and the penalties incurred by crime are to be defined and imposed. Since justice in the commonwealth or civil justice is apprehended as existent in the necessary relations of life, it is to be maintained through its whole extent for all men, and there is to be the recognition of the equality of all men before the law. It is not to assume a different principle of action for different sorts and conditions of men. It is to assert a justice which is impartial, or it becomes itself an organized injustice. It is to establish justice in the authority of law, and to judge the infraction of law as crime. It is to maintain justice for every man; and private revenge is forbidden as the rude justice of an unorganized and barbaric state. The execution of justice is to be regarded as the necessary condition of the commonwealth through its whole extent, and its whole power is to act in its ultimate enforcement. It is to be the guardian of every individual. The object, in the increase of the commonwealth, to be steadily regarded, is that the process of justice shall not be neutralized through old and imperfect judicial organizations, where the abuses tend only to the emolument of a special and conservative profession, as in the commonwealth of Connecticut; and that it shall not become entangled in intricate formalities, to become what Cromwell called the law-system of his age, "a tortuous and ungodly jungle;" nor that it shall affect, beyond the necessity of scientific precision, a phraseology unknown to the people; nor that justice shall be made so costly that any shall be debarred from access to it. Justice is to be open and free to all. It should be the same for all, and thus in the apprehension of crime no special or private rewards should be allowed, but it should be held as the office of the state; and no officer of the state nor of its police, should be allowed to receive a tender of reward from private persons, nor should any gift be made to justice. A system of private rewards gives to wealth and power a special security, which is not open to all, nor promotive of the security of the whole, and is but a slight advance from a system of private revenge. The commonwealth is to bring crime to the light, and its object is to protect rights and not criminals. The fair trial of all charges is to be had, and the evidence of all, the plaintiff and defendant alike, is to be received that all may be known. The object is to make the conviction of crime sure and the punishment inevitable, and to determine the actual injury and the actual degree of guilt. The course of law thus is not to be merely formal and mechanical, as in an imperial code, but it is to regard the varying aspects of human action and the varying conditions of human life. It is to take into account the age and circumstance and mental condition, and all which may be exculpatory in them, and to regard crimes to which different degrees of guilt attach, and for which there must be corresponding degrees in the punishment imposed. Thus the law, instead of an unvarying and mechanical application, presumes the deliberation of those before whom trial is had, and the judgment of a judge.

The commonwealth has the institution of its procedure in the common law. This is its exclusive province. It is this law which has been instituted in the ascertainment of the justice involved in the necessary relations of men. It recognizes a solid justice existent in the development of these relations. It is shaped in the jural definition of these relations. It acknowledges, therefore, as a prescriptive right, that which by long continuance has been wrought in the use and wont of men. It holds the right of ways which are open to all alike, and fair to all, and have been long trodden by the steps of men. It is this recognition of justice as existent in the necessary relations of men, which is the precedent of the common law, and the condition of its legal positivism. It is not the tradition of any code nor commandment, however ancient.

The principles to be regarded in the constitution of the commonwealth are those which define its unity and its scope. The unity of the commonwealth is that of the unitary organization of justice. Its authority is to have within itself no formal restriction and no sectional limitation. It is as a crime against the whole that the violation of its law is to be regarded and punished. The denial of the unity of the organization of the commonwealth was the ground of opposition to the important legislation of the commonwealth of Pennsylvania, in the succession of crimes and outbreaks of violence in Schuylkill County in 1867, and also to a system of metropolitan police in certain separate districts. But the commonwealth fails of its end when crime is allowed to remain unpunished, or rights become insecure through defect in its organization. There is no sectional right in the outlawry of a certain locality, to preclude the action of the commonwealth through its whole extent.

The scope of the commonwealth has also no restriction in the institution of civil rights, and the determination of the whole civil order is within its sphere. The reason and the right of the legislation of the commonwealth of Pennsylvania, which modified the whole tenure of property, and was so great an advance in establishing the freedom of property, placing real property upon the same basis in certain respects as personal property,[1] was opposed with the argument, not that the act was in itself unjust, but that it was beyond the scope of the commonwealth. But this rests in a deficient apprehension of the commonwealth, for in the normal civil order and civil administration, there is no formal limit to its action.

The territorial extent of the commonwealth is commonly shaped by some circumstance, or some consideration of civil administration. It conforms mainly to the content of the commonwealth, and when once established it is to be

[1] Price Act, April 18, 1853.

held stably, as if it were itself bottomed in the common law, and as describing old and established interests which have grown up and repose in it.

The nation in its civil organization may constitute a single commonwealth, or it may be divided into many and separate commonwealths, and these may increase in number, with the extension of the national domain, and the change and growth of population.

The conception of the commonwealth, as it has been represented in political science, has had its precedent in the slow advance of civilization. Its organization is not new nor strange, nor did it come forth at once complete in all its powers in the beginning of the American state. The form may be discerned in its germ in the first unfolding of the civilization of the Teuton, and may be traced in the succeeding institutions of our ancestors as they emerge from the shadows of German forests. It appears in the structure of the constitution of England, in the organization of counties for civil administration and the management of local and special concerns, while embraced in the kingdom, and subject to the Crown and the Parliament, in whom is the determination of the political whole. It appears in the distinction of the Hundred, and however rude and imperfect may have been the form of this, and however widely writers may differ in defining its character and limitations, they all agree in the reference to it of the transaction of judicial, and the management of local concerns; its primary object is that of civil administration. There is, in the "Lives of the Chief Justices," an illustration of the manner in which this distinction was guarded. The writer says of the office of Chief Justiciar, as introduced by William the Conqueror from Normandy, "The functions of such an office would have ill accorded with the notions of our Anglo-Saxon ancestors, who had a great antipathy to centralization, and prided themselves upon enjoying the rights and advantages of self-government. The shires being parcelled into Hundreds and other subdivisions, each of these had courts in which suits both civil and criminal might be commenced."[1] It was not by a single assembly of men, however great, that so vast and noble a structure was conceived, nor in any single age has it been perfectly realized. It has been formed slowly in the long struggle of society toward the better attainment of its end. It will always obtain a more perfect form with the progress of the people.

The commonwealth has, in the historical development of the United States, its amplest and its highest organization. There has been the illustration of its strength and its conformance in the order of the whole; and also of its evil, when, severed from the whole, it has sought to build a civilization in the furtherance of some separate and special interest, and to base in that the foundation of society.

The sphere of the commonwealth must be ascertained by its content; by what it is, and not by what it is assumed to be; by its actualization, and not by any abstract conception of law, or empty theory of society. In the illustration of the nature of the commonwealth, reference is made to the constitution of the commonwealth of Pennsylvania, not only because it lies nearest at hand, but as that of one of the original thirteen commonwealths, — a commonwealth as central, and as conservative in the habit of the community as any, and comprehensive of as great and varied interests as any, and it has had in the revision of its constitution the aid of lawyers of singular eminence.[2] And since what is assumed for one com-

1 *Lives of the Chief Justices*, vol. i. p. 33. The distinction may be traced in its outline in defining the nation and the commonwealth, in the distinction of public rights and duties as supreme and subordinate. — See Christian's *Bl. Comm.* chart. iii.

2 The commonwealth, as the civil organization of society, opens a more immediate field to lawyers; but then, also, by the same influence, they may be withdrawn too exclusively within its contemplation, and are apt to become, and for the same reason, — that is as also withdrawn exclusively in it, — what Dr.

monwealth, in its nature, is assumed for all, the constitution of this may be taken as a legal instrument to furnish its illustration.

The formal organization of the commonwealth is in legislative, executive, and judicial powers, through which its order is construed. The legislative department has its province presumed in the nature of the commonwealth, and its special limitation in the judicial department. The judicial organization and form of procedure is necessarily more amply defined in the object of the commonwealth. The executive department is defined in the office of the governor, — a name not indicative of political precedence, nor suggestive of the sovereignty of the state, but denoting the direction of the internal administration, and the regulative or magisterial character of the civil office.

The commonwealth is the institution of the authority of law in the civil order. It forbids that any shall be arraigned but by due process of law.[1] It allows neither private revenge nor private judgment to assume the behest of justice. It regards crime as a violation of the

Arnold called the political economists, — "those one-eyed men." But their services have indeed been conspicuous in the formation of the constitution of the commonwealth of Pennsylvania; and there is no commonwealth in which the jural scope has been more clearly maintained, or the province of its judicial in distinction from legislative powers more carefully and wisely guarded, and where the constitution has been so little cumbered with the detail which belongs to the sphere of legislative enactment. It bears the impress of the work of Wilson, and Gibbons, and Chauncey, and Sargeant, and Price, and Binney, and Wallace.

[1] The earliest historical assertion of law is not in the enunciation of a principle, but in a judgment on a case (see Maine's *Ancient Law*, p. 3), and there is in it, whatever else there may be, the presumption of a substantial order in the necessary relations of life, and crime is adjudged in the interruption or violation of this; in this may be traced the historical development of the common law. Its origin is in no formal code, nor in the tradition of a formal code.

"There have been," Mr. Maine says, "three agencies which, in its historical course, have shaped the process of the common law, legal fiction, equity, and legislation." The first, whatever its advantage in some periods, is a rude device, and belongs mainly to the past; the second must constantly seek the aid of legislation, as it finds expression in a positive form; and the third becomes the more potent agency. It is only within a very recent period that legislation has been brought to shape the course or to act in the explication of the common law in the commonwealth of Pennsylvania.

peace, and therefore as against the commonwealth, and in its name it is judged.[1]

The commonwealth is to institute courts for the admin istration of the civil order.[2] The historical origin and formation of courts affords the widest illustration and evidence of its province. The court is constituted for the assertion and protection of civil rights.

There is for every one subject to the authority of the commonwealth, the right to bring his cause into court, and each may be required to appear before the court, and the award of justice is rendered by it. The access to the court is for all, and "every man for an injury done him in his lands, goods, person or reputation, shall have remedy by the due course of law, and right and justice administered without sale, denial, or delay."[3] Before the court a trial of the cause is had, that justice in the matter may be ascertained. The method is demonstrative, and evidence is given and the facts in the case examined. The parties bring in witnesses to their suit, and everything concerning it is laid before the knowledge of the judge and the jury by whom the verdict is rendered. These successive steps are themselves rights, and belong to every one subject to the authority of the commonwealth. There is for each the right to appeal to the court, to call witnesses, to have council in law, and to bring before the judge and jury all that may concern the action. Every individual in the commonwealth to whom its writ may come, is required to

[1] *Constitution of the Commonwealth,* Art. I. sec. 1. Art. II. sec. 1. Art. VI. sec. 10.

"The style of all process shall be, 'The Commonwealth of Pennsylvania,' and all prosecutions shall be carried on in the name and by the authority of the Commonwealth of Pennsylvania, and conclude 'against the peace and dignity of the same.'" — *Ibid,* Art. V. sec. 11.

[2] "The judicial power of this commonwealth shall be invested in the supreme court, in courts of oyer and terminer, and general jail delivery, in a court of common pleas, orphan's court, register's court, and a court of quarter sessions of the peace for each county; in justices of the peace; and in such other courts as the legislature may from time to time establish." — *Ibid,* Art. V. sec. 1.

[3] *Ibid,* Art. IX. sec. 11.

answer the summons of the court. In the feudal age, the nobility regarded it as an injustice that they should be held to obey this summons, or that the evidence of all men should be received in respect to them, but in the new Parliament House in London, a painting by the side of the throne represents the arrest of the heir to the throne by a London constable. The facts are to be brought out, and that only can be held as authentic which is brought to the knowledge of the judge and jury.[1]

In the court the method of procedure is formal and exact. This formality gives to the cause of every man the same dignity. It invests every charge and every suit, by whomsoever it is brought, with the same solemnity. The same summons sets forth the claim alike of all, whether rich or poor or citizen or stranger. This formality secures justice from abuse, and forbids that the cause of any should be passed by hurriedly or slightingly.

In the court the procedure is open to all. Its sessions are announced, and the whole action is public, since the crime is not alone against the individual, but against the peace and dignity of the whole; and although the cause is between certain parties, yet the justice involved affects the whole; and the punishment is not alone the satisfaction of a private wrong, but the consequence of the violation of the law.

In the court the examination is before a jury, and judgment is rendered by it, and the verdict it returns when the offense is proven, is called a conviction. This is the office of the jury.[2] The trial by a jury is not, as De Lolme described it, simply to resign the individual to the judgment of a few persons; but as Hegel says, it is the demand of the conscience of the individual that justice be meted out to him, and the conviction is rendered as expressive alike of the conscience of the individual, and the conscience of the community which the jury represent. It is the claim

1 *Constitution of the Commonwealth*, Art. IX. secs. 9 and 11.

2 *Ibid*, Art. IX. sec. 6.

over impulse and desire, of the conscience of every man, and the witness of his own, his true and better nature, which no crime can wholly silence, and which by crime has been most wronged. The punishment which follows is the manifestation of crime. It is not primarily reformatory, and it may not always of itself have that effect upon the individual, but it is the sequence of crime in which its nature is manifested. The conscience of the individual and of the whole demands that crime shall be brought to light, and that punishment shall be inevitable, and the commonwealth fails of its end in so far as this is not accomplished. The significance of punishment by solitary confinement, is in the fact that it is the reflex of the nature of crime itself, for evil, as the subversion of personality, involves the loss of freedom, and is the separation of one from his fellows, and the severance of relationships, and is itself an isolation: thus solitary imprisonment is but the manifestation of the sequence of crime. The adoption of this mode of punishment indicates an advance in civilization.

The commonwealth is to make provision for the institution of officers in the civil administration, as for instance, the district attorney and the justice of the peace. The former office in its very imperfect construction, has some of the best elements of jural progress; and of the latter, Stahl says, that the office embodies perhaps the highest conception in the Anglican civil system. It represents the peace of society as conditioned in justice. It is to consider in its inception the charge of the interruption of the peace of society, and there was a deep significance in the formula in which the old writs ran: "In the peace of God, and the commonwealth." It has to provide also for the institution of all offices of civil order, as sheriffs, justices, constables, coroners, prothonotaries, registrars, and recorders.[1]

It belongs to the commonwealth, in the guardianship of

[1] *Constitution of the Commonwealth*, Art. VI. secs. 6, 7; Art. IV. sec. 6.

interests, to enforce the execution of contracts and of wills, and the administration of estates. It has in its scope those institutions, so fundamental in the civil order, — the contract and the will. The form in which these are executed is of consequence, since they are to be maintained and enforced as positive law. It is thus requisite that all wills shall be proven, and all deeds and titles are to be given in the name of the commonwealth, and it is to provide for the probate of wills and the recording of deeds.[1]

It belongs to the commonwealth, in the securance of interests, to regulate the relations of capital and labor, and to maintain and protect the division and coöperation and freedom of labor. It is to adjust the legal rate of interest upon capital. It is to charter corporations and to provide for their privileges, immunities, and estates. In the direction of intercourse in trade and exchange, it has the supervision of roads and highways, excepting only military and post-roads which are in the immediate control of the nation. In the security of health and in sanitary provisions, it is to institute officers and boards of health, and hospitals, and asylums, and homes for the infirm or incapable, or aged or insane, and it is to provide for the poor and to appoint overseers of them.[2]

It is for the commonwealth to establish municipalities, and to grant and convey municipal rights or privileges, and to institute the order and confer the powers which are requisite for the civil administration, in the organization of counties, towns, and boroughs within its limits. The execution of its powers is through a police and constabulary.

There is in this summary the substantial content of the constitution of the commonwealth of Pennsylvania, to which reference was made in illustration of the commonwealth in itself. This which was ascertained to be its necessary conception, has been its realization in its normal

[1] *Constitution of the Commonwealth*, Art. V. sec. 10. [2] *Ibid*, Art. VII. sec. 6.

process. With the formal exception which is to be noticed, and which is not in all respects inconsistent with its administration, this is all there is in it. There is no power beyond this that could be actualized or strive for actualization in it without involving some contradiction. There is beyond this only the sphere of legal fictions, of empty theories, and political abstractions. There is beyond no solid ground. It is the field of restless visionaries and political dreamers; and instead of the domain of substantial order, it has proven the confine of anarchy and secession and rebellion. In it an evil ambition has wrought, and the forces of disorder and division have mustered.

The powers which alone remain to be noticed, and which constitute an exception to the preceding, are those which refer to divorce, to education, to the resident qualifications of an elector, and to the militia as a local or constabulary force. These powers are such as in part are properly related to the normal administration and economy of the commonwealth, and therefore in certain aspects may be referred to it, or they are powers which, when left to the commonwealth, fail to obtain any substantial actualization. There is nothing in them to justify the speculation, which has assigned the most limitless scope to the commonwealth. The limitless in human affairs is indeed that only which is untravelled by thought. There is, in the civil and political life, no sphere of arbitrary and indefinite powers; the arbitrary is without the domain of law, and the indefinite is the unformed thought and purpose, the vagueness and weakness which appears in incapacity of thought and irresolution of will.

There is an article on divorce, defining certain restrictions of the legislative power in its action upon it, and then referring it to the courts. The administration in divorce, in its connection with the common law, passes consistently to the commonwealth; but the nation has an immediate obligation in the maintenance of the family in its moral unity and moral order, and if it fails to attain this in its action through the commonwealth, it is imperative that it shall assume its immediate authority. There is no form that can intervene by which it can be divested of its obligation to maintain a moral order.

There is an article on public instruction, which provides for the institution of schools, so that all may be taught free. But while the administration of a system of education may be referred to the commonwealth, its institution is of national importance, and also of national obligation, and in the defect of the commonwealth, its authorization should proceed from the nation.

There is an article on the qualifications of an elector, in which the conditions of electoral power in the commonwealth are defined, while its electors are described as "citizens of the United States," and its special provision in respect to the commonwealth, is the limitation of the term of residence necessary before any election for "a citizen of the United States who had previously been a qualified voter" in the commonwealth, in order to vote at an ensuing election. The constitution of the United States describes the qualifications of an elector, but its definition is simply inclusive of the qualifications of the lower house in each commonwealth, and the more specific qualification is referred to the commonwealth; but since the right to vote is a political right, and integral in the nation, the provision for it should be in the fundamental law, and its guaranty in the supreme law of the people. The terms and conditions of electoral power cannot be left to the discretion of each separate commonwealth, without the risk of unequal qualifications which might act as a disturbing force, or tend to create alienation or division, and the definition of political power belongs to the nation.

There is an article which provides for the arming, organizing, and disciplining of the militia, and describes the governor as the commander-in-chief of the army and navy of the commonwealth. Of this it is only to be said that the commonwealth has no right to declare war, and over the militia the governor has power only within the limits of the commonwealth, and he is thus only commander-in-chief, "except when they are carried into the service of the United States." It is only for internal order and administration that the governor has immediate command, and as the militia acts as a constabulary or police, to prevent a breach of the peace of the commonwealth within its borders. When the governor is represented as the "commander-in-chief of the army and navy of the commonwealth," the office is not further defined. Since the commonwealths of the nation have for the most part no sea-ports and no sailors, and, in some instances, no navigable waters, the title can scarcely be supported. It is a name for which there is no reality, and except for lawyers it leads beyond all soundings. No navy has ever set sail, and no sailor has ever trod its deck, only constitutional lawyers have exchanged its signals and answered its salutes. It is as a legal fiction, if it can make that claim, but a painted ship upon a painted ocean, although for the lawyers who sail upon it, out on the limitless expanse, it is as good as oak and iron. And the governor in this character, on the streams to which he may often be confined, is like Wordsworth's fisherman, "tricked out in proud disguise." But this assumption of military and naval authority in its consequent weakness, is indicative of the neglect of the nation in its own sphere, to provide for the instruction and organization of the whole people, as a military force, which is its express obligation. The commonwealth is necessarily itself concerned with the militia only as a constabulary; and when the military organization has been left to it, it has been at the most defective, and its display a masquerade to fill an idle holiday. There is in the commonwealth no conception, and no power of war, and it may neither declare war nor conclude peace.

These powers, in divorce, in education, in the definition of electoral laws, and in the instruction and organization of the militia for local purposes, are alone those which have any description in the constitution of the commonwealth, that are not exclusively within its normal conception, and they in certain respects are not inconsistent with its administrative order. But they are in a necessary and immediate relation to the nation, and their exclusive reference to the commonwealth becomes the defect in their institution, or the source of weakness and of radical error in the organization of the whole.

The nation and the commonwealth exist in a two-fold relation: firstly, the nation is immanent in the commonwealth; and secondly, the nation is external to the commonwealth.

The nation is immanent in the commonwealth.

The commonwealth of itself is incomplete, and presumes the being of the nation in which it subsists. The commonwealth of itself has no permanence, and in the nation alone it has its consistent end. It is only as the nation is immanent in it, that it is brought into relation to its object in the unity of the whole. Then it is no longer simply the private interest of the individual which is its end, but it is the end of the nation itself, — a moral interest which gives to justice alone its strength. It still institutes and administers justice with reference to the individual, and acts in the maintenance of private interests; but its work is no more for a private end alone, nor simply that each individual shall be secure in his special rights, but that all sources of disorder shall be removed, and all that hinders the administration of justice shall be overcome. It is thus, as the commonwealth subsists in the nation and its moral order, that it brings to individual rights a permanence.

The civil order which may have the highest formal completeness, when the life of the nation is no longer present in it as a sustaining power, is merely abstract. The most perfect institutes of a civil system have of themselves no enduring power. The historian of Roman jurisprudence may justly describe the great worth to society of those civil institutions — the contract and the will, — but there was in them no inherent strength to save the society of Rome when the nation was crumbling beneath the weight of empire. In them there was no renovating energy to stay the corruption, or to check the swift decay that was undermining all within. It is thus that in imperial ages there may be a higher culture and structure of the civil order, as in France under the empire. It is thus, also, that the study of the civil law of itself has the attraction only of an external symmetry, and impresses one only as a formal system and as a cold and lifeless anatomy. It has not the spirit of an historic power. The genius of the great masters of the Justinian era can throw over it only a faint glow, and the energy of a living spirit is wanting in the most splendid development of the civil organization of society.[1]

It is only in the immanence of the nation that the commonwealth has its continuance in history. The structure, which is a combination of private interests, could not exist of itself in the strenuous conflict of the moral forces of history. There can exist in history no mere negation; and the commonwealth of itself can have no place among those powers which, in the life of humanity, bear its issues to their close. The assumption of the foundation of society in the commonwealth has been the precedent of a false civilization. Since the commonwealth exists only as the organization of the individual and collective interests of private persons, when the foundation of society has been sought in it, it has assumed a selfish principle as its law,

[1] See Merivale's *History of the Romans*, vol. vii. p. 429.

and its end has been the predominance of a selfish interest. And as the commonwealth is formed in the necessary relations of life, it cannot become of itself a power in history which is a moral order, and in the realization of freedom. It holds the web and the woof in which those historic figures appear; but it apprehends not the unity of that design which through centuries, is wrought in the conscious purpose of nations.

The nation in its sovereignty is immanent in the commonwealth. Its determination is the supreme law; the law of the nation is the law in every commonwealth. The constitution of the United States is the constitution of every State. The real sovereignty is in the nation, and the will of the organic people is prevalent through the whole. The power, as in any organism, acts through every member, and thus conversely the injury to a part involves the injury of the whole, and the peril to any commonwealth is the peril of the nation.

The nation in its freedom is immanent in the commonwealth. This freedom is not simply the securance of civil rights, and that in some transition may be better effected in an imperialism, but it is in the nation in its moral being. The life of the nation thus may become imperilled through the commonwealth when its freedom is not realized in it; since then its spirit is no longer apprehended in it, and there is a separation from the consciousness of its historical aim, and that corruption which is consequent when one existing among the parts acts upon the whole without any comprehension of the whole. The unity also of the nation is imperilled, if the freedom of the people is not realized through the whole, and slavery has its sequence in dissolution and division.

The nation is external to the commonwealth.

The commonwealth is invested with a formal sovereignty. It is not the sovereignty of the people, in its organic being, but a formal sovereignty, limited to a certain process and to the formal exercise of certain powers for the prosecution of that process. The power is existent in the sovereignty of the organic people, and it is only in reference to the formal process in which the commonwealth is constituted, that the nation is external to it.

The commonwealth has a formal, but not an organic unity. It is a whole only in its relation to the nation, and through it, to the other commonwealths of the nation.

The commonwealth is defined by boundaries which are formal, that is, they are not the natural boundaries which divide nations, as oceans, or mountains, or rivers; nor the historical boundaries which separate one people from another, in their integral life, and are shaped in the struggle and conflict of history; but they are the lines and angles which are traced in the formal demarkation of an estate, such lines as are drawn by the surveyor and the engineer. They cross rivers and mountains, and stretch away from the sea, and sweep by points of external defense, where one people might make a stand against another people. If there be an uncertainty as to these boundaries, the commonwealth cannot maintain its position against what might be presumed an invasion, by any declaration of war on the invader, since it cannot declare war, nor can it determine its own boundaries in dispute, but the settlement of them is with the nation. These boundaries thus cannot be conceived as those of a separate political people in its historical course, and illustrate the fact that the commonwealth has in itself no elements of permanence in history. In the agitation in its movements, they would be obliterated as lines drawn in the sand.

The nation exists in an external relation to the commonwealth; but the commonwealth has in itself no external relation, excepting only to the nation and to the other commonwealths through the nation. It comprehends no foreign relation, that is, a relation to an international state. It can enter into no league nor alliance, nor form any treaty. If a crime has been committed against its peace by any person escaping to a foreign state, it is only through the nation that extradition is obtained, while on any commonwealth in the nation direct requisition may be made. If there be any invasion, it is the nation which is invaded, and the peril is for the whole people, and with its whole physical power it is to meet the invader.

The commonwealth as constituted in this formal system, as a civil corporation, that is, as an artificial person, has certain formal rights, or more exactly, immunities. If the divided, and in the development of the nation so rapidly increasing commonwealths, have each a necessary continuity, and the capacities of an organic people, in its organic being in history, then the rights of each are the rights of a nation in its sovereignty, and each may assume correspondent duties and obligations. But the commonwealth has no continuance in its separation from the nation, and its rights are existent in its formal organization, and it is the nation alone which can recognize these rights. These rights are maintained for the commonwealth, only as the commonwealth exists in the nation.

Firstly; There is for the commonwealth the right that the nation shall maintain it as integral in itself. It can detach no commonwealth, and allow none to be detached from itself. It can withdraw its authority from none, and can alienate or transfer none. It is not only existent in each, but it is existent in its unity and its entirety in each. It is thus that in the invasion or peril of one, it is the whole that is invaded or imperilled.

Secondly; There is for each the right to the maintenance of its organization, in its normal action as a commonwealth. The order and the execution of justice is to be maintained in each, and if necessary by invoking the strength of the whole. The due form of law in the privilege and protection of courts, and the trial by jury, is to be sustained in each. The validity of contracts is to be enjoined in each, and through the separate commonwealths, the nation is to maintain for each full faith for its reports and judicial procedure.

Thirdly; There is the right to the maintenance in each, of the freedom of the nation. None can be reduced to a condition of mere subjection, as to some imperial power which is over and isolated from it. The right to the freedom of the nation is in so far a condition of unity that if it be not realized in the commonwealth, the latter becomes in fact only a province, separated from the sovereignty and consequent freedom of the whole, and its members have no real citizenship.

Fourthly; There is the right in each to the maintenance of a definite boundary and domain. The lines are those which define the order of the organized administration of justice in the securance of private rights, that is, the rights defined in a civil system and the maintenance of private interests. These boundaries, while they are not such as separate one historical people from another, are such as appear in a vested or a customary right. They are the lines which are marked in the survey of property as in a private estate, and property requires exact limits and seeks security and stability in them, while change might tend to disorder, and occasion conflicting forms and titles and unsettle values. These lines are therefore to be carefully defined. While there is thus no moral ground which could hold them in the supreme necessity of the people, in the normal condition they are to be maintained in the order of the whole. It is thus that there is in them that attraction of association, and that wealth which gathers with the course of the generations, and they become like the lines of an homestead. They are to be so regarded, that no new commonwealth shall be formed out of another, but with the concurrence of its own consent and of the authority of the nation.

Fifthly; There is the right to the maintenance in every

commonwealth of a form of government and organization corresponding to that of the nation. There is to be in none the incongruity which would appear in discordant forms. There is to be in none a form of government which shall isolate it from the order of the nation and of the commonwealths coexistent with it in the nation. The republic is to maintain for every commonwealth a republican form of government.

These rights in their maintenance necessarily presume the being of the nation, and have apart from it no actualization. They are defined and established in the constitution of the nation and in its supreme law, and form the high guarantees of the constitution.

The more definite enumeration of rights is consequent from the formal process of the commonwealth, or from the formal equality of one commonwealth with another in the maintenance of interests; as for instance, the right that for every crime committed within its limits as against its own peace and dignity, and in violation of its order, the trial shall be had within its limits; that every criminal, whereever he may be in the nation, shall be remanded to it on the requisition of its governor; that upon the seas, rivers, and highways of the nation each alike shall have the same right of way; that each shall be regarded alike in every regulation of commerce and revenue, and in these none have precedence to another; that no vessels bound to or from one, shall clear or pay duty to another; that the citizens of each shall alike be eligible for the offices and trusts of the nation; and the right, when its corporate rights and interests are endangered, to enter as a party in court, and the corresponding necessity to appear and answer a summons as a party in court, but it is only in a court instituted by the nation that this right of the commonwealth is construed; and the right finally that to the citizens of each in its normal order there shall be given and secured all the rights, privileges, and immunities which belong to those of any of the several commonwealths in the nation, or the right to a formal equality in the commonwealth.

The commonwealth is a formal organization. If the order of the commonwealth is overthrown in anarchy or rebellion, and its course is interrupted or overborne, it is in and through the nation alone that there is the power of reconstruction. The organization is formal, and it is upon the people in its organic and moral being, that is, the nation, that there is the ultimate obligation, although not always the immediate action, in the institution of rights through the whole and for the whole. The nation can therefore allow no civil formula to intervene between it and a condition in which civil rights are utterly destroyed through anarchy, or to restrain its action when robbery and murder and violence and crime in every shape prevail, but tried by no process of law and deterred by no punishment; and there is not in this condition the maintenance of the commonwealth, nor can it claim even the name. The curse of impotence would be upon the government of a people, which should aid or abet such a condition. There would be the failure of government to obtain its primary ends, and whatever theory of civil relations was adduced to justify it, it would denote the imbecility of a people. The theory would be a theory of anarchy and not of the state. The government restrained from its end in this formalism could not long endure. It would be itself the greater criminal. The commonwealth is only formal, and the subversion of the civil order within it empties it, and there remains only a territory and an unorganized population among the vestiges of a past civil system.

The nation and the commonwealth, in the coincidence of the civil and political organization, hold certain necessary powers, which are involved in their order and administration. These are the concurrent powers of the constitution. Their ultimate ground is in the sovereignty of the people in its organic unity; but they are necessary to executive action alike in the civil and the political sphere.

The illustration of these powers is in the power to levy taxes, and the power to call out and employ for its object physical force. But the power of taxation in the commonwealth is strictly internal, and the force it calls out can act in its immediate direction only as a constabulary for internal order.

The principle determinative of these powers is implied in the nature of the nation and the commonwealth. The power in the commonwealth is subordinate and dependent. Kent says, "Although the State legislatures have a concurrent jurisdiction in the case of taxation, except as to imposts, yet in effect though not in terms this concurrent power becomes a subordinate and dependent one. In any other case of legislation, the concurrent power in the State would seem to be entirely dependent," etc.[1]

The distinction in the nation and the commonwealth becomes more apparent in those powers in each, which have in their procedure a more immediate correspondence, as the judiciary. The distinct nature of each has determined the object of the action of this power in each, while the form of action is the same. It is thus, in the words of Kent, that "the judicial power of the United States is necessarily limited to national objects." It has for its province the application in cases involving a conflict of rights, of the constitution as the supreme law, and of the acts of Congress as laws, and it is to give judgment in cases which arise in a controversy between separate commonwealths, and when action is brought by a member of one commonwealth against another, and in cases arising in the external sovereignty of the nation under treaties and in revenue or admiralty practice. But Kent says, of a principle which, involved in the necessary conception of

[1] 1 Kent's *Comm.* p. 393.

the commonwealth, has struggled toward a clearer recognition, "the United States has no common-law jurisdiction in criminal cases." [1] To this he adds, in explication of the same principle, "the vast field of the law of property, the very extensive head of equity jurisdiction, and the principal rights and duties which flow from our civil and domestic relations, fall within the control, and we might almost say, the exclusive cognizance of the State governments." [1]

The earlier decisions of the judiciary of the United States were the embodiment of a profound national spirit, and the contrast appears, as we turn from the weight of their decisions to the bulk of the later, and pass from their large and solid conceptions to notions which only obtain consistency in the writings of Calhoun and Tucker's Blackstone. There was in these earlier decisions a conception of the being of the nation, which the nation in its progress could advance in, but which it could only by its retrogression reject, and by its dissolution obliterate. They laid the foundations in which the people can build. The precedents which they established apprehended clearly the substance and object of the nation and the commonwealth, and they embodied in a massive and symmetric order the conception to which the masters in political science had sought to give expression.

The relation of the nation and the commonwealth, the international and the civil state, is fundamental. It is only in their necessary conception that this relation is ascertained. It is only in their substance that this relation is realized. In contrast to the exposition of their necessary relation, which has its premise in their content, there are certain theories which comprise mainly the phases which the subject has assumed in abstract speculations and legal presumptions. These theories are mainly significant in their contrast to the principle which has been established.

[1] 1 Kent's *Comm.* pp. 367, 500.

Firstly; There is a theory in which the States are represented as simply vast corporations which had their origin in some charter or patent, and continue with substantially the same privileges and prerogatives once vested in them. They are corporations overgrown with time, a mass of undefined forms and an accumulation of interests, but in conformance to no consistent principle, and constructive of no consistent order.

But in immediate answer to this it may be said,—Firstly; These powers are not thus undefined and unlimited, but exist in a clear limitation, and are the same in each commonwealth, and are part of the same order. The theory would indicate a condition which ought not to be maintained if it existed, and would imply the social disorder, not the organization of a free people. The theory presents the opposite of their actual condition. Secondly; It is not to be presumed that these civil states could continue only as vast corporations, whose charters had lapsed, and which then remained with these positive but indefinite and miscellaneous powers. There is no country that could exist in the confusion that this would involve, and the civil states could not occupy the place which they have with no other ground or content. Thirdly; There has never been an historical people that would refer its whole civil system to an organization which had no other character than this. To entrust the security of civil rights, of life and liberty and property, to such a power as this presents, and to abide in its judgment upon them, involves that which no people would allow. It would contradict every conception of civil order, and it has in civil society no parallel. Governments in every form have been imposed upon a people, but no people have ever conceded to an organization such as this assumes, the powers existent in a commonwealth of the United States.

Secondly; There is a theory in which the States or commonwealths are represented as separate societies, each possessed of the sovereignty and independence and continuous being of a separate political power; each is possessed of the highest political attributes; each may claim the ultimate obligation of all its members, and to it their ultimate obedience is due; there is for each a distinct historical place and destination, and each has immanent in itself all the capacities of an international power. These States are connected in a government to which they have delegated certain powers, expressed in a written contract, while all other powers, which can attach to the most unlimited conception of political action, remain resident in themselves. The government established through this agreement is formed as their common bureau, or general agency, for certain objects. This theory was the postulate of the action of Calhoun and Davis and Stephens. It led the former, in 1831, to assert the right in each State, within its own limits, to nullify any act of the national Congress which it might deem unconstitutional or unjust, and it led the latter, in 1861, to assert the right in each State to secede, and to maintain in itself a sovereign, independent and continuous existence.

There is in this theory the explicit assertion of a confederate and the rejection of a national principle, and it presumes its inconsistence with the unity and being of the nation. This will involve a separate consideration. But the only answer to this theory, which is beyond all controversy, and is that of the realism of history, is that the separate commonwealths have no realization in history in conformance to this conception. The right, for instance, which in history is the crucial test of political sovereignty, the right to enter into relations with other nations, and to recognize them and be recognized by them, has never been possessed by these communities, and the power apparent in the inception of national existence is wanting to them. The theory is unreal; but it is that evil theory which apprehending the commonwealth as identical with the political people and apprehending nothing beyond, had its logical sequence in the subordination of the whole to a special interest, and consistently assuming slavery as that interest, induced the effort for that object, to effect the destruction of the whole. The events of history in the guidance of the people in its organic and moral being, are the witness to that unity, the rejection of which is blindness to the actual life and relations in which men exist. This assumption of a political contradiction — the presence of a real sovereignty in the nation and also in the commonwealth — has its result told in the impassioned words: —

> "My soul aches
> To know when two authorities are up,
> Neither supreme, how soon confusion
> May enter 'twixt the gap of both and take
> The one by the other." [1]

This theory sought to obtain realization in the articles of the confederation, which was precedent to the constitution; but these articles failed, because they were an abstraction and had no correspondence to the real constitution of the people. And the constitution which was then enacted is the exponent of the people only because it is the supreme law, and the government instituted in it is not one of separate States, but it is ordained and established by the people, and represents an organic relation to persons as members of it; that is, it is the constitution of a nation. The real sovereignty is in the organic people, whose will is the supreme law; but it is the people of the United States, and not of each or any particular State, whose will is the supreme law. And sovereignty exists in the people in its organic continuity; the people in no separate State is thus formed, but the citizens of one State are the citizens of every State, and since a state cannot exist as an abstraction, it follows that none can be regarded as separate from the organic whole.

[1] *Coriolanus*, Act 3, sc. 1.

This theory had its consistent representative in Mr. Calhoun, who avoided none of its necessary conclusions; but he gave no conception of a political life beyond the commonwealth, and the state for him was only a society existing in jural relations, and composed of individuals related to it as private persons, and having for its end the securance of private interests in their individual or collective character. This theory is beyond consideration in itself, since it involves conclusions which it would be the unreason of things to allow, and would deny the conscious spirit and life of the people, the organic being of the nation in history.[1]

Thirdly; There is a theory which represents the people as existent as an organic whole, while in its complex political organism the States are each an integral and original part. The sovereignty is in the organic people, while in the necessary organization of the people the States are integral; or in other words, the sovereignty is in the political people, in whose real political constitution the States are necessary. This is the position of Mr. Brownson, and apparently of Mr. Hurd. Mr. Brownson says, "the sovereignty is in the States united, not in the States severally." Mr. Hurd says, "The constitution as a political fact is the evidence of the investiture of certain sovereign national powers in the united people of the States antecedent to the constitution, as well as of the residue of sovereignty

[1] On the false origin of civilization in the conception of the commonwealth as separate from the nation, see Maurice's *Prophets and Kings*, passim.

"The commonwealth presumes the nation and subsists in it. When the state is represented as only a union of various individuals, or an association, it is only the commonwealth that is apprehended. There are modern publicists who have given no other view of the state." — Hegel, *Philosophie des Rechts*, p. 241. This criticism mainly applies to the view of the state in an empirical school. It is given in the writings of Mr. Macaulay, and it is reiterated in the political writings of Mr. Mill, and the political conception is constantly in the exclusive representation of the commonwealth, and this may be at least the consistent ground of the admiration of the latter for the political speculations of Mr Calhoun.

in the same people in their several condition of the people of distinct States." [1]

This theory is more thorough, and may claim an higher historical consistence than either of the preceding. But it is defective if it may be conceived to place the form of the state above the life of the state, or to condition the life upon the form. There is no preconceived political form to which the being of the political people is to correspond. The real sovereignty of the people can be predetermined by no form, but it is itself to determine the form of its political life. The fact that in a certain period it acts in a certain form does not therefore make that form necessary to its being, nor forbid that it may be changed. And sovereignty subsists in a unity, not in an aggregate, and is existent in the people not simply as a territorial people, although it is in the people of the land, but in the people as organic and moral. There is also a formal sovereignty, and the exercise of certain powers necessary to its normal executive action, that is, vested powers, in the commonwealth, and it is because the organic people forming the nation has a real sovereignty that the powers existent in the commonwealth cannot be wholly beyond its recall, or utterly detached from it, as would follow, for instance, in the secession of a commonwealth. And if, as this theory implies, the existence of the several civil States is necessary in the realization of the sovereignty of the organic whole, then the acts performed and the laws enacted in the interval of the action of each and all might be reversed or annulled, as transpiring in some interregnum and void of sovereignty. And the order of the separate commonwealths is formal, and in the supreme necessity of the organic people they may be merged and remerged into each other. The nation is not conditioned upon the existence and continuance of the separate civil States in their extant form. It could

[1] Brownson, *The American Republic*, p. 220. Hurd, *Law of Freedom*, etc., vol. i. p. 408.

exist through one as through another political form, and even while all the commonwealths included in it were changed. It has not the condition of its being in any form, nor its limitation in an external order.[1]

But there is in none of these schemes the exposition of the nature and relation of the commonwealth and the nation. The realization of the commonwealth and the nation in conformance to their necessary conception, — the commonwealth as the civil organism, subsistent only in the nation, and in its formal order invested with a formal sovereignty, but with the ample sphere of the civil organization, in which individuals have the institution of their private relations; and the nation, as the moral organism, the being of the organic people in its freedom; — the result in this is before and beyond any theories or any formulas. In the realization of history it cannot be changed by them so as to be made as if it were not, but in their prevalence its development may be disturbed or detained.

The premise of the distinction in the nation and the commonwealth — the United States and a particular State, — has been assumed in certain propositions which claim a separate notice.

Mr. Calhoun defines the principle on which the distinction is based, "The division of the powers of the government was effected by leaving subject to the control of the several States, all powers, which it was believed they could advantageously exercise, without incurring the hazard of bringing them in conflict, and by delegating others specifically to the United States."[2] This is the application of a

[1] Hurd, *Law of Freedom*, etc., vol. i. pp. 400–415. Mr. Hurd's exposition of the historical course of the state is indeed masterly; and one cannot avoid regret that the writer, who has shown the widest political learning and the finest freedom of thought of any American publicist, should have been led to and through this long compilation of laws on slavery. It only indicates in how many ways the system has been the source of loss to us.

[2] Calhoun's *Works*, vol. ii. p. 420.

mere empiricism, which proceeds only on the principle of an avoidance of conflict. It is for the keeping of the peace between the separate commonwealths. It presents the commonwealth as the integral and original power, and the government of the whole is not ordained and established by the organic people in its sovereignty, but constituted by the delegation of certain powers of and from the several States; and it again illustrates the fact that Mr. Calhoun apprehended nothing beyond the commonwealth. It is also the assumption of only a negative principle, the avoidance of the risk of conflict, and therefore cannot become the ground of a positive order, nor constructive of anything. It prescribes also only the form of the commonwealth, and the principle in which the powers of the whole are left to be determined is not given, but they are merely represented as "others." In the principle assumed, moreover, instead of escaping the hazard of conflict, in its political conception it has become the inevitable source of conflict, and has borne in itself the elements of dissolution to the whole.

The distinction is often represented as that of a central government and a self-government, meaning by the latter simply a local administration. But this is obviously defective, since the distinction is not one of government and administration. There is government and administration alike in the parts and in the whole. There are in the nation necessarily immediate administrative powers, and these affect every individual in the whole, and there is a central government and strictly central system, as of a wheel within a wheel, in the civil organization. There is indeed in the commonwealth the administration of its order, or a local administration, but this distinction fails to ascertain the principle in which its order consists. The work of De Tocqueville, so profound in its apprehension of the thought of another people, the gift of a citizen of France to the United States, has illustrated the worth of a central government and local administration, or a self-government in the meaning of the local administration of local affairs; but there has been beneath this the development of a far grander and more complex order.

There is in the writings of Mr. Choate a significant illustration of the principle which has been ascertained. In endeavoring to sustain the separate political sovereignty of the separate States, when he defines the powers existent in the commonwealth he says, " one of the prerogatives of sovereignty — the prerogative to take life and liberty for crime, — is theirs without dispute."[1] It is indicative of the principle in their distinction, that on the assumption of their sovereign powers this only can be cited without dispute which is itself not strictly, in the conception which has been ascertained, the act of political sovereignty, but belongs to the commonwealth in its formal sovereignty, and is necessary to its executive action as the civil system in the nation.

There is an apparent objection to this principle in a declaratory statement of the constitution describing powers as reserved to the States, or to the people. But this, while not in immediate variance with this distinction, has no immediate application. The constitution asserts in the amplest measure national powers, and prohibits powers to the commonwealth. The powers are not reserved by the States to themselves, since inasmuch as the States did not grant powers, they could reserve none; and the power asserting itself, is of the people, whose will is alone the supreme law over the whole. The phrase also, " the States," while it is represented as identical with the people, by a common principle of interpretation in law, must be explained as congruous with the same term in the preceding sentences of the legal document in which it appears.

[1] Choate's *Works*, vol. i. p. 197.

The importance of the definite consideration of the distinction of the nation and the commonwealth constantly appears. A senator said of the Civil Rights Bill, that it opened "a new epoch in the legislation of America;" and while that great bill had its constructive principle in the immanence of the nation in the commonwealth, and the nation is to maintain not the pretense of civil order, but the commonwealth in its reality organized in the unity of the nation, yet whatever should tend to bring the nation to assume in itself the immediate sphere of the commonwealth and its permanent retention, would involve the most grave disaster. It might, as in the institution of an imperialism, secure a more perfect civil order for a certain period, but it would not continue long. In its close it would be destructive of the noblest civil and political order that society has yet attained.

The clearer recognition of this distinction is the condition of the higher development of the commonwealth itself. There can be but an imperfect advance while its nature is undefined and its province is undetermined. Its object must be clearly apprehended. There devolves upon it, says Kent, "the duty that its jurisprudence be cultivated, cherished, and exalted," and this, while not strictly comprehensive of it, indicates its immediate design. The legislature has not in the civil organization the relative position and precedence which it has in the political body. The best elements of stability in the commonwealth of Pennsylvania, have been in the withdrawal of that which was not clearly to be referred to the legislature and its reference to the courts. The securance of civil rights is the immediate act of the judiciary, and it is vain to divide its responsibility, or to construct a power to act in its stead, or to merge its offices or functions with those of the legislature. If it becomes weak or corrupt, the only remedy is its reconstruction in the commonwealth, and not the accumulation of its powers in the legislature.

As the commonwealth is formed in the jural relations of society, the common law, through the common working of many commonwealths in a political whole, may have before it in their varied process an higher attainment. Its aim is to be the administration of justice. The better civil order is in the higher manifestation of justice, and the clearer assertion of the nature and doom of crime. Punishment is to be made inevitable as the manifestation of crime. Justice is imperative, and perfect justice alone truly imperial. There are false theories of conscience and crime which make the one a mere negation, and the other only an imperfect stage of development, and hold the conflict of good and evil as a neutral field; and there is a necessitarianism in which there is the denial of the reality of crime, and there is a humanitarianism which is consistent with no just and holy conception of the origin or the destination of humanity, which are undermining the order of society, and converting into a poor pretense its most awful institutions. There is the demand for a more manifest justice. It is a day of evil for a people, when it comes to regard the punishment of crime only as the sequence in some legal formula, or determined in some social contract or some law of expediency, and when its statesmen lose all consciousness of a divine obligation, that crime must be punished, and wicked men must meet the consequence of their deeds. This is the end in the commonwealth, and in its failure to realize this it is separated from its ground in the nation, and its organization no longer corresponds to its end.

There has been in the historical course of the United States the higher development of the civil and political organization of society, — the commonwealth and the nation. Their sequence is not the mere accident of history, nor the induction of an arbitrary theory, nor the assumption of a legal formula; but it has been justified in the reason of the state. It is an organization ampler and nobler than they who in the generations have builded in it, could wholly comprehend; and working steadily and faithfully in their own day, they have wrought in the ages, building better than they knew. It has been vindicated in political science in the pages of its few masters. It fills the almost prophetic conception of Milton, — "not many sovereignties united in one commonwealth, but many commonwealths in one united and intrusted sovereignty."

The commonwealth is poor and empty, as are all things else, in seeking to be something other than itself. When it assumes a national place and national relations, it is severed from its consistent strength and its symmetric order, and is weak in the assumption of unreal powers. It becomes the caricature of the state, moving with a deceptive pomp in a disastrous pageant. In the building of a false civilization, in the accumulation of merely material interests, it bears with it the ruin of a people. The family has its own place, and the commonwealth has its own dignity; but the worth of each is in the fulfillment of its own law. And if the commonwealth, instead of its maintenance in the unity of the nation in which its interests alone have a moral ground, and are formed in the spirit of a moral interest, is broken and dissevered from it, it is when material possessions are counted as beyond freedom, and gold is more precious than humanity, — the golden wedge of Ophir more precious than a man.

CHAPTER XVII.

THE NATION THE ANTAGONIST OF THE CONFEDERACY.

THE nation and the confederacy represent the forces in conflict in human society.

The nation in its organic and moral being in history may recognize other nations, and may enter into certain relations and assume certain obligations with them; it may form an alliance or join in a league with them, for certain objects defined, for instance by a treaty between them; but each is subsistent in itself, and the convention which they form obtains its only force from the sovereignty of each persisting in it, and is conditioned upon their continuance, and expires with its own limitation or with their retirement. But this presumes the existence and affects only the powers and obligations of separate nations.[1] It is apart from the principle of confederatism.

The confederacy is the construction of society in its own exclusive type. It defines the origin of society in the voluntary action of certain separate parties, and it is formed in their contract; its powers proceed from the contract of those who are associated as private persons in it, and the authority of its government is derivative from the arrangement of the articles of this contract. The formation of society is artificial, and the government and order of the world are of human contrivance, — certain expedients for the accomplishment of secular and separate ends. The

[1] A principle of politics of increasing strength in this age is "freedom from alliances," and this is indicative not only of changes in the character and relation of nations, but of the stronger personal life of the nation. There was this consciousness of freedom in the advice of the fathers of the republic, as in the words of President Washington, "avoid all entangling alliances."

state is the exclusive possession of those who have constructed it; its government is their agent; its justice the scheme of their legislators; its freedom the resultant consequent from the exchange conducted on the entrance to it; and each is limited to the proprietors who are joint parties in it. The end of society is the securance and furtherance of private interests; its order is the balance of these interests; its government is the representation of these interests; its primary and exclusive function is their protection.

The confederacy may be defined as the combination of separate individuals or societies who enter into a voluntary agreement, and in the arrangement which they have formed there is the source of government; the limitation of its action is with the several parties, and in the express terms of their arrangement, that is, it is the origin and institution of society in conformance to the civil contract. The highest principle in it is not the institution of justice which is in itself before all legislation, and is not created by it; nor the organization of rights which it may recognize but cannot bestow, nor the realization of freedom which although posited in an external order is of the spirit of man, and can no more be conferred by the lawyer than by the preacher or prelate or king, but it is the law of combination after which it is constructed. The confederacy has been called by its historian, "the most polished and the most artificial production of human ingenuity," and defined as a system in which each party, "as an independent and sovereign power, and as in itself absolute, enters into a compact with others."[1] Montesquieu, while regarding its primary object as security, which is assumed as belonging to it in a greater degree, describes it as "an assemblage of societies which is to arrive at such a degree of power as to provide for the security of the whole."[2]

[1] Freeman's *History of Federal Government*, vol. i. p. 6.
[2] Montesquieu's *Spirit of Laws*, bk. ix. ch. i.

The end is here only that of the commonwealth with which the state is identified. In the period in which Montesquieu wrote, it was presented as a formal system, — a precedent to oppose the formal system which identified the state with the prince, and in the conflict with the legal assumptions of feudalism, the social contract had a value while maintained as a legal fiction.

The formal constitution of a people in some period of transition — as in an early stage of political development, or a later stage of political degeneracy, — may take the shape of a summary of articles in conformance to a confederate system, but its characteristic is always the lack of permanence. If the people exist in the unity of a conscious and organic life, and in the continuity of an integral power in history, it is set aside as not representing the reality, and in the development of the people in its national being, with which it cannot consist, it is necessarily rejected; or if through the ascendency of a selfish power the unity of the nation is broken by it, there is in the lapse into the confederacy only the evidence in its external condition of that which has been wrought within in its moral dissolution.

The confederate is the immediate antithesis to the national principle, as the confederacy is the necessary antagonist to the nation in history. This antithesis becomes apparent in every aspect in which they may be regarded. The nation, as the organism of human society, presumes an organic unity; and its being, as organic, is that which no man can impart. The confederacy assumes the existence of society as artificial, as formed through an association of men in a certain copartnership of interests, and as only the aggregate of those who, before living separately, voluntarily entered it. The nation is formed in the development of the historical life of the people in its unity; the confederacy is a temporary arrangement which is formed in the pursuance of certain separate and secular ends. The nation in its necessary being can have its origin only in the divine will, and its realization only in that. The confederacy assumes the origin of society in the voluntary act of those who separately or collectively enter it, and its institution has only this formal precedent. The nation is constituted in a vocation in history, and therefore has its own purpose and work; and of this it cannot divest itself, as if it was an external thing, nor alienate, nor transfer it to another. The confederacy is the device of a transient expediency, and in conformance to certain abstract or legal notions, or formulas, as the exposition of a scheme. The nation exists as a relationship, as it is in and through relations that personality is realized; and it can neither have its origin in, nor consist with, a mere individualism. The confederacy comports only with an extreme individualism, — the association of private persons, the accumulation of special interests, to be terminated when these may dictate or suggest. The nation exists in an organic and moral relation to its members, and between the nation and the individual no power of earth can intervene. The confederacy is only a formal bond, and the individual has no more, in the state, an end in correspondence to his moral being; and it is thus that the word confederate has become stamped with a certain moral reprobation. The nation exists in its unity in the divine guidance of the people. The confederacy allows only the formal unity which is created in the conjunction of certain men or associations of men.

Their antithesis appears the more obvious, the more intimately they are regarded. The confederacy assumes only the aggregation of separate parties, as individuals or societies, but allows no principle in which a real unity may consist, nor the continuity in history of the generations of men. It is a formal order whose condition is a temporary expediency, and its limitation is defined in that, and not in the conditions of an organic and moral being. It is not the guidance of the people in its vocation, in the realization of its being in history, but its structure is framed after its own device, and out of the material which it has heaped together. It builds of its own brick and mortar — which it has accumulated, — what it alone can build, although its brick be as venerable as that upon which Mr. Carlyle has pronounced his political eulogium, building after its own schemes in the structure of society a Babel, and the result, which is not only a recurrent fact but a moral necessity, is that the work fails of all permanence in history, and the builders are driven away, or if it be preferred, they go away with confusion and division.

The antithesis which appears in the national and confederate principle has its manifestation in history. The confederate principle in its necessary sequence can bring only division, and unity and order are established only in the same measure in which it is overcome. The security, which it has made its single aim, it has failed to obtain; and in the furtherance of private and special interests it has been rent and broken by them. The pages of history contain everywhere the record of its disaster. The illustration of its course and its consequence appears — as in these lands also it had its widest construction — in Greece and in Germany. The termination of the history of Greece is abrupt, as if the sudden and violent issue of crime. It was as the confederate spirit came to prevail, in the division of her separate communities, and in the exclusive assumptions and supremacies of these communities, in the precedence of Athenian, and Spartan, and Theban, and Macedonian power, that the strength, which in its unity of spirit had triumphed over the multitudes of Asia, was lost; and in the dissension of these communities, which preferred alliance with a foreign power, so entirely was the national purpose effaced, and in the rivalries and jealousies of private ambition and devotion to private ends, the life of Greece was destroyed. The only union sought or allowed was in that fatal device, a balance of power, which was always irregular and disturbed, while separate communities with their separate interests alternately contended for the supremacy. The disease in the members could be overcome by no organific force working in the whole, for this was prevented by the assumption of a merely formal relation. Then followed a succession of internal wars, interrupted only by transient intervals of peace. The greater power of the confederate principle was then also in those communities, where a system of slavery predominated, as in Sparta; while in Athens there remained until the close the memories and hopes of a national life. This has left its expression in some of the noblest political conceptions in literature. And still it is in Athens that the national life of Greece is slowly reillumined. But the issue of the confederacy was a disaster from which none were exempt. The citizens of Athens themselves were disfranchised. The separate communities sank into the condition of Roman provinces, and the ruin involved the whole, and the subjection of the whole to a foreign power. The termination of the drama has been fitly represented by the historian, when the last great patriotic statesman of Greece went alone into the temple of Poseidon, to hail and welcome death. The most complete recent illustration of this principle is in the German Confederation. The assumption of the rights of sovereignty by petty states and municipalities, each with its claim to independence and legitimacy, divided the people, and in its resultant weakness left it through centuries the ally or the subject to some imperial power. The mockery of the power of a great people was in the construction of the German Bund. It was the prop of weak and pretentious sovereignties — mere lords of division at home and agents of imperial powers abroad. It led the people across every frontier as the antagonist of nations; and France, and Italy, and Denmark, in turn, have felt its assault. It could not protect the people from domestic tyranny, nor avert foreign invasion. In the most immediate danger to the people it could not act; while the Turks were before Vienna, Diet after Diet was held, but no common action followed. There are none of the great highways of Germany over which her own soldiers have not been compelled to march as the ally of a foreign power, and none of her capitals over which they have not aided to hoist a foreign flag. It is only after long humiliation that there comes the dawning of the unity and freedom of the German nation. There is alike in ancient and modern history, the evidence how deadly a foe the confederate spirit has been; how close its alliance has been with slavery and with the predominance of every selfish interest; how, through the division and resultant weakness of the people, it has opened the way to foreign supremacy and to imperialism, and how long has been the battle which the nation has had to fight.

The nation attains the realization of its sovereignty and its freedom only as it strives to overcome this false principle, and yet as its root is in a selfish tendency it is only at last overcome in the close of the conflict of history. The confederacy in itself has no permanence, but the evil principle, the bite of the serpent, remains, and in some sudden moment it may rise and strike at the life of the nation. With the people of the United States the conflict of the nation and the confederacy passed through a long period of years, until the character of the principle and purpose in each was to become manifest, and they were to meet face to face, and over a continent from its centre to the sea their armies were to be gathered, and in a struggle of life and death, not only for those who are, but for those who shall be, the issue was to come forth in the judgment of Him, with whom are the issues of eternal conflicts.

On the postulate of a confederate principle, it was assumed that the people constitute a confederate association of separate political societies, that each of these is sovereign, and each has a separate, integral and continuous existence, being associated with the others in a formal agreement for certain defined ends and the securance of certain interests; and that from this joint agreement expressed in the stipulations of certain articles formed by each as a party with the others, there is derived the authority of the government and the powers of the people. The inference in logic, and the result in fact, was the attempted secession of one or several of these societies, when any deemed that it was justified to itself in the exercise of its sovereignty, and in the consequent maintenance of its continuous existence, — in necessary coincidence with the extinction of the organization of the whole, which was regarded as only formal, and in which the separate societies were combined. There was assumed for each a sovereign and continuous existence, and an ultimate authority over its population, who were primarily constituted as the citizens of each society, and each could be conceived to exist without the others; but the relation of the people in and of the whole was formal, and it could not be conceived apart from the separate societies upon whose existence in their independence and sovereignty and continuous existence it was thus conditioned.

There has been in the history of no people the witness to a higher unity. The divine guidance of the people has nowhere had ampler evidence, and in the consciousness of the people it has been held in a purpose transmitted from the fathers to the children, in the faith of succeeding generations. The unity of the people has been moulded in the unity of a history so perfect, that apart from it the succession of events is a discord and not a development. If this unity be denied, the history holds no significance, and the people have acted with so long toil and sacrifice in a false masque, — a poor but fatal comedy of errors.

The foundations were to be laid in a new world, not in the age of imperialism, when the Roman empire was the central power in the world, nor in the age of medievalism, when the power in the same centre was transferred to papal ecclesiasticism, but in the age of the coming of the life of nations. It was the age of national development. Its gates were opened in the age of that protestantism which was formed in the struggle and endeavor of nations, against a universal domination whose capital was Rome. It was the national age of England, the age of her highest development, the age also of Shakespeare, and Raleigh, and Bacon, and Milton; in this age there was the beginning of the positive development in the history of the American people. There was the inception of the historical unity and historical life of America.

The people, in the colonial period, was formed under one government — that of Great Britain; and all were constituted under one sovereignty, as they were comprehended in one colonial system. Through the years preceding the War of Independence, the colonies, which were the plantations of Great Britain, were in an integral relation to one power, and subject to one authority. The government of Great Britain was over and inclusive of the whole. The formal investiture of the colonies with certain sovereign powers, was confined mainly to the administrative powers, which are necessary in the organization of civil society, that is, the order of the commonwealth.

From England the people was to inherit those elements which consist with a common relation. There were only those forces, which tend to the community of men, and there was mingled with them no element of variance. There was an inheritance of one language and one literature, and common manners and arts and laws.

The War of Independence, while it cannot be strictly called a revolution, was in the development in its unity of the people planted here, and here to unfold its life. The separation from Great Britain was a single political act; it was the act of the whole people, and involved the assumption by the whole of the sovereignty, which before was asserted over the whole by Great Britain.[1] It was occasioned by the same single course of events. The people had been subject through their lives to the same fortunes. Its complaint was of the same grievances, and it had suffered the same wrongs and endured the same humiliation. There was the same purpose animating the whole, and it advanced toward the same end. The period of colonial dependence was succeeded by the independence of the whole.

The action of the people was naturally, in the first instance, through the existent social forms, but it was none the less the action of the whole people. The people acted necessarily in the organizations in which it stood, — as the town meeting, the county, the municipality, the commonwealth, — and its action must have been through these forms, unless all forms were obliterated in some social devastation; but this action through the extant forms in this transition, instead of being conclusive of the separate political sovereignty and continuity of each community as an integral political power, when considered in its political aspects, is wholly inconsistent with it.[2]

1 "The association of the American people took place while they were colonies of the British empire, and owed allegiance to the British crown." — 1 Kent's *Comm.* 201.

2 De Tocqueville inferred that the people and freemen of each township constitute the political integer, and that its existence is independent of the collective people of the commonwealth. — *Democracy in America*, vol. i. pp. 40, 67, 68. Mr. Bancroft maintains the same position. — *History*, vol. ii. pp. 59, 60. See also Hurd's *Law of Freedom, etc.*, vol. i. p. 405. "These views have been expressed by them without sufficient reflection or examination, and are not correct in principle, nor sustained by our colonial records, nor by any adjudication of our courts."—Butler, J., in *Webster* v. *Harrington*, 32 Connecticut R. 136. The assumption of the town meeting as the integral political power, or the political monad, is described as the merest fiction, and as destitute of foundation in both fact and law, and this is illustrated by a wide survey of evidence. The argument is conclusive against the integral political character of the township; but there is more apparently to justify the inference of M. De Tocqueville and Mr. Bancroft, that the integral political power is resident in the township, than may be cited to maintain the same claim for the commonwealth.

There is in its continuance the unfolding of a still grander and more imposing unity. The War of Independence, with its years of suffering and devotion and sacrifice, was the war of one people. It was fought from its opening to its close before the inception of the Constitution, and with no formal constitution, but they "stood all together, and they marched all together." They went forth to battle under one leader, and under him they won a common victory. The power of the whole was instituted in one Congress. The language it used in its official acts, spoke of "country and America." The names which the political power assumed, were the "Continental Congress" and "Continental Army" and "Continental money." The name "United America" was often repeated. The relation toward other political powers was that always of one people forming a nation, and the recognition by other nations was not of each community as a separate political power, but it was the recognition of the people as one nation. It was the organic people forming a nation that sent forth its ministers, and with it treaties were made and international relations were established. Thus its ministers were received by France as the ministers of the United States, and at the conclusion of the treaty made between the two governments in 1778, the King of France spoke to its ministers of "the two nations." The authority asserted was of the whole people, and the delegates in the Revolutionary Congress proclaimed its power "*in the name and by the authority of* THE GOOD PEOPLE of these colonies." The Declaration of Independence was the act of the whole people; it calls the Americans one people, and its salutation is to them as fellow citizens. There is in it the assumption of no separate rights, and the record of no separate wrongs. The Declaration in its conception transcends the spirit of any of these separate communities, and was beyond their separate grasp. It was by the whole people that the war was carried on, and victory was won, and peace was established for the people. There was in these events beyond argument the evidence of the divine guidance of the people. And the witness to this providential guidance of the people in the realization of the nation, was to be given by one whose words are more than those of an isolated individual. President Washington said, in his first inaugural to the people, "Every step by which they have advanced to the character of an independent nation, seems to have been distinguished by some token of providential agency."

The subsequent circumstance of the deepest significance is that the people sought to realize its purpose under the articles of a confederation. It was the assumption of a confederate principle, although in the nature of things it induced inevitable contradictions; thus, while the separate States are represented as sovereign, they are not so in reality, but the attributes of political sovereignty are withdrawn from them; then also the articles are called the Articles of Confederation, but they are also described as articles of perpetual union; the acts which were then performed under the articles were incongruous with a confederate conception, and thus the Congress of the people proceeded to enact laws as if invested with positive powers, and thus the great seal of the United States with its legend of unity was adopted; and treaties were confirmed by the Congress, in which the nation was bound by obligations to other nations, and the whole people was held by them; under these articles also, — so far was the condition removed from an actual sovereignty in the separate communities, — in the highest issues, and those which involved the very being of the people, the ultimate determination was with nine of the thirteen communities, and this formal political action was imperative over the whole. But the fact of the most enduring import is that these articles of confederation had no continuance; but after a very brief period of confusion and disaster they fell away, partly through their inherent weakness, and partly because they did not correspond to the real constitution, and could not embody the real spirit and purpose of the people.[1]

There was formed by the people a national constitution. It was ordained and established by the people, and in the institution of a national government, "We the people of the United States, — for the United States of America." It is called "the Constitution," and not, as before, "the Articles," as in a compact. The end which it places before it is a national object, — "to provide for the common defense, to promote the general welfare, to secure the blessings of liberty to ourselves and our posterity." The ordination of the government is in a national legislature, whose laws are authority for the whole land; and a national judiciary, to which is referred the subject and administration of public law, and before which the separate communities in a conflict of rights appear by summons or appeal; and a national executive vested in one person in the unity of the personality of the nation. It is the enumeration of national rights and of national powers. It is ignorant of and indifferent to the very names, and the number and the extent of the separate civil communities comprehended in it.

The illustration of this history is in the necessary political development of the people. The formal argument in every phase admits no other conclusion, as in its course there can be traced no divergent event.

[1] President Madison says of the character of the confederation, after describing the Amphictyonic and Achæan leagues, which he represents as in analogy with it, "The inevitable result of all was imbecility in the government, discord among the provinces, foreign influences and indignities, a precarious existence in peace, and peculiar calamities in war." — *The Federalist*, No. xx.

President Washington, who held the conception of the organic and moral being of the nation with a more profound sincerity and grasp of thought than any American statesman — certainly before President Lincoln — wrote to John Jay, March 10, 1787, of: "a thirst for power, and the bantling — I had liked to have said — the monster sovereignty, which has taken such fast hold of the States individually."

Firstly, The separate societies or commonwealths have each of itself no integral historical life, and there is no separate historical aim which may be apprehended in them. The whole historical development is of the people of the United States, and upon the people its work has been laid. Apart from the people of the United States, and apart from a relation in and to that, history is ignorant of these separate communities. They have no separate ground in history.

Secondly, The object and end toward which the people has moved, has been the realization of a common end, and that the end of the being of the nation, the realization of freedom. The aim has been to place beyond all aggression the inalienable right of personality, the freedom of conscience and of thought, and to embody in more enduring institutions the rights of man; and this in the course of the people has been increasingly apparent. The end was not the false and negative conception of what is called freedom, which was to exist only in their relative independence in respect to each other, a freedom of alienation and division, but there was the unity of a moral aim, and for this the toil and conflict and sacrifice of years have been offered and this has been given to the people. The immortal words in which Washington was called by the Continental Congress to the head of the Continental Army were, "to command all forces raised or to be raised for the defense of American liberty."

Thirdly, The societies, with the interval of a brief and most significant period of transition, have existed under a positive national constitution. It is a constitution which proceeds from the political people in its unity. The supreme law is the assertion necessarily in its organic character of the sovereign political power. The constitution is the supreme law. The names of the separate societies are unknown to it, and there is no recognition of a separate sovereignty, and no assumption of a divided sovereignty.

The words are not in it, and it is only a school which claims the specious pretense of a literal construction, that reads of State sovereignties between the lines. The form in which the change or amendment of the Constitution may be effected, precludes a separate sovereignty in the separate communities. While it can only be effected in a form which is established, yet the act is ultimate and the whole is subject to it, but no sovereignty can consist with this ultimate subjection, whether the conclusion in its procedure be determined as a political act, by a political majority of one, or of two thirds.

Fourthly, The physical power, the organized might of the people, is formed by and in obedience to the authority of the people as a whole. It is organized as a national power. And as war is the act of the nation in its entirety, it is also beyond the capacity of a separate society to declare war or to conclude peace. The military oath, which every officer registers, is, " That he owes faith and true allegiance to the United States, and agrees to maintain its freedom, sovereignty, and independence."

Fifthly, The separate societies have no existence each as a separate society in international relations. The capacity to recognize other nations, and to be recognized by them, to form treaties and enter into the relations defined by international law with them, is the note or the crucial test of the sovereignty of a political people, and in its formal and external relations a positive test, but there is for this action no capacity in the separate societies, and this power has no existence in them.

Sixthly, There have been certain of these societies, correspondent in every actual capacity, and in their character and organization to the other communities, and invested with all their powers and immunities, which have been constituted by the nation, that is, by the people as a whole. This is the condition of an increasing number of them. They have been formed by the formal act and enactment of the nation, and to assume for these an original and independent existence, and an actual sovereignty, is a contradiction. It places the created above the creator.

Seventhly, These societies are so constituted that citizenship exists in all its rights and powers in the whole, and the citizens of the United States are the citizens of every State. It is one political body, to which the members are individually related. There is no expatriation on passing from one society to another; and no naturalization is requisite in the change from one section to another, and there is in no separate society the power for such action. But to apprehend a State as existent, apart from the people comprehended in it, is an abstraction, and can appear only in the vision of political speculations.

Eighthly, The separate societies have not the constituent elements of political power. The rights which appear in a national sovereignty and the correspondent powers, are not possessed by them. They have not separately the capacities of an independent political people. Their construction is in a civil system, and they are without the conditions of integral political supremacy. Whatever may be the inference of speculations and the course of legal hypotheses, this is the fact of their condition.

Ninthly, They have no external relation apart from the United States. It is the latter alone which is manifest in an external sovereignty. They are constituted in a form necessary to internal order and administration, and have none of the indices of power in which a nation appears in its external sovereignty, maintaining its own relations, and acknowledging on earth no external control beyond itself.

Tenthly, The separate societies have not the physical unity which appears in the being of an independent nation. They have in their existence no conformance to its geographical law. They are defined by no natural and no historical boundaries, but every natural and historical boundary is erased in their interrelation. There are none of those lines that demark the existence of a separate people on the earth. In the collision of events, and the conflict and migration of races, and the crush of the forces of history, which are mightier in their duration than those of physical nature, if a separate existence was assumed they would become in the first shock so changed as to lose their identity, and history could not recognize them.

But while the argument in its conclusion allows no digression, and has in the records of scarcely any years in the existence of a people, a parallel in height and fullness, yet an argument is only illustrative, and in the presence of the being of the people, and in the realization of history, there is presumption in any argument. The evidence is in the being of the people, and from its conscious unity there is no appeal, and it allows no inquiry. If there be not the consciousness of the unity and sovereignty and freedom which subsist in the organic being of the people, then all argument is empty, and all inquiry is vain. The realization of history can be determined by no political abstractions, and events conform to no individual preconceptions. Facts do not defer to theories; in the strong image of the poet, "words are men's daughters, but God's sons are things."

The principle in which the character and relation of the separate civil societies are defined, whatever its form, necessarily affects the foundation of society, and is constructive of its whole process. If there be assumed for each a necessary and continuous existence, then each is a self-subsistent power, and then the bond which holds them as collective, that is, as a combination of certain separate and self-subsistent societies, is formal, and the principle in which their relation is formed must be necessarily the confederate principle. To maintain then the continuous union of each with all, and to compel each to persist continuously in connection with another or with all in this formal relation, would not only be destructive of the sovereignty and independence presumed in each, but when this compulsion was made against its clearly and persistently expressed intent, it would become the institution of human society in force. It would involve in human society the maintenance through physical force of a formal order, and not the existence of an integral or organic and moral being.

The principle which is the necessary postulate of the confederacy has been defined clearly, and has been held strenuously. There was nothing vague in the attempt at secession, nor in the premise on which it proceeded. It was the assumption of the sovereignty and independence and continuous existence of each separate community, and the act of secession was the necessary sequence as each or any deemed itself justified to itself by the grievance it bore, or by the advantage it was to secure. The secessionists regarded themselves primarily as the citizens of these separate communities, and subject to the ultimate authority of each, and became confederate in and for the protection and furtherance of a special interest, which was assumed as the immediate object.

The confederate principle which was manifest in the denial of the organic and moral being of the nation, could appear only as a destructive force. It had its necessary sequence, as it sought its realization, in an attempt at the dissolution of the whole.

The conflict of the confederate principle with the nation has been borne on through all the years of the people. There are memorials and declarations, and enactments and proclamations, and judicial decisions and state papers, which are framed in conformance to the scheme of a confederacy, or formed in the realization of the being of the nation.[1] And still in the devices of parties and the expe-

[1] There is a force often imputed to some textual statement, in which it is so construed as to compel history, and thus a notion or dogma counter to all reality may be built upon some political memorial, as the phrase of a state paper. There is an illustration of this in the speculations of Mr. Calhoun. An article

dients of priests, and the forms of legists and the opinions of jurists, the conflict appears. The construction of government has sometimes been conceived to exist in a compromise, but the fact has been their inevitable conflict. As in their conception each involves the negation of the other, there has been in history their incessant antagonism. As the nation is formed in its unity in the will of God in history, and is manifest in the divine guidance of the people, and advances in its continuity in the transmission of its purpose from the fathers to the children, in the fulfillment of the vocation of the whole people, and exists in the realization in its organic and moral being of a moral order in history, so the confederacy denies the unity and con-

of the Confederation reads, "each State retains its sovereignty, freedom and independence, and every power, etc.," and thus it is assumed as the reality in history that each State or society possessed a real sovereignty and independence, and all the political powers involved in a sovereign and independent political being. There is then maintained in strict consistency and as the immediate inference of this postulate, the necessary and continuous existence of each State or society as a political power, and having all political powers immanent in the political body. It is on the phrase of a state document that the whole fabric is constructed, and for all time. — See Calhoun's *Works*, vol. i. p. 148. The original sovereignty is not the creation of a legal formula, since it is itself the power which can affirm its will as law, and thus in France, for instance, at one period, the most various constitutions, each having the authority of law, succeeded each other; but it is not presumed that the actual condition changed with each state document, that appeared, as it was said, so rapidly as to form a periodical literature.

Mr. Hurd says, "Declaring a state of things does not make it. Since no declaration of sovereignty can be more than evidence, it may as such be compared with other testimony. The declaration of July 4th asserted the colonies to be 'free and independent states.' The accompanying declarations of an existing condition of private persons that 'all men are created equal, etc.,' all men have 'inalienable rights,' did not determine any private conditions, even though the state of private persons is the effect, and not like sovereignty, the cause of law." — *Law of Freedom, etc.*, vol. i. p. 407.

"The possession of sovereignty, being a fact and not an effect of law, whatever written memorials of the rightfulness of any national sovereignty may exist, they can only proceed from itself, and they can only be taken as historical evidences of its existence; not as law controlling that possession of sovereign power which they assert. And the authors of these declarations must always be supposed to have the right to substitute others of different term and of equal juridical authority. There can therefore be no written constitution of government so authoritative in its nature or its expression as to determine the rightful sovereignty, the rightful holders of that rightful supreme power." — *Ibid.* vol. i. p. 396.

tinuity in the being of the organic people, and assumes the origin and foundation of society in the convention of men, and its construction in the combination of separate interests, and its continuance in the dictation of interests, it is conditioned in the law of a temporary expediency, and as a power in the exclusive possession of a class or of a race, and for the furtherance of separate and specia ends.

It cannot be too often repeated that the War was not primarily between freedom and slavery. It was the war of the nation and the confederacy.

The nation and the confederacy meet at last in mortal conflict. It is the battle of the nation for life. Confederatism, in its attack upon the nation, is in league with hell. It severs the children from the fathers. It erases the sacred memories which are their common heritage. It passes over violated oaths. It rejects a law of righteousness in the realization of society. It denies the divine origin of humanity, and the sacred rights it bears in its divine image. It refuses the foundation of its unity in the corner-stone, which is the "foundation which is lying." It forms its alliance with slavery, and that dam got its brood. It gathers to itself the pride, the treachery and infidelity of men, the worship of money, the vulgarity of fashion, and the distinction of caste. It collects its supporters out of all parties and factions and churches and sects. It is the conflict of history, the battle of Judæa with Babylon, which sweeps through all the centuries. In its awful significance, it can find but an imperfect expression in the symbols of human thought. It is but faintly imaged in the fight of the eagle and the serpent. It may never wholly cease until the end of history. The confederacy is the embodiment of the evil spirit, in which there is the destruction of the being of the nation, the organic and moral unity and continuity of society, and the subversion of the whole to selfish ends. It strives to subvert the nation to serve its end in the perpetuance of slavery, or the pride of birth, or hatred of race. It turns from defeat on the field to cheat men with its lies and its frauds. It retreats slowly from every hold. There is no people but has felt the poison of its fangs, and none but has been deceived and seduced by its sorceries. The nation in the realization of its being has always to contend with it, and in the subjection or the resistance to it is the sign of weakness or of power. The nation is to bear the conflict to the close of history, as it is to strive for the realization in its moral fulfillment of the life of humanity, to which every advance in its history will call it, and of which every new age may be the revelation, as the days of the Son of Man.

In every age the character and result of the conflict becomes more clear, as its issue is revealed in the judgment of history. It is not alone the conflict of ideas, for it is in another than an intellectual arena, and reaches the very passion and contradiction of life. It is not alone the conflict of freedom and slavery, excepting only as freedom is realized in the realization of the being of the nation, and slavery, as divisive or destructive, is to be overcome by it. It is the nation contending for its unity, which is in God, and for its continuity, in which the generations from the fathers to the children bear its holy purpose, and for the fulfillment in humanity of a law of righteousness. The nation was battling for her very being, as she rose to victory, from the fields of Vicksburg and Gettysburg and Atlanta, and the lines before Richmond.

CHAPTER XVIII.

THE NATION THE ANTAGONIST OF THE EMPIRE.

The nation has its immediate antithesis in the empire. The nation is formed in the freedom of the people, as an organic whole, and it comprehends the whole in its action and end as a moral organism; the law of the empire, or the imperial principle, is the formation of the order of society in the subjection of the whole to an individual or a separate collection of individuals.

In the empire, there is strictly the realization of the freedom of only one or a few. The will of the people has no expression in it, and there is substituted in its stead the will of an individual, or a class, to whom alone action is allowed. The government is not of the people, but apart from the people. They are the subjects of it, but are not participants in it, and have no place in its positive determination. The empire allows no real expression to the will of the people, but only to an individual or a family or a class. Thus its government becomes repressive, and tends to efface the conscious life and spirit of the people.

The nation is in identity with the people, but the empire identifies an individual or a class, with the political body. Its language is always in the phrase of Louis XIV. The ruler is not regarded simply as a member of the political body, but is himself the state. There is no law and no power beyond his individual authority; there is no voice except his individual proclamation, and no rights beyond his individual rights. The public good is not the immediate aim, and the common welfare is not an object in itself, nor the well being of the people the end of the whole, except only as it goes well with him.

The government of the empire is not in the will of the organic people, expressed through the organic powers of the political body, but the sole authority is the private judgment and the executive act of the imperator. It is a necessary absolutism, and the law of the empire is concluded in the Roman aphorism, quod Principi placuit, legis habet vigorem.

The empire may conform to the physical being of the state, and has the conditions of an external order, but not of the development of the nation as a moral order. There is the action only of an imperial will, and its process is an imperial edict. There is in the people no evocation of a moral spirit, and no education of an individual character in them. The capacity of each is not called forth, and his powers are not awakened; he is in no immediate relation to the state; he does not act in the determination of its course; he cannot realize in it his own purpose, nor strive for the embodiment in it of his moral aim. The life of the state is withdrawn from him, and its conduct is secret from him; he cannot comprehend it, as in his individual existence he is not comprehended by it. There is thus no development of the individual personality, no moral life and spirit in the people. This appears in China, which is perhaps in all its aspects the most complete illustration of the empire. In China, says Hegel, "the ground of moral action is entirely obliterated. Such is the fearful condition of things in regard to responsibility and non-responsibility; all subjective freedom and moral accountability and concernment in an action is lost sight of." [1] The consequence is seen in the subversion of moral responsibility. In its criminal code there is no individual

[1] Hegel, *Philosophie der Geschichte*, p. 156.

"Die autokratie wird allerdings ausgeschlossen, durch die Representative verfassung, und durch den Begriff des Staats selbst." — Rothe, *Theologische Ethik*, vol. ii. p. 126.

accountability recognized for crime, and there is a confusion of the moral judgment and indifference to moral distinctions. In its civil system, punishment is not necessarily imposed upon offenders, but is a formal satisfaction of the law. Thus for instance, one who has committed a crime to which the penalty of death is affixed, and is condemned, may, and with slight expense almost always can find one who will suffer the penalty in his stead, and the law is then satisfied, no regard being had to the exposition of justice, nor in the infliction of punishment, to individual guilt. Thus also if a resident on a certain street commits a certain crime, the penalty is imposed on the street, and all the houses, for instance, are demolished. There is thus the destruction of the moral life of the people, and there is no consideration of the individual character. There is thus in the empire no wide and complex life, and no diversitude in thought and action. There is nothing of that wealth in art and literature and laws, which appears when the energies of the people are called forth with the fresh and free development of the individuality of each. Its life thus has no depth, and its action is mechanical, and there is only a wide and superficial uniformity. In its best epochs, the empire can present only a few isolated figures, — the greatness of a solitary individual or a family which are lifted far above the people, and their greatness is transient. This desolation of the life and spirit of the people in imperialism is reflected in some of the darkest pages in history, and where the gloom is deepened by the greatness of some solitary form or some line of rulers in its lonely exaltation. The annals of Tacitus disclose the condition in Rome, when the conviction of individual obligation, and of the authority of law, and of continuity with the past, and of the relations of men was lost, and there remained only the sense of subjection to the will of a single individual which was external to the people.

The tendency in imperialism is not only to undermine the moral life and spirit of the people, in its immediate action in the subversion of personality, but also to subvert it as it is formed in the relations of life. In Rome, the decay of the family was in immediate connection with the merging of the nation in the empire. The object is not the strengthening of the sacredness of the family relations, which are in correlation with the nation in its moral being, but it aims at the solitary grandeur and permanence of a dynasty.

The empire tends to obliterate, when it cannot identify with itself, the historical memorials which have gathered in the history of the people. It seeks to substitute for them the associations and traditions of a dynasty. The thought of the people is diverted from its achievements in the past, and there is inculcated only the sense of dependence upon the existent power. There is in this condition no spirit through memory to inform the mind of the people. There is nothing also to incite their forethought. In this dependence there is no longer robustness of spirit or moral hardihood; and in the empire the people are regarded, and through its forms are addressed, as children.

The progression of the empire is in contrast with the law of development in the integral unity of the nation. It tends to increase by aggregation, and its extension is in its material aggrandizement. There is no unific force acting from within to shape and determine the whole, but only the decree of the imperator, which is an external affair. The sovereignty of the people forming the nation is limited in its own organic law, and through its subsistence in the organic whole; but in the assumption of an individual will as in identity in its domination with the state, there is no necessary limitation and no restriction to the widest circle, to which this will may extend its authority. While the sovereignty of the people in the nation presumes the organization of the whole people, the organization of the empire is established in the edict of the imperator. The pale of the empire is the boundary of the power affirmed in the imperial decree. The tendency of imperialism is thus always to pass the natural and historical boundaries by which a people is described, and it becomes an accumulation of peoples, and is formed not in an organic relation, but held by a formal and external bond, which is the imperial decree. This was the career of Rome in the empire. It did not intend so vast or so remote a conquest; but losing the consciousness of the moral unity of the nation in its integral and historical life, and apprehending only a formal relation in the law or edict of the empire, it was borne on in the accumulation of peoples and lands under its authority, until overpowered by the mass it sunk beneath its weight and tumbled in ruins. The same impulse appears in the course of England in its empire in India. The limit to its sway is constantly being drawn only to be erased. Wellington said it was the Indus, but it was long since passed, to move on to Peshawur and on to Burmah, and to secure the possession obtained which is held by no cohesive power, it is still hurried on with alarm at external aggression. When once the will asserts its own individual power as a domination in the world, it seems, in the consequent evil, to be emptied of its own freedom, and it moves as if impelled by some fate.

The destruction of nations thus may be traced in this loss of their moral unity and freedom in the transition to empire. The decline and fall of Rome appears as it ceases to be a nation and becomes an empire. Its imperial power had always certain material attractions, and in its inception it was not without certain advantages; it instituted a more perfect civil order; it terminated social wars which had long continued; it brought an immediate security, and there was a check upon the frauds and corruptions of a prætorial and proconsular administration; it relieved the people from the agitation and concern in public affairs; but there was the decay of public spirit, and the beginning of those tendencies which were to effect in their gradual course the decline in which the acquisitions of the centuries of its national development were to perish. The power which once in its discipline had been irresistible, at last could defend no section of its territory from the inroad of a single tribe out of the many once embraced in its conquest. As its public spirit was destroyed, and its marvelous organization was broken, and the energy which had moulded and pervaded its action was undermined, there was in imperialism no creative force to renew it, and no recuperative strength to overcome its decay. The same consequence with the advance of imperialism may be seen in Spain. The record of her imperial dominion under Philip II. is told in the proud story of the chronicler of that day; "he held in Europe the kingdoms of Castile, Aragon, and Navarre, those of Sicily and Naples, Sardinia, Milan, Roussilon, the Low Countries, the Balearic Islands, and Franche Comté; on the western coast of Africa he held the Canaries, Cape Verde, Oran, Bujiya, and Tunis; in Asia he held the Philippines, and a part of the Moluccas; in the new world the vast kingdoms of Peru, Mexico, Chili, and the provinces conquered in the last years of Charles V. with Cuba, Hispaniola, and other Islands." But this enumeration of so vast an apparent material power is the preface to disaster, and the beginning in Spain of centuries of humiliation. There is a more recent illustration of the same tendency in imperialism in Austria. In the long roll of soldiers whom Francis Joseph saluted on the field of Sadowa, as his faithful children, there was the German, the Italian, the Magyar, the Croat, the Slovak, the Pole, the Rouman; but in this multitudinous mass, there was no organic unity. They were the representatives on the field of only a vast aggregate of peoples and states, and the bond which held them was formal, and whether that bond be in a confederate compact or an imperial edict, it can have no unific force.

The empire is formed in the subjection of peoples and races. It thus embraces those in the state who are isolated from the state. It is a dominion, and is without the conscious unity and aim of the nation. The nation may break down the division and antagonism of races, in a moral order and organism, but this principle is wanting in the empire, and thus it can only embrace subject races as inferior. It is this which tends always to bring the empire into alliance with slavery. The government is not formed in the institution of rights, since no rights are recognized beyond the imperial will, nor in freedom since only the will of the imperator is allowed freedom, nor is it in the protection of the weak and the poor, but it is the sign of their subjection to the strong. It comprehends the people not as integral in the state, but as masses and fragments, and sects and parties and races, and in these conditions they are subject, and the government is an external affair.

The empire, since it is a government external to the people, tends to form an external life. The moral strength and energy of the people is not called forth, and there is the suppression of their spirit. There is a uniformity of action, and the people move mechanically, and the government is not a power in which the people acts. It is thus that the people in the empire are withdrawn from actual life by amusements, and are to be diverted by shows and pageants gotten up for them, and having the attraction of an external magnificence.

As in the empire the government is isolated from the people, the people in their isolation become at length no longer affected by it. Their lives become independent of it, and it is powerless to influence their actual condition. There is thus in the decline of Rome, in the empire, no fact more sad than that the actual condition of the people is unchanged under the most brutal and sensual, and the most humane and gentle of rulers. It remains the same under Aulus Vitellius, and M. Antoninus Aurelius.[1]

The empire creates a false conception of human power and human greatness. There is the assertion of power not in the service of humanity, but in separation from it. In the elevation of an individual or a class, the distance between them and the people is widened, and there gathers about the imperial presence a distant grandeur which removes it from the common condition of humanity. The dignity of the empire is sought, not in its moral, but its material power. It is estimated in the extent of its dominion, or the vastness of its possessions, or the number of its armies, or the strength of its armament.

There may be in the empire, in its immediate inauguration, an apparent advantage; it may enable men to devote themselves more exclusively to the pursuit of their private affairs and their private ends; it may relieve them from attention to public duties and the direction of public events; it may introduce a more regular routine, and more uniform method and system in the public administration; it may display a greater external splendor, and construct vast works of public utility; there may be a greater care for the physical condition of the people; but these may be connected with the degradation of the spirit of the people, and there are in these no elements of political permanence. The traces of the possession of England by the Romans, under the empire, still may be found in the almost obliterated ruins of the bridges, and roads, and public works, which they constructed; but it was in the coming of a power which sought to awaken the spiritual life

[1] There seems, in the fate which instead of freedom is the principle of the empire, the reflex of the lives of the people in the life of the individual imperator. Gibbon says, "Such was the unhappy condition of the Roman emperors, that whatever might be their conduct, their fate was commonly the same. A life of pleasure or virtue, of severity or mildness, of indolence or glory, alike led to an untimely grave, and almost every reign is closed by the same repetition of treason and murder." — *History, etc.*, vol. i. ch. 12.

and energies of men, and wrought in the common people, that there was the elements of an enduring strength. There may be in the empire, also, works of great excellence in literature and art; but these will more often have had their root in some earlier period of national energy, and the creative power in all literature and art can appear only in the development of a native strength. There may be, also, a greater civil code, although instituted from the precedents formed more often in an earlier period; but this is the condition of the civil corporation, and can have only the attraction of an external system.

The result of the empire is not always the creation of a vast or permanent material wealth. It has been said that the empire creates wealth, although it destroys credit. The latter certainly follows, since the people cannot ascertain the intent of the ruler; and the secret course of the government gives rise to distrust and foreboding, and business enterprise is checked, and men will not risk large undertakings. But the empire does not create wealth. It does not stimulate human activity, nor incite the thrift and forethought and shrewdness of the people. The people in the empire are not rich. There is greater inequality of fortune, and wealth becomes useless in the hands of the few, and the poverty of the mass is in contrast with the vast riches of a few individuals or families. In Great Britain the increase of pauperism and the disappearance of the yeomanry—that is the larger number of proprietors—has been in proportion to the accumulation of lands in the possession of a few. In Rome, under the empire, the nobles and farmers of the revenue were rich, while the people were poor. "They fight," said a tribune, "to maintain the luxury and wealth of others, and they die, with the title of lords of the earth, without possessing a single clod to call their own."

The condition of the people in an imperialism is not one of happiness. In the midst of the external power of imperial Rome, there was in the people no satisfaction of the spirit. This exists only in the conscious energy, — the freedom of the people ; but in the empire there is the depression of the spirit. There is no comprehension of a moral end. The imperial government, if it acts in respect to the people, acts only in doing what is good for them, while in the nation the individual is called, in its organic and moral being, to act in the realization of that which is in itself good.

There is in the empire the creation of a love of power for its own sake, and of domination for itself. It is the view of powers and principalities. The people exist for the government, and not the government for the people. The former is not the servitor of the people, but the people is only its instrument, — the means for its end. It is thus that it is only in its inception, or in certain transient intervals, that the "empire is peace," and the tendency of mere power acting itself out is to impel the people into war.

The influence of imperialism, in the subversion of the freedom of the individual personality, tends to induce an impression of fate. The people when it acts, acts in an order which is external to it, and mechanically and blindly, as if impelled by some external power, and not in the conscious determination of men. There thus arises a sense of incapacity in the presence of the evils weighing upon it. There is the want of responsibility in respect to them, and as the people is excluded from public affairs, the decay of public conscience follows, and there is no energy nor effort toward the reform of abuses or the removal of wrongs. The government, in the destruction of the freedom of the individual person, is led to invade the sphere of the individual, and to assume the immediate conduct of life, destroying all individuality, and determining the vocation, the home, the marriage, the work and rest of men. The government also tends to become a mere system of police,

— although as in its civil system its police may be very highly organized, — since in its isolation from the people, in order that their course may not also become secret from it, it has to set spies over them, and gradually comes to regard them with suspicion and distrust. There is a tendency also to regulate life by a formal and artificial standard, to introduce some scale of virtues to denote the relative excellence of deportment, and the reward of virtue is in some ribbon or prize, and the periods of life, as of marriage, or rest from labor in age, are assigned in conformance to some uniform and external scheme of notation. It is thus in the empire that life becomes superficial and frivolous, and men are diverted with toys and playthings, as in China. Then the order of the state becomes mechanical, and this is the character of administration in China, with its competitive examinations, where political trusts and civil offices are assigned by a graduated scale in a pedantic system. It is thus also in the empire that there is the absence of all event in their history, and there is in the people an apathy, and in their long chronological records only a monotony. The tendency of imperialism has thus always been, to induce a fatalism.

The nation may exist in some transient period, through confederate or imperial forms,[1] but their characteristic, if

1 In Russia there has been, with an imperial form, the advance of the people in the development of a national life and in freedom; but in its imperfect development the immediate danger to civilization is in the identification of the state, with the physical power of a race. In France, the imperial policy has been involved with constant contradictions. It established in universal suffrage the strongest guaranty of the rights of the people, and in its constitution, says Bluntschli, "full deference is given to the majesty of the people of France, as the source of the power of the state, the legislative body is made immediately dependent upon its confidence, and the imperial power derived from its will." The title of the emperor is "par la grâce de Dieu et la volenté nationale, Empereur des Francais." Its strength also has been in holding through imperial forms the conception of the nation, and its disaster has been in its later abandonment of it, as in its policy in Mexico and in its later course in Italy. In England the tendency in imperialism is more apparent. Its sympathy, Michelet says, its "grosses mitgefuhl," was with the confederacy. Its main alliance in this age

the nation does not fail in its integral organic and moral power, is the lack of permanence. The nation has always to contend with them and to meet them sometimes in secret

is with the empire of the Turks, and with an historical fitness, but with no consciousness of its propriety, it received the Sultan at a banquet, at the expense of the Indian administration, and at a table covered with the plunder of Rajas' palaces. The influence of imperialism may be traced in the increase in it of Roman ecclesiasticism, and in its literature not more in the open avowal of its old men, as Mr. Carlyle and Mr. Ruskin, than in the more than pagan fatalism of its younger men. It has built an empire in India, whose policy has been to crush every germ of national spirit in its native populations; and as the national spirit in England, in the defect of moral strength, has diminished, the power in India has been held as the power in a race, and that race the English; in its Indian administration it has had no power to overcome caste, since its own government is imbedded in caste; it has degraded the people, and while under Moghul rule, the highest offices in the army and the state were open to them, all participation in the government has been denied them under English rule; it has destroyed the physical condition of national well being, in a varied industry, instead of encouraging this as a securance against famine or accident, as in Orissa it suppressed the salt manufacture, which had existed for ages, in order to swell British revenue, and in the single failure of the rice crop, there was nothing for the people to fall back on; in its constitutional formalism it established a system of civil justice, which a people, before prompt to punish crime, found so alien that they preferred to submit to crime rather than the infliction of the civil system; in its own action it found in the superstition of ignorant Sepoys its instrument, with which to send them to meet death; in its contact with a people from whom has sprung in literature the speculative hymns of the Vedas, and the delicate purity of Kalidasas verse, and the subtle metaphysical contemplation of the Maha Bahrata, and which in art has filled India with cities of architecture so imposing; it has not sought to develop the spirit of the people, but to crush and deface it. Thus under English rule, while it may conceal a real weakness, there has been an apparent increase in Hinduism, and a more lavish consumption of gold on its idols; and even Mohammedanism has increased under it, but the latter has come to discern elements of peril, only in the advance of Russia, while England's relation toward it is regarded as one of indifference. In its foreign policy it left Denmark, when every higher principle would have led it to sustain it; it might fight for the independence of Belgium, which is more integral to France than Scotland or Ireland to England, and whose independence, as R. von Mohl says, in its origin is laughable, since this is an outpost for itself on the continent; it might fight to prevent the independence of Egypt, since this is on the way to its Indian empire; it opposes a vast work, of continental beneficence, as the Suez Canal, and the most effectual check to the slave trade, with secret and bitter diplomacy. The measure of reform in its suffrage may tend to check its imperialism; but its main characteristic is the incapacity to deal with the evils which it recognizes, in its suffrage, and education, and lease of land, and military organization. There seems to be no consciousness of responsibility in the people for them. The characteristic of its policy is the destitution of conscience. "In the eyes of her people," says M.

and again open alliance, and in many disguisements; it is not on a single field, nor in a single age that the conflict is over. The close of the history of two of the great nations, in the ancient world, is the warning of the evil. The life of the nation perished,—in Greece, in the confederacy, in Rome, in the empire. The nation has always to contend with the dissolution of a confederate principal, and the domination of an imperial principal.

De Tocqueville, "that which is most useful to England is always the cause of justice, and the criterion of justice is to be found in the degree of favor or opposition to English interests."

CHAPTER XIX.

THE NATION THE INTEGRAL ELEMENT IN HISTORY.

THE nation is the integral element in history. It is as old as history. The phrase which describes "the new doctrine of nationalities," has scarcely a superficial justification.

The process of history is a development in the realization of the moral order of the world. There is in it an organic unity and growth, which is the condition of its continuous life. There is the unity of the divine idea, and it holds a purpose appearing in and through and uniting the ages. It is a moral order, and thus it has been said, "the history of the world cannot be understood apart from the government of the world."

It is in history as the realization of the moral order of the world, that the nation is formed as an integral power. It is in this that the vocation of the nation is given to it, as in the fulfilling of its vocation its being as a moral person is realized. This is also implied in the realization of a moral order, since its condition is in freedom, and there can be no history in the law and sequence of a physical necessity. The nation is not then of itself a righteous power, but the realization of its being through its vocation in a moral order is in righteousness; not only the law of its being, but the condition of the realization of its being, is in righteousness. In its necessary being it moves toward this end. Thus in anarchy and oppression and violence and crime there is the negation of its being. Thus, also, in so far as it fails of its end, it passes from history. As history is in the realization of a moral order, in the unity of a divine purpose, when the nation ceases to work in its own vocation in it, and to act as a constructive power in the harmony of its design, then it no more has a place in it. It is this constant possibility of evil in the nation that involves the most real obligation, and is the incitement to the utmost energy and vigilance, and it is this which gives solemnity to history.

The continuous process of history is in the nation. There is formed in it the transition from the vague and the indefinite to the determinate spirit of a conscious life. That which lies beyond it has for its characteristic the undefined. The life of the nation in its beginning, as in the individual, holds the slow awakening of a conscious aim. It is in the moments of its existence, hidden from sight, as are the changes in the process of life in every form. The early incident and circumstance in the life of the people offer but the faint premonition of its course, and there is but the dim dawning of that vocation, which in the retrospect of a fulfilled purpose, rises into clearer light. But as the indication of its spirit, these events may be wrought in traditions, or again, in the type they hold, while in their immediate event of no significance, they are kept in reverent memory, and are cherished in the reminiscence of the people. They are often, in the purpose which they prefigure, and through the refraction of events, invested with a light "which was not on sea or shore," but become always more clear in the march of the people. Then in the advance of its conscious life, it may be that language has a more unitary and ampler development; but while language may of itself often indicate the boundary of a people, it is yet only the incident and not the foundation of its unity. Then tribunals and institutions of justice, and codes and instruments of law, are defined and established. There are in its services and solemnities, in its days and festivals, the memorials of the greater events in its course. There is, then, in literature and art, the work of its creative power, the impress of its character and the reflection of its spirit. There is indeed in each of these, and in all their forms, — in law and literature and art, — a universal element, and their excellence is in its more perfect expression, but this instead of forming an external limitation to the being of the nation as a moral person, is implied in personality, and is more manifest in its higher realization. Then law and literature and art have their continuous development in the nation, and their conservation in it; it is thus that one speaks not only of the Greek and Roman mind, its quality and character, but of the unity apparent through the polity and literature and art of Greece and Rome.

The nation is formed in the elevation of man above an animal existence. It is not defined in a merely physical basis, and in certain physical relations. Its end is not the satisfaction of physical wants alone, nor is it comprehended in the sequence of physical necessity. It is as the course of freedom that it becomes the expression of a determinate spirit, and the assertion of the dominion of man over nature. It is in its free spirit that man is raised from the stupidity of an animal condition. There is the inspiration of a conscious energy. Thus in Greek and Roman art there is the expression of the exaltation of humanity, — a victory which it gains, — which gives to it its highest type. In the Greek it is the victory of the human over the earthly and sensual; and in the Roman it is a moral discipline and virtue, in which there is the sign of a conquest over the merely unorganized and undisciplined mass, and it is this in each which gives a spiritual element to its ideal.

The nation, as it is the power in history, is formed in the conditions of history. Its course must be one of conflict and endeavor. Its battle and victory is in no aimless conquest. Its vocation is no indefeasible inheritance. Its freedom is realized only in its ceaseless work; it does not come, as things are let to fare on. Its strength is not born out of the sky, nor wrought in dreams. It is indeed maintained only by eternal vigilance. The nation must always strive, and it is not here nor now that it can cease from its labor nor enter its rest. There can be no danger so great as that in which it shall dream in any moment that it is saved, and that its struggle is over, and its conflict is closed. It is with many doubts and many fears, and with discipline and sacrifice, that it is to work out its salvation.

The nation is the work of God in history. Its unity and its continuity through the generations is in Him. He is present with it as with the individual person, and this is the condition of its being, as a moral person. Its vocation is from God, and its obligation is only to God, and its freedom is His gift. The transmitted purpose which it bears in its vocation, is in the fulfillment of His will. The procession of history is in the life of nations, and in the perfected nation, is the goal of history.

There is before the nation the attainment of the end of history. It is the constituent power in which history is borne to its end. It is to act not only in but for the order of God. This is apparent in its relations. It is given to the nation to act in the realization of the individual personality — the formation of human character. The individual first becomes a person in the nation. The powers of the individual are called forth, in the sphere of its law and its freedom. The nation has also to maintain in conformance to their moral conception all the relations of life as integral in a moral order.[1]

It is given to the nation to assert and establish its authority as law. It is a law regulative of the action of the individual. This power belongs to no individual, and to no collection of individuals, but it is in the nation.

[1] "Ein kosmopolitisches menschliches Leben, ist eine leere werthlose Abstraction." — Rothe, *Anfange der Christlichen Kirche*, p. 16.

It is given to the nation to bear to its issue, the conflict with slavery. It is not only formed in the determination of the spirit in its freedom, but it has to contend with the dominations over men, in the bondage of the world. To contend with slavery is the work which through providence in history has been given to the nation. This is only the statement of an historical fact; the work has been given to no individual, and to no special or ecclesiastical association of men, but to the nation. The nation in the realization of its own being, — in the maintenance of its own unity and its own life, — is borne on to an inevitable conflict with slavery. It may be for the nation gradually to overcome it by ameliorating laws and institutions, or in some sudden moment to meet it in direct conflict, when slavery aims at its life, and it is only through convulsive effort that it uproots it in order to live. Yet it is never utterly removed, but will take root in other fields and in other forms. The forces in antagonism to the nation it joins in its alliance. The struggle of Greece was with slavery as the ally of confederatism, and of Rome with slavery as the ally of imperialism. The conflict has followed with clearer issue in the new world, and victory has been given to the nation in its redemptive years.

There is given to the nation no separate and special end, but its vocation and its work is for humanity. This end is presumed in its being as a constituent element in and for the moral order of the world, for the moral order of the world is the fulfillment of humanity in God. The conception and realization of the life of humanity does not exclude the being of the nation, as if it was simply external to it, nor as if it was to disappear merged into it.

The nation on the contrary comes forth in the realization of the life of humanity. The life of humanity is not a restriction, as in some external limitation, to the nation as a moral person, but its fulfillment is in the nation as a moral person. It is thus that there is in the nation a constant exclusion of a selfish egoism instead of a construction of society out of it. It is thus also — as becomes more apparent in the course of the modern world — that it is not in the power of men to hold the nation in their own exclusive possession, nor to have their own way in it, nor to warp it after their own arbitrary schemes and designs, nor to identify it with their own selfish and private ends. It is thus also that it cannot be retained in the exclusive claim of a family or a race. In its work for humanity, and its fulfillment in its divine origin and relations, the nation has been formed in the modern world. The Turks appear as a power in identity with a race, but there is apparent the absence of a national being, and there is wanting the organization of law and freedom and rights.

There is, in a certain school, a tendency to refer the whole course and development of civilization to races, and to regard separate races in their racial character, as the integral powers in history. In this assumption the history of the world is apprehended as consequent not from the special and physical properties of the soil, the climate, and the like, but from the properties of races. The development of history is presumed in the institution of the power and supremacy of a race. The most complete construction of history is traced through the suggestion of names in ancient genealogical records, and the most elaborate and far-reaching theories are literally built upon no other foundation than the scattered bricks of the ruins of the tower of Babel, in whose hieroglyphics modern philologists decipher the whole course of history, and find the key that opens all its changes. The only exodus of nations which it allows, is in the judgment on the dispersion of the builders, and the only genesis is in the confusion of their language. The same tendency appears in the shaping of history, after theories of Aryan spirit and Aryan life. There may be in the physical distinction of races the elements of diversitude, and of an ampler and more opulent culture and character, and the physical laws and properties of races are to be studied and not to be disregarded; but to assert the identity of the nation with a race is to assume for it a physical foundation, and involves the denial of its moral unity and moral order. If the utmost that language and architecture and art and every mode of culture may indicate, be allowed to racial characteristics, the conclusion yet remains, which has the universality of a law, that there may be the widest possible contrast in respect to civilization in the same race, alike in the same age, or in mainly the same condition of soil and climate in succeeding ages, and that this contrast will be in exact proportion to the development of the life of the nation. It also conversely remains, that in the destruction of the nation there will appear anarchy, violence, slavery, and the want of a continuity of purpose, that is the extinction of civilization, whatever be the racial capacities and characteristics of men. The conception also of a power whose strength is in a race, and whose distinction is in the separation of a race, does not represent the hope which is moving in history, and is in direct antagonism to the historical course of the modern world. The dream of a vast federation of the Anglo-Saxon race, which recent English publicists have told, in which certain nations were to act and to subsist, as the defense of the deposit of modern civilization, is an illusion which could only arise with the decay of national spirit in England. The project of a federation of the Latin race which the Emperor of the French may at one time have indulged, which was to embrace two continents, and to hold in security the same deposit, met with immediate disaster, and its weakness was apparent as it came in conflict with the nations. The attempt to organize as a political power the Slavonic races, becomes a source of the utmost peril, and not of progress in civilization; and there is nothing in the cry of Panslavism which will move the spirits of men and inspire the courage of armies, as do the words which express the moral being of the nation, — the cry of "Holy Russia!" It is the nation in its organic and moral unity, which acts as a power in history, and not a race in its special and separate physical character. The fact in correspondence with this has always been, that the nation has been rent and broken in its strength and swept from the foundation on which it alone can subsist, when it has assumed to identify itself exclusively with a race, or to build upon the distinction of races. It has no longer a moral foundation, nor a universal end when it asserts as its ground the rights of a race, and not the rights of man; and the government which no longer recognizes justice as necessary, nor subsists in the sovereignty and freedom of the people in a moral organism, but is in identity with a race, is the sign of an expiring civilization.[1]

The nation is the power on which is laid the work of history. The power has not been with the more vast populations, nor extensive territories, nor long dynasties, but in the nation. The empires lie apart from the line of the historical development of humanity. It is not in them that its purpose is discerned, nor in their years

[1] "The thought — that every one, even the least, his welfare, his rights, his dignity, is the concern of the state — that every one in his own personality is to be regarded, and protected, and honored, and esteemed, without respect to ancestry, or rank, or race, or gifts, if only he bear the human face and form; this is the characteristic principle of the age, and its true distinction. This principle is alien to the earlier ages, and even to the age of the Reformation. It is first in the modern age, that humanity in its full conception has become an energizing principle of right and duty, determining the whole order of society." — Stahl, *Philosophie des Rechts*, vol. ii. sec. 1, p. 345.

"The inner life of man is manifested in the evolution of society; the love of the family passes into the love of the state, and the love of the state rises into the all-embracing love of humanity." — Comte, *Politique Positive*, ii. 14.

Bluntschli, writing simply as the historian of political movements, says of "nationality and humanity as the two conceptions at once limit and fill each other. In the earlier ages a national spirit has had an apparent influence in politics and the formation of the state; but in none has it wrought with the conscious energy of this age. Clearly discerned as the guiding-star of coming political life appears the highest conception of humanity." — *Geschichte des Allegem. Statsrechts und der Politik*, p. 659.

that its continuous design is traced, nor in their conquests has there appeared the progress of mankind. There has not been in them the awakening of the spiritual energies of men. The discovery of all that remains of them, the colossal fragments of the architecture which they raised, indicate as their characteristic the representation of animal existence, and the worship of animal forms. Their spiritual powers were sunk in an animal condition, with them there was no Odyssey of the adventure of a moral life, and no Iliad of march and battle to maintain the relations of a moral order. Their names, in the monotony of their existence, often owe their preservation to a passing allusion in the literature of some nation with whom in some moment they were brought in contact, or the bare record of the dates in their cycles is deciphered in the fading lines on the broken and scattered stones of their buildings. Thus in the ancient ages it was not in the vast empires of the east, as Nineveh and Babylon and Assyria, that there was the work of history, nor that the development of the spirit appears, but it was almost alone in three nations,—in Judæa and Greece and Rome. Their advance was the progress of civilization. In them was kept the prophecy of humanity in history, their victory was its moral conquest, and its imperishable renown. In the modern ages the course of history is in the peoples in whom is the realization of the national being. It is thus in France and in England. With the unfolding of the ages this becomes more manifest. The movements of this age apart from it are incomprehensible, its battles have no significance, and its crises no decision. Thus Italy, from weakness and division in her separate provinces and rival cities, with the call of a united Italy, is struggling toward a national unity. Germany, from its narrow communities and sovereignties, each with its pedantic pretensions to legitimacy, and the trivial forms of its courts, with their orders of scholars and soldiers, is rising to the unity of the German nation; and on the United States was laid the call to that battle, in which victory through long sacrifice is the manifestation of the unity and being of the nation in the realization of the freedom of humanity. These events are indeed the witness borne through the sacrifice of nations, to the resurrection of the spiritual powers of man, and the deliverance of the redemptive life.[1] They are the dawning of the new ages of humanity. They who live in them stand in an Apocalypse.

It is because the nation is formed as a power in history that in its decay it passes from history. Its decay is the dissolution of the moral order and the severance of the moral relations, in which the individual exists. The outward circumstance may remain the same. There is the same race or races, the same people who dwell among the memorials of the toil and sacrifice of their fathers, and the same land which was their ancient inheritance. The mountains and field and sky are still the same, but in the con trast with that which has been, they who dwell among them in the course of physical nature that changes not, are as those that "'gin to be a'weary o' the sun." The presence has vanished in whose light all things were transfigured. There is no more the glory they have known. They hold no more in the strength of a conscious purpose, the hope of humanity. This dissolution of the moral being and unity of the nation, can follow only in the most awful crime and corruption of a people, and its consequence is in the most far-reaching disaster. There is in it a consuming of power, and withering of energy, which only evil can effect. It is only in the denial of the calling, which has been borne toward its fulfillment by the fathers, and in the consequent degradation of humanity, that the

[1] "Whoever does not assume unconditionally the might of goodness in the world, and its ultimate victory; whoever starts from moral unbelief, not only cannot lead in human affairs, but must follow with reluctant steps. We live indeed in the kingdoms of the redemption, and no more in the kingdoms of this world." — Rothe, *Theologische Ethik*, vol. iii. sec. 2, p. 901.

nation can perish. There is in it the judgment of history. The convulsions of the physical world have no correspondence for it; in the words of the Roman statesman, it is as if "the whole world were to perish, and to tumble in ruins."[1] The voice of no prophet, however tremulous with the burden of its sorrow, can express the woe to come. It is the severance from the generations which have been, and from the generations which are to be; it is "a day of woe unto them that are with child, and there shall be great distress in the land, and wrath upon this people, and they shall fall by the edge of the sword, and shall be led away captive into all nations." The doom falls upon the whole land, and there is none exempt. Judæa, when the life of the nation was dying, and its calling was forgotten, and its unity broken in the assumption of sects and the pretension of parties, and it was to reject in its royal line One who came to it as the eternal King and Priest and Prophet of humanity, who wept over its Capital at the vision of its approaching desolation, is no longer a power in history, and the people pass from the gates of its immortal city, not yet returning again. It is scattered over the world, and among nations is as no nation. The days come to them as to the stranger, and their path through distant lands is marked by persecution. There was in Greece, in the conflict with the multitudes of the East and their empires, a conscious moral spirit, which has placed the scene of them among the immortal battle-fields of the world; but when there succeeded the contention of her separate communities, in which the life of the nation perished, the ideal fades from her art, while there yet remains the versatile and crafty skill, and the supple cunning of the hand. The character of the people becomes frivolous, and their purpose vain and empty; they become traders and tricksters in words, the sophists and

[1] "Simile est quodam modo, ac si omnis hic mundus intereat et concidat." — Cicero, *De Republica*, iii. 23.

rhetoricians who wander from city to city, and are led away as slaves by other peoples to be made their tutors; their land is converted into a province of a foreign empire, and for centuries they are subject to the dominion of the Turks.[1] The decadence of the national life of Rome was the beginning of the end of its history. The figures of noble dignity and severity pass away with her triumphal processions. The elements of the moral being of the nation, the unity of organization, the devotion to public ends, the strength of discipline, the reverence for law, the sacredness of the family, all perish. The people are overcome by invaders whom once two or three legions could hold in easy subjection; and the land is open to foreign peoples, and shakes with the tread of foreign armies. The fall of the nation in its influence upon the individual is reflected through centuries, and the crimes which occasioned it leave their impress upon him. As its maintenance in its unity and moral being is the highest blessing, and for those who are to be, so also in its destruction the disaster sweeps on and embraces them.

While the destruction of the nation can come only in the issue of the most awful crime, and is manifest in the judgment of history, it has not in history its final close. The life whose unity was revealed in sacrifice, does not wholly perish. There may intervene centuries of humiliation and defeat, and the people be scattered or carried into distant captivities, but its spirit still lives. Though it is overborne by the migrations of races and the vicissi-

[1] Niebuhr says of Greece: "All its ancient institutions, nay its faith itself, had vanished, and there was nothing to compensate for the loss. The Greeks possessed no less intelligence, perhaps even more than before; there was more knowledge, insight, etc. Whatever can be made they did make; but what cannot be made by every one who has diligence and ambition to exert his powers, such as epic and lyric poetry, these were lacking. Instead of the venerable tragedies of old, they had comedies. But on the other hand they were further advanced in the arts and the mechanical skill which belongs to practical life. Their speculations were more subtle and logical, but there was no more grand philosophy of nature; they still possessed political cleverness, but we find no political orators." — *Ancient History*, vol. iii. p. 18.

tudes of empires, yet the type of its being is not effaced. The faith of the fathers and the hope of the children does not all fail. The words of its prophets are not all vain. There may come in the life of nations the renewal of its years, and there is manifest in them the power which can "restore the leaves which the locust has eaten." There is the faith that the nation is immortal. There is in nations the witness to the power of a resurrection. In some hour its sleep is broken by the gray of the new dawn, and its sealed springs are touched again. This is no allusive phrase and no vague imagery, drawn from the sphere of the spiritual life of the individual, but it is the reality of history, and its recognition is in the conscious life of nations. There is in this age an increasing testimony to it, and not only in the later, but in the ancient nations. Judæa through centuries of wandering does not lose her national character; and the last words of her prophets spoke of the restoration of Israel. In Greece, so long overborne by a foreign domination, there is yet a sleep that is full of dreams, and the stirrings of a new energy, and the broken signs of a new spirit. The life of Rome in its historic unity, is yet apparent in the purpose of a people, and is being renewed in its ancient seats. In the evidence of history the most utter and isolated individualism, the most exclusive and distant ecclesiasticism, cannot affirm the extinction of the life of nations.[1]

The moral order of the world is the fulfillment of humanity in God. This is the development of history. The

[1] "The key to the political movements in Europe is obviously the resurrection of nationalities." — *Mr. Bancroft's Letter*, 1867.

The evidence of the power of a resurrection in nations has been stated, not apparently by any design nor with any reference to a real presence, as the characteristic of the modern world, that is, the world since the manifestation of the Christ. "All ancient states were short-lived. Once declining they never recovered. Their course was that of a projectile, — a rise, a maximum, a precipitate descent. Modern nations are long lived, and possess recuperative powers wholly unknown to antiquity." — Dr. Lieber, *Amer. Presb. Rev.*, 1868.

realization of the moral is toward a definitely Christian principle. This is necessarily implied in the Christian principle, as the universal and the immutable, that is the moral. As the nation is called to be a power in history, it is in the realization of its being the Christian nation. It is this in its necessary conception. It has not in its option the alternative to determine whether it shall be, but yet shall or shall not be this, but its necessary realization is the Christian nation. And conversely, as history is in its development the realization of a moral order, it is only as the nation acts in and for that order that the nation has its being in history. It is thus that its freedom has been wrought in the power of the redemption, and its renewal in the power of the resurrection. In other words, the only completion of the state is in the Christian state, and it is as a power in history, which is the redemptive life of humanity, that it has its vocation and its destination.[1]

The nations of the ancient ages, Judæa and Greece and Rome, in their historical calling, held in their ongoing toward the coming of the Christ, the fulfillment of the divine purpose. In the new ages, the ages of the Christ and his coming, the nations have existed in the historical Christian development. The formative principle of their life has been derivative from the Life. The nation conversely, has no realization in the new ages beyond the line of the historical Christian development. Whatever may be the preconception of events, or the inference of political theories or speculations, this is the realism of history.

[1] "We know nothing of an antithesis between the moral and the political. The state in which the Christian is to live must be bound by the same divine will that binds him, and it must have the same for its nature which he recognizes as his innermost nature." — Schleiermacher, *Christliche Sitte*, p. 279.

"There is, *in concreto*, no state corresponding to the conception that can be conceived, but the Christian state, that is, the state as determined through the moral principle, which is definitely Christian.

"Christianity is essentially a political principle, and a political power. It is constructive of the state, and bears in itself the power of forming the state and of developing it to its full completeness." — Rothe, *Theologische Ethik*, vol. iii. sec. 2, p. 968.

And there has been no people in whom the life revealed in the Christian development has been implanted, and has become a living energy, but it has acted as a formative political principle, and formative of the nation. There is no fact more significant than that in the same centuries, in the lands in which Mohammedanism has existed, there has been no national life. It has prevailed among vast populations, and races who in every racial characteristic were incomparably beyond the rude races of Northern Europe, and it has had long continued possession of the most varied and fertile territories, but it has created no nation. Its central and representative power stands now on the verge of Christendom, a tottering and discordant empire, sustained by other peoples, and identified with a race and degenerating into a mere horde.[1] The same absence of a spirit formative of a national development appears in Buddhism. This has consisted only with the power of a race or an empire. Thus cultivated Hindus complain of the want of a power of political continuity, a power which the continuation of tradition does not supply. But the absence of a formative political principle and national life is more apparent in Mohammedanism, and more significant from its immediate contact with the historical Christian development.

The ancient nations stood in the prophecy of the coming of the Christ, the manifestation of the divine origin and unity and affinity of humanity. It was in the conditions of a moral life, that is through conflict and sacrifice, that the later nations came into being, whose calling was in the coming of Him of whom the ancient nations held the prophecy. The church in its unity and its power was the realization of a spiritual kingdom in the world. Its end was universal. There was in it the assertion of the divine origin and relations and destination of humanity. It was

[1] See Goldwin Smith, *The Empire*, pp. 223–225.

24

in identity with no family and no race. It was the church of the people. The spiritual was not the abstract, and because it was the spiritual it was not therefore the unreal; but in it there was the revelation of the real, — the foundation which is lying, and other can no man lay. There was the manifestation of a spiritual kingdom on the earth, in the unfolding of the spiritual powers of man. The church was formed, in the realization of a spiritual kingdom in the world, in the new ages. It was the witness to the redemption of the spiritual powers of man, from all that had dominion over them. It was the conflict of the Christ, the true Lord of man, in whom alone is freedom, with principalities and powers of evil. The battle of the church with the empire in the Middle Age was in the endeavor toward the realization of a spiritual kingdom on the earth. It was in its spiritual freedom that the nations were called into being. The germ of their life was hidden in it. In the redemption of the spirit of man there was the development of the life of nations. The realization of freedom was in the individual and in the nation, — the realization of the individual personality, and the moral personality of the nation.

The power which was central in the world, and proceeding from Rome asserted a universal dominion over all men and all nations, proclaiming that Cæsar is king, and that humanity is to recognize no other and higher, was to fall before the power of a spiritual kingdom, in which was the manifestation of the eternal king, whose coming is the deliverance of humanity. The church rose over the ruins of the empire, which had striven to establish a universal dominion, in the witness to the deliverance of the spiritual powers of man in the Christ; in this was the sign of its conquest. But it succeeded to claim the dominion in itself, which it had denied in the empire. It proclaimed no longer the deliverance of man. Then when it assumed in and for itself the life which was revealed in the Christ, when it refused to recognize a spiritual life in men and in nations, it became itself something external. It was the divine order, in the redemptive process of history, that the spiritual should become manifest as the real. The realization of the individual personality, and of the moral personality of the nation, was in the manifest power of the redemption. The denial of the realization of the spiritual life and powers of the individual personality and the moral personality of the nation, apart from the external order of the church, involved a necessary conflict. The power of Rome in its denial confronted the realization of the spiritual life of man. It was the church which assumed to stand in the place of the Christ, and it denied an immediate relation in the individual and the nation in their freedom and their life, through the Christ, to God. It became the contradiction of the spiritual and the catholic, itself the unspiritual and the uncatholic. It asserted in itself a dominion over men, and not their deliverance. The bonds and fetters it forged were so subtle and strong, that it would seem that the mightiest spiritual effort of humanity could not break them, and no power in heaven or earth could rend them.

The conflict in the realization of spiritual freedom, becomes then, the beginning of a new age. The central fact in the Reformation is the realization of personality, its freedom, its duties, its rights, in the individual and the nation. It is the conflict of the individual and the nation in the realization of their being, with the dominion of Rome as the force of principalities and powers had been wrought in that to crush human freedom. The witness to the redemption of the world, the sign of the conquest of the Christ, was not in the church against the world, but it was in the nations of Christendom in their conflict with the church. The spiritual conflict was the conflict of the nations.

This has its repeated illustration in modern history, and appears through the complications of its events and the commingling of its actors, and its record is in pages which are not yet closed. The nations have been involved in a conflict with Rome for their integral unity and being. The struggle has been for their existence, their order, their freedom. There is none as it has sought to realize its freedom, that has been exempt from the secret or open assault of Rome. Its attack has taken on every form, and there is no weapon however cruel, and no device however false, which it has not used, and no ally however evil, which it has not engaged. It has appeared on every field as the foe of the life and liberties of nations. The record is in the earlier as in the later nations, and is crowded with its evidence. In Italy no other fact has wider or more patent illustration. It is there indeed more complex in its phases, since upon her was bestowed the fatal gift which wrung from Dante his sad and bitter protest. The result is summed up in the conclusion of a recent writer, "The papacy has been the eternal, implacable foe of Italian independence and Italian unity. It never would permit a powerful native kingdom to unite Italy."[1] Macchiavelli, who inscribed his "History of Florence" to Clement VII., says, "all the wars which were brought upon Italy by the barbarians," — that is, foreigners, — "were caused mainly by the Popes, and all the barbarians who overrun Italy were invited in by them. This has kept Italy in a state of disunion and weakness." In France the conflict appears in varying forms, through century after century. The life of the nation was maintained by none with a higher purpose, and its powers were guarded by none with a profounder spirit than by the holiest of her kings, Louis IX. The edict, in the name of "Louis, by the Grace of God, King of the French," has been called "the great charter of independence to the Gallican Church;"

[1] Milman's *Latin Christianity*, vol. i. p. 477.

and in its course, it has been said of it that, "seized by the Parliaments, defended, interpreted, extended by the lawyers, it became the barrier against which the encroachments of the ecclesiastical power were destined to break; nor was it swept away until a stronger barrier had arisen in the unlimited power of the French crown." The issue was never more clear than in the long drawn battle of Boniface and Philip the Fair. It has been continued by her Crown and Parliaments and Courts; it has suffered interruption neither in monarchical nor republican epochs; it underlay the prolonged controversy of the canon and the civil lawyers; it was to justify the language of a philosophic historian, — "the Gallican liberties are the standing anti-Pope." In England, the conflict of Rome with the nation, through all her better centuries, has been borne in the front of her battles. It has summoned her Kings and people to the field more often than any other cause. The strife of the Tudor age, which made the mightiest of her kings, Henry VIII., "the only supreme head in earth of the Church of England," and the wars of the fifteenth and sixteenth centuries, whatever the immediate form they took, were the battle of the nations against the universal domination of Rome, and in them the nations were contending for their very being and freedom. The wars of the Low Countries, of Elizabeth, and of William of Orange, which, so frequently renewed, closed for at least one epoch on the field of Blenheim, involved this for their actual issue. The alliance of Rome against the nations was with imperialism. It is with that her power has combined, and she has wielded that to crush nations. It is thus that she found her instrument in Philip II., in Louis XIV., in Napoleon III. As Spain, in her imperial age, sought to fasten the domination of Rome upon the nations, in her swift decline the fetters she strove to rivet upon them were drawn more closely upon her, and France has fortified within and against herself the power she went to Italy to sustain. It is this conflict which has never been absent from the thought of the greater modern statesmen, as William of Orange and Cromwell.[1] In Germany the conflict has been more apparent with the German nation. The work of Luther was the awakening of a national spirit. The power of the Electors was his constant support. The issue is continued in the most recent events. The alliance of Rome with imperialism in Austria has been always in antagonism to the unity of Germany and its freedom. The battle of Sadowa was the triumph of Protestantism, the triumph of the German nation, the Germany of Luther and Hegel. Its immediate result was the widest disaster to Rome.

In every nation where Rome has a vestige of authority, the conflict appears. The irreconcilable hostility of Rome to the being of nations has never had more open avowal than in this century.[2] In Italy it is still the unceasing antagonist to the nation. It does not acknowledge the existence of the nation of Italy, and recruits an army out of

1 "The conservation of that, 'namely', our national being, is first to be viewed with respect to those that seek to undo it, and so make it not to be." "Whatever could serve the glory of God and the interests of his people, they see more eminently in this nation than in all the nations in the world; this is the common ground of the common enmity entertained against the prosperity of our nation, against the very being of it. All the honest interests, all the interests of Protestants in Germany, Denmark, etc., are the same as yours. Therefore the danger is from the common enemy abroad, who is the head of the Papal interest." — Cromwell's *Letters and Speeches*, vol. iii. p. 150.

2 In the Encyclical of December 6, 1864, Pius claims the exemption of the clergy from the authority of secular tribunals, and asserts a divine sanction in "refusing to permit their cases to be subject to the judgment of the latter." The traditions of ecclesiastical supremacy are not forgotten for one moment, and it is asserted that "rulers are subject to the jurisdiction of the church," and even that "in the state, internal municipal laws are involved in the same subjection." The necessary antagonism to modern civilization is indicated, and the syllabus in its close deems it a fatal error, that "Romanus Pontifex potest ac debet cum progressu, cum liberalismo, et cum recenti civilitate sese reconciliare, et componere." — Pii, P. P. IX., *Syllab.*, December 6, 1864.

Milman, in his conclusion on the condition of the Latin Church, says: "The clergy in general, there were noble exceptions, were first the subjects of the Pope, then the subjects of the temporal sovereign." — *History of Latin Christianity*, vol. viii. p. 158.

all lands, and its drum beats the roll-call of a motley crowd, and once more, in alliance with imperialism and with foreign soldiers, its flag is borne before them to battle with the people of Italy. In America, with some eminent individual exceptions, the influence of Rome was with confederatism, and while it is not clear whether the act was in her spiritual or temporal capacity, nor what guise was worn, Rome was the only power to recognize the confederacy. In Mexico and the South American Republics, it is the unceasing foe of their unity and freedom. In every sphere of diplomacy its emissaries are engaged, and its policy seeks supremacy. It is the so-called clerical party in these unhappy and disordered states, that is always in league with secession; there is no power that works so secretly through municipalities and provinces, and in combinations with factions and parties, to subvert the whole to its own ends. It is the foe in all to their progress and education and order and freedom.

This antagonism of Roman ecclesiasticism to the nation is involved in its necessary postulate. The domination it has assumed, its authority, its scope, cannot consist with the realization of moral freedom. The Reformation was in the realization of freedom. There was in Protestant history the development of a positive principle. It was not a merely negative movement, only the protest against certain errors and abuses, but there was the manifestation of moral freedom, — the positive realization of personality in the individual and the nation,[1] — the life, the being of each as existent in its origin in God, and in its unity and continuity derivative only from God. The great postulate of Protestantism is the assertion of the immediate relation of the human spirit to the Christ, and between the human soul and Him, there can stand neither priest nor book. It

1 "The principle of moral individualism stamps the movement with its characteristic impress.

"It was the reality of moral freedom in Christ, that more than all else gave triumph to the Reformation." — Tulloch, *Leaders of the Reformation*, p. 135.

is the assertion in the life of humanity in history, not of a formal but a real theocracy, — the divine order of the world in the Christendom of nations.

This antagonism is necessary also in the assumption of Roman ecclesiasticism, since it denies to the individual and to the nation a real and integral moral being, — the realization of a divine vocation in the moral order of the world — which is not formulated through it. The individual and the nation apart from the church, are regarded as in identity with the world, — only the kingdoms of this world, — and the church will concede to them, therefore, no spiritual life or powers, no real freedom, no fulfillment of a divine vocation, in conscious obedience to a divine will. It assumes the working of the divine energy, and the fulfillment of the divine purpose in itself alone, and in the individual and the nation only as formulated through it, and the moral — that is in its definite Christian realization, the moral order of history, apart from itself is unreal, only the legal, the unspiritual condition of man. It assumes that in and through itself alone the redemptive life is formed, and in it alone is manifest the power of the redemption and the power of the resurrection. It alone is built upon "the foundation which is lying;" and itself external, all which is external to it, is a baseless structure. It alone stands in the living and eternal will, and that only has a real and a moral continuity which is formed in it. It will not concede that in the individual and the nation as separate from itself, there is wrought the work of righteousness on the earth. Therefore when Protestantism asserts that the nation has the condition of its being in righteousness, and in righteousness alone its strength and exaltation, and that its unity and continuity is only in the will of One, who will establish righteousness on the earth, and its freedom in the obedience to that will, and its being and responsibilities in an immediate relation to that, — these truths Roman ecclesiasticism, in its primary assumption, denies and discards.

The inevitable character of this antagonism in Roman ecclesiasticism appears also in the fact that it will not concede a real and immediate relation in the individual or the nation to God, — to God as manifest in the Christ, — nor that their life and personality are immediately and only derivative from Him. The life of the individual, the moral life as definitely Christian, it asserts to be mediated and formulated in it, and that the nation is only the province of physical forces, the combination of material interests, a secular kingdom, in whose course there is only what it calls a phenomenal morality.[1] It will not admit the divine guidance of the people in its history, and holding the light only in itself, it discerns not the presence which goes before the march of the people. It does not allow in the nation a means or agency of actual good, nor that it derives its wisdom and courage and understanding only from God, nor that its obligation is to no other power on earth, but only to Him. It will not admit in it a vocation, whose duty cannot be transferred to another. In its assumption, the nation is not a power in the realization of the divine kingdom in the world, but in its origin and end is in alienation from it, — only a kingdom of this world.

The church, in this conception, comes to regard the being, the unity and the freedom of the nation with indifference, when it is not its avowed antagonist. The nation is regarded at the most as only formal and abstract, and existent in indifference to right and wrong, and the church is not to stoop to what it represents as the secular

1 "The Catholic confession, although sharing the Christian name with the Protestant, does not concede to the state an inherent justice and morality — a concession which in the Protestant principle is fundamental. This severance of the political morality, which is necessary to the being of the state from its natural connection, is characteristic of that religion, since it does not recognize justice and righteousness as something integral and substantial. But thus isolated and torn away from their inner centre, the sanctuary of conscience which is their last refuge, and the still retreat where religion has its abode, the principles and institutions of political legislation are destitute of a real unity in the same measure in which they are compelled to remain abstract and undefined." — Hegel, *Philosophie der Geschichte*, p. 64.

aims in the life of humanity. In its view, the unity and continuity of the nation in which the fathers are turned to the children and the children to the fathers, the authority of government and the reverence for law, and the punishment of crime on the earth, and the triumph over oppression, over principalities and powers which have held dominion over men, involve no immediate and divine obligation. The aim of the statesman is no longer the conformance of legislation to a divine law of righteousness, and the end of the state is no longer the fulfillment of an order which he did not create, but whose principle he is to obey. The faith of the people, the fulfillment of its work through all the trials of its years, the very devotion and sacrifice of its children, the wisdom and courage of its leaders, have no real moral significance, but are only the continuance of a sacrilegious course, the circumstance of a profane history.[1]

[1] This is also the attitude of many of the sects, and the conclusion of their logic, when it does not avoid its premise. A recent writer says: "The secular career of man is a violation of sacred obligations and of a divinely established order. In reference to the divine idea and intent, it is a sacrilege — well denominated profane — the history of the world as the opposite and antagonist of the church, only the ordinary workings of the human mind, and such products as are confessedly in its competence to originate, etc." Then the construction of the Nicene formula is described in its parallel, in the sæculum necessary to it, "As long a time as was required for pagan Rome to conquer and subjugate the Italian tribes, and to lay the foundations of a nationality that was to last a millennium in its own particular form; as long a time as was required for the thorough mixing and fusion of British, Saxon, and Norman elements into that modern national character which in the Englishman and Anglo-American is perhaps destined to mould and rule the future, more than even Rome has the past." Then the parallel of the Nicene formula is continued. "The one is metaphysical, the other is political and relates to the rise and formation of merely secular sovereignties, exceedingly impressive to the natural mind and dazzling to the carnal eye; these metaphysical victories secured a correct faith, etc." — Shedd's *History of Christian Doctrine*, vol. i. p. 18, p. 374. This is the conception, in which, in the consistent and necessary sequence of its premise, national life is apprehended.

It is evident that the character of the appeal to the eye is consequent upon the content of the object; but there has never been in the life of nations an immediate appeal to the carnal eye to compare with that made in the centuries included in this parallel, by the visible church.

There is the assumption in this description also of the apprehension of truth

There is a so-called catholic church, beyond the pale of Rome, which assumes the same. If a nation is struggling for its unity and being against forces of division and dissolution, it is a subject of no moral concernment. The life of the nation and the sacred obligations of its citizenship, which so inspire common men that they will die for them, and pass those gates of holy and willing sacrifice with the sacrament of the nation upon their lips, it regards only with moral indifference. If a people in a great crisis are redeemed from slavery, it sees not the glory of their deliverance. It heeds not the roll of the waves parted by the right hand of Majesty on high, but asks only that it still may catch the murmur of waters, breaking on the shores of ancient wrong. It repeats its protest against sedition, conspiracy, and rebellion, but to their reality its conscience is dead. It asks in the litany of human hopes and sorrows, for the unity of all nations, but for those who hold the unity of the nation as a divine

only as a proposition. It is represented in its scientific precision as an abstract formula, and the contrast is with the real conflict of history. The analogy in the centuries of the construction of this formula may have another presentation. This metaphysical speculation never had more exclusive control of the thoughts of men, nor more regard for its scientific precision than in the city of Constantine, under Heraclius, in the beginning of the seventh century. It passed on to the controversy as to the two wills; but the impressiveness of its themes did not affect the lives of men. It was the sign of the division of the schools, it separated society in the avenues of fashion, it started the mob and tumult in the streets, it was the signal of parties in miserable circus-fights; but it awakened no moral energy. It was apprehended only as a dogma — an abstraction — and with no reference to the actual condition of men. It was a strife only measured by the scientific accuracy of terms, in which a dogma was held. It was then that their foundations on which they built — the foundations of a system, but not of a living Person whose Will had been revealed to men — were shaken by the coming of a conqueror, as a voice from the desert. It has been said by an historical writer, "his words and deeds carried out the moral of the previous history. Mohammed proclaimed an actual God, to men who were disputing concerning his nature and attributes. Mohammed affirmed that there was an actual will, before which the will of man must bow down. It was a tremendous proclamation. Philosophy shrinks and shrivels before it. All ethical speculations are concluded by the one maxim, — that God's commands are to be obeyed; all metaphysical speculations are silenced by the shout of a host, "He is, and we are sent to establish his authority over the earth."

gift, it is silent and offers only the drowsy opiates of this world that drug the spirits of men. Its hierarchy will not soil itself with these common aims, although St. Peter could ask with longing for the time of the restoration of Israel, and St. John could trace in the historical order of the nation, the symbols of eternal things, and St. Paul could dwell upon its historical events as the sacraments of the divine presence, and the voices of Prophets have been lifted in exultation at the nation's deliverance, or burdened with its sorrow since the world began. It wearies of the symbols of the prophetic office when the reality is gone. It concerns itself with a ritual and processions, but they are no longer the ritual, nor the processions of a people. It finds no longer a significance in the name of Protestant, since it has no place in the great process of Protestant history.

Whether the United States will be involved in an immediate conflict with Rome, lies in her future. While there are noble, but still few exceptions, her unity and education and freedom will meet in Roman catholicism, it may be a guarded and often concealed, but an unceasing antagonist. Those who see in the course of the Christian centuries only the development of a dogma, and regard Protestantism as an intellectual conflict, can find no ground of apprehension. M. Guizot turns from speculations on the essence of Christianity, to advocate a confederacy in Italy, and the maintenance of the temporal power of the Popes; but to those for whom the conflict of so many centuries has a deeper reality, the ecclesiasticism of Rome bears another character. Milton was the statesman of a greater age, and was a wider scholar, and of fairer sympathies, but for him it was "the old red dragon." It was to be met by the nation in a struggle of life and death. And the nation will not maintain its unity or its being if it meet it only as a material force. The church will not give place to an atheistic state, nor to a material civilization. The end of history is not attained, and the destination of humanity is not realized in that.

The nation can meet the forces with which it has to contend only as it realizes its own moral being, and recognizes its origin and end in God. If it be held in a merely material conception, it can bring no strength to the real battle of history, where moral forces contend. If it be regarded as only formal, it will be broken by that held in a subtler bond. The nation is called to a conflict in every age, where the result does not depend upon the strength of its chariots, nor the swiftness of its horses. It is to contend with weapons wrought not alone in earthly forges — it is to go forth clothed with celestial armor, and of celestial temper. It is to fulfill a divine calling. It is to keep a holy purpose. It is to enter the battle for righteousness and freedom. It is to contend through suffering and sacrifice, with faith in the redemption of humanity, for the rights of humanity, — rights given to it by Him whose image it bears.

NOTE. — The morality of a people, and so also its politics, will always correspond to its actual theology, and will be but the sequence of that. The assertion that men are saved, not by faith in a divine person, but by faith in a dogma or a system of dogmas, induces a formalism, which is reflected in politics, in the notion that a political form or dogma will save the nation. Thus we are told as before by the theological doctors, now by the political doctrinaires, not that the people are saved by faith in God and his righteousness, but that the only safety is in the constitution, inclusive of a certain scientific formula, defining the correct relation of the states.

The discussion as to the formal recognition of God in the written or enacted constitution has scarcely a better ground. In the historical or providential — the real and unwritten constitution, — it is the very condition of the being of the nation. But the written or enacted constitution defines only the formal organization, and relations of the powers of the state, and then also it is an instrument of law, and subject to amendment, etc., and the divine recognition might be required with the same propriety in every legislative enactment.

CHAPTER XX.

THE NATION THE BEGINNING AND GOAL OF HISTORY.

THE aim of political science is the presentation of the nation, as it is in its necessary conception. Its object is to define it in that unity and law which alone is the condition of science. This necessitates an inner and critical justification of its representation.

The nation is organic, and has therefore the unity of an organism, and in its continuity persists in and through the generations of men; it is a moral organism, it is formed of persons in the relations in which there is the realization of personality, it is not limited to the necessary sequence of a physical development, but transcends a merely physical condition, and in it there is the realization of freedom and the manifestation of rights; it consists in the moral order of the world, and its vocation is in the fulfillment of the divine purpose in humanity in history.

The nation as it exists in its necessary conception, is the Christian nation.

The Book which illustrates from the beginning of history the divine purpose, and the divine order in the world, has been and is the book of the life of nations. It is not a book which belongs to the childhood of the race and outgrown is to be left with stories and pictures to children; it is not a book of abstractions, to be shaped in the systems of schools; it does not hold the life of nations in indifference, as do the hierarchs of ancient and modern religions, to find their sanctity in their external isolation. It contains in the order of history from its beginning to its close, the revelation of the origin and unity of the nation, and the law of its being. It is the record of the revelation through history of the divine economy. It is not to construe the polity of one age, but of the ages. There is the unfolding of principles which are deeper than a formal order and a formal organization. They are not concluded in the transient and local. In the succession of events they do not become isolated, and in the changes of time they do not become obsolete. They are the revelation of an authority which no tyrant can suspend, and no anarchy subvert.[1]

This has its clearest assertion from those who have been called to their work in the foundations of nations; it has been, in the crises of nations, their strength and their stay, and its words have wrought with the power of a divine inspiration in the spirit of the people. There is in the liter-

[1] There is much that is suggestive in the comparison of those great contemporaries — Spinoza and Hobbes; and it has been often traced, and in many ways; but it is in no respect more significant than in the consideration which they give in their political writings to the Hebrew Scriptures. In their political inquiry, neither of them can avoid the fact of the wide and continuous influence of the Hebrew Scriptures upon politics, and each sets honestly to work to account for it, and to ascertain some principle of reconciliation between them and their own theories. There is reflected in each the thought of schools and sects in this age, who hold their names in distrust.

The result of their attempt to reconcile their political conceptions with the Hebrew Scriptures, is stated by a recent historian of philosophy: "All the ingenuity and courageous dogmatism of Hobbes, could not hinder him from appearing awkward and sophistical when he tried to reconcile his theory of society and of government, with that which represents God as constituting the family; God as forming the people whom He had delivered from bondage into a nation; God as himself governing it, whatever subordinate instruments — priests, kings, prophets — He employs; God as preparing them for the manifestation of a divine kingdom, wherein men should be governed by a Father, be united to each other in a Mediator, by an in-dwelling Spirit.

"Spinoza is still more embarrassed, precisely because he has more sense of a divine economy, and is less able to divest himself of early associations. The strange dream of a people, persuaded by their law-giver to regard God as their King, and to bind themselves under a covenant to Him, has to be maintained under all difficulties that he may show how peculiar the Hebrew state was, how little it can be a model for other states, and yet what lessons it may teach them respecting the dangers of monarchical, still more of priestly or prophetical usurpation. Having once got rid of the primary idea of the Jewish state, he could have no difficulty whatever in disjoining its history from the history of all other nations." — Maurice, *History of Modern Philosophy*, p. 410.

ature of the world no other expression of the ground and being of the nation, as it is found here in the beginning of history; — no other expression of the glory and honor of the nation as it is unfolded here in the goal of history. Its words have been kept, —

> "As better teaching,
> The solid rules of civil government,
> In their majestic, unaffected style,
> Than all the oratory of Greece and Rome;
> In them is plainest taught and easiest learnt,
> What makes a nation happy and keeps it so,
> What ruins kingdoms and lays cities flat."

There has been no more constant recognition of its political principle than is repeated in the writings of the fathers and founders of the republic. In their confession of the divine presence and the divine guidance, there is an accordance as of the psalms of a nation. The recognition of the origin and continuity of the nation in God, is repeated in the inaugurals of the earlier Presidents. It is not the utterance of empty phrases in some indifferent moment, it is spoken in the hour of the assumption of the most sacred trust, the imposition of the most sacred obligation. The words of its great citizen Franklin, which reach to the foundations of political thought, in the most critical hour, in the Convention of the Representatives of the people for the formation of the constitution, were, "We have been answered in the sacred writings, that 'except the Lord build the house, they labor in vain that build it.' I firmly believe this; and I also firmly believe this, that without his concurring aid, we shall succeed in this political building no better than the builders of Babel. We shall be divided by our little partial local interests; our projects will be confounded; and we ourselves shall become a reproach and a by-word down to future ages."[1] President Washington said in his first inaugural, "No people can be bound to adore the hand which conducts the affairs

[1] The Convention, June 28, 1787.

of men more than the people of the United States."[1] There is no language deeper in its analogy than that of President Jefferson at the close of his inaugural, "I shall need, too, the favor of that Being, in whose hands we all are, who led our fathers as Israel of old from their native land, and planted them in a country flowing with all the comforts and the necessaries of life; who has covered our infancy with his providence, and our riper years with his wisdom and power, and to whose goodness I ask you to join in supplications with me."[2] The last inaugural of President Lincoln was the unbroken expression of the spirit of these Scriptures, and its whole thought was gathered up in their words, in the recognition of one who will establish righteousness on the earth, "whose judgments are righteous and just."[3] And if there be in the beginning of nations a prescience, the words on the lips of the Pilgrims were not of a state formed in the poor figment of the social contract, nor a condition in which there was merely a negative freedom where conscience was released from all obligation, but they were of a life in which these principles become a living power.[4]

There is, however, a preconception in two opposite forms, each of which, while recognizing in these Scriptures the representation of the nation, limits it in its principle and its end.

1 President Washington's *Inaugural*, April 30, 1789.

2 President Jefferson's *Inaugural*, March 4, 1805.

3 President Lincoln's *Inaugural*, March 4, 1864.

4 See *Lectures* by members of the Massachusetts Historical Society, 1869. *The Aims and Purposes of the Founders of the Massachusetts Colony*, by Rev George E. Ellis, pp. 50, 55, 63. This statement of the object of the founders of Massachusetts has a singular historical value. It is the true Puritan tradition, and beyond the empty theories of freedom and law and the state, which a later age sought to assume as historical in its stead. The law of suffrage, however defective its form, had a true and consistent principle. The expression of Winthrop was, "The civil state must be raised out of the churches." This also could not consist with a negative or formal conception of freedom, and Winthrop always condemns such a conception.

It is said, in the one form, that Judæa was a theocracy, and then the inference is drawn that, by this fact, it is isolated from other nations, and for them has no immediate significance. The word theocracy, in this connection, is traced from Josephus, a Jew of an imperial age, and if it represents the isolation of one nation from another in the divine government of the world, or the exclusion of any nation from the universal law manifested in that government, then it is the assumption against which the prophets constantly contended.

And the principles in which Judæa is formed, are represented as the universal and immutable laws which are the condition of the life of a nation. If it had not a divine origin and unity, if there had not been in it the presence of an invisible King, it would then have been the exception, and its course the singular circumstance, the abnormal condition in history.

It is said, however, that the divine vocation of the people, and the foundation of the nation in a righteous Will which was manifest in Judæa, is limited to the past, to the prophetical ages, but with the coming of the Christ, in whom, those ages are fulfilled, it ceases to be real. There is no more a divine presence and guidance of the people, nor the foundation of its unity in a righteous Will, nor the condition of the being of the nation in righteousness. Then in the later manifestation the divine power is further removed. Judæa was a nation called and chosen in history, but in the fuller years there are none. The end is changed from the beginning, that history is to be read as the letters in the Hebrew books. But the Christ is represented in his coming as the only King, and as nearer to humanity than in the earlier ages, and as revealing in his own life the foundation of its eternal relationships. The Christ is called the only King, the Deliverer, in obedience to whom the freedom of the individual and the nation consists. And as there has been in nations the recognition of the Christ as the King, there has been the formation of a national life, and the unity in which alone the divisions of races are overcome; and as the nations have rejected the Christ as the King, no more a power in his Kingdom, they have passed from history.

It is because Judæa was a real theocracy that it is not detached from the government and history of the world, and its record is of worth for every nation, and the presence of which it is the witness is not more distant but nearer than of old, — the Christ is the King from whose authority no nation is excluded. But it is allowed that, in a certain conception, the Christ is the King, and then the conception is assumed to be one to which the nation may give no further heed. It is held as an abstraction, and withdrawn from the actual lives of men and nations. It is referred to the province of the dogmatist and the ecclesiast, and is presumed no longer to concern the man of affairs; the statesman may recognize it only as in some rhetorical phrase, he strengthens his appeal in conformance to popular impressions not yet worn out; the journalist is to dismiss it as belonging to the dream of the mystic, but having no relation to events as the days go by; the economist, apprehending the nation only as the commonwealth, may insist upon a sustained indifference to it, as alone consistent in politics, until there comes some crisis, when the maxims of economy are unheeded, and the craft of parties is confounded, and the systems of theorists and the devices of legists are burned as stubble in the flames that try all things.

The nation is constituted not in a formal but a real theocracy, and there is nothing more to be considered in certain phases of modern thought than the negation of the real theocratic idea in connection with the avowal of its abstract postulate and abstract conclusion. It eliminates the whole content of the Gospels in their constant representation of the Christ as the King, while deferring to its abstract conception.

If further it be assumed that Judæa, in the recognition and presence of the divine King, becomes the anomaly in history, this is controverted by the fact that it is a nation.[1] This is its historical condition, whatever may be the drift of historical abstractions. The laws of the life of nations are illustrated in it, but it is not exempt from them. There is no presentation of the formulas of political science, in the construction of a system, but there is the being of the nation in history. There is no formal organization defined in necessary correspondence to the nation, but it exists in its identity under the lawgiver, the judges, the kings; and the peril, which is always near, is that the people will lose the consciousness of the unity and continuity of the nation in its invisible king, and apprehend it only as a formal and external organization.

In the opposite form to this, — in which the representation of Judæa as a theocracy has been made the premise of its detachment in history, — its representation as a nation is made the premise of the same conclusion.

It is admitted that Judæa was a nation, but there is the conception of the nation as only in identity with an exclusive form or principle, and the denial of its universality. The nation is regarded as formed only in a separative

1 "The true spiritual life of the world commenced in the chosen people. He who denies this would seem to deny not a theory of inspiration, but a great and manifest fact of history. But the spiritual life commenced under an earthly mould of national life, similar in all respects, political, social, and literary, to those of other races. The Jewish nation, in short, was a nation and not a miracle. Had it been a miracle, it might have shown forth the power of God, like the stars in Heaven, but it would have been nothing to the rest of mankind, nor could its spiritual life have helped to awaken theirs." — Goldwin Smith, *The Bible on Slavery*, etc., p. 5.

Spinoza represents the position of Judæa as isolated in history. The second inquiry in the introduction to the *Tractatus Theologico Politicus* is, "Why the Hebrews were called and chosen of God?" to which the answer is, "When I saw that this meant nothing more than that God gave them a certain spot of the earth, where they might dwell securely and commodiously, I learned that the laws revealed to Moses by God, were nothing but the laws of the special Hebrew empire, and therefore that none except the Hebrews were bound to receive them; nay, that even they were not bound by them, except so long as their empire in Palestine lasted."

principle. It is the local and transient, and is a subject of concernment to a certain people, and therefore of no further concernment. It is only the special circumstance of history, and is comprehended in the special characteristics of a people.

But it is, as containing the revelation of the being of the nation—it is as national, that the Hebrew Scriptures are of worth to every nation. If they represented the being of the nation with indifference, or as simply a formal organization, then they would have no immediate worth for this or for any nation. It is because they reveal the foundation of the unity and continuity of the first nation in history, that they may become also the book of the last.

Mr. Lowell speaks of the mind of Cromwell in certain higher moments, as "working free from Judaic trammels." But in the age to which Cromwell was called, in the battle with unrighteousness in the land and with the allied imperialism and ecclesiasticism of which Spain was the front, it was not trammels which were forged for him in the Old Testament which he knew so well, and had studied as none of England's kings before or since. Would a knowledge of what is described as Aryan civilization have been a substitute for the record of that national life, so deep and so intense and linked to the Throne of God, and finding its unity in Him? There have been those whose thought was without "these trammels"—Julian, with a fair and catholic culture, whose aim was an intellectual imperialism, into which all nations were to be merged, as their images and divinities were to be gathered in one hall;—Spinoza, whose ideal of the state was, that "it should leave the philosophers free to think;"—Goethe, as the courtier at a little principality, who complained that "in the state, no one was willing to live and enjoy, every one wanted to be ruling;"—would Cromwell, working still in the type of his own individuality, have found in the riddance of "Judaic trammels," with these, elements of freedom? If we study the mind of Cromwell, every element of strength was wrought in the faith in which these words become an inspiration. There was another — his secretary — in the same work, who knew these Hebrew Scriptures not as a boy but as a man knows, but in that type of strength and freedom which is only of more worth if it have traces also of an Hellenic spirit, "the Samson Agonistes," still so perfect an expression of undying faith in the triumph of the nation over all its enemies, — is there the restraint of old trammels, — the defect of Milton's freedom? They may not always have separated that which in the earthly vesture of the nation is local and transient, from its real being, but there have been few holding a conception so clear. It is not as men enter into the consciousness of the spirit of the nation that their march is trammelled and their fetters are forged. It is with the free that we are free. There has been no nation but as the mind enters more deeply into its spirit it is imbued with larger freedom. It was not in the Judaic, nor the Roman, nor the Hellenic life, that there was the forging of bonds for men. Thus there is a value for a people, in the study of the literature and art of Greece and Rome, beyond the study of the style and thought of their several poets and historians. It is the contact with the life of the nation which transcends the life of the individual, and is deeper than any separate work in literature and art. This representation of Judaic or Roman or Hellenic trammels has its source in the assumption of a negative notion of freedom.[1]

[1] The Bible has been removed from the course of study in universities, and then from academies, and has no place, corresponding simply as a history and literature, to the history and literature of Greece and Rome. A well-known missionary in Syria, a recent graduate of Yale College, said to me, that scarcely any scholars left their schools in Syria, but with a more thorough knowledge of the Bible than the larger number of the recent graduates of Yale College. This omission of its study is partly the result of the principle which has referred it exclusively to the sphere of the dogmatist and the ecclesiast. The one regards it primarily as a system of dogmas and a collection of isolated proof-texts detached to sustain

There is the record in these Scriptures of the realization of history of the family and the nation. There is the revelation not of a system, but of the divine order in the world.

The nation has its own place and vocation in history. It is as with the individual; the life of none is the same in its outward form and condition, and yet the life of each has the same origin, and is subject to the same law of moral action. There is thus a work for one nation which is not for another, and there is a field of outward circumstance which is the occasion for specific laws and regulations; there is a conduct of affairs which concerns it alone, and

them; and thus it becomes restricted to the schools in which these systems are taught and to their exposition on Sundays; while the other regards it primarily as the record of an ecclesiastical institution, and open only to the knowledge and understanding of a corporation of priests, and requiring the guidance of ecclesiasts for its explanation, and in connection with a ritualism, to be kept in its special sanctity. It is thus removed from its place in the education of the people, and left to the doctor and the priest. It has no place corresponding to that given it by the great masters of thought, in the greater periods of universities, from William of Occam to Hegel. It might be better to study it with the commentary of Spinoza and Hobbes, than to avoid it altogether. The recent tendency is not simply to give their fair place to the physical sciences in their great development, but to exclude the study also of the literature of Greece and Rome; the positivism of science in the revelation of the physical world, is preferred to the positivism of history in the revelation of the moral world, the dynamic is before the divine. For one who makes the phenomenal process of nature and the mind of man as involved in that process, the only object of study and of thought, these Jewish Scriptures can have little value. And since their dates are not always consistent, and their chronology indicates that it has been hopelessly tampered with, what is their value for those whose census is taken in the year 1870? There is also no effort to convey information as to the authorship of the separate documents, and the situation of the writers, and the various questions of the utmost consequence to the critical art of the grammarian. And to those who maintain in a superficial empiricism the only principle in which the state is formed, they must be but a very disjointed collection of documents, containing the record of the migration and fortunes of a very inferior race, who were separated from other races by a narrow and exclusive prejudice, and who have contributed nothing to the questions which are alone prominent — the so-called freedom of trade and the progress of political enlightenment in the combination of wealth and labor, and who in superstitious and theological cycles, holding through poverty and captivity their faith in a calling in history from an invisible King, and their ultimate triumph, refused through every sacrifice wholly to merge themselves into the empires around them, and thereby failed to obtain the vast wealth which the traditions of these empires indicate, and of which the ruins of their buildings and walls bear the trace.

there is a development in the ages in which it is formed; in each age it has to contend with evils which are peculiar to it, and as it rises out of a condition in which slavery and violence and the worship of animal forms everywhere prevail, it is through its own conscious struggle and endeavor.

There is in the divine order the calling and founding of the family. It is the unfolding of the relations of father and brother and son. There is a careful tracing of their descent in the simple succession of names. There are the lives of those who lived as their fathers, and were married, and had sons and daughters, and dying were gathered to their fathers. Even the sins which mainly are described in the book of the Genesis, are those in which there is a violation of the moral unity and order of the family.

There is then the record of the calling and founding of the nation. It has its foundation in God, it subsists in the I am — the everlasting Will. The revelation of God, in the calling of the people, is as the God of their fathers. The words which the leader, who was to go forth in the beginning of their history, was to say to the people, were those in which was the revelation of the Name in which the nation stood, — "Behold, when I come unto the children of Israel, and shall say unto them The God of your fathers hath sent me unto you, and they shall say to me What is his name? what shall I say unto them? And God said unto Moses, I AM THAT I AM, and he said Thus shalt thou say unto the children of Israel, I AM hath sent me unto you."[1] The calling of the people was from God, the nation is formed in no transient and no external circumstance, but in the Eternal, the I AM. It subsists in no compact of men, but in the everlasting Will.

It was in this name they were to confront the tyranny which was over them, and in it they were to stand

[1] Exodus iii. 13, 14.

against all the tyrannies of the world. God was revealed as the Deliverer. It was the redemption of the people; their freedom was a divine gift. The words of triumph were, "I will rid you out of their bondage, and I will redeem you with a stretched out arm, and with great judgments." The words which are repeated beyond all other memorials are, "Thou shalt remember that thou wast a bondman in Egypt, and the Lord thy God redeemed thee thence." The rest of the nation was in peace and freedom, and the goal toward which time was to bear them, was the sabbatical year, the year of jubilee, in which they were to "proclaim liberty throughout the land, and to all the inhabitants thereof." [1]

The succeeding event which is most impressive in their history, and that came in the most solemn circumstance of nature, was the witness to those elements, which can never be separated in the being of the people in a moral order. There was at Sinai, in the giving of the law and the gathering of the people, says Ewald, a twofold significance: there was the witness to the sacredness of the law and the sacredness of the people, — it was an holy law and "an holy nation."

The commandments presume the existence of the nation, as they proceed to define its institutes in a moral order, as the institutes of labor and rest, of property, of marriage. But the people is to remember in its law the living presence, the divine Deliverer. The preamble to the law, which may never rightly be separated from it, is the declaration of their freedom as a divine gift; their freedom is in identity with law and can never become the license in which man is separated from God.

The land which the people were to possess was given to them from God, and was appointed for them. They were to hold it as an inheritance. Yet they were to learn that its possession alone was not the condition of national

[1] Leviticus xxv. 10.

life, that their national being was not the resultant of physical circumstance. The unity of the nation was in no visible bond, and was determined by no confine of land and sea. Their unity and continuity was in God, in the revelation which He made to them, "I am the God of thy fathers."

There is in no literature so deep an expression of the existence of the nation as an heritage to be transmitted from the fathers to the children, but the fulfillment of the divine righteousness is always made the condition of the permanence of the people in the land.

The education of the people through the centuries of their moral and political advancement, was in the knowledge of the relation in which they stood to the visible and the invisible world. They were learning in their national wars and trials, and through all changes and crises, to look to a Being who was not made in the likeness of things in the heaven above or in the earth beneath, and to know Him as their Law-giver and Deliverer and Judge.

The unity of the nation was not defined in any special or temporal limitation. It was not limited to its existent occupants; it was not shut up to "this bank and shoal of time." The nation was not, as in the false civilizations around it, defined in a merely physical condition. It was not as those whose course was only that of a civil corporation, associated by some external fear, or to obtain an individual and common external security, or to promote external interests in pleasure or possession. That was the character of the material civilizations around them, and if the nation was to lose itself in that, it was the destruction of its life. It could not continue merely as the civil commonwealth; if it had no aim beyond that, its vocation as a nation was gone and it was undone. In all its history it was in contrast to the surrounding civilizations. The condition, against the evil of which it was the witness. began with the purpose "Go to, let us build a city," and the unity it opposed was that determined in the measure of the city walls, as if the origin of society was in fear and distrust, and the end was an external security through the division of men. The nation was formed in the relationships of life, and in the recognition of a relation to an invisible one; it did not exist simply as an accumulation of men and in the construction of an external order. The circumstance of its beginning was not with the "building of a city," but on the wide and open plains, and in the journeying through the sea and the wilderness. It was only after struggle, and through trials and vicissitudes, in which there was the recognition of laws, and the institutions of order, and the common organization of the people, with noble memories, and with far hopes for their children, that they came to build a city. Then the memorials of the people were gathered in it. Yet their unity was not in it, nor dependent upon it. The nation lived although its walls were leveled to the ground, and the stones of its temple were scattered and broken.

The life of the nation was through a course of moral conflict and endeavor. It was not as in the civilization of the Philistine — an animal existence, with faith only in visible things and sunk in the worship of animal forms. It was through unceasing wrestling with evil that its advance lay. It was not formed in moral indifference. The awful gates of the mountains were open before it, and through them its journey led. It was tried in great crises. "The Lord hath taken you and brought you forth out of the iron furnace."

The national progress is one in which laws and institutions are acquired; there is the organization of justice, and the form for its administration. Justice is to be executed. "Judges and officers shalt thou make in all thy gates, which the Lord thy God giveth thee, throughout thy tribes: and they shall judge the people with just judgment. Thou shalt not wrest judgment; thou shalt not respect persons, neither take a gift: for a gift doth blind the eyes of the wise, and pervert the words of the righteous."[1] The maintenance of justice is necessary to their continuance in the land.

The universality of law is affirmed — the requisition of all men to a judgment by the law, and the equality of all men before the law. It is repeated from page to page, and there is warning against its denial, and the peril of its forgetfulness. "One law shall be to him that is home-born, and to the stranger that sojourneth among you."[2] "One ordinance shall be for you of the congregation, and also for the stranger that sojourneth with you, —an ordinance forever in your generations; as ye are, so shall the stranger be before the Lord."[3] "Judge righteously between every man and his brother and the stranger that is with him. Ye shall not respect persons in judgment; ye shall hear the small as well as the great; ye shall not be afraid of the face of man, for the judgment is God's."[4] The words of the greatest of its kings, in his farewell to the people, are, "The rock of Israel spake to me, — he that ruleth over men must be just, ruling in the fear of God."[5] There is a singular beauty, among sentences of lofty severity, in the imagery in which the equity of the Judge is portrayed; his judgment must be clear as the light, "as a morning without clouds," and yet, "as the tender grass, springing out of the earth, by clear shining after rain."

The law is represented not as abstract, but as the manifestation of a righteous will, and therefore it is a power which will not conform to the arbitrary schemes, nor subserve the arbitrary aims, of men. It is the affirmation of a righteous will against the self-willed powers which would rend society. It can be severed by no individual caprice

1 Deuteronomy xvi. 18, 19. 2 Exodus xii. 49. 3 Numbers xv. 15
4 Deuteronomy i. 16, 17. 5 Samuel xxiii. 3, 4.

or individual interest. The ruler is not above the law, but is the minister of the law to maintain it unswervingly, and is "to keep the words of this law, and these statutes to do them, that his heart be not lifted up above his brethren, and that he turn not aside from the commandment to the right hand or to the left." [1]

The people in its organization was separated into communities or tribes; but there was one tribe dispersed through the whole as the witness of its unity. Its existence was the witness that the strength of each stood in its relation to the whole, and the strength of the whole in its relation to an eternal King. It was a relationship. It was only in the denial that the unity of the nation was in the living and eternal Will, that they could be separated from God, and therefore from each other. The unity of the nation was not formal, that it should find in society an external limitation in any organization. It was formed as an organic whole. Aaron was chosen as the helper of Moses.

There is the guidance, the care and love which is revealed to nations often in the darkest hours, and in apparent defeat, through the providential history of the people. There were the memorials of the renewal of the nation's faith when it was assailed by foes without and within. "I did bear you on eagle's wings;" and again, "in the wilderness thou hast seen how the Lord thy God did bear thee, as a man doth bear his son, in all the way that ye went, until ye came unto this place."

The nation is inclusive of the whole people in its divine foundation and its divine end. There is no difference of wealth, or race, or physical condition, that can be made the ground of exclusion from it. There is none in it that can be isolated from the privileges and the duties of the covenant in which it is formed. "Ye stand this day, all of you, before the Lord your God; your captains of your tribes, your elders, and your officers, with all the men of

[1] Deuteronomy xvii. 19, 20.

Israel; your little ones, your wives, and the stranger that is in thy camp; from the hewer of thy wood unto the drawer of thy water; that thou shouldest enter into covenant with the Lord thy God, and into his oath which the Lord thy God maketh to thee this day, for a people to himself, and that he may be unto thee a God, as he hath said unto thee, and as he hath sworn unto thy Fathers,— to Abraham, to Isaac, and to Jacob."[1]

The nation was to maintain a divine calling, which was manifest through all its history. It had a work which was its own and which it could not transfer nor abandon. If it betrayed the purpose to which it was called, it was no longer to have place in the power of history, but its name was to become a name of scorn, a proverb and a by-word among men, and it was to meet with shame and contempt. It was not to be diverted from a moral purpose by a lower object, nor to apprehend its end in the mere accumulation of material wealth, nor in the satisfaction of a physical existence. There was the most solemn warning against the gathering of wealth and possession for its own sake, and against the forgetfulness that it was the gift of God and involved duties and obligations.[1] The moral obligation which was manifest in the calling of the nation, was to be maintained in its immeasurable supremacy, as beyond the acquisition of wealth, and to be guarded that it should not be lost in some selfish end. "The graven images of their gods shall ye burn with fire; ye shall not desire the silver or the gold that is on them."[2]

The nation was formed in the conditions of a moral life, and there were powers to be employed and energies to be unfolded. Its freedom was wrought through a divine deliverance, but as in the nature of freedom, it was not in the mere apathy and passivity of the spirit, it was not

[1] Deuteronomy xxix. 10, 13.

Milton says of Deuteronomy xxviii.: "A chapter which should be read again and again by those who have the direction of political affairs."— *Treatise on Christian Doctrine*, etc., ch. xvii.

[2] Deuteronomy viii. 11, 18.

the invitation to repose. It came with the opening of the waves of the sea and the long march, and as men were bidden to "flee by night and by day." Their Passover was to be eaten by men with their loins girded and their staff in their hands, — "ye shall eat it in haste."

Since their course was a moral discipline, every diversion from it was to bring divine judgments upon them, as they had come upon the peoples around them, and these judgments were not in their separation from other peoples but in the manifestation of a universal law. In the forgetfulness of their vocation the doom which had come upon these corrupt communities was to come upon them. "And it shall be if thou do at all forget the Lord thy God, and walk after other gods, and worship them and serve them, I testify against you this day that ye shall surely perish. As the nations which the Lord destroyeth before your face, so shall ye perish, because ye would not be obedient unto the voice of the Lord your God."

The progress of the nation through its own vocation is in the realization of a moral being and order. As it has its own work in its own place and age, there are institutions and regulations especially adapted to it which are transient and local. It is formed in the life of the spirit, and is not to be merely the exposition of a system of unchanging laws and regulations. It is thus that there are laws and regulations which are moulded in the measure of the development of the nation, and thus it is said that Moses gave them certain forms and regulations for the "hardness of their hearts;" — not for their wickedness, which only judgment can follow, but for their rude and obdurate condition. And everywhere there was violence and slavery and rapine and war, and private revenge, and there were evils which were the special characteristic of the age. These were not the institutions of the nation, but they prevailed everywhere on the earth, they were the wickedness in which the world lieth. Thus slavery was not the creation of the law of the nation, but already existed, and the laws and institutions of the nation tended to ameliorate its condition, and ultimately to abolish it. Thus also war and private revenge were not the institutions of the nation, but the nation in its own being was in conflict with them, and its normal process tended to their removal. The nation was called out of a condition of slavery into freedom. It might not, since it was formed in the conditions of history, remove these evils in one moment, but its whole course, its institutions and its order, tend to their mitigation and ultimate extirpation. Thus against wild and unchecked private revenge, it opens cities of asylum, and to a system of slavery it places as a terminus the sabbatical year, which is hailed as the year of jubilee, and while they are called to battle, and confess One who is with them in the battle, that they shall not turn nor be affrighted at their enemies, yet they look forward to the time when there shall be "peace in all their borders."

There is in the progress of the nation the ampler recognition of its calling. It was to bear witness to a divine King and Deliverer and Judge, against those who would subject the spirit of man to the things which are seen. It was to bear witness to a righteous Will, which would establish righteousness on the earth, against those who assumed only a momentary and transient will, or the self-will of men. It was to bear witness to Him and his righteousness against those who corrupted society, those who took bribes, those who removed landmarks. The nation was the witness that these could not have their own way on earth, that there was a righteous Will which would regard them. And if the people were in complicity with these, the judgments they had uttered against others were to fall upon themselves. There was then for them a plague of fire and a plague of blood; that two-handed engine at the door, which smites once and smites no more.

The nation is formed as a moral person. The elements

of the deepest personal being are ascribed to it, and there is no personal quality but is demanded of it. The condition of the moral judgment pronounced against it is in its being as a moral person. It exists in the working out of a divine vocation and a divine election in history. Its conscience is not the reflection of a law of expediency, a mere empiric graduated by expectations of profit and loss, but the voice of very God speaking to the nation in and through its history. Its work in righteousness was not in the conformance to an abstract law, but in the fulfillment of a living, a righteous and eternal Will.

The nation is represented as a moral person. It is declared to be a holy nation. It is called of God; it is called to be holy as He is holy. In view of the evils in the land, to call it a holy nation may seem most unreal. The imbecility of the ruler of a people, the fraud and betrayal introduced into the election of a ruler by a people, the subjection of the individual conscience to the ends of parties and sects, the prevalence of corruption and bribery and robbery among rulers and legislatures, may seem often to bring a doubt of the reality of a divine government on the earth, and to contradict the assertion that the nation is a moral being, and is formed in a divine relation. There is no concealment of the evils spreading through the land by those in whom this assertion is clearest. It is said that "there is no truth and mercy or knowledge of God in the land; by swearing and lying and killing and stealing and committing adultery, they break out; it is like people like priest, and the prophets are with them; the king is glad with their wickedness, the king is a drunkard."[1] The prophet who had declared this condition, yet could declare that the nation existed in a relation to a divine King, and it was this which made the revolt and the corruption of the land so fearful. In its sin there was the violation of the law of its life, the contradiction of its being. It had been

[1] Hosea iv. 1, 2; viii. 3.

called a holy nation. It was bound by holy bonds in a divine relationship. It was brought into a holy estate. In the relationship in which it exists, there is the revelation of its true being and the witness to its unity. The representation which is the sign of its relation to its divine Lord, illustrates the nature and the effect of the sins of the nation, the root of its crimes and the result. They are denounced as the adulteries and the whoredoms of the people. There is the violation of the bond in which its relation is defined. It was the faith that the nation was a holy body, and that it was constituted in a holy relationship, that was the strength and stay of the prophets in the darkest hours. In its analogy with all human relationships, the prophet who gave expression to the divine relation of the nation, was one who was to learn in his own life the truth which was his rest in the evils of the age; when his own house was made desolate, he could not forget that it was a holy bond which bound him to her whose crime was the contradiction of the relation which still in its nature was sacred, and the memory of the past and the existent relation to his children, remained as the evidence to him of this; in this there was the reconciliation of the words which he could utter in the deepening wickedness of the land. The strength of the nation was always in the faith that it was a holy body, that it was formed in a holy relation, that in its very being it was in conflict with the corruption and crime and violence that filled the earth.[1] The peril was always in its forgetting or denying

[1] See Maurice, *Prophets and Kings*, pp. 196–230.

"These bonds might be regarded as artificial and imaginary; they would be regarded so the moment the nation had become incapable of counting anything as real that was not visible; the moment it had passed into an utterly idolatrous condition of mind. But their reality would be proved by the gradual dissolution of all other bonds; by the growing tendency in the members of the nation to deny that they stood in any relation to each other; by the practice of the majority assuming that each man lived for himself; by the strength and popularity of doctrines which justified that practice; by facts which showed that those who treated the divine covenant as a fiction became themselves the sport of every fiction." —Maurice, *Prophets and Kings*, p. 205.

this, or seeking its end in some merely material advancement, in which it could no longer contend with the evil in the world. It was the fact that it was a holy nation, that was the source at once of the hopes and the warnings of the prophets. And in evil days, and the most disastrous periods, and in the most utter corruption, when bribes were taken by those in power, and unjust judgments were rendered, and fraud and oppression and violence filled the land, in the character of the judgments pronounced upon the nation, its nature is revealed. In the awful light of the moral judgments which fill the burden of the prophets, there is alike the manifestation of its real being, and of its eternal relationship, and its divine estate, and its ancestral honors, and the glory it had known, as well as its weakness and pollution and shame.

The course of the nation in history was not itself without illustration of the foes which threaten its destruction. In a later age it was endangered and at last it was divided by secession. The crisis is represented as the consummation of a wickedness which had been increasing in the land; and when the event actually followed, it was but the external manifestation of the sin to which the people had yielded a dominion over themselves. It was in its action and its result the culmination of great crimes. It was when the people had lost their faith in an invisible king, and had sunk into an idolatrous condition of mind. It was when the consciousness of the unity of the nation and its continuity in God had become utterly obliterated. Then its disseverment came from God; the real unity and continuity of the nation in God was already no longer acknowledged, but in its stead only the artificial bond of a formal organization, and there remained only faith in visible things, and the idolatrous condition which is its sequence. There was no longer the consciousness of the divine guidance of the nation and its divine vocation in history, and a living relation in it of the fathers to the children; and the actual secession was then only the outcoming of the actual moral dissolution of the people. The continuance of an external order and décorum might only conceal, while there was no effort to overcome, the internal corruption and the evil consuming all within. But the issue of the event is manifest in the most awful judgments of history. The record is borne on with the heavy burden of the sorrows of the people through all the centuries. There came, as the spirit of secession disclosed its consequences, the loss of all consciousness of a relation to the past, and of the unity and continuity which was in the divine will. The leader whose personal ambition was foremost in the secession, and through whom it was effected, was always referred to in the long refrain, which is repeated by the prophets from year to year, "Jeroboam who made Israel to sin;" and of succeeding kings it is said, "he walked in the way of Jeroboam and of his sin, wherewith he made Israel to sin." The narrative of those who seceded is one of rapid and of deepening degradation, checked by no higher purpose and stayed by no regenerative power. It closes at last in their overthrow and utter destruction. Their idolatry becomes more gross as they sink into a merely animal condition, and as in the empires around them, there is only the recognition and worship of the animal world. Their leader made images of gold, saying, "It is too much for you to go up to Jerusalem: behold thy gods, O Israel, which brought thee up out of the land of Egypt." [1] In the judgment which comes, they are themselves divided and swept utterly away. The most fearful imagery lifts the veil, which falls, not to be lifted again. "The Lord shall smite Israel, as a reed is shaken in the water, and he shall root up Israel out of this good land, which he gave to their fathers, and shall scatter them beyond the river. And he shall give Israel up, because of the sins of Jeroboam, who did sin and who made Israel to

[1] 1 Kings xii. 28.

sin." [1] The result of the secession has the deepest historical significance. There were associated in the secession ten tribes, and only one tribe remained, but the nation itself was not therefore utterly to perish. Its historical work is continued in the one tribe that remained of all the people, and the vocation of the nation and the divine covenant with the fathers in which the nation stood was fulfilled with it. In it there is the unfolding through the advancing years of the purpose of the nation in the world, and in it alone there is maintained an unbroken relation with the past and the future, in the greatness of their ancestral memories and their immortal hopes. Although its life as a people is never again to be what it might have been, yet with it is the history of the people fulfilled. The record of the seceding tribes is one of uncertainty and of gloom deepening in its intensity, until at last they are hidden from sight and pass into outer darkness, beyond the line in which is the development of history. Their steps are gradually obliterated, and there is at last no vestige left. The search for them is a vain and idle inquiry, and becomes the fool's errand of history. To the darkness that overtakes them there is no uplifting.

The immediate result of the spirit which led to the separation of the people, appears in the formation of confederacies. It is the working of a confederate spirit. It is the sequence of secession, and involved in the evil which had led to the dissolution of the whole.[2] The wars which follow are unrelenting and conducted with a hostility which allows no ground of reconciliation. These wars are to settle no question of boundaries, nor are they for the adjustment of interests which had been held in common, but the aim of each is the utter extinction of the other. They engage for this object the aid of enemies, with whom the nation had contended in all its greater epochs. They seek the intervention of foreign powers, and league them-

[1] 1 Kings xiv. 15, 16. [2] 2 Kings xvii. 22, 23.

selves with foreign kings. The treasures of the temple, which was a witness to their unity, are plundered to hire the aid of foreign mercenaries. In these confederacies the seceding tribes are lost, and their record is ended with the words thrice repeated, "The Lord removed them out of his sight," and it is only said of them, "He delivered them into the hands of the spoilers, for they walked in the sins of Jeroboam, which he did; they departed not from them, until the Lord removed Israel from out of his sight, as he had said by all his servants, the prophets."[1] Yet on to the close — and there is scarcely any event of deeper pathos, — the witness that the foundation of the unity of the nation was not in self-will and a self-seeking spirit, but in sacrifice, is continued; wherever the true altar is built, it is still always of "twelve stones, according to the number of the tribes of the sons of Jacob."[2]

The nation is represented as formed in a divine relation. It is not constituted in the distinction of a race, nor in that is there the comprehension of its unity and its aim. In its development it is not determined by a racial law. The glory of its history is not the pride of a race. There were events of the most impressive circumstance in their beginning, to attest that the nation was not born of the flesh, that it was not comprehended in a physical relation to a certain ancestry, and that its continuance was not defined in a certain line of physical descent. The warning not to identify the nation and its rights and privileges

[1] 1 Kings xviii. 31, 33.

[2] "The confederacy of the Samaritans with the Syrians against Judah, was encountered by the confederacy of Judah with Assyria, against Israel. It was no mere border war. Each sought the extermination of the other. These confederacies denoted the spirit at the root of all the crimes, which the Prophet had deplored and denounced.

"The present scheme of Samaria to extinguish its rival even at the cost of giving an ascendency to the uncircumcised king of Damascus, showed clearly enough that the last link of brotherhood was broken, because the last feeling of the divine calling which had made them a nation was gone." — Maurice, *Prophets and Kings*, p. 249.

with a physical succession, stands in awful solemnity in their history, as if in its clear outline wrought in the strong lines of some sculpture, against the stillness of the desert, when the only one in the line of its physical descent, the child of the bondwoman, went forth into the solitude. It was not the child of the flesh, but the child of the promise that was the inheritor of the national covenant. Those whose distinction was only that of a race, were to pass into a merely tribal condition, as the Ishmaelite. In the assumption of its precedent in a racial character, the nation was severed from its divine foundation. Then Abraham and not God was regarded as the founder of the nation.[1] In the assumption of its foundation in a physical condition, and its unity and continuity in a physical basis, it became as the heathen around them, and had no other ground than they. The nation was formed in the divine covenant; its conception was lost in that ethnic claim. Thus their first great statesman made the pride of race and the distinction of physical descent, the object of scorn, and gave expression to it in indelible forms in the service of the people. They were bidden to bring gifts of the fruits of the earth to the altar, with the words, "a Syrian ready to perish was my father."[2] There can be scarcely any measure for the contempt in these words, when a Jew, representing the nation as formed only in a physical condition, is described as a Syrian, and his great ancestor as one "ready to perish." And by all the prophets this pride is denounced, and in the larger humanity of its later ages, there is the ampler expression of the worth of a man. There is the assertion that in assuming a national foundation in the possession of certain racial powers, and claiming it through a pedigree to Abraham, there is the rejection of the divine relation in which the nation subsists. It is a journeying with one who is driven into the solitude

[1] See Maurice, *Prophets and Kings*, p. 309.

[2] Deuteronomy xxvi. 5.

of the desert, and there is no promise beyond. The denunciation of this claim is sometimes repeated, as if in it there was the loss of all which the nation in the fulfillment of its promise could bring, and its end was to be realized by those who were aliens from the house of Israel, — "Doubtless God is our Father, though Abraham be ignorant of us, and Israel acknowledge us not." And when, as the national spirit was decaying, the pride of race became more and more exalted, the last of its prophets was to say to them in the streets of their cities, "God out of these stones can raise up children unto Abraham."

The nation is represented from its beginning, as in its being, in contrast to a false and material condition. It is the conflict of the nation with the spirit which would build a Babel upon the earth. It is a society which is of divine institution, and formed in its unity and continuity in a divine relation, and in the realization of relations in humanity, in contrast with a condition in which fear and self-interest and ill-will are the prevailing motives in the combination of men, which is constituted in the confederation of separate interests, and for the pursuance of selfish ends, to subserve only the pleasure or the possession of men. It is the battle borne on through the centuries of a society which is formed in the recognition of a divine vocation, and of a law of righteousness and freedom, with the forces of dissolution. It is the great battle of humanity with all that oppresses and degrades it, — the battle of Judæa with Babylon. The one apprehends humanity as it is in the divine image, and its rights and its sacredness which society is to realize; the other assumes in humanity an existence only in the physical course of nature, and would stamp upon it the image of a Babylonian spirit. The one is the life of the nation, which can only build on the divine foundation; the other would build of its own materials, the brick and mortar which it has gathered, a city which will reach from the earth to the heavens. It is this with which the nation has to contend in every age, — the spirit which, confessing only a material bond, will bring men at last to worship that.

The formation of the nation in its moral being and order, is the source of the sacredness which attaches always to the land and the capital, and the public memorials and the great events in the history of the people. Their sacredness was derivative from their association with the nation; but the latter was not conditioned upon them. The land was sacred, but they were constituted as a nation before they entered into the possession of it; and there was promised to the nation a permanence beyond that of the mountains and the hills. The events in their national history were the witness of the divine presence, the sacraments of the Lord of Hosts. The capital was the holy city, and yet it was not until far on in their history that it was built, and they were to learn that the foundation of the nation was not in the stones which they had laid, and that its unity was not defined in city walls. The work of history was to be wrought in the advance of the nation, and its triumph was in the exultant anthem, "Open ye the gates, that the righteous nation which keepeth the truth may enter in." The nation persisted through all the vicissitudes of time. The hope of the Prophets was that it was immortal. It was sustained through conquest and captivity. There were those who kept its ancient truth, when they were driven to the secret heights of its mountains, and its life did not wholly perish in oppression, or in the interruption of its government, or the destruction of the city, or the leading away of the people into strange lands. There was still in the most evil days a remnant left. Through changes, in which the whole external fabric and the institution of its government was destroyed, there continued the being of the nation. Its life was beyond the external and the formal constitution, and was not conditioned upon that. It was the spirit of Pharisaism, — and it was originally a political Pharisaism, which holding in identity the moral and the legal, attached a sacredness only to the latter, — the letter of the law, — and conceived the life of the nation as conditioned upon that.

The process which sought its conclusion through the synthesis of political science and the formal definitions of politics, comprehends no representation of the nation as it is found in the record of the first nation. The terms of a formal method are poor and empty before its realism. A writer, who may be taken to represent recent phases in political thought, has described the influence in politics of what he calls "the sentiment of nationality." [1] The analysis of the nature and effect of the "sentiment of nationality," offers no guide to the interpretation of history in the past or in the present age. There is in this ancient record the presentation of the being of the nation in its origin and its realization in the life of humanity. There is the manifestation of the nation, not as the resultant of individual desire or emotion, nor as comprehended in the definitions of a formal science or in the forms of law, but as in its realization in history.

The law and the principle which are presented are universal. They are held in no restrictive conception as in the notion of the ecclesiast, but are sustained in a universal conception. The prophets hold in them the interpretation of all history. They allow no other, but apply these to every people, and in their light alone they judge the widest sweep in their political horizon. The supremacy of their principles is presumed in their universal character. They are declared to be universal, and to show the ground of the life of every nation.[2]

[1] J. S. Mill's *Representative Government*, ch. xvi. on "Nationality."

[2] Jeremiah viii. 7, 10.

There is no form and no external order for the nation which is divinely given as alone valid. It is sometimes said that since the Christ is represented as a King,

The nation in its historical life and calling moved toward the coming of Him in whom there was the manifestation of the real — the divine life of humanity. The work of Judæa and Greece and Rome had its unity in the Christ, who is the centre of history. The title written of Him in his perfected sacrifice, was the King of the Jews, and the words to which history was to bear witness in the ancient nations, were written in Hebrew, and Greek, and Latin. And as the life of the first nations was, so also shall that of the last nations be. As it was toward his coming that the nations of the ancient world moved, so toward Him, and still in his coming, do all the nations move.

and his power in the world as a kingdom, that therefore the form of a monarchy is to be universal, and again from certain expressions in the Prophets, especially in Jeremiah, that the authority is to be that of an elective magistrate, as in a Republic; but the lesson constantly repeated is not of the special validity of an exact and prescribed form, but that the form is moulded by the age and by the spirit of the people, and the nation persists through changes in its external order and administration, and its continuity is maintained through them but is not conditioned upon them.

On the universal application of the representation in the Old Testament, and its relation to the character of the individual, Mr. Maurice says: "I apprehend that we shall learn some day that the call to individual repentance and the promise of individual reformation, has been feeble at one time, productive of turbulent violent transitory effects at another, because it has not been part of a call to national repentance, because it has not been connected with a promise of national reformation."

"We must speak again the ancient language, that God has made a covenant with the nation; if we would have an inward repentance, which will really bring us back to God; which will turn the hearts of the fathers to the children, and the children to the fathers; which will go down to the roots of our life, changing it from a self-seeking life into a life of humility, and love, and cheerful obedience, which will bear fruit upward, giving nobleness to our policy, and literature, and art; to the daily routine of what we shall no more dare to call our secular existence." — *Prophets and Kings*, p. 404.

Mr. Disraeli says, — and this is presented as a principle of universal application in the life of nations, and not in the definition of a racial law, and it is not the language of a mystic or an itinerant thinker, but a statesman who has embodied his thought in the real process of the state, "It may be observed that the decline and disasters in modern communities, have generally been relative to their degree of sedition against the Semitic principle. England, notwithstanding her deficient and meagre theology, has always remembered Zion. The great transatlantic Republic is intensely Semitic, and has prospered accordingly. This sacred principle alone has consolidated the mighty empire of all the Russias." — *Life of Bentinck*, p. 81.

The relation of the Hebrew and the Christian nation is not one of difference, but of development. It has its condition in the higher and ampler revelation. The one was governed by an invisible ruler, and moved toward his coming; the other is governed by a ruler who has manifested himself to the world, and is coming in the world. The one looked with faith toward his coming; the other looks to Him as to one whose power has been revealed on the earth and in its redemption. The one was subject to an external authority,—the "Thus saith" of the divine word; the other is subject to a law which is manifested in the spirit, it is written in the minds and in the hearts of men. The body has become a temple of the spirit. The word is uttered not from heaven above, but is nigh unto men and on their lips. The work is to be the fulfillment of the law of the Christ who is the only and the actual head of the state.

There is always a tendency to return to the Jewish or Grecian, or Latin form, but it is in the denial of the real presence of the Christ,—the rejection of the only and the actual King. In this reaction the nation loses its spiritual power, it is merged in a mere formalism, and is no longer in a living relation to a living and eternal Will.

The law by which the nation is judged, is the law which the Christ has revealed in his humanity. In Him the divine unity and the divine relations of humanity are revealed. He has shared the life of man,—the life of every man. In Him humanity is manifested in that infinite sacredness which it has in the divine and eternal image. It is only as the nation recognizes the law of humanity which He has revealed that it attains the realization of its being. It is only as the nation acknowledges in history the infinite worth of humanity which He has manifested, that it can become a power in history, which is but the realization of the divine redemption which He has wrought.[1]

[1] Matthew xxv. 32, 45.

The crises of the progress of nations in the deliverance of humanity, are described in the sign of his power, — they are the days of the Son of Man, who is revealed as the eternal conqueror. In the overthrow of the tyrannies which have oppressed and degraded men, and of the lies and frauds by which nations have been deceived, and in the rising of new hopes, and the unfolding of new energies, there is the advent of the Christ, — the coming of the Son of Man.

The only foundation then upon which man can build in the life of the individual or of society, is in Him; "other foundation can no man lay than that which is lying." It is in the law which is revealed in the Christ that the solidarity of human society is manifested. It is formed in no selfish principle. It becomes evident that no man liveth for himself. Each is the minister of the whole. In the profound words of M. Comte, it is seen that "to live for others," is but another form "of living by others." The paradox is verified, he that loseth his life shall find it. The foundation is that which the builders rejected. The corner-stone is not in slavery, but in Him who died on this earth as a slave, that He might redeem all. It is the power which is manifested in sacrifice, and the law of service is the law of power. It is the mightier power, and "on whomsoever this rock shall fall it shall grind him to powder."

The nation is lifted above the divisions and distinctions of race. There is the assertion of the physical unity of humanity, and of the divine determination in the times of the existence and the bounds of the dwelling of nations.[1] And the people that comes to believe that there is a purpose in the ages, will watch the "signs of the times," for the attainment of the purpose which is given them, and in the faith that their boundaries in the fulfillment of their vocation are divinely appointed, they will guard them well.

1 Acts xvii. 26.

The nation is formed as a power on the earth. It is invested with power of God; its authority is conveyed through no intermediate hands, but is given of God. It is clothed with his majesty on the earth. It is ordained of God to do his service. It is θεοῦ διάκονος.[1]

The realization of the redemptive purpose in history is represented under a political form. The Christ is a King, and the realization of his redemptive work is a kingdom. The type expressive of his power is drawn from the political life of man. But there is in this only the assumption of the political form which had attained the most nearly to a universality in history. The divine power has, in the Christ in this form, only its earthly representation. It is the power of one who, in his own divine and eternal being, is the only source of power.

The end toward which the nations in the earlier ages moved, and toward which all the nations move,—the centre of history,—is the Christ. The revelation is in a Person. The manifestation which kings and prophets waited for, and which all the types and traditions of the hope and longing in history foreshadowed, is in the divine Person. The revelation is not in a divine system, nor a divine form, nor a divine idea. In the divine relationship, which is manifested in the Father and the Son and the Spirit, there is the foundation of humanity and the realization of the human personality. In the Christ there is the manifestation of the divine origin and relations of humanity, and the eternal life which is given to it; in Him it overcomes the evil of the world, and is victorious over death, and in the power of the resurrection is risen with Him, and ascending with Him, is glorified with Him in the glory which He had with the Father before the world was. Its life is still only in the realization of personality,—in the obedience to his will, in the doing of his work, after the law which He in his own person has revealed.

1 Romans xii. 5.

In this only there is the reconciliation of freedom and law, the law of the spirit, the law which is laid in personality; in this only does personality subsist in those relations which are necessary to its being; in this only there is the unity, without the contradiction, of humanity and personality. Therefore the nation, as it has its end in the moral realization of the life of humanity, is to regard each individual person also as an end, for there is for each the infinite sacredness which is revealed in the Christ, — the Life of humanity. The Christ who is declared to be the head of humanity "is the head of every man." In the Christ, there is the unity and foundation of humanity in its divine origin, and the realization of personality is in its redemptive life.

In the Christ there is the revelation of the divine life of humanity. It is held in no abstract and formal conception as the evolution of a logical sequence; it is held in no vague and empty conception, as in an unhistorical existence; it is the resultant of no numerical estimate; it is no indefinite and unlimited being in which the consciousness of the individual is lost; but there is the revelation of humanity in its realization in personality, in its divine relations. In the Christ as the Prophet, and Priest, and King, there is alone the source of the prophetic, and priestly and kingly powers in humanity. The comprehension of humanity in an isolated individualism is false and unreal. It is the source only of an evil egoism. It is the lord of division.

It is only as the nation has for its end the fulfillment in its moral being of the life of humanity, that it has its realization in history. It is in its work alone, in the fulfillment of the will of the Christ, that it becomes a power in the realization of his redemption, which is the life of history, and in which humanity alone has the foundation of its unity. The work which is for humanity, in its simplest and widest form, is the work for and of the Christ; he has himself declared his very oneness with humanity, as the law by which the nation is to be judged.[1]

The nation is to work in the realization on the earth of his kingdom, who is the only and the eternal King. It becomes then no more the kingdom of this world, but the Kingdom of Him whose reign is of eternal truth, — the reign in which, in the realization of personality, there is the freedom of man. Its advance is only in his advent, its destination is toward Him. Its new ages are the days of the coming of the Son of Man. Its freedom is only in his redemptive strength. It is no more the life of the first man, of the earth earthy.

The nation in the last as in the first age, has still the source of its strength only in its relation to its divine Lord. The danger is still in the denial or forgetfulness, in a material existence, of this relation. The representation of the sins of Judæa, in their principle and their effect, is that of the sins of every nation. In the violation of the divine relation in which the nation is formed, and the rejection of its covenant, the sins of the nation are denounced as its adulteries.[2]

The conflict of the nation is still borne on to the close of history in the antagonism to a false civilization. It is the conflict with a material civilization which would build on the earth a Babylon. It is as the nation yields to the spirit of a Babylon that there is the loss of its freedom and its moral being. It is described as one who is enchanted and demented and besotted and deceived, as "drunk of the wine of the wrath of her fornication." It is only as it contends against this spirit that it becomes a power in the moral life of history, that it follows with the armies of Him, who "in righteousness doth judge and make war." In Him the victory whose sign of conquest is the coming of the Son of Man, — the victory of humanity, — is assured. The imagery illustrative of the most actual condition, por-

[1] Matthew xxiii. 45.

[2] Revelation xviii. 3.

trays the downfall of Babylon in the battles of the centuries. It is described as invested with the circumstance of a false and material civilization, "the great city that glorified herself and lived deliciously," that saith, "I sit a queen, and shall see no sorrow," that was "clothed in fine linen and purple and scarlet, and decked with gold and precious stones and pearls," but in its doom "with violence shall that city be thrown down," for "by thy sorceries were all nations deceived." It is no distant city, so dim and unreal as only to be wrought in spectral imagery, and no imaginary strife, as if fought by phantom armies, and no war of ideas in some intellectual field. It is the reality of history, it is "a city whose merchants were the great men of the earth," and in its overthrow "the company in ships and sailors, and as many as trade by sea, stood afar off, and cried when they saw the smoke of its burning, saying, 'what city is like unto this great city.'" The language which denotes its character, presents no type of individual passion or action, no ideal state, no mystic city of the soul, but it is the type of an inhuman, a material civilization. The victory over it is in the deliverance of humanity, and yet in the description of those who fall upon its battle-field, there is only one word to indicate the moral character of the battle fought, — "there is the flesh of kings and the flesh of captains and the flesh of mighty men, and the flesh of horses and of them that sat on them, and the flesh of all men, both free and bond;" and in the schedule of trade which is given with such detail, as if to compel attention to its real character, there is only one word to indicate its moral condition, — "the merchandise of gold and silver, and precious stones, and of pearls, and fine linen, and purple, and silk, and scarlet, and all thyine wood, and all manner of vessels of ivory, and all manner of vessels of most precious stones, and of brass, and iron, and marble, and cinnamon, and odours, and ointments, and frankincense, and wine, and oil, and fine flour, and wheat, and beasts, and sheep, and horses, and chariots, and slaves and souls of men."[1]

The goal of history is in the fulfillment of the highest political ideal. It is the holy city; it is the new Jerusalem, the end of the toil and conflict of humanity. There is the manifestation of God as the centre of the moral universe. Of that vision it is written in the book which of all others has the voice of anthems and the swell of liturgies, — and amid the confusions of sects and opposing ecclesiasticisms the words are as those of peace, — "I saw no temple there." There is the unity of the universe which has been revealed in the eternal sacrifice, — "the glory of God doth lighten it, and the Lamb is the light thereof." It is toward it that the nations move in the fulfillment of the life of humanity. It is written of the holy city, "they shall bear the glory and honor of the nations into it."[2]

The conflict of the ages of humanity is closed. The battle is ended in eternal triumph. The humiliation has passed into the glorification of the Son of Man, and in that eternal relationship with the Father and the Spirit there is for humanity the realization of that glory which He, who is the Son of God, had before the world was.

The nation is to work as one whose achievement passes beyond time, whose glory and honor are borne into the eternal city. It is not here that it may look for its perfect rest. It has an immortal life. It is no more a kingdom of this world, but it is formed in the realization of the redemptive kingdom of the Christ. The leaders and the prophets of the people can only repeat the ancient lesson, "He is come, and unto Him shall the gathering of the people be."

[1] Revelation xviii.

[2] Revelation xxi. 26.

www.ingramcontent.com/pod-product-compliance
Lightning Source LLC
LaVergne TN
LVHW021146110826
845150LV00005B/1140

* 9 7 8 1 4 2 5 5 4 7 7 3 8 *